"It is difficult to take a fresh appr[...] the people of the Synoptic Gospe[...] find books about groups known fr[...] and other contemporaries, to which few Galileans belonged (Pharisees, Scribes, Sadducees, Essenes, and the like). By contrast, Culpepper spends the bulk of his words on common people. Yes, in his parables, Jesus talked about minority elites but also about children, parents, brides, widows, tenants, laborers, farmers, fishermen, shepherds, and merchants. Such ordinary Galileans are the majority in the pages of *The People of the Parables*. As a result, Culpepper gives us a comprehensive view not only of the Galilean populace but also of the culture and social structures by which Galileans guided human interactions and organized their institutions and systems. Familiarity with such things is a strong foundation on which to build interpretations of Jesus' parables. Culpepper's crystal-clear exposition will make a fine textbook for university and seminary classes on the social world of Jesus, particularly for teachers who want to show students how scholars build arguments. But it is also for anyone, from pastor to layperson to nonspecialist in the Gospels, who aims to understand the world in which Jesus ministered and in which his teachings take on meaning."

—James R. Strange, Charles Jackson Granade and Elizabeth Donald Granade Professor in New Testament, Howard College of Arts and Sciences, Samford University

"Alan Culpepper's *The People of the Parables* is brilliant and fascinating, both in conception and execution. This book enables readers to become richly acquainted with the day laborers, merchants, fishermen, tax collectors, bandits, and others who populate the parables, along with their social circumstances in ancient Galilee, which allows Jesus' parables not only to speak anew but also to resound with the fresh power they held for their first hearers. Culpepper is an insightful interpreter, and this is a highly original and profoundly useful book for any reader of Jesus' parables."

—Thomas G. Long, author of *Proclaiming the Parables: Preaching and Teaching the Kingdom of God*

"With *The People of the Parables*, the reader is transported into the world of first-century Galilee to encounter the people and objects that populate the parables of Jesus—shepherds, estate managers, farmers, tax collectors, vineyards, day laborers, and many more. Culpepper's characterizations are comprehensive and meticulously researched, allowing the reader to fully enter into the dynamics of the parables. *The People of the Parables* fills a critical lacuna in the study of the parables of Jesus. Essential reading."

—John S. Kloppenborg, Professor of Religion, University of Toronto

"Professor Culpepper's latest opus is a one-volume encyclopedia of the social history underlying the people of the parables: well-organized, scrupulously documented, grounded in research both venerable and up-to-date, judicious, and lucid. It illuminates the obvious and probes the unnoticeable. For its insight, concision, and convenience, I shall keep this book at hand in all future study of Jesus' parables. Others are urged to do likewise."
—C. Clifton Black, Otto A. Piper Professor of Biblical Theology, Princeton Theological Seminary

The People of the Parables

The People of the Parables

Galilee in the Time of Jesus

R. Alan Culpepper

WESTMINSTER
JOHN KNOX PRESS
LOUISVILLE • KENTUCKY

First edition
Published by Westminster John Knox Press
Louisville, Kentucky

24 25 26 27 28 29 30 31 32 33—10 9 8 7 6 5 4 3 2 1

Book design by Sharon Adams
Cover design by designpointinc.com
Cover art by Jorge Cocco. Used by permission.

Library of Congress Cataloging-in-Publication Data is on file
at the Library of Congress, Washington, DC.

ISBN: 978-0-664-26884-8

Contents

Part VII: Jesus

Map of Galilee

Preface

*T*he seeds were sown long ago. At the Southern Baptist Theological Seminary in the late 1960s, Harold Songer introduced me to "Jewish and Hellenistic Backgrounds of the New Testament." Yigael Yadin, a visiting lecturer, gave an illustrated lecture on his excavation at Masada. Equally memorable was Joachim Jeremias's lecture on the parable of the two debtors in Luke 7. At Duke, my peers and I read the Apocrypha and Pseudepigrapha with James Charlesworth and the major Dead Sea Scrolls (in Hebrew) with Orval Wintermute. W. D. Davies taught "Paul and Palestinian Judaism." As his research assistant for two years, I did most of the "donkey work" (bibliography and indexes) for his *The Gospel and the Land*. Eric Meyers tried to teach me Mishnaic Hebrew and invited me to dig at Meiron one summer, but other things were more pressing at the time   an opportunity missed! Later trips to Israel introduced me to what W. D. Davies spoke of as the "realia" of history. Conversations with Seán Freyne at Society for New Testament Studies meetings in the 1980s exposed me to his infectious enthusiasm for the history and people of ancient Galilee. Study at the Shalom Hartman Institute as part of the American Jewish Committee's Christian Leadership Initiative in the summers of 2010 and 2011 further deepened my appreciation for Judaism, ancient and modern. Then, the experience of touring archaeological sites with Mordechai Aviam as he guided the Colloquium Ioanneum through Galilee for three days in 2017 germinated the seeds, and the idea for this book began to take shape.

This book is not about the parables per se but about the people of the parables. The more we know about Galilee, the more vivid the parables and Jesus' world become. The subtitle, *Galilee in the Time of Jesus*, deliberately recalls Joachim Jeremias's *Jerusalem in the Time of Jesus* (1923, ET 1969), which drew heavily on rabbinic texts. In the interim, even since its publication in English, appreciation of Galilee's significance for understanding

Jesus' ministry has grown dramatically. The 1970s witnessed an explosion of work that redefined our approaches to the study of Jesus and his historical context. Jacob Neusner questioned the uncritical use of rabbinic materials for understanding Second Temple Judaism in his three-volume work, *The Rabbinic Traditions about the Pharisees before 70* (1971). Géza Vermès turned heads with his *Jesus the Jew* (1973), arguing that Jesus is best understood as a Galilean charismatic. The following year, Martin Hengel's *Judaism and Hellenism: Studies in Their Encounter in Palestine during the Early Hellenistic Period* appeared in English. Eric Meyers, James F. Strange, and others excavated Meiron, then Sepphoris; many other excavations followed. In 1980, Seán Freyne published the first volume from a career devoted to the study of Galilee: *Galilee from Alexander the Great to Hadrian: 323 BCE to 135 CE*. The work of these pioneers has raised fresh questions about Second Temple Judaism and the economics, politics, Hellenization, and Romanization of Galilee. Their work attracted the attention of other scholars, and the flow of important work setting Jesus in his Jewish and Galilean context continued.

My aim in the present volume is to gather the most important findings and new perspectives of the past fifty years, much of which has been published in technical volumes and journals, to make it accessible to students, ministers, and scholars working in other fields.

This project would not have been possible without the support of Mercer University and Emory University. Mercer granted me emeritus status, and Emory invited me to be a visiting professor. Beth Perry, theology librarian at Mercer, and Richard "Bo" Adams, director of Pitts Theology Library at Candler School of Theology, have spared no effort in helping me gain access to research materials. Without the digital resources of these libraries, I could not have written this volume. My appointment as a research fellow in the Department of Old and New Testament at the University of the Free State in Bloemfontein, South Africa, offered further opportunities for international dialogue, travel, and study. I am deeply grateful to each of these institutions, their faculty, and the staff.

Along the way many others have provided much-needed and appreciated guidance, encouragement, and assistance. Dan Braden, editor at Westminster John Knox, helped shape this volume from its inception, especially its design and intended readership. I am also grateful to Julie Tonini, who guided the volume through the editorial process, and David Garber, the copyeditor. The care and attention to detail that they brought to the manuscript ensured the highest possible standards for the final text. Shannon Li prepared the subject index, often including a second level of specificity, so that readers can easily find what they are looking for. Working with this team and seeing the book emerge under their professional direction has been a joy.

Mordechai Aviam, Clifton Black, Eugene Boring, David Fiensy, and James R. Strange read the manuscript as it was nearing completion, helping me catch errors and fill gaps, but of course I alone am responsible for the remaining deficiencies and inaccuracies.

Works cited are listed at the end of each chapter, providing bibliographies for discrete subjects. Important ancient texts are quoted, generally from the Loeb Classical Library, with translations and modern editions listed in the Bibliography of Ancient Sources and Translations. Biblical quotations are taken from the New Revised Standard Version unless otherwise noted. The map of Galilee was created and copyrighted by A. D. Riddle and James R. Strange; I am grateful to both for permission to reproduce it in this volume.

Parts of this volume have been published or used in articles and contributions to Festschriften while I continued to work on it: "Babatha: The Woman of Letters Who 'Knew No Letters,'" *Perspectives in Religious Studies* 50 (2023): 167–79; and "Women in Second Temple Fiction," *Review and Expositor* 120, 4 (2023).

Above all, the support, encouragement, and love of my bride of fifty-six years, Jacquelyn Culpepper, has been unfailing, filling our home with joy even when, day after day for the past several years, I have been at the computer "in Galilee."

R. Alan Culpepper
Memorial Day, 2023

The Canonical Parables and Their Characters

Parable	Text Location	Category
1. Children in the Marketplace	Matt 11:16–17// Luke 7:31–32	children
2. Sower	Matt 13:3–8// Mark 4:3–8// Luke 8:5–8	farmer
3. Planted Weeds	Matt 13:24–30	householder, servants, reapers
4. Mustard Seed	Matt 13:31–32// Mark 4:30–32// Luke 13:18–19	householder
5. Leaven	Matt 13:33// Luke 13:20–21	woman
6. Treasure in a Field	Matt 13:44	man
7. Pearl	Matt 13:45–46	merchant
8. Fishnet	Matt 13:47–48	fishermen
9. Lost Sheep	Matt 18:12–13// Luke 15:4–6	shepherd
10. Unmerciful Servant	Matt 18:23–34	king, servants
11. Vineyard Laborers	Matt 20:1–15	householder, laborers, steward
12. Two Sons	Matt 21:28–32	father, sons
13. Tenants	Matt 21:33–43// Mark 12:1–9// Luke 20:9–16	householder, tenants
14. Feast	Matt 22:2–13// Luke 14:16–24	king, servants, guests
15. Wise and Wicked Servants	Matt 24:45–51// Luke 12:42–46	master and steward
16. Ten Maidens	Matt 25:1–12	maidens, bridegroom
17. Talents	Matt 25:14–30// Luke 19:12–27	master, servants
18. Sheep and Goats	Matt 25:31–46	king, shepherd

Parable	Text Location	Category
19. Seed Growing Secretly	Mark 4:26–29	farmer
20. Returning Master	Mark 13:34–36	householder, servants
21. Two Debtors	Luke 7:41–42	master, debtor
22. Good Samaritan	Luke 10:30–35	traveler, thieves, priest, Levite, Samaritan, innkeeper
23. Friend at Night	Luke 11:5–8	father, traveler, neighbor
24. Rich Farmer	Luke 12:16–20	rich man
25. Barren Fig Tree	Luke 13:6–9	vineyard owner, vinedresser
26. Choice Places at Table	Luke 14:7–11	host and guest
27. Tower Builder	Luke 14:28–30	landowner
28. Warring King	Luke 14:31–32	king
29. Lost Coin	Luke 15:8–9	woman
30. Prodigal Son	Luke 15:11–32	father, sons, servants
31. Unjust Steward	Luke 16:1–7	rich man, steward, debtors
32. Rich Man and Lazarus	Luke 16:19–31	rich man, beggar
33. Servant's Reward	Luke 17:7–10	servants
34. Unjust Judge	Luke 18:2–5	judge, widow
35. Pharisee and Tax Collector	Luke 18:10–13	Pharisee, tax collector
36. Sower and Reaper	John 4:35–38	sower, reaper
37. Good Shepherd	John 10:1–5	shepherd, hireling, thief
38. Vine and Vinedresser	John 15:1–8	vinedresser

Abbreviations

Ancient Sources

Pseudepigrapha

1 En.	1 Enoch
Jos. Asen.	Joseph and Aseneth
Jub.	Jubilees
LAB	Liber antiquitatum biblicarum (Pseudo-Philo)
Let. Aris.	Letter of Aristeas
Mart. Isa.	Martyrdom of Isaiah
Ps.-Phoc.	Pseudo-Phocylides
Sib. Or.	Sibylline Oracles
T. Ab.	Testament of Abraham
T. Job	Testament of Job
T. Jos.	Testament of Joseph
T. Jud.	Testament of Judah
T. Levi	Testament of Levi
T. Mos.	Testament of Moses

Dead Sea Scrolls

CD	Damascus Document
DSS	Dead Sea Scrolls = Qumran scrolls
1QapGen	Genesis Apocryphon
1QH	Hodayot (Thanksgiving Scroll)
1QpHab	Pesher Habakkuk
1QS	Manual of Discipline
1QSa	Manual of Discipline (appendix a)
3Q15	Copper Scroll
4QD	Damascus Document
4QFlor	Florilegium

4QMMT	Halakhic Letter (*Miqṣat Ma'aseh ha-Torah*)
4QpHos	Pesher Hosea
4QpNah	Pesher Nahum
4Q242	Prayer of Nabonidus
11QTemple	Temple Scroll

Rabbinic Sources

'Abod. Zar.	Avodah Zarah
'Abot	Avot
'Arak.	Arakhin
ARN	Avot of Rabbi Nathan
b.	Babylonian Talmud
B. Bat.	Bava Batra
B. Meṣ.	Bava Metzi'a
B. Qam.	Bava Qamma
Ber.	Berakhot
Beṣah	Betzah
Bik.	Bikkurim
'Ed.	Eduyyot
'Erub.	Eruvin
Giṭ	Gittin
Ḥag.	Hagigah
Ḥal.	Hallah
Ḥul.	Hullin
Ker.	Kerithot
Ketub.	Ketubbot
Kil.	Kil'ayim
Lam. Rab.	Lamentations Rabbah
m.	Mishnah
Ma'aś.	Ma'aserot
Meg.	Megillah
Menaḥ.	Menahot
Mid.	Middot
Mo'ed Qaṭ.	Mo'ed Qatan
Ned.	Nedarim
Neg.	Nega'im
Nid.	Niddah
Pe'ah	Pe'ah
Pesaḥ.	Pesahim
Qidd.	Qiddushin
Rosh. Hash.	Rosh Hashanah
Sanh.	Sanhedrin

Shabb.	Shabbat
Sheb.	Shevi'it
Shebu.	Shevu'ot
Song Rab.	Song of Songs Rabbah
Soṭah	Sotah
t.	Tosefta
Taʿan.	Taʾanit
Ṭehar.	Teharot
Ter.	Terumot
y.	Jerusalem Talmud
Yad.	Yadayim
Yebam.	Yevamot

Apostolic Fathers

Barn.	Barnabas
Did.	Didache
Ign. *Eph.*	Ignatius, *To the Ephesians*

New Testament Apocrypha and Pseudepigrapha

Apos. Con.	Apostolic Constitutions and Canons
Gos. Thom.	Gospel of Thomas
Prot. Jas.	Protoevangelium of James
Ps.-Mt.	Gospel of Pseudo-Matthew

Greek and Latin Works

Appian
| *Bell. civ.* | *Civil Wars* |
| *Hist. rom.* | *Roman History* |

Apuleius
| *Apol.* | *Apologia* |
| *Metam.* | *Metamorphoses* |

Aristotle
| *Gen. an.* | *Generation of Animals* |
| *Pol.* | *Politics* |

Athenaeus
| *Deipn.* | *Deipnosophistae (Sophists at Dinner)* |

Augustine
| *Trac. Ev. Jo.* | *Tractates on the Gospel of John* |

Aulus Gellius
| *Noct. att.* | *Attic Nights* |

Cato
Agr.   *Agriculture*

Celsus
Med.   *On Medicine*

Cicero
Fin.   *On the Ends of Good and Evil*
Off.   *On Duties*
Sen.   *On Old Age*

Clement of Alexandria
Paed.   *Paedagogus*

Columella
Rust.   *On Agriculture*

Dio Cassius
Hist.   *Roman History*

Dio Chrysostom
Or.   *Discourses*

Diodorus Siculus
Hist.   *History*

Dionysius of Halicarnassus
1 Amm.   *Letters to Ammaeus, 1*
Ant. rom.   *Roman History*
Comp.   *On Literary Composition*

Epictetus
Diatr.   *Discourses*
Ench.   *Enchiridion*

Eusebius
Hist. eccl.   *Ecclesiastical History*
Onom.   *Onomasticon*

Herodotus
Hist.   *Histories*

Homer
Il.   *Iliad*
Od.   *Odyssey*

Horace
Sat.   *Satires*

Josephus
Ag. Ap.   *Against Apion*

Ant.	*Jewish Antiquities*
J.W.	*Jewish War*
Life	*The Life*

Justin Martyr
Dial.	*Dialogue with Trypho*

Livy
Ab urbe	*History of Rome*

Musonius Rufus
Frag.	*Fragment(s)*

Oppian
Hal.	*Halieutica*

Origen
Cels.	*Against Celsus*
Hom. Jer.	*Homilies in Jeremiah*
Hom. Lev.	*Homilies in Leviticus*

Pausanius
Descr.	*Description of Greece*

Paulus
Dig.	*Digesta*
Sent.	*Sententiae*

Philo
Abr.	*On the Life of Abraham*
Agr.	*On Agriculture*
Alleg. Interp.	*Allegorical Interpretation*
Contempl. Life	*On the Contemplative Life*
Creation	*On the Creation of the World*
Embassy	*On the Embassy to Gaius*
Good Person	*That Every Good Person Is Free*
Joseph	*On the Life of Joseph*
Moses	*On the Life of Moses*
QG	*Questions and Answers on Genesis*
Spec. Laws	*On the Special Laws*
Virt.	*On the Virtues*

Philostratus
Vit. Apoll.	*Life of Apollonius of Tyana*

Plato
Soph.	*Sophist*
Symp.	*Symposium*

Pliny the Elder
Nat.   *Natural History*

Pliny the Younger
Ep.   *Epistles*

Plutarch
Conj. praec.   *Advice to Bride and Groom*

Polybius
Hist.   *Histories*

Strabo
Geogr.   *Geography*

Suetonius
Cal.   *Gaius Caligula*

Tacitus
Ann.   *Annals*
Dial.   *Dialogue on Oratory*
Hist.   *Histories*

Terence
Haut.   *Hauton timorumenos (The Self-Tormentor)*

Tertullian
Bapt.   *On Baptism*
Marc.   *Against Marcion*
Pud.   *On Modesty*
Virg.   *The Veiling of Virgins*

Varro
Rust.   *On Agriculture*

Vitruvius
Archi.   *On Architecture*

Xenophon
Mem.   *Memorabilia*
Symp.   *Symposium*

Papyri

P.Bas.   *Papyrusurkunden der Öffentlichen Bibliothek der Universität zu Basel*, 1917
P.Coll.Youtie   *Collectanea Papyrologica: Texts Published in honor of H. C. Youtie*, ed. A. E. Hanson et al. Bonn, 1976
P.Corn.   papyrus inventoried by Cornell University

P.Jud.Des.Misc.   *Miscellaneous Texts from the Judaean Desert*, ed. J. Charlesworth, 2000

P.Lille   Papyrus grecs (Institut Papyrologique de l'Université de Lille), journal, 1907–

P.Mich.   *Michigan Papyri*, journal, 1931–

P.Mur.   *Murabba'at Papyri. Les grottes de Murabba'ât*, ed. P. Benoit, J. T. Milik, and R. de Vaux. Oxford, 1961

P.Oxf.   *Some Oxford Papyri*, ed. E. P. Wegener, 1941

P.Oxy.   Oxyrhynchus papyri

P.Petaus   A papyrus from the archive of Petaus, a village scribe

P.Şe'el.   Şe'elim papyri

PSI   papyri inventoried by Papiri della Società Italiana

P.XHev/Se Nab 1   Papyrus Starcky (P.Yadin 36)

P.Yad.   Yadin papyri. *The Documents from the Bar Kochba Period in the Cave of Letters*, 1963–2002

P.Yale   Yale Papyrus Collection, Beinecke Rare Book and Manuscript Library

Modern Sources

AB   Anchor Bible

ABD   *Anchor Bible Dictionary*. Edited by D. N. Freedman. 6 vols. New York: Doubleday, 1992

ABRL   Anchor Bible Resource Library

ABS   Archaeology and Biblical Studies

AIL   Ancient Israel and Its Literature

AJA   *American Journal of Archaeology*

AJEC   Ancient Judaism and Early Christianity

ANET   *Ancient Near Eastern Texts Relating to the Old Testament*. Edited by James B. Pritchard. 3rd ed. Princeton: Princeton University Press, 1969

ANF   *Ante-Nicene Fathers*

ASP   American Studies in Papyrology

AYBRL   Anchor Yale Bible Reference Library

BAR   *Biblical Archaeology Review*

BASP   *Bulletin of the American Society of Papyrologists*

BDAG   Danker, F. W., W. Bauer, W. F. Arndt, and F. W. Gingrich. *Greek-English Lexicon of the New Testament and Other Early Christian Literature*. 3rd ed. Chicago: University of Chicago Press, 2000

BETL	Bibliotheca Ephemeridum Theologicarum Lovaniensium
Bib	*Biblica*
BibInt	Biblical Interpretation Series
BJRL	*Bulletin of the John Rylands University Library of Manchester*
BJS	Brown Judaic Studies
BRev	*Bible Review*
BTB	*Biblical Theology Bulletin*
CAP	Cowley, Arthur E. *Aramaic Papyri of the Fifth Century B.C.* Oxford: Clarendon Press, 1923
CBQ	*Catholic Biblical Quarterly*
CIJ	*Corpus Inscriptionum Judaicarum.* Edited by Jean-Baptiste Frey. 2 vols. Rome: Pontifical Biblical Institute, 1936–1952
ConBNT	Coniectanea Biblica: New Testament Series
CPJ	*Corpus Papyrorum Judaicarum.* Edited by V. A. Tcherikover. 3 vols. Cambridge, MA: Harvard University Press, 1957–64
CSCT	Columbia Studies in the Classical Tradition
DJD	Discoveries in the Judaean Desert
ECL	Early Christianity and Its Literature
EDEJ	*The Eerdmans Dictionary of Early Judaism.* Edited by J. J. Collins and D. C. Harlow. Grand Rapids: Eerdmans, 2010
FRLANT	Forschungen zur Religion und Literatur des Alten und Neuen Testaments
HdO	Handbuch der Orientalistik
HSCP	*Harvard Studies in Classical Philology*
HSM	Harvard Semitic Monographs
HTR	*Harvard Theological Review*
HUCA	*Hebrew Union College Annual*
HvTSt	*Hervormde teologiese studies*
ICC	International Critical Commentary
IDB	*The Interpreter's Dictionary of the Bible.* Edited by G. A. Buttrick. 4 vols. New York: Abingdon, 1962
IDS	*In die Skriflig / In Luce Verbi*
IEJ	*Israel Exploration Journal*
IEph	*Die Inschriften von Ephesos.* Edited by H. Wankel. Bonn: Rudolf Habelt Verlag, 1979–84
ILS	*Inscriptiones latinae selectae.* Edited by H. Dessau. 1892–1916

ISBE	*International Standard Bible Encyclopedia.* Edited by G. W. Bromiley. 4 vols. Grand Rapids: Eerdmans, 1979–**88**
JAJ	*Journal of Ancient Judaism*
JAJSup	Journal of Ancient Judaism Supplements
JAS	*Journal of Archaeological Science*
JBL	*Journal of Biblical Literature*
JBV	*Journal of Belief and Values*
JDS	Judean Desert Studies
JHMAS	*Journal of the History of Medicine and Allied Sciences*
JJS	*Journal of Jewish Studies*
JMR	*Journal of Mosaic Research*
JQR	*Jewish Quarterly Review*
JRASup	Journal of Roman Archaeology Supplementary Series
JRS	*Journal of Roman Studies*
JSHJ	*Journal for the Study of the Historical Jesus*
JSJ	*Journal for the Study of Judaism*
JSJSup	Journal for the Study of Judaism Supplements
JSNT	*Journal for the Study of the New Testament*
JSNTSup	Journal for the Study of the New Testament Supplement Series
JSOT	*Journal for the Study of the Old Testament*
JSP	Judea and Samaria Publications
JSPSup	Journal for the Study of the Pseudepigrapha Supplement Series
JTS	*Journal of Theological Studies*
KJV	King James Version
LCL	Loeb Classical Library
LNTS	Library of New Testament Studies
LSJ	Liddell, H. G., R. Scott, H. S. Jones. *A Greek-English Lexicon.* 9th ed. with revised supplement. Oxford: Clarendon Press, 1996
NAB	New American Bible
NASB	New American Standard Bible, 1995
NGTT	*Nederduitse gereformeerde teologiese tydskrif*
NIB	*New Interpreter's Bible*
NIDB	*New Interpreter's Dictionary of the Bible.* Edited by K. D. Sakenfeld. 5 vols. Nashville: Abingdon, 2006–9

NIV	New International Version
NovT	*Novum Testamentum*
NRSV	New Revised Standard Version
NRSVue	New Revised Standard Version, updated edition
NTL	New Testament Library
NTS	*New Testament Studies*
OeO	Oriens et Occidens
OTP	*The Old Testament Pseudepigrapha.* Edited by J. H. Charlesworth. 2 vols. Garden City, NY: Doubleday, 1983–85
P&P	*Past and Present*
PEQ	*Palestine Exploration Quarterly*
PJ	*Palästina-Jahrbuch*
PL	Patrologia Latina [= *Patrologiae Cursus Completus*: Series Latina]. Edited by Jacques-Paul Migne. 217 vols. Paris, 1844–1864
RBS	Resources for Biblical Study
RMCS	Routledge Monographs in Classical Studies
RSV	Revised Standard Version
SB	*Sammelbuch griechischer Urkunden aus Aegypten.* Edited by F. Preisigke et al. 21 vols. Wiesbaden: Harrassowitz, 1915–2002
SBEC	Studies in the Bible and Early Christianity
SBFCMi	Studium Biblicum Franciscanum, Collectio Minor
SBLABS	Society of Biblical Literature Archaeology and Biblical Studies
SBLDS	Society of Biblical Literature Dissertation Series
SCI	*Scripta Classica Israelica*
SEMA	Studies in Eastern Mediterranean Archaeology
SFSHJ	South Florida Studies in the History of Judaism
SHBC	Smyth & Helwys Bible Commentary
SJ	Studia Judaica
SJT	*Scottish Journal of Theology*
SNTSMS	Society for New Testament Studies Monograph Series
SR	*Studies in Religion / Sciences religieuses*
SS	Studia Samaritana
StPB	Studia Post-biblica
TANZ	Texte und Arbeiten zum neutestamentlichen Zeitalter
TBT	*The Bible Today*

TDNT	*Theological Dictionary of the New Testament.* Edited by G. Kittel and G. Friedrich. Translated by G. W. Bromiley. 10 vols. Grand Rapids: Eerdmans, 1964–76
TENTS	Texts and Editions for New Testament Study
TSAJ	Texte und Studien zum antiken Judentum
WAW	Writings from the Ancient World
WUNT	Wissenschaftliche Untersuchungen zum Neuen Testament
ZNW	*Zeitschrift für die neutestamentliche Wissenschaft*
ZPE	*Zeitschrift für Papyrologie und Epigraphik*

Bibliography of Ancient Sources and Translations

Translations of ancient sources are taken from the following unless otherwise noted.

Ante-Nicene Fathers. 10 vols. Translated by Alexander Roberts and James Donaldson. Repr. Grand Rapids: Eerdmans, 1985.

The Apostolic Fathers. 2 vols. Translated by Bart D. Ehrman. LCL 24 and 25. Cambridge, MA: Harvard University Press, 2003.

Apuleius. *Metamorphoses* (*The Golden Ass*), *Volume I: Books 1–6*. Edited and translated by J. Arthur Hanson. LCL 44. Cambridge, MA: Harvard University Press, 1996.

Aristotle. *Generation of Animals*. Translated by A. L. Peck. LCL 366. Cambridge, MA: Harvard University Press, 1942.

Babylonian Talmud. Translated and edited by I. Epstein. London: Soncino, 1961.

Catallus: Poems 61–68. Edited by John Godwin. Warminster, UK: Aris & Philipps.

Celsus. *On Medicine, Volume I: Books 1–4*. Translated by W. G. Spencer. LCL 292. Cambridge, MA: Harvard University Press, 1935.

Chariton. *Callirhoe*. Edited and translated by G. P. Goold. LCL 481. Cambridge, MA: Harvard University Press, 1995.

Charles, R. H. *The Apocrypha and Pseudepigrapha of the Old Testament*. 2 vols. Oxford: Clarendon Press, 1913.

Charlesworth, James H., ed. *The Old Testament Pseudepigrapha*. 2 vols. Garden City, NY: Doubleday, 1983–85.

Cicero. *On Duties*. Translated by Walter Miller. LCL 30. Cambridge, MA: Harvard University Press, 1913.

———. *On Old Age. On Friendship. On Divination*. Translated by W. A. Falconer. LCL 154. Cambridge, MA: Harvard University Press, 1923.

Columella. *On Agriculture, Volume I: Books 1–4*. Translated by Harrison Boyd Ash. LCL 361. Cambridge, MA: Harvard University Press, 1941.

Dead Sea Scrolls Translated, The. *See* García Martínez

Dio Cassius. *Roman History, Volume IV: Books 41–45*. Translated by Earnest Cary and Herbert B. Foster. LCL 66. Cambridge, MA: Harvard University Press, 1916.

Dio Chrysostom. *Discourses 12–30*. Translated by J. W. Cohoon. LCL 339. Cambridge, MA: Harvard University Press, 1939.

Diodorus Siculus. *Library of History, Volume XII: Fragments of Books 33–40*. Translated by Francis R. Walton. LCL 423. Cambridge, MA: Harvard University Press, 1967.

Dionysius of Halicarnassus. *Critical Essays, Volume II: On Literary Composition. Dinarchus. Letters to Ammaeus and Pompeius*. Translated by Stephen Usher. LCL 466. Cambridge, MA: Harvard University Press, 1985.

———. *Roman Antiquities, Volume I: Books 1–2*. Translated by Earnest Cary. LCL 319. Cambridge, MA: Harvard University Press, 1937.

Dupont-Sommer, A. *The Essene Writings from Qumran*. Translated by G. Vermès. Cleveland: World Publishing Co., 1961.

Epictetus. *Discourses, Books 1–2*. Translated by W. A. Oldfather. LCL 131. Cambridge, MA: Harvard University Press, 1925.

———. *Discourses, Books 3–4. Fragments. The Enchiridion*. Translated by W. A. Oldfather. LCL 218. Cambridge, MA: Harvard University Press, 1928.

Eusebius. *Onomasticon: The Place Names of Divine Scripture; Including the Latin Edition of Jerome*. Edited by R. Steven Notley and Ze'ev Safrai. Boston: Brill, 2005.

Fronto, Marcus Cornelius. *The Correspondence of Marcus Cornelius Fronto*. Translated by C. R. Haines. LCL 112. London: Heinemann, 1919.

García Martínez, Florentino. *The Dead Sea Scrolls Translated: The Qumran Texts in English*. Translated by Wilfred G. E. Watson. Leiden: Brill, 1994.

Gellius. *Attic Nights, Volume I: Books 1–5*. Translated by J. C. Rolfe. LCL 195. Cambridge, MA: Harvard University Press, 1927.

Goldin, Judah, trans. *The Fathers according to Rabbi Nathan*. New Haven: Yale University Press, 1955.

Horace. *Satires. Epistles. The Art of Poetry*. Translated by H. Rushton Fairclough. LCL 194. Cambridge, MA: Harvard University Press, 1926.

Josephus. *Jewish Antiquities: Books I–IV*. Translated by H. St. J. Thackeray. LCL 242. Cambridge, MA: Harvard University Press, 1930.

———. *Jewish Antiquities: Books XII–XIV*. Translated by Ralph Marcus. LCL 365. Cambridge, MA: Harvard University Press, 1943.

———. *Jewish Antiquities: Books XVIII–XX*. Translated by Louis H. Feldman. LCL. Cambridge, MA: Harvard University Press, 1965.

———. *Jewish War: Books I–III*. Translated by H. St. J. Thackeray. LCL 203. Cambridge, MA: Harvard University Press, 1927.

———. *Jewish War: Books IV–VII*. Translated by H. St. J. Thackeray. LCL 210. Cambridge, MA: Harvard University Press, 1928.

———. *Judean Antiquities, Books 8–10: Translation and Commentary*. By Christopher T. Begg and Paul Spilsbury. Vol. 5 of *Flavius Josephus*. Edited by Steve Mason. Leiden: Brill, 2005.

———. *The Life; Against Apion*. Translated by H. St. J. Thackeray. LCL 186. Cambridge, MA: Harvard University Press, 1926.

Mishnah, The. Translated by Herbert Danby. Oxford: Oxford University Press, 1933.

Oates, John F., Alan E. Samuel, and C. Bradford Welles, eds. *Yale Papyri in the Beineck Rare Book and Manuscript Library*. Vol. I. ASP 2. New Haven: American Society of Papyrologists, 1967.

Philo. *Every Good Man Is Free. On the Contemplative Life. On the Eternity of the World. Flaccus. Hypothetica. On Providence*. Translated by F. H. Colson. LCL 363. Cambridge, MA: Harvard University Press, 1941.

———. *On Abraham. On Joseph. On Moses*. Translated by F. H. Colson. LCL 289. Cambridge, MA: Harvard University Press, 1935.

———. *On the Creation. Allegorical Interpretation of Genesis 2 and 3.* Translated by F. H. Colson and G. H. Whitaker. LCL 226. Cambridge, MA: Harvard University Press, 1929.

———. *On the Decalogue. On the Special Laws, Books 1–3.* Translated by F. H. Colson. LCL 320. Cambridge, MA: Harvard University Press, 1937.

———. *On the Embassy to Gaius. General Indexes.* Translated by F. H. Colson. Index by J. W. Earp. LCL 379. Cambridge, MA: Harvard University Press, 1962.

———. *On the Special Laws, Book 4. On the Virtues. On Rewards and Punishments.* Translated by F. H. Colson. LCL 341. Cambridge, MA: Harvard University Press, 1939.

———. *On the Unchangeableness of God. On Husbandry. Concerning Noah's Work as a Planter. On Drunkenness. On Sobriety.* Translated by F. H. Colson and G. H. Whitaker. LCL 247. Cambridge, MA: Harvard University Press, 1930.

Philostratus. *Apollonius of Tyana, Volume I: Life of Apollonius of Tyana, Books 1–4.* Edited and translated by Christopher P. Jones. LCL 16. Cambridge, MA: Harvard University Press, 2005.

———. *Apollonius of Tyana, Volume II: Life of Apollonius of Tyana, Books 5–8.* Edited and translated by Christopher P. Jones. LCL 17. Cambridge, MA: Harvard University Press, 2005.

Pliny the Elder. *Natural History, Volume II: Books 3–7.* Translated by H. Rackham. LCL 352. Cambridge, MA: Harvard University Press, 1942.

———. *Natural History, Volume III: Books 8–11.* Translated by H. Rackham. LCL 353. Cambridge, MA: Harvard University Press, 1940.

———. *Natural History, Volume IV: Books 12–16.* Translated by H. Rackham. LCL 370. Cambridge, MA: Harvard University Press, 1945.

Pliny the Younger. *Letters, Volume I: Books 1–7.* Translated by Betty Radice. LCL 55. Cambridge, MA: Harvard University Press, 1969.

———. *Letters, Volume II: Books 8–10. Panegyricus.* Translated by Betty Radice. LCL 59. Cambridge, MA: Harvard University Press, 1969.

Plutarch. *Moralia, Volume II: How to Profit by One's Enemies. On Having Many Friends. Chance. Virtue and Vice. Letter of Condolence to Apollonius. Advice about Keeping Well. Advice to Bride and Groom. The Dinner of the Seven Wise Men. Superstition.* Translated by Frank Cole Babbitt. LCL 222. Cambridge, MA: Harvard University Press, 1928.

Polybius. *The Histories, Volume I: Books 1–2.* Translated by W. R. Paton. Revised by F. W. Walbank and Christian Habicht. LCL 128. Cambridge, MA: Harvard University Press, 2010.

Polybius. *The Histories, Volume VI: Books 28–39. Fragments.* Edited and translated by S. Douglas Olson. Translated by W. R. Paton. Revised by F. W. Walbank and Christian Habicht. LCL 161. Cambridge, MA: Harvard University Press, 2012.

Schneemelcher, Wilhelm, ed. *New Testament Apocrypha.* 2 vols. Translated by R. McL. Wilson. Louisville: Westminster/John Knox Press, 1991.

Strabo. *Geography, Volume VII: Books 15–16.* Translated by Horace Leonard Jones. LCL 241. Cambridge, MA: Harvard University Press, 1930.

Tacitus. *Agricola. Germania. Dialogue on Oratory.* Translated by M. Hutton, W. Peterson. Revised by R. M. Ogilvie, E. H. Warmington, and Michael Winterbottom. LCL 35. Cambridge, MA: Harvard University Press, 1914.

———. *Histories: Books 4–5. Annals: Books 1–3.* Translated by Clifford H. Moore and John Jackson. LCL 249. Cambridge, MA: Harvard University Press, 1931.

Varro. *On Agriculture.* Translated by W. D. Hooper. Revised by Harrison Boyd Ash. LCL 283. Cambridge, MA: Harvard University Press, 1934.

Part 1

Introduction

Chapter 1

Getting Oriented

*F*irst-century Galilee furnished the cast for Jesus' parables. His repertoire drew from everyday life in Galilee's towns and villages as Jesus creatively portrayed recognizable figures: a tax collector and a Pharisee, farmers, fishermen, absentee landowners and tenants, unjust stewards and debtors, children and day laborers in the marketplace, a Samaritan, a woman hoarding a few coins, shepherds and hired hands, widows and judges, and neighbors awakened at night (Dodd, 10; Scott, 79). In this social world, Jesus announced the kingdom of God, God's justice, and vindication of the poor.

From its northeast corner, Galilee extends from Lake Hule, only the southern tip of which is visible on the Map of Galilee and which was drained in the 1950s, west to the edge of the coastal plain, south to the Mount Carmel range, southeast along the southern edge of the Jezreel Valley, east along the border of Samaria, zigzagging northeast to the southern end of the Sea of Galilee. Josephus (*J.W.* 3.35–43) distinguishes upper Galilee from Kefar Hananya north, which is mountainous, where sycamores do not grow; and lower Galilee, where sycamores do grow (m. Sheb. 9:2; cf. Avi-Yonah, 133–39).

A brief overview of major events in the history of Palestine is essential if one is to understand the setting of Jesus' parables early in the first century CE. Could someone in the remote future really understand American culture today if they did not know something about the major wars in our history: the Revolutionary War, the Civil War, World Wars I and II, and the Vietnam War? In the same way, each era in its history shaped the character of first-century Galilee.

1.1 The Ptolemies and Seleucids

As a small land bridge between Egypt and empires in the north, Palestine was dominated in turn by Assyria, Babylonia, Persia, the Ptolemies, and the

Seleucids. After nearly a century of independence under the Maccabees and their descendants, the Hasmoneans, eventually Judea, Samaria, and Galilee fell under Roman rule. Each period left its mark on the region. The legacy of the Persians (538–332 BCE) was Aramaic, the primary language of the Near East from 600 BCE to 700 CE and the common language of first-century Jews. Alexander the Great defeated Darius III, first at Issus (333 BCE) and again at Gaugamela (331 BCE), bringing an end to the Persian Empire. Following his death in 323 BCE, Alexander's companions staked out their claims to portions of his conquests and spent the next twenty years fighting each other. By 301 BCE, following the Battle of Ipsus, the territories of Alexander's empire were divided among his successors: the Antigonids held Macedonia, the Ptolemies ruled Egypt and Libya, and the Seleucids controlled Syria and Persia.

The Ptolemies dominated Palestine for the next century, during which they set social and economic patterns that continued into the Roman period. In many ways, Jesus' parables reflect these patterns with large landowners, tenants, stewards, moneylenders, and day laborers. Jerusalem became a temple state governed by a high-priestly aristocracy. Travel between Jerusalem and Alexandria was common, and the Hebrew Scriptures were translated into Greek during this period (the Septuagint; see Letter of Aristeas).

A century later, the scene shifted again. Rome was beginning its expansion in the East with campaigns in Macedonia. The Seleucid king, Antiochus III ("the Great," ruling 222–187 BCE), was preparing for the inevitable conflict with Rome and annihilated the Ptolemaic army at Panium (later called Caesarea Philippi) in 200 BCE, establishing Seleucid control over Palestine. Egypt would never again control Palestine. In 188 BCE, Antiochus was forced to sign a peace treaty with the Romans at Apamea, under which his son, who would become Antiochus IV (Epiphanes, [God] Manifest, but called by some Epimanes, the Mad One), was sent to Rome as a hostage; Antiochus agreed to pay Rome 15,000 talents over a period of twelve years. His successor, Seleucus IV (187–175 BCE), attempted to plunder the temple in Jerusalem, but his emissary, Heliodorus, returned, saying he had been prevented from doing so by supernatural beings (2 Macc 3:22–30).

1.2 The Maccabean Revolt and the Hasmoneans

Antiochus IV was influenced by the time he spent in Rome and Athens; he never opposed Roman power, and he became a proponent of Hellenism.

When Antiochus IV came to power (175 BCE), he immediately began to shore up his control of Palestine and push back the Ptolemies. When the Romans stopped him from taking Alexandria, Antiochus returned to Jerusalem, where Jason had deposed Menelaus, whom Antiochus had appointed as high priest.

> So, raging inwardly, he [Antiochus] left Egypt and took the city by storm. He commanded his soldiers to cut down relentlessly everyone they met and to kill those who went into their houses. Then there was massacre of young and old, destruction of boys, women, and children, and slaughter of young girls and infants. Within the total of three days eighty thousand were destroyed, forty thousand in hand-to-hand fighting, and as many were sold into slavery as were killed. Not content with this, Antiochus dared to enter the most holy temple in all the world, guided by Menelaus, who had become a traitor both to the laws and to his country. He took the holy vessels with his polluted hands, and swept away with profane hands the votive offerings that other kings had made to enhance the glory and honor of the place. (2 Macc 5:11–16; cf. 1 Macc 1:16–24. Note: Numbers in ancient sources are often exaggerated.)

The stage was set for revolt. Seeking to solidify his control of Judea and raise revenues for his impending conflict with Rome, Antiochus IV

> sent letters by messengers to Jerusalem and the towns of Judah; he directed them to follow customs strange to the land, to forbid burnt offerings and sacrifices and drink offerings in the sanctuary, to profane sabbaths and festivals, to defile the sanctuary and the priests, to build altars and sacred precincts and shrines for idols, to sacrifice swine and other unclean animals, and to leave their sons uncircumcised. They were to make themselves abominable by everything unclean and profane, so that they would forget the law and change all the ordinances. He added, "And whoever does not obey the command of the king shall die." In such words he wrote to his whole kingdom. He appointed inspectors over all the people and commanded the towns of Judah to offer sacrifice, town by town. (1 Macc 1:44–51)

Although his objectives were military and financial, Antiochus recognized that to establish his control over Judea, his southern border with Egypt, he would need to abolish Jewish religious loyalties. Temples were commonly believed to be residences of the local god, whom the people worshiped to assure their protection and prosperity. When the king's officers came to the town of Modein, they ordered Mattathias to be the first to offer the idolatrous sacrifice.

But Mattathias answered and said in a loud voice: "Even if all the nations that live under the rule of the king obey him, and have chosen to obey his commandments, everyone of them abandoning the religion of their ancestors, I and my sons and my brothers will continue to live by the covenant of our ancestors. Far be it from us to desert the law and the ordinances. We will not obey the king's words by turning aside from our religion to the right hand or to the left."

When he had finished speaking these words, a Jew came forward in the sight of all to offer sacrifice on the altar in Modein, according to the king's command. When Mattathias saw it, he burned with zeal and his heart was stirred. He gave vent to righteous anger; he ran and killed him on the altar. At the same time he killed the king's officer who was forcing them to sacrifice, and he tore down the altar. Thus he burned with zeal for the law, just as Phinehas did against Zimri son of Salu [see Num 25:6–15].

Then Mattathias cried out in the town with a loud voice, saying: "Let every one who is zealous for the law and supports the covenant come out with me!" Then he and his sons fled to the hills and left all that they had in the town. (1 Macc 2:19–28)

Three and a half years of fighting followed (167–164 BCE), with the rebels and the Hasidim (the pious ones) led by Mattathias's sons. When Mattathias died, Judas Maccabeus (the Hammer) became the rebels' commander. Judas soon drove the Seleucids out of Jerusalem, regaining control of the temple, and delivering it from "an abomination that desolates" (Dan 9:27; 11:31; 12:11; see Mark 13:14 par.).

He chose blameless priests devoted to the law, and they cleansed the sanctuary and removed the defiled stones to an unclean place. They deliberated what to do about the altar of burnt offering, which had been profaned. And they thought it best to tear it down, so that it would not be a lasting shame to them that the Gentiles had defiled it. So they tore down the altar, and stored the stones in a convenient place on the temple hill until a prophet should come to tell what to do with them. (1 Macc 4:42–46)

In these accounts we see loyalties and flash points that persisted into the first century, including adherence to the law, zeal for the traditions of their ancestors, and protection of holiness and purity from the profane and unclean, especially the temple.

The formative significance of the second century BCE was profound. In response to Antiochus IV's threat to their ancestral traditions, Judeans coalesced around the Torah, and specifically the Torah as law. John J. Collins has traced this development, which he called "the *halakic turn* toward rigorous observance of the details of the Law, in the wake of the Maccabean revolt" (vii, 170), in the Temple Scroll, Jubilees, and 4QMMT (97–113). In *The Origins of Judaism*, Yonatan Adler sought to determine the earliest dates for which there is archaeological and literary evidence of Judaism's defining practices: Torah observance through dietary laws, ritual purity, avoidance of figural art, Sabbath observance, circumcision, and the synagogue. In essence, when does "Judaism" first appear as "a distinct way of life *governed by a legal system* composed of commandments, prohibitions, and assorted regulations founded on the Pentateuch" (Adler, 207, with his italics)? He concludes: "The Torah came to be widely known to the masses and regarded as authoritative law only in the Late Hellenistic period, following the cataclysmic events surrounding the Hasmonean revolt toward the middle of the second century BCE" (190, 234–36). In the following chapters we cite many of the documents and material remains from the first and second centuries BCE that support Adler's conclusion.

The practices and prohibitions that marked Jewish identity and distinguished Jews from gentiles continued to reverberate. In the New Testament, echoes of the zeal of Mattathias and the Maccabees persist in the Jerusalem leaders' response to Jesus and his earliest followers. Thus the chief priests and the Pharisees say, "If we let him [Jesus] go on like this, everyone will believe in him, and the Romans will come and destroy both our holy place and our nation" (John 11:48). False witnesses report, "This man [Stephen] never stops saying things against this holy place and the law; for we have heard him say that this Jesus of Nazareth will destroy this place and will change the customs that Moses handed on to us" (Acts 6:13–14).

The rededication of the temple in 164 BCE was celebrated annually at Hanukkah (see John 10:22). When Judas Maccabeus died (160 BCE), he was succeeded by his brother Jonathan (160–142 BCE). In the late 140s BCE, following the death of Ptolemy VI in 145, Seleucid contenders battled for power, with devastating effects on Galilee: "The epicenter of the chaos appears to have been the Galilee, where more than a dozen sites of various size were destroyed or abandoned" (Berlin, 38). Following Jonathan's death in 142, Simon seized the opportunity presented by the weakness of both the Ptolemies and the Seleucids, captured Jerusalem, and established the Hasmonean kingdom, becoming "leader and high priest forever, until a trustworthy prophet should arise" (1 Macc 14:41). The Hasmoneans were a succession of priest-kings. Josephus traces the name "Hasmonean" to the great-grandfather of Mattathias (*Ant.* 12.265).

- John Hyrcanus (134–104)
- Aristobulus I (104–103)
- Alexander Jannaeus (103–76)

- Shelamzion (Salome) Alexandra (queen; her son, Hyrcanus I, was high priest, 76–67)
- Conflict between Hyrcanus II and Aristobulus II (67–63)

John Hyrcanus ceased to pay tribute to the Seleucids and captured Shechem, then Idumea and Samaria.

If the Torah received a new prominence as the law by which Jews regulated their lives during the Hasmonean period, as Collins and Adler argue, it is not surprising that Jewish sectarianism appears almost immediately. Some of the Essenes established the community at Qumran probably during the reign of John Hyrcanus, and Josephus first mentions the Pharisees and Sadducees during the reign of John Hyrcanus, saying that he initially supported the Pharisees, then renounced them, supporting the Sadducees (*Ant.* 13.288–298). Aristobulus I continued his father's program of expansion by annexing Galilee: he "compelled the inhabitants, if they wished to remain in their country, to be circumcised and to live in accordance with the laws of the Jews" (*Ant.* 13.318–319; cf. 13.257). Alexander Jannaeus crucified 800 Pharisees and executed their families in front of his dying victims (*Ant.* 13.380). Salome Alexandra, Alexander Jannaeus's widow, provided a period of relative peace and prosperity following her husband's wars. In 63 BCE, when both Hyrcanus II and Aristobulus II sent emissaries to Damascus to appeal for Pompey's support, that Roman general seized Jerusalem and freed the cities conquered by the Hasmoneans (*J.W.* 1.155–158; *Ant.* 14.74–76), leaving only Galilee to the Jews, making Judea a vassal to Rome, subjecting it to Roman taxation, and appointing Hyrcanus II as high priest (*Ant.* 14.73–79). Judea's brief period of independence (164–63 BCE) thus ended.

1.3 Roman Domination

Julius Caesar removed the burdens imposed by Pompey and named Antipater, the governor of Idumea, to be procurator of Judea. Shortly before his death, Antipater appointed his sons to be governors: Herod, governor of Galilee; his brother, Phasael, governor of Jerusalem. When the Parthians invaded Syria and Palestine in 40 BCE, Herod fled to Rome. There, supported by Mark Antony and Octavian, he was declared king of Judah (37 BCE). Returning to Judea, Herod seized Jerusalem and married Mariamme (Mariamne), a Hasmonean princess (granddaughter of Hyrcanus II), and proceeded to root out rebels and rivals. When Mark Antony was killed at Philippi (30 BCE), following the assassination of Julius Caesar (44 BCE),

Herod pledged his loyalty to Octavian, who became Caesar Augustus (27 BCE–14 CE). Cleopatra fostered conflict between the Idumeans and the Hasmoneans in Herod's court. Never fully accepted by the Jews because he was an Idumean, Herod hired a mercenary army and wiped out any suspected opposition, including eventually Hyrcanus II (d. 30 BCE) and other descendants of the Hasmoneans, including Mariamme and three of his own sons.

Styling himself as a Hellenistic monarch, patron, and benefactor, Herod was a great builder of cities, including Sebaste (in Samaria) and Caesarea Maritima, along with the aqueduct to bring water from Mount Carmel to that city. He transformed Jerusalem, erecting a palace, hippodrome, and theater; his greatest project was the rebuilding of the temple. Josephus describes its magnificence.

> The exterior of the building wanted nothing that could astound either mind or eye. For, being covered on all sides with massive plates of gold, the sun was no sooner up than it radiated so fiery a flash that persons straining to look at it were compelled to avert their eyes, as from the solar rays. To approaching strangers it appeared from a distance like a snow-clad mountain; for all that was not overlaid with gold was of purest white. (*J.W.* 5.222–223)

Philo agrees: "Foreign visitors . . . are amazed both at their [the temple buildings'] beauty and magnificence" (*Spec. Laws* 1.73). Herod's benefactions to cities abroad proclaimed his loyalty to his Roman patrons as well as his place on the world stage.

Still, Herod never felt secure. He built fortresses across the land, including the fortress of Antonia, named for Mark Antony, in Jerusalem; Machaerus, east of the Dead Sea; Herodium, eight miles south of Jerusalem; and palaces at Jericho and Masada. Intrigue and rivalry among his wives and sons led to brutal reprisals and eventually Herod's own deterioration. Before his death he planned a lavish funeral and ordered mass executions when he died, so there would be mourning throughout the land (*Ant.* 17.176–181). The executions were not carried out.

Augustus ratified Herod's will, yet denied the title "king" to Herod's sons. The emperor appointed Archelaus tetrarch of the provinces south of Galilee: Samaria, Judea, and Idumea (4 BCE–6 CE); Herod Antipas tetrarch of Galilee and Perea, which was across the Jordan River (4 BCE–39 CE); and Philip tetrarch of regions north and east of the Sea of Galilee (4 BCE–34 CE). Archelaus was removed from office for excessive brutality in 6 CE (see Matt 2:22). Philip built Caesarea Philippi and Bethsaida.

Herod Antipas, "that fox" (Luke 13:32), built Sepphoris, then forcibly brought new settlers to Tiberias (*Ant.* 18.36–38), aspiring continually to succeed his father as king of Judea (Chilton, xv, 147, 171).

Following Archelaus's removal, Judea was governed by Roman prefects (6–41 CE), then procurators (44–66 CE). Pontius Pilate, neither the best nor the worst of the Roman prefects (Brown, 1:722), was prefect from 26 to 36 CE. A partially intact inscription that mentions Pilate, probably from the decade of his prefecture and now preserved at the Israel Museum in Jerusalem, was recovered at Caesarea Martima. By the end of this period, Judea was sinking into anarchy, with rebel groups fighting one another. In contrast, Galilee remained under Herodian rule: Herod Antipas, then Agrippa I (39–44 CE). In response to Gaius Caligula's order to erect his statue in the temple (39 CE), Galilean peasants petitioned Petronius, governor of Syria, to intervene and refused to till the land (*Ant.* 18.273).

The procurator, Gessius Florus (64–66 CE), who was worse than his predecessors, "stripped whole cities, ruined entire populations, . . . proclaiming throughout the country that all were at liberty to practice brigandage" (*J.W.* 2.278). Then he pillaged seventeen talents from the temple (*J.W.* 2.293) and marched on Jerusalem to quell the uproar that followed, actions that precipitated the Jewish Revolt of 66–70 CE. The revolutionary council in Jerusalem sent Josephus to Galilee to maintain peace while preparing to confront the Romans. When some men seized a large quantity of silver and gold from the wife of Agrippa II's finance officer, Josephus dispatched most of the plunder to Jerusalem to fund work on the city's walls and said he kept the rest to fortify Taricheae. When Vespasian marched through Galilee in 67 CE, taking Sepphoris without a fight, Josephus retreated to Tiberias, then to Yodefat, before defecting to the Romans. Standing before Vespasian and Titus, Josephus predicted that they would both become Caesars, a prophecy for which they spared his life. Vespasian then besieged Jerusalem and called in additional legions from Alexandria. After the succession of three claimants to the throne in Rome following the murder of Nero, Vespasian's troops acclaimed *him* as emperor. When Vespasian returned to Rome, his son, Titus, carried out the destruction of Jerusalem and its temple in 70 CE, then besieged the Zealots at Herodium and Machaerus, and finally took Masada (ca. 73 CE). One can hardly imagine a more turbulent time or place for "a marginal Jew" (John Meier's term) to announce the coming of the kingdom of God.

Works Cited in Chapter 1

Adler, Yonatan. 2022. *The Origins of Judaism: An Archaeological-Historical Reappraisal.* AYBRL. New Haven: Yale University Press.

Avi-Yonah, Michael. 2002. *The Holy Land from the Persian to the Arab Conquest (536 B.C.–A.D. 640): A Historical Geography.* Rev. ed. Jerusalem: Carta.

Berlin, Andrea M. 2023. "The Rise of the Maccabees." *BAR* 49.2:32–39.

Brown, Raymond E. 1994. *The Death of the Messiah.* 2 vols. New York: Doubleday.

Chilton, Bruce. 2021. *The Herods: Murder, Politics, and the Art of Succession.* Minneapolis: Fortress.

Collins, John J. 2017. *The Invention of Judaism: Torah and Jewish Identity from Deuteronomy to Paul.* Oakland: University of California Press.

Dodd, C. H. 1935. *The Parables of the Kingdom.* London: Nisbet.

Meier, John P. 1994. *A Marginal Jew: Rethinking the Historical Jesus.* Vol. 2, *Mentor, Message, and Miracles.* New York: Doubleday.

Scott, Brandon Bernard. 1989. *Hear Then the Parable: A Commentary on the Parables of Jesus.* Minneapolis: Augsburg Fortress.

Chapter 2

Reading Our Sources

*I*f we were dependent on sources written in Galilee in the first century, we would have very little to work with. The Gospels themselves are among our best sources since they preserve Jesus' teachings and were written in the latter part of the first century, although their places of composition are debated. Q (the parables and sayings found in Matthew and Luke but not Mark) may have been composed in Galilee (see esp. Bazzana; Keddie, 217–67). Josephus wrote of his experiences in Galilee. Beyond the Gospels and Josephus, the available sources come from elsewhere, earlier or later than Jesus' ministry: the writings of the Apocrypha and Pseudepigrapha; Philo; Josephus; the Dead Sea Scrolls; rabbinic writings, especially the Mishnah (the collection from the oral tradition of the Pharisees); and papyri from Egypt and near the Dead Sea. Each has its limitations.

As we have seen, Galilee changed under the Hasmoneans and the Herods, and the destruction of Jerusalem in 70 CE brought marked changes throughout Palestine. As a result, the available sources for the history and culture of first-century Galilee require careful handling. Greco-Roman literature, generally written by the elites of Athens and Rome, is of limited value. Yet it may preserve descriptions applicable to life in antiquity generally or economic patterns that influenced Galilee, such as estates and absentee landowners or the authority of the paterfamilias. Philo of Alexandria was roughly contemporaneous with Jesus, but as a wealthy, urban, Hellenistic, diaspora Jew, his writings are of limited value for understanding Galilean village life. As a rule, where reflections of daily life and culture are similar in earlier and later sources—as, for example, in Sirach (early 2nd c. BCE) and the Mishnah (200 CE, with sayings attributed to earlier rabbis)—we may assume that what they show us about Jewish life would have been true for first-century Jews in Galilee also. For example, the similarity between the attitude expressed by the servant girl who identified Peter as a Galilean (Matt 26:69; Mark 14:70; Luke 22:59) and the much later slur, "foolish

Galilean" (b. 'Erub. 53b), directed at Jose the Galilean, a contemporary of Akiva (early 2nd c.)—this similarity suggests a common Judean sentiment toward Galileans throughout this period. On the other hand, many rabbinic rulings did not apply before 70 CE.

Interpreters must be sensitive not only to the geographical and chronological contexts of our sources but also their ethnic, religious, and social locations. For example, only in the Gospel of Luke, which was probably addressed to a more affluent, Greco-Roman audience than Matthew or Mark ("most excellent Theophilus," Luke 1:3), do we find Jesus saying, "Who among you would say to your slave who has just come in from plowing or tending sheep in the field, 'Come here at once and take your place at the table'? Would you not rather say to him, 'Prepare supper for me, put on your apron and serve me while I eat and drink; later you may eat and drink'?" (Luke 17:7–8). In most of Jesus' sayings and parables, landowners and slaveholders are outsiders, not his audience.

Some of our sources are earlier or later than the first century, but some of what they record would have been true for the first century also. The same can be said for sources written in Jerusalem, Egypt, or elsewhere. Apocryphal stories often project ideals and virtues, yet incidental details about life in antiquity also. Historians, especially Josephus, used sources and had biases that influenced their writings. Rabbinic texts may reflect first-century practice, but more often they retroject later traditions and practices. Many texts are quoted or cited in the following chapters, so the reader must continually ask whether what they tell us is relevant to understanding life in first-century Galilee or not. Nevertheless, a more accurate picture of Galilean culture is emerging from the sources and data as historians sift them *chronologically*, exposing the differences between Galilee in the early first century and the second and later centuries; *geographically*, exposing the differences between upper Galilee and lower Galilee, and between villages, towns, and cities; and *socially*, distinguishing the elites from the great majority of the population, who were farmers and artisans. Still, the sources are so sparse that we often catch only glimpses of life in Galilee at this time. With these cautions in mind, we turn to a survey of our available sources.

2.1 Galilee in the Old Testament and the Gospels

Galilee appears only a handful of times in the Old Testament: Joshua 20:7 lists "Kedesh in Galilee in the hill country of Naphtali" among the cities of refuge; 21:32 says, "Out of the tribe of Naphtali: Kedesh in [upper] Galilee with its pasture lands, the city of refuge for the slayer" was given to the

Levites (cf. 1 Chr 6:76). King Solomon gave King Hiram of Tyre twenty cities in Galilee, but "they did not please him" (1 Kgs 9:11–12). Tiglath-pileser of Assyria captured strongholds in the region, including "Kedesh, Hazor, Gilead, and Galilee, all the land of Naphtali; and he carried the people captive to Assyria" (2 Kgs 15:29). Yet Isaiah prophesies, "In the former time [the LORD] brought into contempt the land of Zebulun and the land of Naphtali, but in the latter time he will make glorious the way of the sea, the land beyond the Jordan, Galilee of the nations" (9:1).

The Gospels, especially the parables, provide rare glimpses into everyday life in Galilee. Mark, the earliest of the Gospels, collects a group of agricultural parables in Mark 4 and others in Mark 12:1–11; 13:28–29, 33–37. Matthew and Luke, drawing on a common "source" (Q = *Quelle* [German]), contain more parables than Mark, both in Galilee and in Jerusalem; in Luke, Jesus speaks many of them on the way to Jerusalem. Jesus' conflict with the Pharisees is especially sharp in Matthew (see ch. 23). In contrast, the Gospel of John contains little of Jesus' Galilean ministry, only the wedding at Cana (2:1–11), the healing of the royal official's son (4:46–54), and the feeding of the five thousand and Jesus' walking on the water (John 6). John 21 reports the risen Lord's appearance by the Sea of Galilee. John also contains figurative sayings (*paroimia*, e.g., 3:8, 29–30; 5:19; 8:35–36; 10:1–5; 15:1–8) but none of the synoptic parables. Surprisingly, Acts seldom mentions Galilee. The disciples are instructed to remain in Jerusalem after Jesus' resurrection (Luke 24:49; Acts 1:4). Then, they are charged to be witnesses "in Jerusalem, in all Judea and Samaria, and to the ends of the earth" (Acts 1:8), but this commission does not mention Galilee, which appears only in Acts 1:11, "Men of Galilee"; 9:31, "the church throughout Judea, Galilee, and Samaria"; 10:37, the gospel "spread throughout Judea, beginning in Galilee after the baptism that John announced"; and 13:31, Jesus "appeared to those who came up with him from Galilee to Jerusalem."

2.2 The Apocrypha

The Old and New Testaments are supplemented by the (OT) Apocrypha, generally the books that appear in the Septuagint (LXX) but not in the Hebrew Bible. Jerome included these books in the Latin Vulgate. Although some of these writings are difficult to date, most of them originated in the second or first centuries BCE. They include historical writings (esp. 1 and 2 Maccabees), additions to Esther and Daniel, wisdom writings (Wisdom of Solomon, Sirach), expansions of biblical tradition (Baruch, Letter of Jeremiah), and edifying folktales (Tobit, Judith).

Tobit presents a vivid description of Jewish piety prior to the Maccabean era. Tobit's family was from the tribe of Naphtali in upper Galilee:

> All my kindred and our ancestral house of Naphtali sacrificed to the calf that King Jeroboam of Israel had erected in Dan and on all the mountains of Galilee [1 Kgs 12:25–33]. But I alone went often to Jerusalem for the festivals, as it is prescribed for all Israel by an everlasting decree. I would hurry off to Jerusalem with the first fruits of the crops and the firstlings of the flock, the tithes of the cattle, and the first shearings of the sheep. (Tob 1:5–6; cf. Exod 13:12; Lev 27:32; Deut 14:22–27; 18:4; 26:1–11; Culpepper, 451–52)

Tobit gives readers an expansive window onto Jewish piety and its social world as it encourages not only paying the tithes, giving alms, and journeying to Jerusalem for the festivals but also such expressions of piety as burying the dead and marrying within one's tribe. At the end, Raphael, Tobias's angel companion, offers the following summation:

> Bless God and acknowledge him in the presence of all the living for the good things he has done for you. Bless and sing praise to his name. With fitting honor declare to all people the deeds of God. Do not be slow to acknowledge him. It is good to conceal the secret of a king, but to acknowledge and reveal the works of God, and with fitting honor to acknowledge him. Do good and evil will not overtake you. Prayer with fasting is good, but better than both is almsgiving with righteousness. A little with righteousness is better than wealth with wrongdoing. It is better to give alms than to lay up gold. For almsgiving saves from death and purges away every sin. Those who give alms will enjoy a full life, but those who commit sin and do wrong are their own worst enemies. (Tob 12:6–10)

Galilee appears at the beginning and end of Judith (1:8; 15:5), the spellbinding story of a heroine who delivers her town from the siege of Holofernes, a Persian general. Judith's religion is vigorously nationalistic, a blend of patriotism and piety. She scrupulously obeys the law of Moses regarding dietary laws, fasting, prayer at fixed times, and ritual ablutions.

First and Second Maccabees are our primary sources for the events of the Maccabean Revolt (167–164 BCE), although they present sharply contrasting views. First Maccabees, "composed by a historian working in the circle of John Hyrcanus" (Berlin and Kosmin, 406), tells the story from the outbreak of the revolt to the reign of John Hyrcanus, lauding Mattathias and his sons, "the family of those men through whom deliverance was given to Israel" (1 Macc 5:62), and drawing parallels between King David and Mattathias to establish the legitimacy of the Hasmonean dynasty. Second Maccabees abridges the work of Jason of Cyrene, who is otherwise unknown, denigrating the high priests Jason and Menelaus and the brothers of Judas Maccabaeus, while praising the high priest Onias III and emphasizing the purification of the temple, the deaths of the martyrs, the miraculous victories that followed, and beneficial covenants with righteous gentiles (Goldstein, 3–36). "Galilee" occurs eleven times in 1 Maccabees but never in 2 Maccabees. Especially notable is the report that "the people of Ptolemais and Tyre and Sidon, and all Galilee of the Gentiles, had gathered together against them 'to annihilate us [the Israelites]'" (1 Macc 5:15). When Judas heard this, he sent his brother Simon to rescue the Jews in Galilee, which he did, pursuing the gentiles to the coast (Ptolemais) before leading "the Jews of Galilee and Arbatta" to Judea (1 Macc 5:16–23, 55).

Fourth Maccabees contains a discourse on religious reason and the Mosaic law, followed by the stories of the Maccabean martyrs: the priest Eleazar (5:1–7:23), the seven brothers (8:1–14:10), and their mother (14:11–18:19). Other books of the Apocrypha contain wisdom traditions and materials that offer insights into Jewish culture and ethics during the period immediately preceding the New Testament.

The books of the Pseudepigrapha contain a wide variety of Jewish and Christian writings from 200 BCE to 200 CE that circulated in early Jewish and Christian communities (Charlesworth; Bauckham, Davila, and Panayotov). Although Galilee seldom appears in these writings, they furnish valuable reflections of the diversity of thought and practice among Jews during this period.

2.3 Josephus

Beyond the New Testament itself, the most important source is Flavius Josephus (born in 37 CE), an aristocrat from Jerusalem, and commander of the Jewish forces in Galilee during the First Jewish Revolt (66–70) before he defected to the Romans in 70. After the war, Josephus was granted Roman citizenship and a pension in Rome. There he wrote *The Jewish War* (about 79 CE), in which he depends on Nicolaus of Damascus, Herod's adviser; he attributes the war not to the Jewish people generally but to a small group of revolutionary leaders, especially Eleazar ben Simon, John of Gischala, and Simon bar Giora (Rhoads, 101–5, 122–36, 140–47). This account of the war was followed later by *The Antiquities of the Jews*, which recounts their history through the Old Testament and up to the outbreak of the war in 66. The latter part of this longer history overlaps the first two books of *The Jewish*

War: while they contain some differences in perspective, both works present the history, religion, and practices of the Jews to the Roman public in the most positive light. Two other works followed later: his *Life*, a brief (and poorly written) autobiography; and *Against Apion*, which responds to slanderous accusations against the Jews. Josephus's descriptions of Galilee are remarkably consistent in these works, but his references to the revolutionary leaders, relations between the cities and the rural towns and villages, and population figures are suspect because of his personal agendas (Root, 10–20).

2.4 The Dead Sea Scrolls

The Dead Sea Scrolls, from caves near Qumran, contain writings of that community, a Zadokite sect generally identified as Essene. These scrolls include works peculiar to their community, such as rules, hymns, prayers, and liturgical materials; as well as the earliest known biblical scrolls (3rd c. BCE scrolls taken to Qumran) and books of the Apocrypha and Pseudepigrapha. Some of the scrolls are distinctly sectarian; others offer glimpses of practices shared by other Jewish communities. The Romans' destruction of Qumran in 68 CE furnishes a firm terminus for the dating of the scrolls, but questions remain concerning the existence of Essene communities elsewhere and the ways in which their practices reflect or differ from the practices of other Jews.

2.5 Philo

Philo Judaeus (ca. 20 BCE–50 CE) was a prolific interpreter of Scripture and Jewish tradition. Writing for Jews in Alexandria and elsewhere, Philo argued that Jewish tradition and learning was as sophisticated as that of the Greeks. He is therefore a leading representative of Hellenistic Judaism as he mediates between Hellenism and Jewish Scriptures and teachings. Again, we must ask: To what extent and in what ways was such dialogue occurring in Galilee during this time? Galilee appears in Philo's writings only in passing (*Embassy* 326).

2.6 Rabbinic Sources

The oral tradition of the Pharisees is preserved in parts of the Mishnah, a collection encompassing six tractates, as committed to writing around 200

CE by Judah the Prince in Galilee. Although the Mishnah occasionally attributes teachings and traditions to pre-70 teachers, its traditions were shaped following the destruction of the temple; the continuity between Second Temple Pharisees and the later rabbis is not as strong or clear as was once thought (see ch. 17 below).

Rabbinic tradition remembers Galilean charismatic holy men who could pray for the sick and for rain: Honi the Circle-Drawer (*Ant.* 14.22; m. Taʻan. 3:8), Hanina ben Dosa (m. Ber. 5:5), and Jose the Galilean: "When, for their sins, there is drought in Israel, and such a one as Jose the Galilean prays for rain, the rain comes straightway" (y. Ber. 9b; see Vermès, 72–78; Meier, 2:581–88; Avery-Peck; below, in 21.6). The first challenge is to distinguish the traditions and sayings that reflect practices in the early part of the first century from those that reflect a later period. The second is to determine which ones give us a window onto Galilean as well as Judean practices. The usefulness of rabbinic sources for our purposes is further complicated by considering that this literature is "the product of an intellectual and religious elite and therefore not necessarily reflective of a wider population" (Lapin, 241).

2.7 Papyri

Papyri are emerging as another valuable source of information. Sabine Huebner, a leading papyrologist, describes problems facing research into the lives of ordinary people in the New Testament period.

> Common people held no high offices and composed no histories, epics, or poems—in fact, most were not able to write at all. Their everyday lives and deeds were generally of no importance to the writing of history. Roman law had little personal relevance to those who did not own or bequeath anything and could not afford to start legal proceedings. A commoner did not have the means to dedicate a portico to the public forum; nor did the city have any reason to honor them publicly with a monument. Their offspring could rarely afford to mark their tombs with a stone inscription. (1)

Nevertheless, they did pay taxes; they, their families, and any property they owned were entered on census and tax records. Many letters and business documents written on papyrus also survive, but due to the susceptibility of papyrus to dampness, most of these materials come from the sands of Egypt. "Hundreds of thousands of papyri, preserved by favorable environmental conditions, report on details of life in Roman times, including individuals' daily fears and worries, which are unavailable with this degree of quality and in this quantity in any other sources" (Huebner, 3). Although there were pronounced differences between Egypt and Galilee, study of the papyri and ostraca (inscribed pottery fragments) reveals much about the ages, health, life expectancy, families, work, travel, and business activities that would have been true in Galilee as well as Egypt (Kloppenborg 2006; 2010). In addition, many of the Qumran scrolls are papyrus texts, other papyri have been recovered from the "Cave of Letters" (see 7.8 below), and 4th c. BCE Samaritan Aramaic papyri were found at Wadi ed-Daliyeh, about 9 miles north of Jericho (see below, 19.1.3).

2.8 Inscriptions

Scholars lament the dearth of Galilean inscriptions and other documentary evidence (Lapin; Knauf, 337–38). Nevertheless, the few that can be dated to the Second Temple period provide valuable data. Ancient Palestinian inscriptions are generally burial inscriptions or dedications on public buildings, especially synagogues, written in Hebrew, Aramaic, or Greek; most of these postdate the destruction of the temple in 70 CE.

A set of Greek inscriptions (ca. 202–195 BCE) discovered at Hefzibah in the Bet She'an/Scythopolis Valley contains orders from Antiochus III; Antiochus IV; and Ptolemaios, the region's *strategos*. These orders shed light on the administration of Seleucid estates (see 9.3 below). An ostracon from the second century BCE found at Sepphoris contains part of the term *epimelētēs*, a general term for an administrator; two lead weights contain the title *agoranomos*, "market overseer" (117/116 BCE and 29/30 CE), the latter from Tiberias (see 12.5; Chancey, 30–31, 135). A decree from Caesar, probably from the period following the death of Agrippa I in 44 CE, is recorded on a Greek inscription that may have originated in Galilee; it forbids grave robbery, promising the penalty of death for transgressors (Chancey, 56–58). The construction of Roman roads can be dated by inscriptions on milestones (see 13.1). Only one inscribed ossuary (a limestone box for secondary burial of bones) from Galilee can be dated to the first century or early second (Chancey, 130), but affluent Galileans may have collected the bones of family members in Judean ossuaries. The Galilean synagogue inscriptions are all later (3rd/4th c. and later; cf. Chancey, 139–55; Lapin). A translation of the Theodotos Inscription, which documents a first-century synagogue in Jerusalem, is discussed below (3.2).

2.9 Archaeology

These written sources can now be supplemented by a constantly increasing volume of information from archaeological excavations of Galilean sites (see esp. Fiensy and Strange; Fiensy 2020). Each new discovery tells us more about the people of Galilee, economic conditions, how they lived, what they did, where they gathered, and even what they ate. The challenge now is correlating the record of material remains with written historical sources.

All this material, much of it published by specialists in various disciplines, requires careful study. The purpose of this volume is to gather relevant findings and interpret them for those who study, teach, and preach the parables: all who wish to know more about the setting of Jesus' Galilean ministry.

Works Cited in Chapter 2

Avery-Peck, Alan J. 2007. "The Galilean Charismatic and Rabbinic Piety: The Holy Man in the Talmudic Literature." Pages 149–65 in *The Historical Jesus in Context*. Edited by Amy-Jill Levine, Dale C. Allison Jr., and John Dominic Crossan. Princeton: Princeton University Press.

Bauckham, Richard, James R. Davila, and Alexander Panayotov, eds. 2013. *Old Testament Pseudepigrapha: More Noncanonical Scriptures.* Grand Rapids: Eerdmans.

Bazzana, Giovanni B. 2015. *Kingdom of Bureaucracy: The Political Theology of Village Scribes in the Sayings Gospel Q.* BETL 274. Leuven: Peeters.

Berlin, Andrea M., and Paul J. Kosmin, eds. 2021. *The Middle Maccabees: Archaeology, History, and the Rise of the Hasmonean Kingdom.* SBLABS 28. Atlanta: SBL Press.

Chancey, Mark A. 2005. *Greco-Roman Culture and the Galilee of Jesus.* SNTSMS 134. Cambridge: Cambridge University Press.

Charlesworth, James H., ed. 1983–85. *The Old Testament Pseudepigrapha.* 2 vols. Garden City, NY: Doubleday.

Culpepper, R. Alan. 2021. *Matthew.* NTL. Louisville: Westminster John Knox.

Fiensy, David A. 2020. *The Archaeology of Daily Life: Ordinary Persons in Late Second Temple Israel.* Eugene, OR: Cascade.

Fiensy, David A., and James R. Strange, eds. 2014–15. *Galilee in the Late Second Temple and Mishnaic Periods.* 2 vols. Minneapolis: Fortress.

Goldstein, Jonathan. 1976. *I Maccabees.* AB 41. Garden City, NY: Doubleday.

Huebner, Sabine R. 2019. *Papyri and the Social World of the New Testament.* Cambridge: Cambridge University Press.

Keddie, G. Anthony. 2018. *Revelations of Ideology: Apocalyptic Class Politics in Early Roman Palestine.* JSJSup 189. Leiden: Brill.

Kloppenborg, John S. 2006. *The Tenants in the Vineyard: Ideology, Economics and Agrarian Conflict in Jewish Palestine.* WUNT 195. Tübingen: Mohr Siebeck.

———. 2010. "Pastoralism, Papyri, and the Parable of the Shepherd." Pages 47–70 in *Light from the East: Papyrologische Kommentare zum Neuen Testament*. Edited by Peter Arzt-Grabner and Christina M. Kreineker. Wiesbaden: Harrassowitz.

Knauf, Ernst Axel. 2003. "Writing and Speaking in Galilee." Pages 336–50 in *Zeichen aus Text und Stein: Studien auf dem Weg zu einer Archäologie des Neuen Testaments*. Edited by S. Alkier and J. K. Zangenberg. TANZ 42. Tübingen: Francke.

Lapin, Hayim. 1999. "Palestinian Inscriptions and Jewish Ethnicity." Pages 239–68 in *Galilee through the Centuries: Confluence of Cultures*. Edited by Eric M. Meyers. Winona Lake: Eisenbrauns.

Meier, John P. 1994. *Mentor, Message, and Miracles*. Vol. 2 of *A Marginal Jew: Rethinking the Historical Jesus*. New York: Doubleday.

Rhoads, David M. 1976. *Israel in Revolution, 6–74 CE: A Political History Based on the Writings of Josephus*. Philadelphia: Fortress.

Root, Bradley W. 2014. *First-Century Galilee: A Fresh Examination of the Sources*. WUNT 378. Tübingen: Mohr Siebeck.

Vermès, Géza. 1973. *Jesus the Jew*. London: Collins.

Chapter 3

Introduction to First-Century Galilee

*T*he historical events that shaped first-century Galilee introduced move-ments of peoples, cultural changes, population growth, new cities, and smaller towns connected by a network of roads. Material remains from the early Roman period provide clues to the culture, religious practices, and responses to gentile influences. This chapter surveys these demographic and cultural shifts and the artifacts they left behind.

3.1 Galilee before the Hasmoneans

Greco-Roman writers seldom mention Galilee. Pliny the Elder (23/24–79 CE) says only, "The part of Judaea adjoining Syria is called Galilee" (*Nat.* 5.15). Strabo (64/63 BCE–21 CE) identifies its inhabitants not very accu-rately, as follows:

> This region lies towards the north; and it is inhabited in general, as is each place in particular, by mixed stocks of people from Aegyptian and Arabian and Phoenician tribes; for such are those who occupy Galilee and Hiericus [Jericho] and Philadelphia and Samaria, which last Herod surnamed Sebaste. But though the inhabitants are mixed up thus, the most prevalent of the accredited reports in regard to the temple at Jerusalem represents the ancestors of the present Judaeans, as they are called, as Aegyptians. (*Geogr.* 16.34)

Galilee was only sparsely settled after it was overrun by the Assyrians in the eighth century BCE, and little is known about the area during this period. Indeed, "there is a nearly complete absence of historical sources concern-ing eastern Galilee during the 550 years between the Eastern conquest and the Hasmonean rebellion" (Leibner 2009, 315). Palestine was exposed to

Hellenism after its conquest by Alexander the Great (about 332 BCE) and Roman occupation following Pompey (63 BCE). Nevertheless, while these events shaped the future of the eastern Mediterranean world, they had little effect on rural Galilee.

The Mishnah lists "the old castle of Sepphoris, the fortress of Gush-Halab, old Yodpat, [and] Gamla" among the fortified towns in Galilee (m. 'Arak. 9:6). A series of Hasmonean campaigns led to the abandonment of Galilean settlements and repopulation by Jewish settlers (Leibner 2021, 142–43). Aristobulus I (104–103 BCE), who continued John Hyrcanus's (135–104 BCE) expansion of Jewish territory, annexed Iturea (southern Lebanon) and Galilee (Goodman, 599–600). Immediately, new towns and villages began to appear, including many referred to frequently below: Capernaum, Gamla, Yodefat, Nazareth (see below, 21.1), and Sepphoris (Reed 1999, 97). Hasmonean fortresses made the region safer (Moreland, 158), and the Judeans who settled in Galilee maintained connections with Jerusalem (Aviam 2004a, 54; Aviam 2004b, 7–15). Magdala (Migdal/Taricheae), strategically located on the shore of the Sea of Galilee at the eastern end of Wadi Hammam, was established by the Hasmoneans (De Luca and Lena, 280–83), and the population of Capernaum increased greatly (Mattila, 244; Zwickel, 172).

3.2 The Jewish Character of First-Century Galilee

Population growth accompanied by modest economic expansion continued in the early part of the first century. Galilean villages "thrived and expanded" under Antipas, and the iconography on his coins displays sensitivity to Jewish religious feelings (Jensen 2007, 29; Jensen 2012, 51–55). The population of Galilee more than doubled between 50 BCE and 50 CE. Increased security and political stability fueled limited social mobility (Edwards 2007, 359–62; Leibner 2009, 333–35; Reed 2010, 351, 364–65; Root, 156–58). Capernaum and Magdala became centers of the fishing and fish-processing industry. Construction at Sepphoris and Tiberias provided employment; the growth of these cities created new markets. Roads from villages and towns to the cities were the veins and arteries of the economy: farmers and artisans brought their goods to the markets, and traveling merchants brought their wares and imported items to the villages (Edwards 1992; see below, 13.1). As Edwards observes, "Villages were not static bastions of tradition but rather fluid entities that reflected as well as participated in the economic and cultural currents swirling around them" (2007, 374).

Josephus reports there were 204 "cities and villages in Galilee" (*Life* 235). Material remains confirm that Galilean villages in the first century were predominantly Jewish (Bonnie, 11–12). Religious markers begin to appear in the first century BCE, including *miqva'ot* (stepped pools for ritual cleansing; Aviam 2004b, 17; Magness, 16–17; Luff, 78–86), stone vessels (which did not retain impurity; see Edwards 2002, 114–15; Miller 2003; Reed 2003; Zangenberg; Berlin 2011, esp. 92–96), Hasmonean coins, Judean oil lamps (attesting a close affinity with Jerusalem; Jensen 2012, 61; Jensen 2013, 21–22; Luff, 86–91), Judean ossuaries (bone boxes made of Judean limestone and carried to Galilee), and the absence of images and pig bones. Although secondary burial of bones dates back to the Chalcolithic Period (4500–3400 BCE; Luff, 91), Judean ossuaries begin to appear in 20–15 BCE in Judea, disappear from Jerusalem after 70 CE, but continue to be found in fewer numbers in Galilee until the third century (Magness, 151). About seventy-five ossuaries have been found in Galilee (Aviam 2013b, 109).

The stress on Jewish identity in early first-century Galilee may well have been an expression of social protest. Galilean Jews built *miqva'ot* to maintain their ritual purity; refused to use coins with images of gods, temples, or political leaders; and used stone vessels while refusing gentile ceramics (Richardson and Edwards, 249–50; Edwards 2007, 370–73; Jensen 2013; Miller 2015, 45–55; Fiensy 2020, 286). The majority of coins found in lower Galilee are Hasmonean coins that did not bear human images, and Herod Antipas did not put his image on coins he struck. Nevertheless, coins with images clearly circulated in Jewish areas (Mark 12:15–17), and the Tyrian shekel, which bore the image of the Phoenician god Melqart, was, ironically, the preferred coin for payment of the temple tax (Sanders, 400–401; Richardson, 246–47; Culpepper, 334–35). After the Romans established a colony for veterans on the ruins of the Phoenician city Berytus in 15 BCE, red-slipped table vessels, which were identified with Roman culture and domination, quickly disappeared from Galilean homes (Berlin 2002, 69; Berlin 2011, 96–99).

The sheer number of *miqva'ot* in Judea and Galilee—over 1,000 (Adler, 61–66; cf. De Luca and Lena, 306), many of which are in homes—illustrates the heightened concern for purity among Jews during this period (Bonnie, 287–313, 329–32). In contrast, no such pools have been found along the coast or in the Decapolis. *Miqva'ot* have not been found at Capernaum, probably because the lake could be used for ritual purification, but Magdala had at least two.

The Hasmonean conquest of Galilee under Aristobulus I (see above, 1.2) was followed by settlement of Judeans in Galilee (see 3.1 above; Cromhout).

It is not surprising, therefore, that the earliest Galilean synagogues date from the first century BCE. Anders Runesson distinguishes between public synagogues and private or association synagogues (Runesson 2001, 213–35, 361; Runesson 2017; Miller 2015, 45; Runesson and Cirafesi). In addition, some synagogues were in private homes. The remains at Tel Rekhesh are a private synagogue: "There is no doubt that this is an assembly room, in a Jewish farmstead, and therefore we can easily suggest that this is a synagogue, where the owner of the estate gathered his family and workers for reading the Torah and study [of] the law" (Aviam and Safrai, 101). This discovery suggests further "that synagogues were common in every village[,] even the small ones" (Aviam and Safrai, 101). Remains of synagogues from the early Roman period have been found at Magdala, Wadi Hammam, Tel Rekhesh, Shikhin, Cana (Khirbet Qana), Gamla, and Magdala (Aviam 2019, 298–99; Bonnie, 172–74, 177–78; Catto, 93–96, 102–3; Edwards 2002, 111–14; Hachlili, 23–42; Leibner 2015, 348–50; McCollough 2015, 141; McCollough 2021; McCollough 2022, 115; Richardson, 66, 104; Runesson 2017; Runesson, Binder, and Olsson, passim; Ryan 2017, 61–67; Ryan 2023). The Gospel references to a first-century synagogue in Capernaum (Mark 1:21; John 6:59) may also be corroborated by probes beneath the existing limestone synagogue (Catto, 99–102; Cirafesi; Runesson 2001, 182–85; Runesson 2017, 164; Runesson, Binder, and Olsson, 29–32; see, however, Bonnie, 181–84). Synagogues served primarily as places for public reading and interpretation of the Scriptures. As such, "the synagogue functioned primarily as a kind of *educational* institution," where the Torah was taught and interpreted (Adler, 170, with his italics; cf. Runesson 2001, 213–35, 342–50). Secondarily, public synagogues also functioned as community centers: "These new institutions probably helped standardize religious customs within each community" (Root, 168). The Migdal Stone, discovered in the synagogue at Magdala that was destroyed during the revolt of 66–70 CE, is especially exciting because it gives us the earliest representation in Galilee of the Menorah in the temple in Jerusalem and other images that confirm a close connection between the Jews in Galilee and Jerusalem.

The Theodotos Inscription, discovered in a cistern filled with rubbish south of the temple in Jerusalem, is generally dated to the Herodian period. Because other inscribed stones were found in the same cistern, they were apparently placed there after the destruction of Jerusalem in 70 CE. The inscription describes the functions of a synagogue, at least of that synagogue:

Theodotos son of Vettenus, priest and *archisynagōgos*, son of an *archisynagōgos* and grandson of an *archisynagōgos*, built the assembly hall (*synagōgē*) for the reading of the Law and for the teaching of the commandments, and the guest room, the chambers, and water fittings, as an inn for those in need from foreign parts, (the synagogue) which his fathers founded with the elders and Simonides. (Kloppenborg, 252–53)

The "water fittings" could have been facilities for washing and purification, and these may have been unique to the function of the synagogue in Jerusalem, where visitors would have been common (Hachlili, 523–26).

The influence of Greco-Roman culture in Galilee during the lifetime of Jesus has often been greatly exaggerated. The inroads of Hellenism were actually quite modest. Herod the Great built extensively at Caesarea, Sebaste, Jerusalem, and elsewhere but left Galilee almost wholly untouched. Prior to Herod Antipas, who started building Sepphoris shortly after Herod's death in 4 BCE and Tiberias in 19 CE, Galilee had no cities, and none of the edifices of Hellenistic culture: theaters, amphitheaters, hippodromes, or gymnasia (Freyne, 53). In the early part of the first century, Galilee enjoyed an increase in population, economic growth, and relative political stability during Herod Antipas's 43-year reign (4 BCE–39 CE): "He was not a *remaker* of Galilee, but rather a modest *developer*" (Jensen 2007, 31). While the establishment of Sepphoris and Tiberias as administrative centers was important, their influence in the early first century was not as pronounced as it would become (Meyers 1997, 59; McCollough 2013, 55–57). Throughout the first century, Sepphoris "remained overwhelmingly Jewish" (Meyers 1997, 64). Rather than being oriented toward the West and absorbing the influence of the cities, it now appears increasingly that the Jewish population of Galilee came from Judea during the period of the Hasmoneans and retained its ties with Jerusalem and the temple.

Mark Chancey contends that "the processes of Romanization were in only their nascent stages under Herod the Great and Antipas" (142; so also Keddie, 25; and Bonnie, esp. 319–23). Josephus records that Herod Antipas's palace at Tiberias contained representations of animals (*Life* 65), but Antipas's coins did not bear animal or human images (Adler, 93). Because imported pottery (Eastern terra sigillata or red-slipped pottery, popular in Galilee during the late Hellenistic period), mold-made lamps, brass, public inscriptions, and marble were associated with Greco-Roman culture, their disappearance in Galilee at the same time as the appearance of markers of Jewish religious identity discussed above may be evidence of Galilee's resistance to Roman culture in the first century (Magness, 54–59; Root,

132–35). Ernst Knauf notes the dramatic increase in Greek inscriptions in northern Israel and the Transjordan, from only four in the first centuries BCE/CE to thirty-seven in the second and third centuries CE (344–45; cf. Lapin, 263; Bonnie, 115–20).

Aristocratic Jews in Jerusalem began to adopt Hellenism at least by the Maccabean period (1 Macc 1:11–15), but the Hellenization of Galilee did not make great advances until the Roman period, and then not until the settlement of Roman garrisons in Galilee around 120 CE. The story of Jesus and the centurion (Matt 8:5–13//Luke 7:1–10) is the only record of an encounter between Jesus and a gentile in Galilee; the centurion was probably a Herodian officer rather than a Roman soldier. Jesus met the Canaanite woman in the region of Tyre and Sidon (Matt 15:21–28), and the Gadarene demoniac on the east side of the Sea of Galilee (Mark 5:1–20). Direct Roman administration of Galilee did not begin until after the death of Agrippa I in 44 CE, and even then the influence of Roman culture is evident first in the cities and among the elites.

3.3 Towns and Villages

"Lakeside Galilee" developed its own subculture with its fishing industry, nascent urban centers (Magdala and Tiberias), and intersections with interregional trade routes (Root, 171–73). Josephus extolls the idyllic fruitfulness of Galilee.

> For the land is everywhere so rich in soil and pasturage and produces such a variety of trees, that even the most indolent are tempted by these facilities to devote themselves to agriculture. In fact, every inch of the soil has been cultivated by the inhabitants; there is not a parcel of wasteland. The towns, too, are thickly distributed, and even the villages, thanks to the fertility of the soil, are all so densely populated that the smallest of them contains fifteen thousand inhabitants. (*J.W.* 3.42–43)

Even granting Josephus's penchant for exaggeration—certainly his estimate of the population of the villages is grossly exaggerated—Galilee *is* more fertile than the surrounding regions. Most Galileans lived in villages with fewer than 2,000 inhabitants, which were more homogeneous than larger cities. David Fiensy, who estimates populations based on 160 persons per acre, suggests three categories: village, town, and city.

Figure 1

Nomenclature	Examples	Size (acres)	Population
Village (<2,000)	Nazareth	200–400	
	Capernaum	10–12	600–1,500
	Cana (Khirbet Qana)	8–9	1,200–1,400
	Yodefat	10	1,600
Town (2,000–4,000)	Chorazin		
	Gamla	15	2,400
Small City (4,000–6,000)	Magdala	22.5	4,000–5,000
	Sepphoris	50	2,500–5,000
	Tiberias		5,000–6,000

(Fiensy 2014, esp. 185; Fiensy 2020, 52, 58; cf. Crossan and Reed, 119; De Luca, 169; McCollough 2013, 58; 2022, 112; Reed 2000, 152; Richardson, 76, 81; Schumer)

Size and population estimates vary for different periods of occupation. For example, although it is common to say that Sepphoris and Tiberias were the only two cities in Galilee, the former established beginning in 4 BCE and the latter in 19 CE, estimates of their size, population, and influence may be greatly exaggerated in light of their later development. Josephus says, "Herod [Antipas] fortified Sepphoris to be the ornament of all Galilee" (*Ant.* 18.27); actually, "Herod Antipas renovated only the city wall and did not construct or finance any other building projects there"; and "None of the Roman-style public buildings unearthed at the site so far dates to the early first century CE" (Weiss, 54, 55). These buildings and the monumental theater, seating 4,500, were built during "the city's massive development in the late first and early second centuries CE" (Weiss, 67). The "simple buildings" that Zeev Weiss and his team excavated on the eastern summit and its slopes "resembled the typical rural construction of the Galilee" (55). Technically, Sepphoris did not become a Roman city until the royal bank moved there in 61 CE (Keddie, 51). While most estimates of the population of Sepphoris are 8,000 to 12,000, a recent reassessment, based on dating the lower city to the second century, places the first-century population at 2,500 to 5,000 (Schumer). Keddie concludes that, in the early Roman period, Magdala was "a more significant urban-type settlement than Sepphoris. . . . After Antipas moved his capital to Tiberias in

19 CE, Sepphoris and Magdala were comparable settlements, and Magdala may even have overshadowed Sepphoris in economic significance" (64).

Little evidence of first-century buildings has been found at Tiberias: possibly the first phase of a Roman theater seating 5,000–6,000; an agora (1st–2nd c.), "a luxurious structure" under a Byzantine building; and an early Roman stadium (Cytryn-Silverman, 192–97; Luff, 154–55). Nevertheless, at least during the pre-70 period, the population of Tiberias may also have been less than the commonly accepted estimates of 8,000 to 10,000. Given these reassessments, the divide between villages and cities in Galilee was also less significant in the early part of the first century, emerging clearly only in the second century (Chancey, discussed above; Schumer; and Keddie, 51–53).

Drawing on his excavations at Yodefat and elsewhere, Mordechai Aviam finds evidence that Galilean villagers represented a broad spectrum of poor and middle- to upper-middle-class inhabitants. They were wool workers, weavers, potters, shop owners with flour mills and olive presses, and elites (probably high officials, oligarchs, and tax collectors) who lived in frescoed houses (Aviam 2004b, 17; Aviam 2013a, 44; see also McCollough 2013, 62, 71–72). At the same time, general prosperity does not mean there was an equitable distribution of goods. Nevertheless, the rapid increase in the population of Galilee and the expansion of settlements and cultivated land in the first century (Leibner 2009, 332–35) probably fueled a rise in the standard of living for many (Root, 118–20).

3.4 Galilean Houses

From the Gospels themselves, we can begin to sketch the houses, furnishings, and surroundings of a Galilean village. In the parable of the neighbor at night, the family sleeps together, and the door is shut, locked, or barred (*kekleistai*, Luke 11:7). Four men, friends or relatives, carried the paralyzed man up on the roof, where they "dug it up" (*exoryxantes*), made an opening by digging through the sun-baked clay of the flat roof, and lowered the man into the house (Mark 2:4). Luke, picturing the house as one typical of a Mediterranean city rather than a Galilean village, describes the roof as made of tile (Luke 5:19): hence, a pitched roof. The wedding at Cana was held at an elite's home or at the synagogue; few if any private houses in Cana would have had six large stone vessels and a dining room (*triclinium*) supervised by a head waiter (*architriklinos*, John 2:2–9; see 8.3 below). The dining area in Simon the Pharisee's home is open so that people from the community can see the banquet in progress (Luke 7:36–38). A master could assign a slave to watch the door (Mark 13:34; cf. Luke 12:35–38). Houses are furnished with an oil lamp (*lychnos*), a lampstand (*lychnia*), and a bed or couch (*klinē*; Matt 5:15; Mark 4:21; Luke 8:16; 11:33). Millstones are common (Matt 18:6//Mark 9:42//Luke 17:2).

Excavations at Capernaum, Khirbet Qana, Magdala (Migdal), Yodefat, and Gamla are filling out the picture (Luff, 149–58). These sites are diverse in location: Capernaum and Magdala by the lake, others on hilltops. In population, they range from 1,000 to 2,000 inhabitants (see above, 3.3). Yodefat and Gamla were destroyed by Vespasian in 67 CE and not rebuilt, so these sites provide time capsules for pre-70 Galilean villages. Khirbet Qana contained ceramics from the early Roman period, a prominent rectangular building, Hasmonean coins, pottery like that produced at Shikhin, stone vessels, a possible *miqveh*, an Aramaic abecedary, and a cave with Greek inscriptions showing that it was frequented by later pilgrims (Negev and Gibson, 109–10).

Villages were generally unwalled and did not have an agora (marketplace) or public buildings. Josephus fortified Gamla, Yodefat, and Magdala/Taricheae (*J.W.* 3.462–465; 4.9). Although most villages did not have communal cisterns, Khirbet Qana and Yodefat were exceptions (Edwards 2002, 114–15).

Families lived in villages and worked in fields and vineyards nearby. The basic styles include simple houses, often one multipurpose room with a storage area and a side courtyard; complex houses built around three or more sides of a courtyard; and terrace houses built on steep hillsides (Hirschfeld, 22, 99–103). In Capernaum, small houses were built with dry-set basalt stones around a courtyard. From the street, one entered through a wooden door. The houses typically had dirt or stone floors, flat roofs, and either no windows or small windows facing the courtyard. Mortar consisted of clay or soil and water, sometimes mixed with straw for greater strength (Hirschfeld, 222–23). The roofs were made of wattle-and-daub construction: clay pressed down between bundles of reeds or brush, which are laid over and at right angles to wooden beams. Fixed stairs or portable ladders provided access to the roof, which could be used for a variety of activities (Acts 10:9). Some houses shared a courtyard, where most domestic activities took place. Courtyards often contained hearths, ovens, millstones, handpresses, and cisterns collecting rainwater from the roofs. Several types of ovens were used, but generally bread was baked in the same chamber as the fire (Frankel, 236–37; Frank). Those sharing a courtyard might be extended families, although by the first century extended families may have been declining because of the economic pressure on small landholders (Fiensy 1991, 126–32). Courtyard neighbors were therefore not necessarily related (Hezser, 38). Some rooms around a courtyard were used for storage or for animals. Chickens and dogs ranged freely and inhabited courtyards and other open areas (Horwitz, 519). Villagers relieved themselves "outside the fence" or used chamber pots (Hirschfeld, 276–77). Families lived, worked, ate, and often slept outside, moving inside only in inclement weather. Rooms were dimly lit by oil lamps. Only two-room or larger houses had beds. Poor families in one-room houses rolled out mats at night for the family to sleep on—hence the predicament of the father whose neighbor knocked on the door while the family was asleep.

Rabbinic judgments illustrate the kinds of disputes that arose in such community settings: "If two joint holders [partners] would make a partition in a courtyard, they should build the wall in the middle. Where the custom is to build of unshaped stones, or of hewn stones, of half-bricks, or of whole bricks, so they should build it: everything should follow local use" (m. B. Bat. 1:1).

Similarly, we find rulings regarding what must be done if the wall falls down: the joint holders must rebuild it (1:4); who is responsible for building a gatehouse or door to the courtyard: everyone who uses it (1:5); how close to another's cistern may one dig a cistern: no closer than three handbreadths away (2:1). Moreover, "If a man sold a courtyard, he has sold also its houses, cisterns, trenches, and vaults, but not the movable property" (4:4).

Terrace houses without courtyards were the norm in villages built on hillsides (Gamla, Yodefat, and Cana). Josephus says that at Gamla "the houses were built against the steep mountain flank and astonishingly huddled together, one on top of the other, and this perpendicular site gave the city the appearance of being suspended in air and falling headlong upon itself" (*J.W.* 4.6–7). With terrace houses, a family would use the roof of the house below it as its outdoor space. Some homes had an upper room or underground storage. In places (Nazareth), some houses backed up to caves. Poor families also lived in tents or makeshift shelters on the edge of the town or outside the gates of a walled city (Fiensy 2014; Richardson, 77–79, 103–4; Corbo, 1:867). More affluent homes have been found also, notably the frescoed house at Yodefat, an elite house (early Roman) at Cana (McCollough 2022, 118), the erroneously named "triple courtyard house" (with one inner courtyard) at Capernaum (1st–3rd c. CE; Hirschfeld, 68–69), two large houses at Magdala (Aviam 2022, 98–99), and a farmstead at Tel Rekesh (Aviam 2022, 99).

3.5 Reflections

The locus of Jesus' ministry was Galilee (Mark 1:14, 39) and more specifically Galilean towns and villages, so we turn now to meet the people through whose lives and life situations Jesus preached the kingdom of God, the people of the parables. Jesus recalled the promises to Israel in the prophets and proclaimed the Power and Authority (God) higher than the Romans and their Herodian vassals. Jesus no doubt tapped the economic distress and unrest of struggling Galileans, but the Jesus movement was no revolt of the poor (Schröter, 260). Although he subverted Roman and Herodian authority, that was not the driving focus of his ministry. Jesus announced the coming of a kingdom that transcends earthly powers. Israel would be delivered from its oppressors, not by open revolt but by the God who had faithfully guided Israel in the past and would soon establish divine justice and sovereignty on the earth. Although essentially religious and apocalyptic, the social and political implications of this message continue to reverberate twenty centuries later.

Works Cited in Chapter 3

Adler, Yonatan. 2022. *The Origins of Judaism: An Archaeological-Historical Reappraisal.* AYBRL. New Haven: Yale University Press.

Alkier, S., and J. K. Zangenberg, eds. *Zeichen aus Text und Stein: Studien auf dem Weg zu einer Archäologie des Neuen Testaments.* TANZ 42. Tübingen: Francke.

Aviam, Mordechai. 2004a. *Jews, Pagans, and Christians in the Galilee.* Rochester, NY: University of Rochester Press.

———. 2004b. "First-Century Jewish Galilee: An Archaeological Perspective." Pages 7–27 in *Religion and Society in Roman Palestine: Old Questions, New Approaches.* Edited by Douglas R. Edwards. New York: Routledge.

———. 2013a. "People, Land, Economy, and Belief in First-Century Galilee and Its Origins: A Comprehensive Archaeological Synthesis." Pages 5–48 in Fiensy and Hawkins.

———. 2013b. "Burial Customs in Judea and Galilee in the Late Second Temple Period: An Important Component in the Discussion about 'Jesus' Family Tomb.'" Pages 108–11 in *The Tomb of Jesus and His Family? Exploring Ancient Jewish Tombs near Jerusalem's Walls.* Edited by James H. Charlesworth. Grand Rapids: Eerdmans.

———. 2019. "The Ancient Synagogues in Galilee." *Early Christianity* 10:292–314.

———. 2022. "The Economic Impact of the First Jewish Revolt on the Galilee." Pages 95–107 in Blanton, Choi, and Liu.

Aviam, Mordechai, and Ze'ev Safrai. 2021. "Private Synagogues: What Were They Used For?" *Judaïsme Ancien/Ancient Judaism* 9:97–126.

Berlin, Andrea M. 2002. "Romanization and Anti-Romanization in Pre-Revolt Galilee." Pages 57–73 in *The First Jewish Revolt: Archaeology, History, and Ideology.* Edited by Andrea M. Berlin and J. Andrew Overman. New York: Routledge.

————. 2011. "Identity Politics in Early Roman Galilee." Pages 69–106 in *The Jewish Revolt against Rome: Interdisciplinary Perspectives*. Edited by M. Popovic. JSJSup 154. Leiden: Brill.

Blanton, Thomas R., IV, Agnes Choi, and Jinyu Liu, eds. 2022. *Taxation, Economy, and Revolt in Ancient Rome, Galilee, and Egypt*. RMCS. London: Routledge.

Bonnie, Rick. 2019. *Being Jewish in Galilee, 100–200 CE*. SEMA 11. Turnhout, Belgium: Brepols.

Bonnie, Rick, Raimo Hakola, and Ulla Tervahauta, eds. 2021. *The Synagogue in Ancient Palestine: Current Issues and Emerging Trends*. FRLANT 37. Göttingen: Vandenhoeck & Ruprecht.

Catto, Stephen K. 2007. *Reconstructing the First-Century Synagogue: A Critical Analysis of Current Research*. LNTS 363. London: T&T Clark.

Chancey, Mark A. 2005. *Greco-Roman Culture and the Galilee of Jesus*. SNTSMS 134. Cambridge: Cambridge University Press.

Cirafesi, Wally V. 2021. "A First-Century Synagogue in Capernaum? Issues of Historical Method in the Interpretation of the Archaeological and Literary Data." *Judaïsme Ancien/Ancient Judaism* 9:7–48.

Corbo, Virgilio C. 1992. "Capernaum." *ABD* 1:866–69.

Cromhout, Markus. 2008. "Were the Galileans 'Religious Jews' or 'Ethnic Judeans'?" *HvTSt 64, 3*.

Crossan, John Dominic, and Jonathan L. Reed. 2001. *Excavating Jesus: Beneath the Stones, Behind the Texts*. Rev. ed. San Francisco: HarperSanFrancisco.

Culpepper, R. Alan. 2021. *Matthew*. NTL. Louisville: Westminster John Knox.

Cytryn-Silverman, Katia. 2015. "Tiberias, from Its Foundation to the End of the Early Islamic Period." Pages 186–210 in Fiensy and Strange.

De Luca, Stefano. 2013. "Capernaum." Pages 168–80 in vol. 1 of *The Oxford Encyclopedia of the Bible and Archaeology*. 2 vols. Oxford: Oxford University Press.

De Luca, Stefano, and Anna Lena. 2015. "Magdala/Taricheae." Pages 280–342 in Fiensy and Strange.

Edwards, Douglas R. 1992. "The Socio-Economic and Cultural Ethos of the Lower Galilee in the First Century: Implications for the Nascent Jesus Movement." Pages 53–73 in *The Galilee in Late Antiquity*. Edited by Lee I. Levine. New York: Jewish Theological Seminary of America.

————. 2002. "Khirbet Qana: From Jewish Village to Christian Pilgrim Site." Pages 101–32 in *The Roman and Byzantine Near East*. Vol. 3. Edited by J. D. Humphrey. JRASup 49. Portsmouth, RI: Journal of Roman Archaeology.

————. 2007. "Identity and Social Location in Roman Galilean Villages." Pages 357–74 in *Religion, Ethnicity, and Identity in Ancient Galilee: A Region in Transition*. Edited by Jürgen Zangenberg, Harold W. Attridge, and Dale B. Martin. WUNT 210. Tübingen: Mohr Siebeck.

Edwards, Douglas R., and C. Thomas McCollough, eds. 1997. *Archaeology and the Galilee: Texts and Contexts in the Graeco-Roman and Byzantine Periods*. Atlanta: Scholars Press.

Fiensy, David A. 1991. *The Social History of Palestine in the Herodian Period: The Land Is Mine*. Lewiston, NY: Mellen.

————. 2014. "The Galilean Village in the Late Second Temple and Mishnaic Periods." Pages 177–207 in Fiensy and Strange.

————. 2020. *The Archaeology of Daily Life: Ordinary Persons in Later Second Temple Israel*. Eugene, OR: Cascade.

Fiensy, David A., and Ralph K. Hawkins, eds. 2013. *The Galilean Economy in the Time of Jesus*. ECL 11. Atlanta: Society of Biblical Literature.

Fiensy, David A., and James R. Strange, eds. 2014–15. *Galilee in the Late Second Temple and Mishnaic Periods*. 2 vols. Minneapolis: Fortress.

Frank, Tim. 2022. "Cooking Installations." Pages 237–49 in *T&T Clark Handbook of Food in the Hebrew Bible and Ancient Israel*. Edited by Janling Fu, Cynthia Shafer-Elliott, and Carol Meyers. New York: Bloomsbury.

Frankel, Rafael. 2013. "Corn, Oil, and Wine Production." Pages 233–44 in *The Oxford Encyclopedia of the Bible and Archaeology*. Edited by Daniel M. Master. New York: Oxford University Press.

Freyne, Seán. 1997. "Town and Country Once More: The Case of Roman Galilee." Pages 49–56 in Edwards and McCollough.

Goodman, Martin. 1999. "Galilean and Judaean Judaism." Pages 596–617 in *The Cambridge History of Judaism*. Vol. 3, *The Early Roman Period*. Edited by William Horbury et al. Cambridge: Cambridge University Press.

Hachlili, Rachel. 2013. *Ancient Synagogues—Archaeology and Art: New Discoveries and Current Trends*. HdO 105. Leiden: Brill.

Hezser, Catherine. 2010. "The Graeco-Roman Context of Jewish Daily Life in Roman Palestine." Pages 28–47 in *The Oxford Handbook of Jewish Daily Life in Roman Palestine*. Edited by Catherine Hezser. Oxford: Oxford University Press.

Hirschfeld, Yizhar. 1995. *The Palestinian Dwelling in the Roman-Byzantine Period*. SBF-CMi 34. Jerusalem: Franciscan Printing Press.

Horwitz, Liora K. 2000. "The Animal Economy of Ḥorvat 'Eleq." Pages 511–28 in *Ramat Hanadiv Excavations: Final Report of the 1984–1998 Seasons*. Edited by Yizhar Hirschfeld. Jerusalem: The Israel Exploration Society.

Jensen, Morten Hørning. 2007. "Herod Antipas in Galilee: Friend or Foe of the Historical Jesus?" *JSHJ* 5:7–32.

———. 2012. "Rural Galilee and Rapid Changes: An Investigation of the Socio-Economic Dynamics and Developments in Roman Galilee." *Bib* 93.1:43–67.

———. 2013. "Purity and Politics in Herod Antipas's Galilee: The Case for Religious Motivation." *JSHJ* 11:3–34.

Keddie, G. Anthony. 2019. *Class and Power in Roman Palestine: The Socioeconomic Setting of Judaism and Christian Origins*. Cambridge: Cambridge University Press.

Kloppenborg, John S. 2006. "The Theodotos Synagogue Inscription and the Problem of First-Century Synagogue Buildings." Pages 236–82 in *Jesus and Archaeology*. Edited by James H. Charlesworth. Grand Rapids: Eerdmans.

Knauf, Ernst Axel. 2003. "Writing and Speaking in Galilee." Pages 336–50 in Alkier and Zangenberg.

Lapin, Hayim. 1999. "Palestinian Inscriptions and Jewish Ethnicity." Pages 239–68 in Meyers 1999.

Leibner, Uzi. 2009. *Settlement and History in Hellenistic, Roman, and Byzantine Galilee*. TSAJ 127. Tübingen: Mohr Siebeck.

———. 2015. "Khirbet Wadi Ḥamam in the Early and Middle Roman Periods." Pages 343–61 in Fiensy and Strange.

———. 2021. "Galilee in the Second Century BCE: Material Culture and Ethnic Identity." Pages 123–44 in *The Middle Maccabees: Archaeology, History, and the Rise of the Hasmonean Kingdom*. Edited by Andrea M. Berlin and Paul J. Kosmin. SBLABS 28. Atlanta: SBL Press.

Luff, Rosemary Margaret. 2019. *The Impact of Jesus in First-Century Palestine: Textual and Archaeological Evidence for Long-Standing Discontent.* Cambridge: Cambridge University Press.

Magness, Jodi. 2011. *Stone and Dung, Oil and Spit: Jewish Daily Life in the Time of Jesus.* Grand Rapids: Eerdmans.

Mattila, Sharon Lea. 2015. "Capernaum, Village of Naḥum, from Hellenistic to Byzantine Times." Pages 217–57 in Fiensy and Strange.

McCollough, C. Thomas. 2013. "City and Village in Lower Galilee: The Import of the Archaeological Excavations at Sepphoris and Khirbet Qana (Cana) for Framing the Economic Context of Jesus." Pages 49–74 in Fiensy and Hawkins.

———. 2015. "Khirbet Qana." Pages 127–45 in Fiensy and Strange.

———. 2021. "The Synagogue at Khirbet Qana in Its Village Context." Pages 81–95 in Bonnie, Hakola, and Tervahauta.

———. 2022. "The Economic Transformation of an Early Roman Galilean Village: A Keynesian Approach." Pages 108–25 in Blanton, Choi, and Liu.

Meyers, Eric M. 1997. "Jesus and His Galilean Context." Pages 57–66 in Edwards and McCollough.

———, ed. 1999. *Galilee through the Centuries: Confluence of Cultures.* Winona Lake: Eisenbrauns.

Miller, Stuart S. 2003. "Some Observations on Stone Vessel Finds and Ritual Purity in Light of Talmudic Sources." Pages 402–19 in Alkier and Zangenberg.

———. 2015. *At the Intersection of Texts and Material Finds: Stepped Pools, Stone Vessels, and Ritual Purity.* JAJSup 16. Göttingen: Vandenhoeck & Ruprecht.

Moreland, Milton. 2007. "The Inhabitants of Galilee in the Hellenistic and Early Roman Periods: Probes into the Archaeological and Literary Evidence." Pages 133–59 in *Religion, Ethnicity, and Identity in Ancient Galilee: A Region in Transition.* Edited by Jürgen Zangenberg, H. Attridge, and D. Martin. WUNT 210. Tübingen: Mohr Siebeck.

Negev, Avraham, and Shimon Gibson, eds. 2001. *Archaeological Encyclopedia of the Holy Land.* New York: Continuum.

Reed, Jonathan L. 1999. "Galileans, 'Israelite Village Communities,' and the Sayings Gospel Q." Pages 87–108 in Meyers 1999.

———. 2000. *Archaeology and the Galilean Jesus: A Re-Examination of the Evidence.* Harrisburg, PA: Trinity Press International.

———. 2003. "Stone Vessels and Gospel Texts: Purity and Socio-Economics in John 2." Pages 381–401 in Alkier and Zangenberg.

———. 2010. "Instability in Jesus' Galilee: A Demographic Perspective." *JBL* 129:343–65.

Richardson, Peter. 2004. *Building Jewish in the Roman East.* Waco, TX: Baylor University Press.

Richardson, Peter, and Douglas Edwards. 2002. "Jesus and Palestinian Social Protest: Archaeological and Literary Perspectives." Pages 247–66 in *Handbook of Early Christianity: Social Science Approaches.* Edited by Anthony J. Blasi, Jean Duhaime, and Paul-André Turcotte. Walnut Creek, CA: AltaMira.

Root, Bradley W. 2014. *First Century Galilee: A Fresh Examination of the Sources.* WUNT 378. Tübingen: Mohr Siebeck.

Runesson, Anders. 2001. *The Origins of the Synagogue: A Socio-Historical Study.* ConBNT 37. Stockholm: Almqvist & Wiksell.

———. 2017. "Synagogues without Rabbis or Christians? Ancient Institutions beyond Normative Discourses." *JBV* 38:159–72.

Runesson, Anders, Donald D. Binder, and Birger Olsson. 2008. *The Ancient Synagogue from Its Origins to 200 C.E.: A Source Book*. AJEC 72. Leiden: Brill.

Runesson, Anders, and Wally V. Cirafesi. 2021. "Reassessing the Impact of 70 CE on the Origins and Development of Palestinian Synagogues." Pages 37–57 in Bonnie, Hakola, and Tervahauta.

Ryan, Jordan J. 2017. *The Role of the Synagogue in the Aims of Jesus*. Minneapolis: Fortress.

———. 2023. "Jesus in the Synagogue." *BAR* 49.1:34–41.

Sanders, E. P. 2016. *Judaism: Practice and Belief, 63 BCE–66 CE.* Minneapolis: Fortress.

Schröter, Jens. 2008. "Jesus aus Galiläa." Pages 245–70 in *Jesus und die Archäologie Galiläas*. Edited by Carsten Claussen and Jörg Frey. Biblisch-Theologische Studien 87. Neukirchen-Vluyn: Neukirchener.

Schumer, Nathan. 2017. "The Population of Sepphoris: Rethinking Urbanization in Early and Middle Roman Galilee." *JAJ* 8:90–111.

Weiss, Zeev. 2015. "Sepphoris: From Galilean Town to Roman City, 100 BCE–200 CE." Pages 53–75 in Fiensy and Strange.

Zangenberg, Jürgen K. 2013. "Pure Stone: Archaeological Evidence for Jewish Purity Practices in Late Second Temple Judaism (Miqwa'ot and Stone Vessels)." Pages 537–72 in *Purity and the Forming of Religious Traditions in the Ancient Mediterranean World and Ancient Judaism*. Edited by Christian Frevel and Christophe Nihan. Leiden: Brill.

Zwickel, Wolfgang. 2013. "Der See Gennesaret in hellenistischer und frührömischer Zeit." *ZNW* 104:153–76.

Part II

Home and Family

Chapter 4

Children

*A*lthough children appear at various places in the Gospels, they are featured in only two parables. With the central role in Matthew 11:16–19, one group of children cannot get another to play, apparently mimicking first a wedding, then a funeral. In Luke 11:5–8, a neighbor responds to a knock on his door during the night, saying he cannot open the door because his children are in bed with him.

Elsewhere, Mary and Elizabeth each have a baby (*brephos*) in their womb (Luke 1:41, 44), and the newborn Christ child (also *brephos*) is wrapped in swaddling clothes (2:12) and laid in a feed trough (a manger; 2:16). People bring infants (*brephē*) for Jesus to bless (18:15). Jesus thanks his Father for hiding the mysteries of kingdom from the wise, while revealing them to infants (*nēpioi*; Matt 11:25//Luke 10:21). Out of the mouths of infants and nursing babes, God has prepared praise (Matt 21:16); yet it will be terrible for women who are pregnant or have nursing babes in the terrors of the last days (Mark 13:17 par.).

The children sitting in the marketplace (agora) are *paidia*, the diminutive of *pais*, although the two terms are often used synonymously to designate children below the age of puberty and slaves or servants. The father's children (Luke 11:7) are also *paidia*. When he was a twelve-year-old *pais*, Jesus sat among the teachers in the temple (2:42–49). Years later, Jesus healed the centurion's *pais* (Matt 8:5–13//John 4:46–54) and raised Jaïrus's *paidion* (Mark 5:40–41). He also cast a demon out of a father's boy (Mark 9:17–27

39

par.) and the Syrophoenician woman's daughter, a *paidion* (Mark 7:25–30). Jesus was often surrounded by crowds that included children. *Paidia* were in the crowds (Matt 14:21; 15:38 par.) that Jesus fed with a youth's (*paidarion*; John 6:9) lunch. On another occasion, Jesus called a child before his disciples and told them that if they sought to enter the kingdom of heaven, they would need to become like the children (*paidia*; Matt 18:1–5), and he blessed the children who were brought to him (19:13–14). In Jerusalem, children (*paides*) in the temple took up the crowd's chant at Jesus' entry into the holy city, "Hosanna to the Son of David" (21:15).

Playing children are the joy of every culture. Epictetus comments that children dance and clap their hands (*Diatr.* 3.24.8). Hellenistic sarcophagi depict children at play, with pet dogs and birds, with a hoop, driving a cart pulled by a small animal, playing ball, and rolling a nut down an incline to scatter a tower of nuts (Veyne, 14–16; Betsworth, 33–34). Epictetus lists various children's games as an illustration of the sort of childish diversion and vacillation his students should avoid: "Sometimes they play wrestlers, again gladiators, again they blow trumpets, and then act a play" (*Ench.* 29.3).

4.1 Galilean Families

In the pages that follow, we will meet various families in Galilee and Roman Palestine. Like modern families in certain respects, some were nuclear, others single-parent or multigenerational families, some better off than others. In many respects, however, they were quite different from modern families. Relationships between men and women were different, and so were courtships and weddings. Marriages were contracts between families. Marriage contracts and certificates of divorce protected the wife's property. Families were patriarchal, and a few men had more than one wife. Yet husbands and wives collaborated, each taking the lead in certain tasks: the man typically led in most activities outside the home. Life expectancies, short by modern standards, and relatively high rates of death in childbirth altered family patterns in antiquity. Eldest sons were especially favored; daughters were reared to become part of another man's household. Most families worked where they lived or walked to nearby farms. A few were wealthy, but most lived at the margin of subsistence, struggling with debts. The chapters in this section explore these and other aspects of family life, reminding us that families in antiquity cannot be stereotyped and often challenge modern preconceptions (see Peskowitz).

4.2 Morbidity and Life Expectancy

Polybius (ca. 200–after 118 BCE) laments the depopulation of Greece during his lifetime, with cities becoming deserted and fields uncultivated, although there had been neither continuous wars nor epidemics. He criticizes men who did not wish to marry or rear children born to them. Some men had only one or two children in order to increase their inheritance, but in such families one child might be carried off by war and the other by sickness. Polybius therefore advocated "passing laws making it compulsory to rear children who are born" (*Hist.* 36.17.5–10).

According to Hillel and Shammai, having two children seems to have been the ideal minimum (m. Yebam. 6:6). Children were valued for the work they contributed to a family, the care they would provide for aging parents, and continuation of the family name and property (Kraemer, 106). The parents' duty was to discipline their children. Josephus writes that the law of Moses counsels parents of rebellious children to remind them that their mother and father

> came together in matrimony not for pleasure's sake, nor to increase their fortunes by uniting their several properties in one, but that they might have children who should tend their old age and who should receive from them everything that they needed. "And when thou wast born," they shall proceed, "it was with joy and deepest thankfulness to God that we raised thee up and devoted our utmost care to thine upbringing, sparing nothing that appeared profitable for thy welfare and training in all that was best." (*Ant.* 4.260–261)

Life was hard in antiquity, and it was especially hard on children. Up to 30 percent died in birth and another 30 percent in infancy (before reaching the age of five). Because of the high rate of infant mortality, life expectancy at birth was only 20 years (Fiensy 2020, 236; Luff, 128–34). A survey of 1,598 individuals from Palestinian tombs shows that 43 percent were 19 years old or younger (Nagar and Torgeë, 166–67; Fiensy 2020, 233). The average life expectancy in late Second Temple Israel, for those who lived to be 20, was 38 for men and 33 for women (Fiensy 2020, 238). Still, about 23 percent of the total population at this time were 40 or older, with a few living into their 60s and older (Fiensy 2020, 246).

The implications of these grim figures are far-reaching. By the time they were sixteen, 70 percent of children had lost one parent; 11 percent were orphans (Malina and Rohrbaugh, 117; Huebner 2013, 523–24; Huebner 2019, 74–76; Betsworth, 11–14): "Almost no children ever knew their grandfathers;

and few adults had fathers who were still alive" (Reed 2010, 365). Frequent pregnancies, death in childbirth, "middle-age" widows, orphans, and single young males were common (Reed 2010, 348–49). A skeleton of a twenty-two-year-old male recovered at Qumran shows that he did hard physical labor with his hands and went barefoot all his life (Fiensy 2020, 191).

Such early deaths were the result of famines, malnutrition, and diseases such as dysentery, which Celsus, a first-century medical writer, says "carries off mostly children up to the age of ten" (*Med.* 2.8.30). Even older children were at risk: "Adolescence is liable to acute diseases, such as fits, especially to consumption; those who spit blood are generally youths" (2.1.21). To have as many living brothers and sisters as Jesus did (Mark 6:3) was unusual. In the burial inscriptions from Leontopolis, Egypt, for example, only one woman has more than one child (Kraemer, 61). Another reason for the limited number of children a woman might bear, of course, was the peril to the mother while giving birth in antiquity. Kraemer notes that the following first-century-BCE inscription from Egypt describes a situation tragically common elsewhere also.

> This is the grave of Arsinoe, wayfarer. Stand by and weep for her, unfortunate in all things, whose lot was hard and terrible. For I was bereaved of my mother when I was a little girl [perhaps in her bearing another child?], and when the flower of my youth made me ready for a bridegroom, my father married me to Phabeis, and fate brought me to the end of my life in bearing my firstborn child. I had a small span of years, but great grace flowered in the beauty of my spirit. This grave hides in its bosom my chaste body, but my soul has flown to the holy ones. Lament for Arsinoe. In the 25th year, Mechir 2. (*CPJ*, no. 1510; Kraemer 1988, *Maenads*, no. 41; Kraemer 1998, 62)

The diseases that plagued Second Temple Israel were internal parasites, tuberculosis, malaria, and leprosy (Luff, 114–37; Fiensy 2020, 199–228). Roundworms, tapeworms, and whipworms sapped nutrients from the body, causing fatigue and susceptibility to other diseases. The deaths of noted tyrants and traitors from severe infestations are described in repulsive detail in our literature. Although these descriptions are stereotypical of the deaths of hated tyrants, the loathsome symptoms were probably commonly known.

Antiochus IV Epiphanes

> The all-seeing Lord, the God of Israel, struck him with an incurable and invisible blow. As soon as he stopped speaking he was seized with a pain in his bowels, for which there was no relief, and with sharp internal tortures.

. . . So the ungodly man's body swarmed with worms, and while he was still living in anguish and pain, his flesh rotted away, and because of the stench the whole army felt revulsion at his decay. Because of his intolerable stench no one was able to carry the man who a little while before had thought that he could touch the stars of heaven. (2 Macc 9:5, 9–10)

Only a little while before, the tyrant "had thought in his superhuman arrogance that he could command the waves of the sea" (cf. Ps 104:6–7; Mark 4:39–41), but now "was brought down to earth and carried in a litter, making the power of God manifest (*phaneran*). In his death, the author hints, Antiochus Epiphanes finally fulfilled his name, "making the power of God manifest" (2 Macc 9:8)!

Herod the Great

[Herod] had fever, though not a raging fever, an intolerable itching of the whole skin, continuous pains in the intestines, tumours in the feet as in dropsy, inflammation of the abdomen and gangrene of the privy parts, engendering worms, in addition to asthma, with great difficulty in breathing, and convulsions in all his limbs. (*J.W.* 1.656; see *Ant.* 17.169)

Agrippa I

And immediately, because he had not given the glory to God, an angel of the Lord struck him down, and he was eaten by worms and died. (Acts 12:23)

Judas Iscariot

Apollinarius of Laodicea (4th c.) quotes a fragment from Papias (2nd c.) that describes the death of Judas Iscariot in similar terms, ostensibly correcting the accounts in Matthew 27:5 and Acts 1:18.

Judas Iscariot was a terrible, walking example of ungodliness in this world, his flesh so bloated that he was not able to pass through a place a wagon passes easily, not even his bloated head by itself. For his eyelids, they say, were so swollen that he could not see the light at all, and his eyes could not be seen, even by a doctor using an optical instrument, so far had they sunk below the outer surface. His genitals appeared more loathsome and larger than anyone else's, and when he relieved himself there passed through it pus and worms from every part of his body, much to his shame. After much agony and punishment, they say, he finally died in his own place, and because of the stench the area is deserted and uninhabitable even now. (Holmes, 316)

Others

Populations in the low-lying areas around the Sea of Galilee—precisely the area of Jesus' itinerant ministry (Bethsaida, Chorazin, Capernaum, and Magdala)—were especially susceptible to malaria, the other chronic illness common in ancient Israel. Josephus describes the atmosphere in this area as "pestilential" (*J.W.* 4.457; cf. Reed 2014; Fiensy 2020, 214–28). Malaria is transmitted by mosquitoes, especially in the summer months. Therefore, where the Gospels report that Jesus healed Peter's mother-in-law (Mark 1:30–31//Luke 4:38–39) and the Capernaum centurion's son (John 4:52) of "a fever," it was probably acute malaria. Parenthetically, symptoms were not clearly distinguished from their causes. Physical anthropologists who studied the skulls found in the tombs of Meiron in upper Galilee found that "almost 50% of the nearly two hundred individuals in the Meiron tombs were children under the age of eighteen and 'most of the children's skulls' had signs of *cribra orbitalia*," lesions that "could have come directly from diseases such as malaria" (Fiensy 2020, 224, citing Smith et al.).

Whether leprosy (Hansen's disease) was known in Palestine in the first century is debated (Hulse; Luff, 115–20), but there is some evidence that it appeared in Egypt around 300 BCE and spread from there (Dols, 314–18). Describing *lepromatous,* Aretaeus of Cappadocia (2nd c. CE), the celebrated Greek physician, grimly comments, "When in such a state, who would not flee;—who would not turn from them, even a father, a son, or a brother? There is danger, also, from the communication of the ailment" (Adams, 372). What the Gospels refer to as leprosy, however, may have been "chronic, patchy, scaly conditions such as psoriasis, fungal infections, seborrheic dermatitis, etc." (Sussman, 11). Nevertheless, *Mycobacterium leprae* and *Mycobacterium tuberculosis* have been identified in the bones of an adult male buried in the cemetery of Akeldama in the Hinnom Valley (Luff, 115–16). In addition to disease, violence also contributed to premature deaths (Luff, 134–36).

4.3 Infanticide

In antiquity, but not among Jews, unwanted children, especially female infants, infants with defects, and those of questionable paternity, were abandoned. Poverty, inability to care for the child, was a common reason for abandonment, but children were also at times abandoned by the wealthy to protect their estate for other children. Scholars debate the prevalence of this practice because it was seldom recorded. In one text (P.Oxy. 744), dated to the year 1 BCE, a worker named Hilarion writes to his wife, Alis, "If it is a boy, let it be, if it is a girl, cast it out [to die]" (Crossan, 20; cf. Caragounis). Excavation of a bathhouse that served as a brothel in Ashkelon in Judea (4th–6th c.) revealed a burial site with the remains of a hundred newborn infants (Faerman et al.). Many abandoned infants were rescued, however, and often adopted if they were boys, fostered if they were girls. Another text (P.Oxy. 37) records a dispute regarding a foundling boy rescued from the gutter. The rescued child became a trope in Greek drama. Romulus and Remus—Rome's founders, according to tradition—were exposed in infancy, as were Oedipus, Agathocles, and Epidaurus (Diodorus Siculus 4.64.1; 8.4.1; 19.2.3–5; Pausanius 2.26.4). The Stoic philosopher Musonius Rufus (b. before 30–d. before 101/2 CE) titled a tractate, "Should Every Child That Is Born Be Raised?" (*Frag.* 15); Pliny the Younger (ca. 61–ca. 112 CE) bequeathed 500,000 sesterces for "the maintenance of free-born boys and girls" (*Ep.* 7.18 [to Caninius Rufus]). After Constantine, Christian leaders taught that infanticide was immoral, and in 374 CE Valentinian I reissued Constantine's edict making infanticide a capital offense (Nathan, 146).

Jews instructed their children to marry and raise children of their own (Tob 4:13; Ps.-Phoc. 175–176). Whatever the situation among gentiles in Galilee, Jewish families did not abandon their children: "The Law orders all the offspring to be brought up, and forbids women either to cause abortion or to make away with the foetus; a woman convicted of this is regarded as an infanticide, because she destroys a soul and diminishes the race" (Josephus, *Ag. Ap.* 2.202; so also Ps.-Phoc. 184–185). Diodorus Siculus (1st c. BCE) also notes that, contrary to other cultures, Jews forbade abandonment of infants: "He [their lawgiver] required those who dwelt in the land to rear their children, and since offspring could be cared for at little cost, the Jews were from the start a populous nation" (40.3.8; cf. 1 Chr 4:27). The prohibition of abortion and abandoning children does not actually appear in the law of Moses, only the repeated command to be fruitful and multiply (Gen 1:22, 28; 9:7; 35:11; Lev 26:9), so Diodorus Siculus and Josephus comment on Jewish practice rather than law (see also Sib. Or. 3.765; Ps.-Phoc. 184). Early Christians also forbade child infanticide (Did. 2.2; 5.2; Barn. 19.5; 20.2).

Abandoning children was a sign of the greatest distress. When Ptolemy IV, king of Egypt (221–204 BCE), attempted to enter the temple, "Mothers and nurses abandoned even newborn children here and there, some in houses and some in the streets, and without a backward look they crowded together at the most high temple" (3 Macc 1:20). The well-being of the mother and the child was so important to Jews that the rabbis allowed midwives to travel on the Sabbath when necessary (m. Shabb. 18:3; m. Rosh. Hash. 2:5). Family and friends gathered to celebrate the circumcision of a male child; by naming a child, the father claimed the infant as his own (Matt 1:21; Luke 1:59–60, 63; 2:21).

Nevertheless, child abandonment appears in the Hebrew Scriptures and was apparently common in ancient Mesopotamia. The Code of Hammurabi (185) declares, "If a man has taken in adoption an infant while still (bathed in) his amniotic fluid and raised him up, that adopted child shall not be (re)claimed!" (Malul, 106). Ishmael was cast under a bush (Gen 21:15). Moses was abandoned, but under extreme circumstances and with his sister watching, to rescue him if necessary (Exod 1:22; 2:2–10). Ezekiel likens Jerusalem to an abandoned daughter:

> As for your birth, on the day you were born your navel cord was not cut, nor were you washed with water to cleanse you, nor rubbed with salt, nor wrapped in cloths. No eye pitied you, to do any of these things for you out of compassion for you; but you were thrown out in the open field, for you were abhorred on the day you were born. I passed by you and saw you flailing about in your blood. As you lay in your blood, I said to you, "Live! and grow up like a plant of the field." (Ezek 16:4–7a; cf. Pss 22:10; 27:9–10; Isa 49:14–15; see Malul, esp. n. 27)

Naming a male heir (Gen 15:1–4) and adopting formulae were also known (Ps 2:7; 2 Sam 7:14), although references to adoption are rare and related to foreign milieus (Exod 2:10; Esth 2:7, 15). Fosterage rather than formal adoption may be in view here: "The reason that formal adoption of a child does not seem to have played a major role in ancient Israelite society may be that other family strategies, such as the practice of polygamy and levirate marriage, also provided a couple with a male heir, or orphans with foster parents" (Huebner 2013, 512). Nevertheless, the manumission and adoption of a Jewish slave in the Jewish colony at Elephantine is attested by an Aramaic papyrus document dated to 416 BCE (Kraeling, no. 8), and catacomb inscriptions attest to Jewish adoptions in Rome (Leon, 232–33).

4.4 Discipline

In the Greco-Roman literature, children were regarded both as deficient and as loveable: "A child was known to understand little, betray petty anger, fear, and lack the measured thoughtfulness that was aspired to. On the other hand, children as a group were enjoyed for small, adorable things: their prattling voices, their frank expressions of tenderness, even their sweet innocence" (Kihlstrom Timpte, 55–56). Children were expected to obey their father, and philosophers debated whether a father should always be obeyed, whatever his commands (Aulus Gellius, *Noct. att.* 2.7.1–13; see Yarbrough, 53–56). Sirach, a Jewish wisdom teacher early in the second century BCE who took a generally dim view of children, said, "It is a disgrace to be the father of an undisciplined son, and the birth of a daughter is a loss" (Sir 22:3; cf. 42:9). Therefore,

> He who loves his son will whip him often,
> so that he may rejoice at the way he turns out.
> He who disciplines his son will profit by him,
> and will boast of him among acquaintances.
> He who teaches his son will make his enemies envious,
> and will glory in him among his friends.
>
> (30:1–3)

On the other hand, "Pamper a child, and he will terrorize you; play with him, and he will grieve you. Do not laugh with him, or you will have sorrow with him" (30:9–10).

Yet, Cicero (*Fin.* 3.19) and Epictetus (*Diatr.* 1.11.17; 1.23.3) also taught that love of children is engendered by nature. Epictetus (ca. 55–135 CE) rejected the counsel of Epicurus, whom he charges with saying, "Let us [wise men] not bring up children," by asking, "But how, then, can we still be social beings, if affection for our own children is not a natural sentiment? . . . Nay[,] he knows, that if once a child is born, it is no longer in our power not to love it or to care for it" (*Diatr.* 1.23). He continues, "Who is not tempted by attractive and wide-awake children to join their sports, and crawl on all fours with them, and talk baby talk with them?" (2.24.18). Yet children are fickle (3.15.12). Ignorance is the defining characteristic of a child, and in that regard a child is a model for all: "For what is a child? Ignorance. What is a child? Want of instruction. For where a child has knowledge, he is no worse than we are" (2.1.16). The same theme appears in the New Testament:

> Brothers and sisters, do not be children in your thinking; rather, be infants in evil, but in thinking be adults. (1 Cor 14:20)

> We must no longer be children, tossed to and fro and blown about by every wind of doctrine, by people's trickery, by their craftiness in deceitful scheming. (Eph 4:14)

> Like obedient children, do not be conformed to the desires that you formerly had in ignorance. (1 Pet 1:14)

4.5 Reflections

Most of the children in Galilee grew up in small agricultural communities, in towns or villages. Their mothers had multiple births and lost many children in birth and infancy. Families were cohesive and often multigenerational; mortality rates were high for parents and grandparents. Intestinal parasites and malaria were common, causing lethargy and widespread misery, and contributing to early mortality. One can imagine anxious parents bringing their children to Jesus so that he might touch them and bless them.

> We must imagine, in light of the above evidence, malnourished children, lethargic toddlers, anemic little ones, even anorexic children—in a word, very sick—among those coming for blessing. They were stunted and wasted (emaciated) children due to parasitic infections. The children were not thriving, were not growing properly, were not as smart as the other children, and the parents did not know why. (Fiensy 2020, 227)

Religious training began at home. Girls learned skills from their mothers, while boys apprenticed with their fathers. And, like children everywhere, they played.

Works Cited in Chapter 4

Adams, Francis, trans. and ed. 1856. *The Extant Works of Aretaeus, the Cappadocian.* London: Sydenham Society.

Betsworth, Sharon. 2015. *Children in Early Christian Narratives.* LNTS 521. London: Bloomsbury.

Caragounis, Chrys C. "Hilarion's Letter to His Wife, Alis (P Oxy 744): A New Suggestion to Solve Its Problem." chrys-caragounis.com/Inscriptions.and.Papyri/Hilarion%20 Letter.pdf.

Cohen, Shaye J. D., ed. 1993. *The Jewish Family in Antiquity.* Atlanta: Scholars Press.

Crossan, John Dominic. 1991. *The Historical Jesus: The Life of a Mediterranean Jewish Peasant.* New York: HarperSanFrancisco.

Dols, Michael W. 1979. "Leprosy in Medieval Arabic Medicine." *JHMAS* 36:314–33.

Faerman, Marina, et al. 1998. "Determining the Sex of Infanticide Victims from the Late Roman Era through Ancient DNA Analysis." *JAS* 25.9:861–65.

Fiensy, David A. 2020. *The Archaeology of Daily Life: Ordinary Persons in Late Second Temple Israel.* Eugene, OR: Cascade.

Holmes, Michael W., trans. and ed. 2006. *The Apostolic Fathers in English.* 3rd ed. Grand Rapids: Baker Academic.

Huebner, Sabine R. 2013. "Adoption and Fosterage in the Ancient Eastern Mediterranean." Pages 510–31 in *The Oxford Handbook of Childhood and Education in the Classical World*. Edited by J. Evans Grubbs and T. Parkin. Oxford: Oxford University Press.

———. 2019. *Papyri and the Social World of the New Testament*. Cambridge: Cambridge University Press.

Hulse, E. V. 1975. "The Nature of Biblical 'Leprosy' and the Use of Alternative Medical Terms in Modern Translations of the Bible." *PEQ* 107:87–105.

Kihlstrom Timpte, Katherine Joy. 2022. *The Transformational Role of Discipleship in Mark 10:13–16: Passage towards Childhood*. LNTS 650. London: T&T Clark.

Kraeling, Emil G. 1953. *The Brooklyn Museum Aramaic Papyri*. New Haven: Yale University Press.

Kraemer, Ross S. 1988. *Maenads, Martyrs, Matrons, Monastics: A Sourcebook on Women's Religions in the Greco-Roman World*. Philadelphia: Fortress.

———. 1998. "Jewish Women in the Diaspora World of Late Antiquity." Pages 46–72 in *Jewish Women in Historical Perspective*. Edited by Judith Baskin. Detroit: Wayne State University Press.

Leon, Harry J. 1960. *The Jews of Ancient Rome*. Philadelphia: Jewish Publication Society.

Luff, Rosemary Margaret. 2019. *The Impact of Jesus in First-Century Palestine: Textual and Archaeological Evidence for Long-Standing Discontent*. Cambridge: Cambridge University Press.

Malina, Bruce J., and Richard L. Rohrbaugh. 1992. *Social-Science Commentary on the Synoptic Gospels*. Minneapolis: Augsburg Fortress.

Malul, Meir. 1990. "Adoption of Foundlings in the Bible and Mesopotamian Documents: A Study of Some Legal Metaphors in Ezekiel 16:1–7." *JSOT* 46:97–126.

Nagar, Yossi, and Hagit Torgeë. 2003. "Biological Characteristics of Jewish Burial in the Hellenistic and Early Roman Periods." *IEJ* 53:164–71.

Nathan, Geoffrey. 2021. "Looking for Children in Late Antiquity." Pages 134–64 in *Children in Antiquity: Perspectives and Experiences of Childhood in the Ancient Mediterranean*. Edited by Lesley A. Beaumont, Matthew Dillon, and Nicola Harrington. New York: Routledge.

Peskowitz, Miriam. 1993. "'Family/ies' in Antiquity: Evidence from Tannaitic Literature and Roman Galilean Architecture." Pages 9–36 in Cohen.

Reed, Jonathan L. 2010. "Instability in Jesus' Galilee: A Demographic Perspective." *JBL* 129:343–65.

———. 2014. "Mortality, Morbidity, and Economics in Jesus' Galilee." Pages 242–52 in *Galilee in the Late Second Temple and Mishnaic Periods*, vol. 1, *Life, Culture, and Society*. Edited by David A. Fiensy and James R. Strange. Minneapolis: Fortress.

Smith, Patricia, et al. 1981. "The Skeletal Remains." Pages 110–20 in *Excavations at Ancient Meiron, Upper Galilee, Israel, 1971–72, 1974–75, 1977*. Edited by Eric M. Meyers et al. Boston: American Schools of Oriental Research.

Sussman, Max. 1992. "Sickness and Disease." *ABD* 6:6–15.

Veyne, Paul, ed. 1987. *From Pagan Rome to Byzantium*. Vol. 1 of *A History of Private Life*. Translated by Arthur Goldhammer. Cambridge, MA: Harvard University Press.

Yarbrough, O. Larry. 1993. "Parents and Children in the Jewish Family in Antiquity." Pages 39–60 in Cohen.

Chapter 5

Education

Both Jewish teachings and Greek philosophers counseled the importance of education, but whatever education the children of peasant and artisan families received was in the home and from their parents. Education was limited by the wealth and abilities of the parents and generally did not go beyond training in their everyday tasks, the family's work (agriculture, fishing, carpentry), and religious education (Prov 6:20; 31:1; Eph 6:4; 2 Tim 1:5; 3:14–15).

5.1 Parental Instruction

Parental instruction was important in Jewish tradition. The Lord commands Moses to assemble the people so that they can hear the Lord's words and teach them to their children: "Teach them to your children, talking about them when you are at home and when you are away, when you lie down and when you rise" (Deut 6:7; 11:19; cf. 4:10; Philo, *Spec. Laws* 4.141). Proverbs contains postexilic tradition for parents and teachers, much of which is presented in direct address.

> Hear, my child, your father's instruction,
> > and do not reject your mother's teaching.
> > > (Prov 1:8)
>
> When I was a son with my father,
> > tender, and my mother's favorite,
> he taught me, and said to me,
> "Let your heart hold fast my words;
> > keep my commandments, and live.
> Get wisdom; get insight: do not forget, nor turn away
> > from the words of my mouth.

Do not forsake her, and she will keep you;
    love her, and she will guard you.
The beginning of wisdom is this:
    Get wisdom,
and whatever else you get,
    get insight."
                        (4:3–7)

"Fear of the Lord" is a recurring theme (Prov 1:7, 29; 3:5; passim), and the instruction is presented in praise of Wisdom, observations about life, proverbs, and positive and negative admonitions.

Tobit gives us a glimpse of what may have been typical parental instruction. Before Tobit sends his son, Tobias, off to recover money he had left in trust in Media, he instructs his son to give him a proper burial when he dies, honor his mother, revere the Lord, live uprightly, give alms, beware of fornication, marry a woman descended from his ancestors, pay workers their wages at the end of the day, discipline himself, seek advice from every wise person, and bless the Lord God at all times (4:3–19; cf. Ahiqar 1.1).

5.2 The Emergence of Torah Literacy

By early in the second century BCE, the teaching of Sirach, a handbook for teachers, combines traditional wisdom teachings with an emphasis on keeping the law:

If you desire wisdom,
    keep the commandments.
                (Sir 1:26)

Whoever fears the Lord will do this,
    and whoever holds to the law will obtain wisdom.
                        (15:1)

The whole of wisdom is fear of the Lord,
    and in all wisdom there is the fulfillment of the law.
                        (19:20)

References to the law are then woven throughout the book (e.g., 2:16; 9:15; 21:11; 45:5). Moses ordained Aaron to serve as a priest, to make sacrifices, to "teach Jacob the testimonies, and to enlighten Israel with his [the Lord's] law" (45:17). Although Sirach was probably written in Jerusalem, these references provide a window onto the nationalism and zeal for the law that characterized the Maccabees and the Hasmoneans and is reflected in the material evidence (stone vessels that did not retain impurity, washing pools, and coins without animal or human images) for the observance of the law in Galilee after its annexation by Aristobulus I (see above, 1.2).

Early references to reading and writing appear in 1 Enoch, where Enoch is instructed to read what is written on "the tablets of heaven," then to instruct his son, Methuselah, and write down all "the signs of wisdom" for him and all those who would come after him (81.1–6; 92.1; 108.1). David Carr suggests that this would have been a plausible picture of "small-scale elite education," especially in priestly families (204). In 4 Maccabees, Eleazar is "a man of priestly family, learned in the law" (5:4).

Jubilees, a retelling of Genesis and the exodus and written in the second century BCE, begins and ends with the revelation of the law to Moses on Mount Sinai. The resurgence of Jewish identity is evident in their zeal for the law, separation from gentiles, keeping the Sabbath, and observing the festivals, sacrifices, and purity. Israel has strayed, and God is calling the people back to the covenant: "Many will be destroyed and seized and will fall into the hand of the enemy because they have forsaken my ordinances and my commandments and the feasts of my covenant and my sabbaths and my sacred place" (Jub. 1.10). Therefore, God calls Moses to the mountain to receive the tablets, "so that you may teach them" (1.1). Parenthetically, in its retelling of the stories of the patriarchs, Jubilees relates that Abraham's father taught him writing when he was fourteen (11.16); while the rustic Esau learned war, Jacob learned writing (19.14). As in 1 Enoch, a priestlike father educates his son. Similarly, Levi charges his children to "walk according to [God's] Law in integrity." The Testament of Levi continues: "Teach your children letters also so that they might have understanding throughout their lives as they ceaselessly read the Law of God. For everyone who knows the Law of God will be honored wherever he goes, . . . and many men will want to serve him and hear the Law from his mouth" (13.1–4). Here we see the pattern of parental instruction, teaching "letters" (*grammata*, reading), and the status that literacy confers. Literacy in the law was adopted by the Hasmoneans as a means of resisting Hellenistic influence. The Seleucids "tore to pieces and burned with fire" the books of the law they found (1 Macc 1:56). In response, Judas Maccabeus, following the example of Nehemiah, "collected all the books that had been lost on account of the war that had come upon us, and they are in our possession" (2 Macc 2:14). The sacred writings were kept in the temple (Josephus, *Ant.* 3.38; 5.61).

Some of the books of the law from the temple probably became the master scrolls that were copied and taught at Qumran and elsewhere (Carr, 233). Reading, interpreting, teaching, and copying the law of Moses were the core activities of the priestly Essenes (1QS VIII, 15). The teacher of righteousness, or "the Righteous Teacher," was called "the interpreter of Torah" (*doresh ha-torah*). The *maskil* was the teacher. The Manual of Discipline (1QS) stipulates, "In the place where the Ten assemble there should not be missing a man to interpret the law day and night, always, each man relieving his fellow. And the Many shall be on watch together for a third of each night of the year in order to read the book, explain the regulation, and bless together" (1QS VI, 6–8). Women and children also received instruction when they came to the community: "They shall assemble all those who come, including children and women, and they shall read into their ea[rs] all the regulations of the covenant, and shall instruct them in all its precepts" (1QSa I, 4–5). A youth should be educated "in the book of HAGY," the "Book of Meditation," probably a reference to the Torah (Carr, 218–19) or a collection of laws or wisdom (Wassen, 353); "according to his age, instruct him in the precepts of the covenant, and he wi[ll receive] [ins]truction in its regulations" (1QSa I, 6–9). At the age of twenty-five, a man could enter the community (1QSa I, 12) after a two-year period of preparation and examination by the community (1QS VI, 21). The council of the community was composed of twelve men and three priests (1QS VIII, 1). The Dead Sea Scrolls, therefore, provide clear evidence of a priestly community teaching the sacred texts to both priests and nonpriests. Wassen concludes that while memorization of Torah was widespread in Jewish homes and communities, "it is less clear that actual reading and writing skills were included in common educational practice" (354). Nevertheless, "given the general character of the [Qumran] community, we may safely assume that the instruction [there] at least included reading [and writing]" (354–55, 358).

5.3 Pedagogy

Philo and Josephus reflect the emerging ideal of universal education in the Scriptures, at least for Jewish men and boys. Philo notes that the Jews alone opposed Emperor Gaius's effort to have his statue placed in a temple (in Jerusalem) because they were trained, "we may say even from the cradle, by parents and tutors and instructors and by the far higher authority of the sacred laws and also the unwritten customs, to acknowledge one God who is the Father and Maker of the world" (*Embassy* 115). While the law is still central for Philo, his instruction regarding the father's role also reflects Hellenistic themes; the father is "to beget good intentions and noble and worthy actions, and then to foster [his] offspring with the water of the truths which education and wisdom abundantly supply" (*Spec. Laws* 2.29). Similarly, Josephus, raised in a priestly family (*Life* 1–6), traces a more developed vision of education to the Mosaic law: "It orders that they [children] shall be taught to read, and shall learn both the laws and the deeds of their forefathers, in order that they may imitate the latter" (*Ag. Ap.* 2.204). Josephus says the Jews take pride in the education of their children (*Ag. Ap.* 1.60): the law (Deut 11:19; cf. *Ant.* 4.211) "orders that [children] shall be taught to read, and shall learn both the laws and the deeds of their forefathers in order that they may imitate the latter" (*Ag. Ap.* 2.204; cf. also Philo, *Embassy* 115).

While Sirach exhorted fathers to be strict, "Discipline your son and make his yoke heavy, so that you may not be offended by his shamelessness" (30:13), Pseudo-Phocylides warned against harshness: "Do not be harsh with your children, but be gentle" (207). Nevertheless, teachers often resorted to corporal punishment. Hence comes Sirach's admonition, "He who loves his son will whip him often" (30:1), and the alliterative aphorism quoted in Hebrews: "He learned obedience through what he suffered" (Heb 5:8, *emathen aph' hōn epathen tēn hypakoēn*). The Shepherd of Hermas (2nd c. CE) underscores the importance of continuous parental instruction: "For as the coppersmith hammers his work to master the material as he wants, so also the upright word spoken every day masters all evil. Do not stop exhorting your children" (Visions 3.2).

Dionysius of Halicarnassus, the Roman educator and historian of the first century BCE, provides the following description of contemporary teaching practices.

> When we are taught to read, first we learn by heart the names of the letters, then their shapes and their values, then, in the same way, the syllables and their effects, and finally words and their properties, by which I mean the ways they are lengthened, shortened, and scanned; and similar functions. And when we have acquired knowledge of these things, we begin to write and read, syllable by syllable and slowly at first. It is only when a considerable lapse of time has implanted firmly in our minds the forms of the words that we execute them with the utmost ease, and we read through any book that is given to us unfalteringly and with incredible confidence and speed. (*Comp.* 25)

Unfortunately, not many ancient Jews had the opportunity to learn to read.

5.4 Levels of Literacy

It is estimated that in antiquity generally only about 10 percent of the population could read (W. Harris, 22, 272), even less among ancient Jews (Hezser 2001, 496). In an early study, Meir Bar-Ilan (1992) cited the correlation between illiteracy and dependence on agriculture, and rabbinic sources support his conclusion that the Jewish literacy rate was less than 3 percent (56). For example, Soferim 11.2 stipulates, "A town in which there is only one who reads; he stands up, reads (the Torah), and sits down, he stands up, reads and sits down, even seven times" (Bar-Ilan 1992, 54). Such estimates provide only a broad context. Literacy rates would have been higher in Jerusalem than in Galilee, higher in cities than in villages and rural areas, higher among elites and priests than among peasants and artisans, and higher among men than women. Consequently, "the large majority of Jews, especially those who lived in the rural areas of the Galilee, would not have had sufficient leisure time and money to engage in any type of learning besides the practical skills needed for subsistence farming and small-scale business" (Hezser 2016, 5). The widespread evidence of literary texts—Torah scrolls and other writings, official documents, and inscriptions—does not necessarily mean a higher percentage of the population could read; hence arises the distinction between textuality and literacy. In contrast to Greek and Roman society, papyrus letters, burial and dedicatory inscriptions, and graffiti are extremely rare in Roman Palestine (Hezser 2001, 500). Complicating the situation, three languages were used in first-century Palestine. Biblical texts and many of the Qumran scrolls were written in Hebrew. Aramaic was the common spoken language, while many also spoke Greek. Only those closely associated with the Romans would have been conversant in Latin.

One must distinguish various levels of literacy: illiteracy (inability to read or write), artisan or craft literacy (a low level of literacy—ability to function in one's work: lists, weights, measurements, names), and scribal literacy (ranging from village scribes with limited abilities to those who could read and write fluently). Similarly, the goal of elementary education was the ability to write one's name (signature literacy). Persons who could not sign their name generally could not read either (Wise, 5). In his groundbreaking study of the signatories of the Bar Kokhba documents, Michael Wise identifies four categories: (1) the alphabetic hand or slow writer, reflecting only a year or two of schooling; (2) the unpracticed hand; (3) the practiced hand or "literary literate," attesting years of study and practice; and (4) the professional scribe (Wise, 59–60; cf. Bazzana, 134–46).

Each of these levels of literacy can be documented from our sources. A cache of second-century (CE) documents belonging to Babatha, a prominent woman, includes a Greek document (P.Yad. 15.35) signed by the scribe Eleazar, with the explanation, "on account of her not knowing letters" (Keith, 92; cf. J. Harris, 95–98). From this, Catherine Hezser concludes, "If even women from wealthy landowning families who managed their own property lacked the most basic practical skills (cf. Babatha and Salome Komaise), one can be certain that illiteracy amongst middle- and lower-class women was almost total" (2001, 498; on Babatha, see below, 7.8).

A piece of a rectangular base with the front hoof of a bull was discovered in Beersheba of Galilee and dated to the Hellenistic period. On it are three inscriptions, one in hieroglyphics, suggesting that the stone was imported from Egypt; one in Aramaic; and one that is unreadable "but looks as if someone copied Greek letters without knowing the language" (Aviam 2004, 8–9). Another artifact, an Aramaic (or Hebrew) abecedary inscription written by an unskilled scribe and dating from the late first or early second century, has been recovered at Khirbet Qana, "the first abecedary found in a Jewish village in the Galilee" (Edwards, 116; Eshel and Edwards). When the Shepherd of Hermas copies the book he was given, he says, "I copied the whole thing, letter by letter, for I could not distinguish between the syllables" (Visions 5.4). Similarly, the scribe Petaus could barely copy the formula, "I, Petaus, village scribe, have received" (P.Petaus 121; Keith, 90, n. 82). On the other hand, Joseph thought Aseneth had fine fingers, "like the fingers of a fast-writing scribe" (Jos. Asen. 20.5).

We do not possess a similar cache of documents from Galilee, but Josephus refers to village scribes in two passages. Describing the infighting about Herod's sons and their wives, Alexander and his associates allegedly threatened, "when they came to the throne, to set the mothers of their brothers to work at the loom along with the slave-girls, and to make the princes themselves village clerks (kōmōn grammateis), sarcastically referring to the careful education which they had received" (J.W. 1.479). The parallel in Jewish Antiquities reads, "[They] continually threatened that if ever they obtained power, they would make village clerks (kōmogrammateis) out of the sons borne to Herod by his other wives, for, they said, their present concern with the education which had carefully been given them fitted them for such a position" (16.203). Clearly, the Herods and their circle of elites looked down on the village scribes even though the latter were literate and educated. Scribes may have enjoyed prestige and limited power in their towns and villages, but they were still far from the seats of power. Assuming that the patterns set by the Seleucids still prevailed in Galilee as they did in Egypt (Bazzana, 9–16), the responsibilities of Herodian scribes included writing reports on the status of land in their area, assessments of taxes due, and complaints and petitions (Bazzana, 40). Babatha's archive of papyrus scrolls (see below, 7.8) found at Nahal Hever includes a similar range of documents: deeds, census records, petitions, court documents, marriage contracts, certificates of divorce, and records of loans. Herodian documents were probably composed in Greek (Bazzana, 120–29). A further clue that this was the case is a market weight found in Tiberias, bearing a Greek inscription that reads, "In the 34th year of the tetrarchy of Herod [i.e., 29/30 CE], being *agoranomos* [official keeping order in the marketplace] Gaius Julius . . ." (Bazzana, 125; see below, 11.5).

Michael Wise determined—from his study of the levels of signature literacy of elite male signatories of the legal texts discovered at Nahal Hever, near the Dead Sea—that Aramaic was the most common spoken language (331), 65 to 80 percent of Judeans spoke a form of Hebrew (296), about 30 percent spoke Greek, and a third to a half of this number could also read Greek (345). "About 16 percent of Judaean adults were signature literate" (347–48), but none of the women in Wise's sample population could sign her name. Illiteracy carried no social stigma; yet literacy was a mark of status and wealth. Extrapolating his results further, Wise concludes that "between 5 and 10 percent of Judean men in the years dividing Pompey from Hadrian were able to read books" (349–50), and many of this elite minority possessed a small collection of sacred books written in Hebrew.

Josephus found copies of the laws of Moses in villages in Galilee (*J.W.* 2.229; *Life* 134). Was more Greek spoken in Galilee than Judea? Chancey surmises that Jesus "would not have needed [Greek] to be a carpenter, to teach the Galilean crowds, to travel around the lake, or to venture into the villages associated with Tyre, Caesarea Philippi, and the Decapolis cities" (163); but Root contends that Lakeside Galilee was "the most urban and Hellenized portion of Galilee," and therefore "a significant portion of the population would probably have known at least a little Greek" (173, 174). Did Jews (some of them priests) bring some level of Hebrew literacy to Galilee? While answers to these questions await further discoveries, it is nevertheless clear that Aramaic, Hebrew, and Greek were present in varying degrees in the Galilean villages.

The ability to compose, transcribe, and communicate written material was a professional competence generally limited to the scribal guilds (Jaffee, 15), and these were associated with the royal courts and the temple in Jerusalem. Scribes who copied the sacred books would have been accorded great respect and authority (Goodman). Books functioned as ritual objects; because of the difficulty in retrieving information from a scroll, scrolling back and forth over unpointed Hebrew to locate a particular passage, with no divisions of chapters and verses, it was useful only to those who "already knew its contents through approximate memorization" (Jaffee, 17). The social implications of such limitations, the expense of producing texts, and limited literacy are profound. "With the exception of scribes actually engaged in book production and copying, the reading of books was commonly connected to ritualized, public ceremonies rather than private study. For most people, a book was a commodity that one 'heard' through the medium of another voice; 'reading' was the activity of declaiming a text before an audience in a social performance approaching the gravity of ceremonial ritual" (Jaffee, 17). For others, reading and writing were limited to retrieving information from lists, business records, and legal contracts.

Most education took place in the home, with fathers instructing their children, or in elite families employing a tutor. Higher levels of literacy reflect a system of schools, greater wealth, and higher status. Although, again, we must be careful about the dates, contexts, and value of our sources for understanding education in first-century Galilean villages, the following overview sets a general perspective. Daniel (2nd c. BCE) says that King Nebuchadnezzar of Babylon (6th c. BCE) "commanded his palace master Ashpenaz to bring some of the Israelites of the royal family and of the nobility, young men without physical defect and handsome, versed in every branch of wisdom, endowed with knowledge and insight, and competent to serve in the king's palace; they were to be taught the literature and language of the Chaldeans" (Dan 1:3–4). Susanna 3 adds that Susanna's parents, righteous and presumably wealthy since she married a very rich man, "trained their daughter according to the law of Moses." During the second century (BCE), a Greek gymnasium was established in Jerusalem to educate "the noblest young men" in athletics and Greek culture (2 Macc 4:9, 12; 1 Macc 1:14).

In response to the spread of Hellenism through the education of Jewish young men in Greek culture, the Hasmoneans adopted the same strategy by emphasizing enculturation in the pre-Hellenistic, Hebrew Scriptures (Carr, 253–72), centered in Jerusalem. By the first century, the reading of Torah in synagogues in Galilee is evident. The synagogue stone discovered in the synagogue at Magdala (1st c. CE) provides clear evidence of the connection with the temple in Jerusalem. Mordechai Aviam (2013) contends that the decorations on the stone represent elements drawn from the Jerusalem temple, including a menorah, and that the stone was used to support a table for the Torah scroll. Others suggest that it was an offering table (De Luca and Lena, 317).

Hearing the Scriptures read would have been a much more remarkable event in an ancient Galilean village than it is today: "Long years of training were required before a person might read publicly without blunder and the accompanying shame" (Wise, 309). This condition raises the question of who read the Scriptures in Galilean synagogues, where such reading was one of their principal functions. Most of those who would read were elites, priests, and scribes. Later, the rabbis forbade certain persons to be readers: deaf-mutes, people in ragged clothes, women, slaves, and minors (m. Meg. 2:4, 6; 4:5–6; Hezser 2001, 453). Those who read and interpreted the Law and the Prophets would have been respected members of their communities. Luke attributes this honor and esteem to Jesus, who, according to Luke, not only read Scripture in his hometown but also sat among the teachers in the temple at age twelve (2:46; 4:15–17; see below, 21.3).

According to the high priest Eleazer in the Letter of Aristeas (127), however, "The good life . . . consisted in observing the laws, and this aim was achieved by hearing much more than by reading." Through the regular reading of Scripture in the synagogues, even those who could not read were instructed in the Law and the Prophets: "He [Moses] appointed the Law to be the most excellent and necessary form of instruction, ordaining, not that it should be heard once for all or twice or on several occasions, but that[,] every week[,] men should desert their other occupations and assemble to listen to the Law and to obtain a thorough and accurate knowledge of it" (Josephus, *Ag. Ap.* 2.175). As these passages suggest, "the emphasis [lay] on Torah observance rather than on study" (Hezser 2001, 460).

5.5 Schools

The origins of the Jewish elementary school (*bet sepher*) are obscure and probably postdate Jesus' ministry. The Palestinian Talmud (Ketub. 8.8) attributes its origin to Simeon ben Shetah (ca. 100 BCE), but this appears to be a case of pressing later rabbinic ideals back to an earlier period. The Babylonian Talmud (B. Bat. 21a) records that Joshua ben Gamla (ca. 64 CE, in the Golan) introduced a decree that teachers should be appointed in every district and town and that children should enter school from the age of six or seven. Neither of these traditions can be authenticated. No contemporary source mentions schools for primary education in Galilee, and Catherine Hezser (2010, 471) questions whether Joshua ben Gamla, one the last high priests, could have carried out such a program before the outbreak of the First Jewish Revolt. Neither have any pre-70 remains of schools been found in Galilee (Poirier, 254). When schools did begin to appear, they were private enterprises. A teacher and his student or students could meet in a variety of places, often in the student's home. Later, ruling on the limits of competition, "R. Joseph said: R. Huna agrees that a teacher cannot prevent [another teacher from setting up in the same alley]" (b. B. Bat. 21b).

"Houses of study" begin to appear in the early centuries, when synagogues became more common and competent readers were needed to read the Torah. The earliest reference to a *bet midrash*, or house of study, occurs in Sirach (2nd c. BCE: "Draw near to me, you who are uneducated, and lodge in the house of instruction" [51:23e]). The earliest sites identified as possible houses of study are small rooms (about 3 × 5 meters) adjacent to the synagogues at Gamla (1st c. BCE; Richardson, 126 and Plate 1), Khirbet Qana (Richardson, 66; McCollough, 116–17), Wadi Hammam, and Magdala (De Luca and Lena, 312; Runesson, 161–62). A lintel discovered in the Golan, dating to the time of Judah the Prince (ca. 200 CE), reads: "The *bet hamidrash* of R. Eliezer ha-Qappar." Still, it is not clear that such rooms were used for instruction in reading the Torah, and synagogue schools were rare in Galilee before the third century CE (Hezser 2001, 497).

5.6 Education in Galilee

Neither the practices at Qumran nor Josephus, a priest from Jerusalem, nor Philo, the Alexandrian scholar, give us much insight into education in Galilean villages. As Josephus self-servingly observes regarding his own proficiency with Jewish and Greek texts, "No one else, either Jew or gentile, would have been equal to the task [of writing *Jewish Antiquities*]. . . . Though many have laboriously undertaken this training, scarcely two or three have succeeded" (*Ant.* 20.262, 265). More illuminating are Sirach's comments on literacy.

> The wisdom of the scribe depends on the opportunity of leisure; only the one who has little business can become wise. How can one become wise who handles the plow, and who glories in the shaft of a goad, who drives oxen and is occupied with their work, and whose talk is about bulls? . . . So too is every artisan [*tektōn*] and master artisan [*architektōn*] who labors by night as well as by day, . . . the smith, . . . the potter. . . . All these rely on their hands, and all are skillful in their own work. Without them no city can be inhabited, and wherever they live, they will not go hungry. Yet they are not sought out for the council of the people, nor do they attain eminence in the public assembly. They do not sit in the judge's seat, nor do they understand the decisions of the courts; they cannot expound discipline or judgment, and they are not found among

the rulers. But they maintain the fabric of the world, and their concern is for the exercise of their trade. How different the one who devotes himself to the study of the law of the Most High! (Sir 38:24–34)

Galilean Jews who practiced ritual washings, avoided unclean foods, and used stone vessels also traveled to Jerusalem for the pilgrimage festivals when they could. Mishnah Hagigah (1:1) describes a father carrying a child on his shoulders or holding his hand as they go from Jerusalem to the Temple Mount. In many places, Galilean Jews went to the synagogue each week to hear the Scriptures read and taught. They also observed the Seder in their homes at Passover (see below, 8.5), thereby passing on the tradition to their children. As the oral tradition of the Pharisees records, "Here the son asks his father (and if the son has not enough understanding, his father instructs him [how to ask]), 'Why is this night different from other nights? . . . And according to the understanding of the son[,] his father instructs him, . . . and he expounds from *A wandering Aramean was my father* [Deut 26:5–11] . . . until he finishes the whole section" (m. Pesaḥ. 10:4).

By around the third century, when a boy entered the *bet sepher* (school, house of letters), at the age of five to seven years, he began to learn to read the Torah. Boys from the age of thirteen participated in the synagogue readings. Rote memorization and repetition continued to play major roles in the learning process. Students read or recited passages aloud until they were able to read the Scriptures accurately. The number of literate women would have been minuscule and limited to women in wealthy families (Bar-Ilan 1998, 43, 50). The rabbis debated teaching Torah to girls; Ben Azzai (ca. 80–120) favored doing so, while Rabbi Eliezer (ca. 120–140) argued that the daughter would misuse the law (m. Soṭah 3:4; m. Ned. 4:3; see Ilan, 59).

5.7 Reflections

In sum, children of peasant and artisan families in Galilee received practical and religious education at home and in the synagogues. Only the children of the elite, landowners, priests, scribes, and the Herodians might receive formal instruction in reading or writing, probably from private instructors. Such skills were a mark of wealth and status. One who read the Scriptures or offered instruction in the synagogue would have been held in high regard. Whatever knowledge of the Law and the Prophets others might gain came through what they had learned from their parents as children and what they heard in this public assembly or in other discussions of the law. It was highly acculturated learning, "the traditions of [their] fathers" (Mark 7:3; Gal 1:14 KJV; 1 Macc 2:16), and had a direct link to the maintenance of Jewish identity, boundaries, and purity.

Works Cited in Chapter 5

Aviam, Mordechai. 2004. "First-Century Jewish Galilee: An Archaeological Perspective." Pages 7–27 in *Religion and Society in Roman Palestine: Old Questions, New Approaches.* Edited by Douglas R. Edwards. New York: Routledge.

———. 2013. "The Decorated Stone from the Synagogue at Migdal." *NovT* 55:205–20.

Bar-Ilan, Meir. 1992. "Illiteracy in the Land of Israel in the First Centuries C.E." Pages 46–61 in vol. 2 of *Essays in the Social Scientific Study of Judaism and Jewish Society.* Edited by Simcha Fishbane and Stuart Schoenfeld with Alain Goldshläger. Hoboken, NJ: Ktav.

———. 1998. *Some Jewish Women in Antiquity.* Atlanta: Scholars Press.

Bazzana, Giovanni B. 2015. *Kingdom of Bureaucracy: The Political Theology of Village Scribes in the Sayings Gospel Q.* BETL 274. Leuven: Peeters.

Carr, David M. 2005. *Writing on the Tablet of the Heart: Origins of Scripture and Literature.* Oxford: Oxford University Press.

Chancey, Mark A. 2005. *Greco-Roman Culture and the Galilee of Jesus.* SNTSMS 134. Cambridge: Cambridge University Press.

De Luca, Stefano, and Anna Lena. 2015. "Magdala/Taricheae." Pages 280–342 in Fiensy and Strange, vol. 2.

Edwards, Douglas R. 2002. "Khirbet Qana: From Jewish Village to Christian Pilgrim Site." Pages 101–32 in *The Roman and Byzantine Near East.* Vol. 3. Edited by J. D. Humphrey. JRASup 49. Portsmouth, RI: Journal of Roman Archaeology.

Eshel, Esther, and Douglas R. Edwards. 2004. "Language and Writing in Early Roman Galilee: Social Location of a Potter's Abecedary from Khirbet Qana." Pages 49–55 in *Religion and Society in Roman Palestine: Old Questions, New Approaches.* Edited by Douglas R. Edwards. New York: Routledge.

Fiensy, David A., and James R. Strange, eds. 2014–15. *Galilee in the Late Second Temple and Mishnaic Periods.* 2 vols. Minneapolis: Fortress.

Goodman, Martin. 1994. "Texts, Scribes, and Power in Roman Judaea." Pages 99–108 in *Literacy and Power in the Ancient World.* Edited by Alan K. Bowman and Greg Woolf. Cambridge: Cambridge University Press.

Harris, Jill. 2010. "Courts and the Judicial System." Pages 85–101 in Hezser 2010.

Harris, William V. 1989. *Ancient Literacy.* Cambridge, MA: Harvard University Press.

Hezser, Catherine. 2001. *Jewish Literacy in Roman Palestine.* TSAJ 81. Tübingen: Mohr Siebeck.

———, ed. 2010. *The Oxford Handbook of Jewish Daily Life in Roman Palestine.* Oxford: Oxford University Press.

———. 2016. "The Torah versus Homer: Jewish and Greco-Roman Education in Late Roman Palestine." Pages 5–24 in *Ancient Education and Early Christianity.* Edited by Matthew Ryan Hauge and Andrew W. Pitts. LNTS 533. London: Bloomsbury T&T Clark.

Ilan, Tal. 2010. "Gender Issues and Daily Life." Pages 48–68 in Hezser 2010.

Jaffee, Martin S. 2001. *Torah in the Mouth: Writing and Oral Tradition in Palestinian Judaism, 200 BCE–400 CE.* Oxford: Oxford University Press.

Keith, Chris. 2011. *Jesus' Literacy: Scribal Culture and the Teacher from Galilee.* LNTS 413. London: T&T Clark.

McCollough, C. Thomas. 2022. "The Economic Transformation of an Early Roman Galilean Village: A Keynesian Approach." Pages 108–25 in *Taxation, Economy, and Revolt in Ancient Rome, Galilee, and Egypt.* Edited by Thomas R. Blanton IV, Agnes Choi, and Jinyu Liu. RMCS. London: Routledge.

Poirier, John C. 2014. "Education/Literacy in Jewish Galilee: Was There Any and at What Level?" Pages 253–60 in vol. 1 of Fiensy and Strange.

Richardson, Peter. 2004. *Building Jewish in the Roman East.* Waco, TX: Baylor University Press.

Root, Bradley W. 2014. *First-Century Galilee: A Fresh Examination of the Sources.* WUNT 378. Tübingen: Mohr Siebeck.

Runesson, Anders. 2017. "Synagogues without Rabbis or Christians? Ancient Institutions beyond Normative Discourses." *JBV* 38:159–72.

Wassen, Cecilia. 2012. "On Education of Children in the Dead Sea Scrolls." *SR* 41:350–63.

Wise, Michael Owen. 2015. *Language and Literacy in Roman Judaea: A Study of the Bar Kokhba Documents.* New Haven: Yale University Press.

Chapter 6

Fathers and Sons

Two Sons (Matt 21:28–32)
Friend at Night (Luke 11:5–8)
Prodigal Son (Luke 15:11b–32)

*F*our parables feature fathers and sons. A father would not give his son
a stone or a snake when he has asked for bread and fish. When the neighbor comes at night, the father is in bed with his young children. When the
father sends the first son to work in the vineyard, his son refuses but then
goes. The second son said he would go but did not. Which one did the will
of his father? The prodigal son asks for his inheritance, which he squanders
in a far country. When he returns home, his father receives him joyfully.
All four parables assume definite expectations about a father's authority
and a son's obligations, which are not likely to have been different in Galilee than in Judea or to have changed greatly over time.

6.1 Parental Duties

Parents were responsible for the education of their children. As Jan van der
Watt observed, "Within an ancient family the transmission of customs that
represented, as well as expressed[,] the 'character' of that particular family, formed a cornerstone of the communal system" (267). Tacitus (*Dial.*
28–29) emphasizes the parents' role in the education of their children (see
above, ch. 5). Horace (65–8 BCE) lovingly describes his father's efforts to
educate him. Because his father was the son of a struggling farmer, he would
not send Horace to the school of Flavius, with the "grand boys" who went
"with slate and satchel hung over the left arm," their fee in hand, on the ides
of each month. Nevertheless, his father instilled in him character that kept

him from shame and scandal. "For this," Horace said, "I owe him praise and thanks the more" (*Sat.* 1.6.65–84).

A statement from the Talmud, although it is later, reflects the traditional duties of the father that would have characterized Jewish families in the first century also: "Our Rabbis taught: The father is bound in respect to his son to circumcise [him], redeem him [if the son is a firstborn], . . . teach him Torah, take a wife for him; and teach him a craft [trade]. Some say, to teach him to swim" (b. Qidd. 29a; Soncino). The sign of circumcision, performed on the eighth day, was rooted in the Abrahamic covenant (Gen 17:10–14), but it received renewed emphasis as a sign of Jewish identity and faithfulness after some in Jerusalem embraced Hellenism, built a gymnasium "according to Gentile custom, . . . removed the marks of circumcision, and abandoned the holy covenant" (1 Macc 1:14–15). In the Seleucid campaign of forced Hellenization and the Maccabean campaign of forced observance of the law that followed, circumcision was the defining boundary marker of Jewish identity:

> *The Seleucids:* "Anyone found possessing the book of the covenant, or anyone who adhered to the law, was condemned to death by decree of the king. . . . According to the decree, they put to death the women who had their children circumcised, and their families and those who circumcised them; and they hung the infants from their mothers' necks." (1 Macc 1:57–61; cf. 2 Macc 6:10; 4 Macc 4:25)

> *The Maccabees:* "Mattathias and his friends went around and tore down the altars; they forcibly circumcised all the uncircumcised boys that they found within the borders of Israel." (1 Macc 2:45–46)

The rabbis' reference to "redeeming" a son applied to the firstborn as a reminder that the Lord had delivered the children of Israel while slaying the firstborn of the Egyptians (Exod 13:13–14). The means of "redeeming" the firstborn male is not specified, although Numbers 18:16 requires five shekels. Faithful observance of the Torah, marriage within the people of Israel, and procreation of children were all essential for the continuation of the people of the covenant and therefore were duties expected of every Jewish father (see ch. 7 on marriage customs). Rabbi Judah ha-Nasi, "the prince," who codified the Mishnah (ca. 200 CE), added that if a father does not teach his son a craft, it is as though he taught him to be a robber, "brigandage." In this regard, Jesus' proverbial saying in John 5:19 reflects the role of parental instruction, and perhaps

Jesus' own experience: "The Son can do nothing on his own, but only what he sees the Father doing; for whatever the Father does, the Son does likewise." The last line in b. Qiddushin 29a, "Some say, to teach him to swim," probably expresses a general admonition to teach sons what they need to survive.

6.2 Family Life

Family life in agricultural communities evolved slowly. First-century Galilean villages were little affected by the ways of the elite in Athens or Rome but drew their way of life from the Hebrew Scriptures and the wisdom teachers. Certain matters were common to families across the ancient world, however, notably the authority of the father and the honor owed to the father. Romulus, to whom the earliest Roman laws were traced, "gave virtually full power to the father over his son, even during his whole life, whether he thought proper to imprison him, to scourge him, to put him in chains and keep him at work in the fields, or to put him to death" (Dionysius of Halicarnassus, *Ant. rom.* 2.26.4). Later, harshness was discouraged, and the killing of a son was outlawed. Reacting to the practice among wealthy families of handing children over to servants to be raised, Tacitus, writing in 100–110 CE, laments the passing of the old ways:

> In the good old days, every man's son, born in wedlock, was brought up not in the chamber of some hireling nurse, but in his mother's lap, and at her knee. And that mother could have no higher praise than that she managed the house and gave herself to her children. Again, some elderly relative would be selected in order that to her, as a person who had been tried and never found wanting, might be entrusted the care of all the youthful scions of the same house; in the presence of such an one no base word could be uttered without grave offence, and no wrong deed done. Religiously and with the utmost delicacy she regulated not only the serious tasks of her youthful charges, but their recreations also and their games. (*Dial.* 28.4–5)

Tacitus's description of "the good old days" probably accords closely with life in a multigenerational peasant household in a Galilean village.

The roles of fathers and sons were little different in Jewish tradition and culture. Honor of father and mother was inscribed in the Decalogue (Exod 20:12; Deut 5:16), and "whoever curses father or mother shall be put to death" (Exod 21:17; cf. 21:15; Deut 21:18–21). Josephus (*Ag. Ap.* 2.206) and Philo (*Spec. Laws* 2.243) interpret the penalties for disobedience of a parent in terms that echo the Roman authority given to the head of the house (*patria potestas*). Cicero, for example, praised Appius because "he maintained not mere authority, but [also] absolute command over his household; his slaves feared him, his children revered him, all loved him, and the customs and discipline of his forefathers flourished beneath his roof" (*Sen.* 11.37).

6.3 Inheritance

Luke recalls a moment when a man called for Jesus to settle a family dispute: "Teacher, tell my brother to divide the family inheritance with me" (12:13). The prodigal son demands his inheritance, as though the father had already died (Luke 15:12); and the wicked tenants of the vineyard conspire to kill the owner's son, "the heir," thinking—wrongly—that they could then claim the vineyard (Matt 21:38//Mark 12:7//Luke 20:14).

The father's role in passing on his property to his heirs was important in both Greco-Roman and Jewish contexts. Under Roman law the father had "a full freedom of testamentary disposition, so that the son did not have to be the heir, whereas in Greek, Egyptian and Hellenistic as well as Jewish law the son, sons or children were the heirs *eo ipso*" (Foerster, 769). For Jews, passing on inherited land had the added significance of covenantal duty, as it pertained to the land of Israel. Inheritance was a feature of God's covenant with Israel (Gen 12:1–3). God gave the land of Canaan to Abraham's descendants (Gen 12:1, 5; 13:14–17; Jub. 13.21; 1QapGen XXI, 8–14), and the prophets projected the promise into the future (Hester, vii–viii).

Each tribe was apportioned a share in the promised land by lot, except the tribe of Levi (Josh 13:14, 33). Shares in one's inheritance were allotted following the law of Moses. The firstborn son received a double portion of the father's property, even if the father preferred another son, or the firstborn of another wife (Deut 21:17). If a father had no son, his inheritance could pass to his daughter (Num 27:8), who was then required to marry into a clan of her father's tribe (36:6). Philo adds the provision that if virgin daughters are left without a dowry, "they should share equally with the males" (*Spec. Laws* 2.125). If a father had no children, his estate would pass to his brothers or nearest kinsman (Num 27:9–11), "so that all Israelites may continue to possess their ancestral inheritance. No inheritance shall be transferred from one tribe to another; for each of the tribes of the Israelites shall retain its own inheritance" (Num 36:8–9).

Although tribal claims to specific territories and membership of families in a particular tribe had faded by the first century, some, like Tobit and the apostle Paul, could still boast of their tribal identity (Tob 5:9–14; Phil 3:5); the ideal was still to choose a wife for one's son from one's tribe, as Tobit charged his son: "Marry a woman from among the descendants of your ancestors; do not marry a foreign woman, who is not of your father's tribe; for we are the descendants of the prophets" (Tob 4:12). Regarding the younger son's return to his father's house in the parable of the prodigal son, Joachim Jeremias observes, "After the legal settlement he [the younger son] has no further claim, not even to food and clothing" (130). A Talmudic reference in a debate regarding rights to property declares, "A son who leaves [his father's roof] and a woman when divorced are on the same footing as strangers [in relation to the father or husband]" (b. B. Bat. 47a).

6.4 Reflections

The characterization of Abraham as father of his descendants became increasingly important during the period in which Jews were defining themselves as a distinct people over against non-Jews. In this context, marks of the ideal father are ascribed to Abraham; in turn, Abraham is cited as the moral exemplar for his descendants. This development is prominently attested in 4 Maccabees, written sometime between Pompey (63 BCE) and Hadrian (120 CE), probably early in the first century CE, likely in Antioch or Alexandria (Anderson, 533–37).

God instructed Abraham to give his sons the mark of the covenant, circumcision (Gen 17:10–14, 23–27), which became the test of observance of the law and therefore a mark worth dying for during the Maccabean Revolt. Antiochus Epiphanes decreed, "Any of them . . . found observing the ancestral law . . . should die" (4 Macc 4:23); but faithful Jews disregarded his decree, "even to the extent that women, because they had circumcised their sons, were thrown headlong from heights along with their infants, though they had known beforehand that they would suffer this" (4:25). These mothers were following the example of Abraham, who was willing to sacrifice his son Isaac in obedience to God's command.

Abraham was blessed because he was faithful when he was tested. Sirach picks up these motifs and comments:

> Abraham was the great father of a multitude of nations, and no one
> has been found like him in glory. He kept the law of the Most High,
> and entered into a covenant with him; he certified the covenant in his
> flesh, and when he was tested he proved faithful. Therefore the Lord
> assured him with an oath that the nations would be blessed through

his offspring; that he would make him as numerous as the dust of the earth, and exalt his offspring like the stars, and give them an inheritance from sea to sea and from the Euphrates to the ends of the earth. (Sir 44:19–21)

Two centuries later, 4 Maccabees echoes the same exhortation to "endure any suffering for the sake of God," adding, "For his sake also our father Abraham was zealous to sacrifice his son Isaac" (16:19–20). The treatise or homily continues, recalling the martyrdom of the mother and her seven sons: "Take courage, therefore, O holy-minded mother, maintaining firm an enduring hope in God. . . . For your children were true descendants of father Abraham" (17:4, 6). "She was of the same mind as Abraham" (14:20), a "daughter of God-fearing Abraham" (15:28). Earlier, Eleazar, in facing his own martyrdom, declared, "Never may we, the children of Abraham, think so basely that out of cowardice we feign a role unbecoming to us!" He exhorted others to follow his example: "Therefore, O children of Abraham, die nobly for your religion!" (6:17, 22).

The rewards of faithfulness will be great. The pious Eleazar prays that his righteous death will atone for sins of God's people: "Make my blood their purification, and take my life in exchange for theirs" (4 Macc 6:29). The faithful will reap the promises God made to Abraham: "All the Israelites who are saved in those days and are truly mindful of God will be gathered together; they will go to Jerusalem and live in safety forever in the land of Abraham, and it will be given over to them" (Tob 14:6–7). Even in death, they will share in the blessings of the patriarchs: "Those who die for the sake of God live to God, as do Abraham and Isaac and Jacob and all the patriarchs" (4 Macc 16:25). Ruth Sheridan defines this motif as follows: "Abraham, Isaac, and Jacob attain an exalted status in the afterlife, from whence they effectively intercede for their 'seed' on earth" (155; see also 165–66). Although there is no evidence of direct dependence, Jesus' argument with the Sadducees presupposes the same assurance of life after death: "As for the resurrection of the dead, have you not read what was said to you by God, 'I am the God of Abraham, the God of Isaac, and the God of Jacob'? He is God not of the dead, but of the living" (Matt 22:31–32).

The importance of "Father Abraham" appears in other passages in the Gospels also. The opening line of Matthew introduces Jesus as "the son of David, the son of Abraham" (1:1). John the Baptist warns the Pharisees and Sadducees, "Do not presume to say to yourselves, 'We have Abraham as our ancestor'; for I tell you, God is able from these stones to raise up children to Abraham" (Matt 3:9//Luke 3:8), but those who are faithful "will come from east and west and will eat with Abraham and Isaac and Jacob in the kingdom of heaven" (Matt 8:11).

Abraham is more prominent in Luke than any of the other Gospels. Mary praises God's faithfulness, saying, "He has helped his servant Israel, in remembrance of his mercy, according to the promise he made to our ancestors, to Abraham and to his descendants forever" (1:54–55; cf. 1:73). Jesus heals a bent woman, whom he affirms as "a daughter of Abraham" (13:16). Then, remarkably, Abraham is named six times in the parable of the rich man and Lazarus, where twice the rich man appeals to "father Abraham" (16:24, 30) for mercy. Yet, there is hope for the rich if they repent; Zacchaeus, a chief tax collector (see below, 15.4), is "too . . . a son of Abraham" (19:9).

Underscoring the importance of Abraham's legacy, Jesus and certain "Jews who had believed in him" (John 8:31) argue over identifying the true descendants of Abraham (8:33–40). Ultimately, the Johannine Jesus claims that Abraham saw Jesus' day and rejoiced (8:56), apparently claiming that the revelation he brought, which would be declared to all the world (17:18), fulfilled God's promise to Abraham that "in you all the families of the earth shall be blessed" (Gen 12:3).

Works Cited in Chapter 6

Anderson, Hugh. 1985. "4 Maccabees." Pages 531–64 in vol. 2 of *The Old Testament Pseudepigrapha*. Edited by James H. Charlesworth. Garden City, NY: Doubleday.

Foerster, Werner. 1965. "*klēros, klēronomos*." *TDNT* 3:758–69.

Hester, James D. 1963. *Paul's Concept of Inheritance: A Contribution to the Understanding of Heilsgeschichte*. SJT Occasional Papers 14. Edinburgh: Oliver & Boyd, 1968.

Jeremias, Joachim. 1963. *The Parables of Jesus*. Rev. ed. Translated by S. H. Hooke. New York: Scribner's Sons.

Sheridan, Ruth. 2020. *The Figure of Abraham in John 8: Text and Intertext*. LNTS 619. London: T&T Clark.

Van der Watt, Jan G. 2000. *Family of the King: Dynamics of Metaphor in the Gospel according to John*. BibInt 47. Leiden: Brill.

Chapter 7

Women: Daughters, Brides, Mothers, and Widows

Leaven (Matt 13:33; Luke 13:20–21; Gospel of Thomas 96.1)
Lost Coin (Luke 15:8–10)
Unjust Judge (Luke 18:1–8)

*W*omen are central characters in three canonical parables. One woman, baking bread, mixes (or "hides") yeast in three measures (*sata*) of flour (ca. 50 lbs., 15 gallons, or a bushel): "No housewife would bake so vast a quantity of meal" (Jeremias 1963, 147). Another has ten coins, drachmas, silver coins each worth about a denarius, a day's wage. When she loses one of the coins, she lights a lamp (because houses, having no windows, are dark), sweeps the floor (probably a dirt floor), and searches until she finds it. Then she invites her friends and neighbors to celebrate with her (see above, 3.4). The third parable focuses on the plight of a widow, pleading with a judge to give her justice, presumably in relation to a third party who owes her money or property (see below, ch. 16). Women baking and hoarding small coins, widows pleading for justice: all, apparently, commonplace in ancient Galilee.

The Gospel of Thomas has a fourth parable featuring a woman in an everyday activity, carrying a jar of meal or flour. "The Kingdom of the [Father] is like a certain woman who was carrying a jar full of meal. While she was walking [on] a road, still some distance from home, the handle on the jar broke and the meal emptied out behind her on the road. She did not realize it; she had noticed no accident. When she reached her house, she set the jar down and found it empty" (Gos. Thom. 97, trans. Crossan, 5).

7.1 The Status of Women

Because of the Jewish and Greco-Roman cultural differences and their inter-actions in Galilee, interpretation of our sources regarding the status and roles of women in first-century Galilee is particularly critical. Each source has its own angle of vision and rhetorical intent. Josephus, for example, portrays the matriarchs Sarah, Rebecca, and Rachel as ideal women whose virtues reflect well on their husbands. Potiphar's wife and the Midianite women are Josephus's villainesses (Amaru). Social norms were negotiated in different ways, often according to the woman's social status, and varied in different periods and locations, at times in contradictory ways (see esp. Hylen, 12–41, 160–63).

Both Greco-Roman and Jewish women lived in a patriarchal, male-dom-inated society. A consistent thread among the opinions of various philoso-phers and physicians, all elite males, was "the assumption that maleness, as recognized by 'masculine' traits, was assumed indicative of full person-hood, orderliness, and therefore, perfection" (Myers, 21). In contrast, femi-ninity represents imperfection and weakness. Aristotle, for example, wrote, "The female is as it were a deformed male" (*Gen. an.* 737a.28; see further Hylen, 5–9). The implications of this patriarchy extended to every area of life and culture: family, state, religion, law, and medicine. Nevertheless, women exercised a central role in household economy and management, child-rearing, and a wide range of work and community activities.

Josephus's descriptions of the reign of Shelamzion Alexandra—"the main female hero of the Hasmonean dynasty" (Ilan 1999, 101), who ruled from 76 until her death in 67 BCE—illustrate the prevailing patriarchal sen-timent and ways it was negotiated. In *The Jewish War*, Josephus praises Shelamzion: "For this frail woman firmly held the reins of government, thanks to her reputation for piety. She was, indeed, the very strictest observer of the national traditions and would deprive of office any offenders against the sacred laws" (1.108). Later, in *Jewish Antiquities*, Josephus portrays Shelamzion negatively, apparently drawing on Nicolaus of Damascus (Ilan 1999, 100–105). Although Josephus concedes that "the queen [lit., "the woman," *hē gynē*] took thought for the welfare of the kingdom" (*Ant.* 13.409) and appends a positive final word (13.432), he follows Nicolaus in his grudging praise and his judgment that women are unfit to rule, alleging that Shelamzion was responsible for the collapse of the Hasmonean dynasty:

> But still they themselves were to blame for their misfortunes, in allow-ing a woman to reign who madly desired it in her unreasonable love of power. . . . (*Ant.* 13.417)

> She was a woman who showed none of the weakness of her sex; for being one of those inordinately desirous of the power to rule, she showed by her deeds the ability to carry out her plans. . . . At least matters turned out so unfortunately for her house that the sovereign power which it had acquired in the face of the greatest dangers and difficulties was not long afterward taken from it because of her desire for things unbecoming a woman. (*Ant.* 13.430–431)

Gender roles and male dominance in war, the priesthood, and leadership (patriarchs, elders, kings) are evident in ancient Israel, but at the village level women shared in "maintenance activities," bearing and raising children, preparing food (especially grinding and baking), spinning and weaving, religious observances in the home, and most other forms of work. As a result, "heterarchy" (mutual dominion, C. Meyers 2013, 196–99) more appropriately describes relationships in which women exercise agency and leadership in certain areas and men in other areas: "The maintenance activities and social structures of ancient Israel meant that daily life was rarely structured according to fixed, hierarchical gender patterns" (C. Meyers 2013, 198).

By the Hellenistic and early Roman periods, however, the status of women was changing (C. Meyers 2013, 203–12). Greco-Roman philosophy began to spread in Palestine in the Hellenistic period. Male and female were viewed as opposites, with masculinity exemplifying perfection and femininity regarded as deficiency: the male superior, the female inferior. Aristotle defined the pattern of social units: states, colonies, villages, and households. According to his view of household management, "There are three parts—one is the rule of a master over slaves, . . . another of a father, and the third of a husband. A husband and father . . . rules over wife and children" (*Pol.* 1.12 [1259a.37–40]; Cohick, 66–67). Other factors changing older patterns included the rise in priestly power in the postexilic, Hasmonean, and early Roman periods; and increased urbanization, primarily in the emergence of Herodian administrative centers in Galilee in the early part of the first century CE. Few women were literate or enjoyed the power that accompanied literacy and written texts (religious and legal).

Judgments on "the weakness of her sex" also appear in Jewish theological constructions, as Jewish understandings of the origin of evil shifted. Philo, for example, declared, "It was fitting that man should rule over immortality and everything good, but woman over death and everything vile" (*QG* 1.37). Moreover, as Alicia Myers observes, "Philo's interpretations of Gen 1–3 reflect a broader shift in the post-exilic and Hellenistic eras from identifying Gen 6 as the story of sin's origins, to focusing on Gen 3" (29). Genesis

6:1–4 claims that "the sons of God" (*bene Elohim*)—or angels, also called the *nephilim*, which may mean "the fallen ones"—married human daughters and raised "warriors of renown." According to 1 Enoch 64, the angels who descended upon the earth "led the children of the people astray to commit sin" (*OTP* 1:44). Jubilees describes how these angels, the Watchers, were sent to "perform judgment and uprightness upon the earth" (4:15); but because of the fornication, pollution, and injustice they brought on the earth, "The Lord blotted out everything from the face of the earth on account of the evil of their deeds" (7.25). With Sirach, the origin of evil shifts from the Watchers to Eve: "From a woman sin had its beginning, and because of her we all die" (25:24). Fourth Ezra does not mention Eve but traces the fall to Adam (7.48 [118]; cf. NRSV, 2 Esd 7:11), The Pauline tradition, if not Paul himself, traces the deception to Eve (2 Cor 11:3; 1 Tim 2:13–14). The Life of Adam and Eve (Greek version: Apocalypse of Moses), probably composed in Palestine late in the first century, contains a detailed account of Eve's deception (9.2; 10.1–11.13; 14.2; 16.3; 19.1–21.6), which ends with Eve saying, "All sin in creation has come about through me" (32.2; *OTP* 2:287).

7.2 Women in the Apocrypha

The apocryphal writings reflect changing and at times conflicting attitudes toward women, yet in some ways they offer more suitable role models for women than the heroines of the biblical accounts. Meir Bar-Ilan observes, "Women were no longer beautiful though passive; they were now beautiful and heroic, delivering themselves and their people from danger. They were also pious and prayed to God. This combination of qualities does not necessarily mean that women changed, but rather that women's self-image and male perception of them changed" (30). The appearance of Jewish heroines challenges the cultural misogyny, at least in terms of the potential of a Jewish queen. Esther (late Persian or early Hellenistic period, with Additions in the Maccabean period), Judith (Hasmonean period), and Susanna (date uncertain) are all fictional heroines set in an imaginary historical setting in the postexilic period.

In the book of Esther, Queen Vashti refuses to be paraded before the king's guests at a banquet after the "drinking was by flagons, without restraint" (1:8). For this, Queen Vashti is removed from her royal position, and the king sends letters to all the royal provinces, "declaring that every man should be master of his own house" (1:22). When Esther wins the beauty contest that followed, she is given "the best place in the harem"

(2:9), then made queen in place of Vashti. Because Mordecai, Esther's cousin and guardian, refuses to bow before the king, Haman conspires to destroy the Jews, charging that they refuse to obey the king's laws (3:8). Esther determines that she must petition the king on behalf of her people, so she invites the king to a banquet at which she petitions him for her life and the life of her people (7:3). The king, having learned of Mordecai's loyalty and Haman's treachery, orders that Haman be hanged, allows Esther to revoke the letters written by Haman ordering the destruction of the Jews, and issues new orders allowing the Jews "to annihilate any armed force of any people or province that might attack them" (8:11).

In a similar fashion, Judith employs both her beauty and her courage to deliver her people. Holofernes, Nebuchadnezzar's general, sets out to exact revenge on the peoples (including "Upper Galilee," Jdt 1:8) who refused to join the king in making war on the Medes. The Judeans, fearing for Jerusalem and their temple, pray and fast, preparing to confront Holofernes's army. Judith, a beautiful and devout widow, maintained the estate of her deceased husband, who had left her "gold and silver, men and women slaves, livestock, and fields" (8:7). Judith sends her maid to the elders of her town, Bethulia, urging them not to put God to the test. Without disclosing her plan, Judith dresses in festive attire and goes out with her maid to Holofernes's camp. Impressed by her beauty, Holofernes's soldiers take her to his tent, where she promises that God has sent her to lead him to Jerusalem. Instead, she pretends to seduce the general, who drinks more than he ever had and lies in a drunken stupor. Judith cuts off his head and returns to Bethulia with his head in her food bag. At daybreak they hang Holofernes's head on the wall and march out to meet the Assyrians, who flee when they discover their general's headless body. All the women of Israel bless Judith (15:12), and many men desire to marry her (16:22), but she remains celibate. "No one ever again spread terror among the Israelites during the lifetime of Judith, or for a long time after her death" (16:25).

Susanna, one of the additions to Daniel, presents a different model, not an empowered heroine but nevertheless one who remains virtuous and trusts in God. Susanna was "a very beautiful woman and one who feared the Lord" (2). Her parents "trained their daughter according to the law of Moses" (3). When two elders seek to force her to submit to their sexual desires, threatening to bring false charges against her, Susanna refuses and cries out loudly. The judges believe the elders rather than Susanna, but God delivers Susanna by stirring Daniel to defend her. When Daniel exposes the elders' false testimony, Susanna's reputation is restored.

We will spend more time with Tobit in the section on weddings; yet it is worth noting the parallels of historical setting, imaginary history, devotion to the law of Moses, and deliverance of a virtuous daughter from false charges in Tobit. Sarah has been married seven times: each of her husbands was killed by the demon Asmodeus on their wedding night. When her father's maids accuse her of killing her bridegrooms and urge her to kill herself, she starts to hang herself but does not do so in order not to grieve her father (Tob 3:10). Instead, she prays, "You know, O Master, that I am innocent of any defilement with a man and that I have not disgraced my name or the name of my father in the land of my exile" (3:14–15). The rest of the story relates how God answers both her prayer and Tobit's and delivers Sarah from the demon's curse.

The Maccabean literature also features pious heroines. When mothers circumcised their children, the Seleucids hung the infants from their mothers' necks, paraded them around, then put them to death (1 Macc 1:60–61; 2 Macc 6:10). In response, faithful Jews told the story of the martyrdom of a mother and her seven sons. When the mother and her sons are brought before "the tyrant" for refusing to eat defiling foods, the tyrant tempts them: "Trust me, then, and you will have positions of authority in my government if you will renounce the ancestral tradition of your national life. Enjoy your youth by adopting the Greek way of life and by changing your manner of living" (4 Macc 8:7–8). Each son refuses and in turn is martyred, yet their mother remains steadfast, even after witnessing their deaths. For this, the author praises her as a model of devotion. "O mother of the nation, vindicator of the law and champion of religion, who carried away the prize of the contest in your heart! O more noble than males in steadfastness, and more courageous than men in endurance!" (4 Macc 15:29–30). In 2 Maccabees' rendering of this story, the mother is "filled with a noble spirit" and "reinforced her woman's reasoning with a man's courage" (7:21). "The mother was especially admirable and worthy of honorable memory. Although she saw her seven sons perish within a single day, she bore it with good courage because of her hope in the Lord. She encouraged each of them in the language of their ancestors" (2 Macc 7:20–21).

These stories from the Hellenistic and Hasmonean periods depict women as models of virtue in their adherence to the laws of Moses, their refusal to submit to "the tyrant" by eating forbidden foods, abandoning circumcision, or worshiping false gods. Like Abraham, they are willing even to sacrifice their children for the sake of their religion. Like Joseph, they flee from sexual defilement. Like Zipporah, they circumcise their sons. Like Jael, they bravely deliver the people of Israel from their enemies. Bar-Ilan makes the salient point: "A woman here sets an example of an ideal role model for Jewish women in similar circumstances" (20).

While women were active in social, economic, and religious activities outside the home, their role was often circumscribed. Josephus and Philo say women could not bear witness in legal matters "because of the levity and temerity of their sex" (*Ant.* 4.219; see also m. Shebu. 4:1; m. Yebam. 16:5, 7) and their "want of sense" (Philo, *Spec. Laws* 2.24). A woman's father or husband could annul her vow (Num 30:3–16; CD XVI, 10–12; m. Ketub. 4:4). Nevertheless, there are references to women bearing witness in certain situations (1QSa I, 11; *Ant.* 17.93; *J.W.* 1.538; see Ilan 1995, 163–66).

Although women played important roles in religious observances in the home, especially pertaining to food and meals, their role in synagogues in first-century Galilee remains unclear (Ilan 2010, 61). The rabbis declared that women were obligated to pray the Eighteen Benedictions and recite the blessing on food (m. Ber. 3:3). Women lit the Sabbath candles (m. Shabb. 2:6–7) and partook in the Passover sacrifice (m. Pesaḥ. 8:1; Ilan 2010, 62), but they were not obligated to go to Jerusalem for the festivals (m. Ḥag. 1:1). The earliest synagogues do not contain separate galleries for women, and inscriptions found in diaspora synagogues dating from the second to the sixth centuries honor women who were leaders in the synagogues (e.g., Rufina, 2nd or 3rd c., in Smyrna; see Brooten; Mathew, 54–63).

7.3 Women at Work

Tobit says that when he lost his eyesight, his wife Anna "earned money at women's work," weaving (2:11). Although weaving was stereotypical "women's work," most women worked constantly at a wide range of domestic, agricultural, and commercial activities and participated in virtually every line of work. Men were not midwives, and women were not soldiers.

The lines between the private and public spheres were blurred, especially in towns and villages, and the private sphere of the household was more expansive and the public sphere more restricted than many interpreters assume (Hylen, 32–35). The architecture of the courtyard and slope houses (see 3.4 above) with shared workspace undermined the distinction between private and public. In a house in Meiron, in upper Galilee, one room contained a workshop for the production of barrels for olive oil; "other rooms and the courtyard contained remains of needles, stone grinders, and cooking utensils, along with three ovens" (Sivertsev, 236, citing E. Meyers, Strange, and C. Meyers, 38). Such archaeological evidence has led to a reconsideration of the traditional view that women lived and worked in the private sphere of home and family: "Public and private are thus overlapping and integrated domains in many aspects of family and community life in traditional societies" (C. Meyers 1999, 115; cf. Baker, 116–22; Esler 2017a, 86–89). Given this reconsideration of "women's work," we will use three distinctively different starting points that lead to both traditional and non-traditional understandings of the daily activities of Galilean women: (1) an often-cited rabbinic list of a wife's duties, (2) archaeological evidence of the Galilean economy, and (3) the items found at Nahal Hever.

The commonly cited list of tasks women performed is found in Mishnah Ketubbot 5:5.

> These are the works which the wife must perform for her husband: grinding flour and baking bread and washing clothes and cooking food and giving suck to her child and making ready his bed and working in wool. If she brought him one bondwoman, she need not grind or bake or wash; if two, she need not cook or give her child suck; if three, she need not make ready his bed or work in wool; and if four, she may sit [all day] in a chair.

Therefore, if a woman had even one maidservant, she was exempt from grinding the flour. Poor women performed this task daily, while apparently any woman who could afford a maidservant assigned such work to her (Weingarten, 291–92). Eliezer adds, however, "Even if she brought him a hundred bondwomen[,] he should compel her to work in wool [weaving], for idleness leads to unchastity."

These "maintenance activities"—grinding, baking, procuring food, cooking, making clothing, washing, and cleaning, along with nursing infants and supervising children—no doubt consumed much of the day for most women. The virtuous woman in Proverbs 31:15 "rises while it is still night and provides food for her household." Other texts mention drawing water (m. Ketub. 1:10; cf. Gen 24:13–20; Exod 2:16; John 4:7), carrying a jar of water (Mark 14:13, where it is unusual that a *man* should carry water), and weaving and spinning (m. Neg. 2:4). The rabbis ruled that one may buy linen goods from women in Galilee because women there worked with flax, whereas wool was more common in Judea, where there were more sheep (m. B. Qam. 10:9; cf. Isa 19:9). Less traditional lines of work also appear in the Mishnah: harvesting (Yebam. 15:2; 'Ed. 1:12), working as a shopkeeper or guardian (Ketub. 9:4), and selling in the marketplace (Ḥal. 2:7).

To prepare four pounds of flour, enough to produce bread for two adults and four children for a day, would have taken two or three hours of grinding. Women consequently often worked together, as suggested by Jesus' saying, "Two women will be grinding meal together" (Matt 24:41//Luke 17:35). The Mishnah also addresses the potential for introducing uncleanness into the house if one of the women was the wife of an *am-haaretz*, one who did not maintain purity as the Pharisees did: "If the wife of an Associate [a fellow Pharisee] left the wife of an *Am-haaretz* grinding flour within her house and she ceased from the grinding, the house becomes unclean; if she did not cease from the grinding, only that part of the house is unclean which she could touch by stretching out her hand" (m. Ṭehar. 7:4). Technological changes affected textile and bread production. The earlier simple, horizontal looms and the warp-weighted vertical looms with the weights tied to the vertical threads, which were found at Yodefat, were replaced by the more efficient two-beam loom in the late first and early second centuries (Leibner, 277–80; Peskowitz, 134–36).

Olynthus mills, rotary hand mills, and the larger donkey mills (Matt 18:6//Mark 9:42//Luke 17:2; Rev 18:21) began to replace the handstone and grindstone, especially in urban centers (Broshi 2010, 542; C. Meyers 2013, 130). Olynthus mills were composed of a lever anchored at one end and attached to the upper stone. Such a mill was operated by moving the lever back and forth, left and right, while grain was fed from a hopper to be crushed between the upper stone and the flat surface beneath it (see Frankel 2003, 8, fig. 6).

The earliest rotary hand mill discovered in Palestine, dating from the first century CE, was found in the Roman camp at Masada (Frankel 2003, 18; citing Netzer, 290–91, figs. 464–65; Frankel 2013, 236). The base or lower stone of a rotary mill rose to a conical point, on which the upper stone sat. The upper stone had a funnel-shaped opening, into which the grain was poured while the upper stone was rotated with a lever or beam. The grain was ground and sifted out between the stones. Rotary mills did not become common among the Jews until the Byzantine period; "an Olynthus mill or donkey mill would have been beyond the means of the peasant farmers typical of Galilee in the Roman period" (C. Meyers 2008, 67–68). The ancient way of grinding with handstone on grindstone persisted in Galilean villages through the Roman period, while Olynthus mills and donkey mills appeared in Sepphoris. Rotary mills of various sizes, probably dating from the early centuries CE, can be seen at Capernaum.

Each of these developments led to increased male dominance and the economic marginalization of women. Bread and textiles began to be produced outside the home and sold in markets, thereby reducing women's roles in the household economy (C. Meyers 2013, 207–9). These changes did not occur uniformly, however. Household patterns dating back to the Iron Age probably continued in remote villages and small towns (C. Meyers 2013, 211).

When coupled with Carol Meyers's findings regarding the role of women in the various types of work in ancient towns and villages, Mordechai Aviam's description of the Galilean economy based on its material remains, especially at Yodefat (destroyed in 67 CE), offers another approach to the kinds of work that Galilean women did.

> The reconstruction of the socioeconomic pyramid in the Galilean society according to archaeological finds places the wool workers (evidenced by the spindle and spindle whorls), weavers (evidenced by the loom weights), and potters (evidenced by the kilns, potter's wheel, and wasters) at the bottom. Owners of shops and workshops (evidenced by the flourmill and olive presses) formed the next socioeconomic level. The owners of the fresco houses formed the uppermost level of the pyramid. (Aviam 2013, 44)

Given the role of women in spinning and weaving (Dorcas, Acts 9:39) as well as agricultural and commercial activities, it is not hard to see evidence of their work in these artifacts.

Philip Esler (2017a, 88–90) has suggested a third vector based on the items found beside Babatha's satchel of legal documents (see below, 7.8). These included a key and two key rings (probably to her house and other buildings, rooms, or boxes), knives, plates, and bowls (probably used in food preparation and consumption), balls of yarn she may have spun, some fine fabrics and kerchiefs, and a sickle she probably used in her orchards.

Taken together, the textual and archaeological evidence illustrates the wide range of work performed by women in agricultural areas. Lynn Cohick (232) aptly characterizes this as "the tough, demanding reality of rural women's lives."

Professional mourners were usually women (Matt 9:23//Mark 5:38; see Josephus, *J.W.* 3.437; Corley, 35–38, 44–56). In Jeremiah, the Lord commands, "Consider, and call for the mourning women to come; send for the skilled women to come. . . . Teach to your daughters a dirge, and each to her neighbor a lament" (Jer 9:17, 20; see also 2 Chr 35:25; Isa 32:11–12; Jer 9:16–20).

The rabbis instructed every husband to mourn his wife's death: "R. Judah says: Even the poorest in Israel should hire not less than two flutes and one wailing woman" (m. Ketub. 4:4; cf. m. Mo'ed Qaṭ. 3:8–9). Zechariah 12:10–14 segregates women in mourning so that women could wail separately, perhaps to maintain their modesty (Bar-Ilan, 75).

Only women could be midwives and wet nurses (m. Shabb. 18:3; m. Rosh. Hash. 2:5; m. Ḥul. 4:3; m. 'Abod. Zar. 2:1). A contract set the terms for a Jewish wet nurse to care for the foundling daughter of a gentile slave owner (*CPJ* 146, 13 BCE, Alexandria), something the rabbis forbade (m. 'Abod. Zar. 2:1). The wet nurse agreed to suckle the child for eighteen months in her own home for eight drachmas and some olive oil each month, during which time she agreed not to have intercourse, conceive, or take another child to suckle.

Prophetesses or mediums of divine revelation appear in Israel (Judg 4:4; 1 Sam 28:7–25; 2 Kgs 22:14; Neh 6:14; Isa 8:3; Acts 21:8–9) as well as in the Greco-Roman world (Sib. Or. 3.818; 4.4–6). Women were also accused of being sorceresses and witches (Exod 22:18; Deut 18:10–12; Isa 57:3). Mishnah Avot 2:7 warns that whoever increases the number of women in his household increases witchcraft; Simeon ben Shetah (1st c. BCE) hanged eighty witches in Ashkelon (m. Sanh. 6:4). Even more extreme, R. Jose the Galilean (2nd c.) "believed that each and every Jewish woman was suspect of practicing witchcraft, of offering incense in idolatrous worship" (Bar-Ilan, 118–19).

Prostitutes could no doubt be found in Galilee also. In Genesis 38, Judah propositioned Tamar, who accepted Judah's signet, cord, and staff as a pledge for the kid he promised to give her from his flock. Rahab the prostitute sheltered Joshua's spies in her house (or inn; Josephus, *Ant.* 5.7) in Jericho (Josh 2:1; 6:17, 25). Jephthah the Gileadite was the son of a prostitute (Judg 11:1). In Jeremiah, the Lord says of Jerusalem, "And you, O desolate one, what do you mean that you dress in crimson, that you deck yourself with ornaments of gold, that you enlarge your eyes with paint? In vain you beautify yourself. Your lovers despise you; they seek your life" (4:30). Following the Lord's command, Hosea marries Gomer and has children with her (1:2). Sirach counsels that one should not even look at a prostitute (41:20).

Luke identifies the woman who anoints Jesus' feet and lets down her hair at a dinner in Simon the Pharisee's house in Galilee as "a woman in the city, who was a sinner" (Luke 7:37). Simon assumes that if Jesus were a prophet, "he would have known who and what kind of woman this is who is touching him—that she is a sinner" (7:39). Several chapters later, when the prodigal son returns from the "far country" (15:13 KJV), among gentiles, his elder brother complains to his father, "This son of yours . . . devoured your property with prostitutes" (15:30). As the elder brother's complaint suggests, prostitution was probably more prevalent in the larger cities and coastal ports, and especially at brothels (see 4.3 above), inns, and bathhouses (Bar-Ilan, 132–55; Cohick, 268–70).

7.4 Daughters

A woman's primary role was to marry and bear children; as a mother it was her duty to guard her daughter's virginity and prepare her for marriage.

Sirach, the misogynistic wisdom teacher, instructed his elite male students at length on the trials of having a daughter.

> Do you have daughters? Be concerned for their chastity, and do not show yourself too indulgent with them. Give a daughter in marriage, and you complete a great task; but give her to a sensible man. (Sir 7:24–25)
>
> It is a disgrace to be the father of an undisciplined son, and the birth of a daughter is a loss. A sensible daughter obtains a husband of her own, but one who acts shamefully is a grief to her father. An impudent daughter disgraces father and husband, and is despised by both. (22:3–5)
>
> Keep strict watch over a headstrong daughter. (26:10)
>
> A daughter is a secret anxiety to her father, and worry over her robs him of sleep; when she is young, for fear she may not marry, or if married, for fear she may be disliked; while a virgin, for fear she may be seduced and become pregnant in her father's house; or having a husband, for fear she may go astray, or, though married, for fear she may be barren. Keep strict watch over a headstrong daughter, or she may make you a laughingstock to your enemies, a byword in the city and the assembly of the people, and put you to shame in public gatherings. (42:9–11)

When Ptolemy IV Philopater (ca. 244–205 BCE) attempted to enter the inner courts of the temple in Jerusalem, the outrage among the people was such that all normal conduct was suspended.

> Young women who had been secluded in their chambers rushed out with their mothers, sprinkled their hair with dust, and filled the streets with groans and lamentations. Those women who had recently been arrayed for marriage abandoned the bridal chambers prepared for wedded union, and, neglecting proper modesty, in a disorderly rush flocked together in the city. Mothers and nurses abandoned even newborn children here and there, some in houses and some in the streets, and without a backward look they crowded together at the most high temple. (3 Macc 1:18–20)

Secluding virgins may have been the practice in elite families (Ps.-Phoc. 215–216), but it is hard to imagine that it was common in agrarian villages in Galilee.

Mother-daughter relationships were particularly complicated. The mother had given birth to a daughter rather than a son. She was expected to raise her daughter in such a way that she avoided bringing shame on her husband while grooming her daughter for the best possible bridegroom. Then, after only twelve to fifteen years, she had to relinquish her daughter to the bridegroom and his family. The frequency with which allusions to preparation of a daughter for marriage appear in our sources confirms both the importance of this parental duty and its poignancy. In Tobit, when Sarah's mother, Edna, prepares the bridal chamber, she weeps, prays for Sarah, and encourages her daughter to take courage (Tob 7:15–17; see 3 Macc 4:6; Kraemer 2020, 91–92).

Pseudo-Philo (LAB)—retelling the horrific story of Jephthah's nameless daughter, whom he sacrificed to God to fulfill the vow he had made (Judg 11:30–40)—grants the daughter a name, Seila; great wisdom; and a mother and nurse to mourn her death. In her lament, Seila recalls her mother's preparations for her wedding.

O Mother, in vain have you borne your only daughter,
    Because Sheol has become my bridal chamber,
And on earth there is only my woman's chamber.
    And may all the blend of oil that you have prepared for me be poured
        out,
and the white robe that my mother has woven, the moth will eat it.
    And the crown of flowers that my nurse plaited for me for the festival,
        may it wither up,
and the coverlet that she wove of hyacinth and purple in my woman's
        chamber,
    may the worm devour it.

(LAB 40.6)

The same imagery appears in Joshua's trepidation at assuming the responsibility of leading Israel in the Testament of Moses. Speaking to Moses, Joshua asks, "How, therefore, can I be (guardian) of this people, as a father is to his only son, or as a mother [Lat. *dominam*, 'mistress of the house'] is to her virgin daughter (who) is being prepared to be given to a husband; a mother who is disquieted, guarding (the daughter's) body from the sun and (seeing to it) that (the daughter's) feet are not without shoes when she runs upon the ground" (11.12).

7.5 Brides

Jewish weddings, which shared with Greco-Roman wedding customs such rituals as bathing and adorning the bride (Kihlstrom Timpte, 76–79), were joyful occasions (Jer 33:11; 3 Macc 4:6, 8; Rev 19:7) with extended festivities. Jews typically practiced endogamy, marriage within their kinship group, which ensured various social values: "retaining property and wealth within the kin-group, consolidating power, maintaining cultic purity, and protection from outsiders" (Hanson, 143). Tobit, of the tribe of Naphtali, married "a member of our own family" (Tob 1:9). Later, Tobit instructs his son, Tobias: "First of all, marry a woman from among the descendants of your ancestors; do not marry a foreign woman, who is not of your father's tribe; for we are the descendants of the prophets. Remember, my son, that Noah, Abraham, Isaac, and Jacob, our ancestors of old, all took wives from among their kindred. They were blessed in their children, and their posterity will inherit the land" (4:12).

Families played well-defined roles. The financial terms were settled at the betrothal or at the time of the marriage and formalized in a marriage contract, which was signed and witnessed (see Babatha's marriage contract, below). Haggling over the marriage contract, the ketubah (m. Ketub. 1:2), was probably common since it represented the bride's value and her family's honor (Tob 7:9b–16). When Tobias reached an agreement with Raguel, Sarah's father, Raguel called in his daughter and said to Tobias, "Take her to be your wife in accordance with the law and decree written in the book of Moses" (7:12); then Raguel wrote out the marriage contract (7:13).

Both families contributed financially to the couple's welfare (Hanson and Oakman, 37–43). The bride's father and family contributed a dowry, while the groom contributed an "indirect dowry" to the bride, her family, or both. The latter is illustrated by the gifts Abraham sent for the family of Isaac's bride (Gen 24:51–53). During the Maccabean period, Alexander Balas, the Seleucid ruler, proposed marriage to Ptolemy VI's daughter, promising an appropriate gift: "Now therefore let us establish friendship with one another; give me now your daughter as my wife, and I will become your son-in-law and will make gifts to you and to her in keeping with your position" (1 Macc 10:54). Ptolemy VI accepted the proposal and took his daughter to Alexander at Ptolemais, along with a reciprocal gift: "He gave him [Alexander] his daughter, and, for her dowry, as much silver and gold as a king was expected to give" (Josephus, *Ant.* 13.82). In Tobit's account of Tobias's marriage to Sarah, after the marriage contract is signed (Tob 7:13) and after the couple survived their wedding night by repelling the demon (Asmodeus), Sarah's father ordered his servants to prepare the wedding feast and gave Tobias half of Sarah's inheritance: "Take at once half of what I own and return in safety to your father; the other half will be yours when my wife and I die" (Tob 8:21).

The typical age for the girl's first marriage was between twelve and eighteen, although she could be even younger when she was betrothed, while the groom was older: "Philo of Alexandria considered a man 'ripe' for marriage between the ages of 28 and 35" (Kraemer 2020, 105, citing Philo, *Creation* 103); when the average life expectancy was not much more than this! Neither of Babatha's husbands lived more than a few years after the wedding (see below, 7.8).

Weddings generally followed the betrothal by a year or longer (m. Ketub. 5:2). Safrai describes the established customs: "The principal stages of the wedding celebration were (1) preparation of the bride, (2) transfer of the bride from her father's home to that of the groom, (3) the bride's introduction into the home of the groom, and (4) blessings and festivities within the husband's home" (Safrai and Stern, 2:757).

In Tobit, where Tobias traveled to another country, the marriage is consummated at the bride's home (8:1–8). The bridegroom normally took the bride to his home, or his father's house, accompanied by his friends (virgins are not mentioned in Tobit, but her maids are: 3:7; 8:12–14). The wise and foolish virgins in Jesus' parable are probably awaiting the bridegroom's arrival at the bride's home (Jeremias 1967, 1100). The wedding procession, carrying the bride to the groom's home, was a public announcement of the marriage. First Maccabees describes the festivity: "The family of Jambri are celebrating a great wedding, and are conducting the bride, a daughter of one of the great nobles of Canaan, from Nadabath with a large escort, . . . a tumultuous procession with a great amount of baggage; and the bridegroom came out with his friends and his brothers to meet them with tambourines and musicians and many weapons" (9:37, 39; see Josephus, *Ant.* 13.20, adding, "as is usual for a wedding" after "large escort"). A typical village wedding would have been less elaborate but probably involved the same elements. Brides and bridegrooms wore their wedding garments, which Isaiah compares to "the garments of salvation": "As a bridegroom decks himself with a garland, and as a bride adorns herself with her jewels" (Isa 61:10; cf. Song 3:11; 3 Macc 4:6; m. Soṭah 9:14).

There was no formal wedding ceremony before a priest, but there are hints of formalities for solemnizing the wedding. In Joseph and Aseneth, which was probably composed in Egypt between 100 BCE and 117 CE but may not reflect actual practices in Egypt or elsewhere (Kraemer 1998, 58), the pharaoh puts crowns on their heads, sets Aseneth on Joseph's right side, puts his hands on their heads and blesses them, saying, "May the Lord God the Most High bless you and multiply you and magnify and glorify you forever" (21.6). Then Joseph and Aseneth kiss, and the pharaoh gives a wedding feast for seven days. The very fragmentary 4Q502 has been identified as a blessing or ritual of marriage (García Martínez, 440–41, 503–4).

The marriage would be consummated at the groom's home or his father's home, where the wedding feast (see Matt 22:1–14) would continue for seven days (Judg 14:12; Tob 11:18; m. Neg. 3:2) or even fourteen days (Tob 8:20; 10:7). Because such elaborate celebrations were more than most families could afford, some families pooled their resources by forming associations with guarantees of mutual assistance (m. B. Bat. 9:4; b. B. Bat. 145b). John's account of the wedding at Cana suggests either that the family was quite wealthy or that several families pooled their resources. Large stone vessels that held twenty to thirty gallons each (John 2:6) were luxury items (Reed, 394). The young men celebrating with the groom, and perhaps protecting him if necessary, were called "the sons of the bridechamber" (Matt 9:15 ASV), or "friend(s) of the bridegroom" (1 Macc 9:39; John 3:29).

Women and even young women apparently joined in the wedding celebration (see Marks, 141–44). Catallus (1st c. BCE) places maidens at the door of the wedding chamber:

> Now husband, you may approach:
> Your wife is in your bedroom.
> . . . .
> Play as you please, and
> Produce children soon. It is not right
> For so ancient a name to
> Be lacking in children, but rather it should always
> Be reproduced from the same stock.
> . . . .
> Maidens, close the doors:
> We have played enough. Good
> Wedded people, live well and
> Keep your youth fit and strong in constant
> Exercise of its functions.
> (Catallus, *Carmina* 61, selected verses from lines 184–228, trans. Godwin)

Late sources refer to the practice of displaying the blood-stained linens as evidence of the bride's virginity (Deut 22:17; see Safrai and Stern, 2:759–60; Satlow, 177). Versions of the Damascus Document found at Qumran say, "And every woman who has had a bad reputation during her maidenhood [in her father's house, no-one should take her, unless on in]spection (the) women are trust[worthy]" (4QD^c I, 1.13–14; 4QD^f IX, 5). The rabbis dictated that weddings should occur on Wednesdays, because the courts were open the next morning and the bridegroom could file a "virginity suit" if he found no evidence of his bride's virginity (m. Ketub. 1:1). Penalties were severe—for the bride if she were not a virgin and for the groom if the charges were false (Deut 22:13–29).

7.6 Wives

Ancient marriages created financial arrangements between families as well as a means of supporting a household and assuring the transfer of property to one's children. Both the husband or the husband's family and the wife's family sought to secure their interests and property, and both contributed to the marriage. The marriage contracts from the Dead Sea area specify a ketubah, the sum of money the wife brought into the marriage and which the husband would repay to the bride if he divorced her or died. The *mohar*, or "bride price," originally paid to the bride's father, was added to the ketubah in the marriage contracts found in the Elephantine papyri (from the 5th c. BCE; Collins, 113–15). The ketubah could also discourage divorce and provide the wife with means to support herself if necessary.

The bride's father could transfer property directly to his daughter by means of a deed of gift (Pfann, 503), to keep it out of the son-in-law's hands. Stephen Pfann explains: "Jewish deeds of gift surviving from antiquity were written only to female members of a family (wives or daughters) who needed such deeds in order to receive family property. They were not counted legal heirs" (503). A wife was expected to work and manage her husband's household, but she also maintained her own property and financial interests: "There were no joint checking accounts in antiquity" (Satlow, 217; see 216–23). Nevertheless, a document (*CPJ* 145, dated 13 BCE, Alexandria) certifying the sale and transfer of property notes that the seller, Protarchos, agreed to the sale "with the assent of his wife." Another Egyptian papyrus (*CPJ* 148, of 10 BCE) acknowledges the payment of a debt by a Jewish freedwoman. These documents attest that Jewish women could manage their own financial interests, borrow and lend money, and buy and sell property.

Proverbs 31:10–31 praises the ideal wife, describing her hard work. The good wife "seeks wool and flax, and works with willing hands" (31:13); she provides food for her household and manages her servant girls (31:15). She can also assess a field, buy it, and plant a vineyard (31:16). This ideal wife works day and night at the spindle (31:18–19), making clothes for her household; she sells linen garments (see Josephus, *Ant.* 11.50), supplying merchants with sashes (Prov 31:21–22, 24). She is also virtuous, generous to the poor, wise, and kind. The husband is therefore instructed: "Give her a share in the fruit of her hands" (31:31).

Josephus summarizes Jewish marriage laws in his response *Against Apion* (2.199–203; cf. *Ant.* 4.244–259), emphasizing that sexual relations should be limited to marriage and then only for procreation of children. A free man was forbidden to marry a female slave or a prostitute. Josephus, for example, describes in detail the affair of Herod's brother, Pheroras, with a slave girl and its consequences (*Ant.* 16.194). One should also not marry a woman for her dowry or deceive her; the woman is to be submissive to her husband. Whether it was practiced or not, Leviticus 20:10 and Deuteronomy 22:22–27 prescribe death for any man who had intercourse with another's wife or a betrothed virgin (*Ant.* 3.274–275). John 8:1–11, however, describes preparation for stoning the woman without any reference to the man. These laws protected the family's line of posterity and title to their land.

If a man desired to divorce his wife, he was required to give her a certificate of divorce (a *git*/*get*) so that she could marry another (Deut 24:1–4; Josephus, *Ant.* 4.253). An Alexandrian bill of divorce dated to 13 BCE (*CPJ* 144) is typical of Hellenistic bills of this kind. It specifies "(a) agreement of divorce; (b) restitution of dowry [in this case sixty drachmae]; (c) annulment of marriage and statement about the illegality of any claim based on the contract of marriage; (d) freedom to marry for both parties; (e) fines for transgression of the deed of divorce" (*CPJ* 2:11). A certificate of divorce from Wadi Murabba'at allows the divorced woman to marry "any Jewish man that you may wish" (P.Mur. 19):

On the [fi]rst of Marḥesh[wan], the year six, at Masada:
  [I] divorce and repudiate of my own free will today,
  I Joseph, son of Na[qsan], you, my wife Miriam, \<daughter\>
  of Jonathan, [fro]m [Ha]nablaṭa, living
  at Masada, who ha[ve be]en my wife
  up to this (time), so that you are free
  on your part to [g]o to become the wife
  of any Jewish man that you please.
  Now you have from me a bill of repudiation
  and a writ of divor[ce. N]ow I give (back) the who[le
  dow]ry and (for) all ru[in]ed [and damaged goods and . . .]. So
  [let it be determined] and [pa]id fourfold. And at (any) time
  [that you] say to me, [I shall] replace for you the document, as long as
    [I am al]ive.
                                                      (Fitzmyer and Harrington, 141)

The Mishnah devotes an entire tractate to bills of divorce (Giṭṭin). Anyone could write a bill of divorce, even the woman, since its validity depended on its witnesses (m. Giṭ. 2:5). Josephus himself was married four times: he divorced his first wife; his second wife deserted him; he divorced his third wife, "being displeased at her behaviour," after they had three children; then lived happily with his fourth wife, who bore him two sons (*Life* 415, 426–428). After a divorce, the children stayed with their father's household. Philo interprets Jewish laws regarding marriage within forbidden degrees of kinship, marrying two sisters, remarrying a wife after divorcing her (*Spec. Laws* 3.12–31), marrying a woman known to be barren (3.34–36), adultery and rape (3.52–78), and false charges of unfaithfulness (3.79–82).

The right of women to divorce their husbands is assumed in the Elephantine papyri, and some women in the Herodian family divorced their husbands (Josephus, *Ant.* 15.259; 18.136). Whether it was common is debated. According to P.Ṣe'el. 13, from Nahal Hever, a woman named Shelamzion received seven items from her former husband, "who received a bill of divorce from her," but the translation is uncertain (Collins, 120).

7.7 Widows

To be a widow was synonymous with being bereaved (Sir 35:18; Bar 4:12; Rev 18:7), poor and in need (Luke 21:3; Acts 6:1; Jas 1:27), forsaken (Ep Jer 38; 2 Esd 2:2, 4), and alone (4 Macc 16:10; 1 Tim 5:5). To become "like a widow" was a metaphor for tragedy and devastation (Lam 1:1; 5:3; Bar 4:12). Caring for widows and orphans was a mark of piety (Deut 14:29; 16:14; 26:12–13; Pss 68:5; 146:9; Isa 1:17; Jer 7:6; 22:3; Sir 35:17–18; 2 Macc 8:28, 30; T. Job 9.5; 10.2), while abusing a widow was an iniquity (Job 22:9; Ps 94:6; Isa 10:2; Ezek 22:7; Mal 3:5; Wis 2:10; 2 Macc 3:10; Mark 12:40//Luke 20:47). The righteous will "guard the rights of the widow, secure justice for the ward, give to the needy, defend the orphan, clothe the naked, care for the injured and weak" (2 Esd 2:20; see Matt 25:31–46; Jas 1:27). The pious widow was especially worthy of praise (Ruth 1:5; 4:5; Jdt 8:4; Luke 2:36–38; Mark 12:42–43//Luke 21:2–3).

Many widows were left destitute at the death of the husband. Life expectancy being what it was, few widows would have had grown sons to care for them. Most widows remarried. Tal Ilan concludes, "Widowhood, then, was a dismal state for a woman to fall into; the rabbis urged widows to remarry and made special efforts to remove the obstacles in their way to this goal. To judge from the sources, not many Jewish women remained widows for very long" (1995, 151).

To receive support from their husband's estate (her ketubah; Ilan 1999, 52–55) or remarry, widows had to prove the death of their husband. What happened if a woman's husband went to sea and did not return, or if there was a report that he had died, or if the "widow" remarried and her husband returned (m. Yebam. 16.5–7)? The rabbis debated the kind of testimony required in such cases (m. 'Ed. 1:12) and ruled that a widow should observe three months of mourning before being betrothed or remarrying (m. Yebam. 4:10). These legal intricacies may not have affected widows in Galilean towns and villages, but their need for support and the limited options open to them would have been no less real.

We may also note that the apostle Paul urged the unmarried and widows not to marry (1 Cor 7:8), but his counsel is clearly influenced by his view of the coming tribulations and imminent end (7:26); given those assumptions, they would be better off not marrying again. Supporting widows also presented the early church with a series of issues that continued long after the first century (Acts 6:1–3; 1 Tim 5:3–16; Tertullian, *Virg.* 9; Apos. Con. 2.2.4; 8.25.2).

7.8 Babatha

Beyond the fictional stories in Esther, Tobit, and Judith, and the interpretations of laws and customs in Philo, Josephus, and the Mishnah, an archive of legal documents provides a glimpse into the life of a Jewish woman living on the border of Judea and Nabatea early in the second century CE. The geographical and chronological proximity of this material make it relevant for our interest in first-century Galilee.

In 1960 Yigael Yadin found "the Cave of Letters" while exploring Nahal Hever, a canyon between Ein-Gedi and Masada, on the west side of the Dead Sea. There he discovered a trove of letters from Bar Kokhba (d. 135 CE), leader of the Jewish rebels, to his subordinates. In addition, the cave contained a variety of items: textiles, including a complete set of clothes; some coins; implements; and human remains. In March of 1961, the same cave yielded a cache of thirty-five papyrus documents (P.Yad. 1–35) belonging to Babatha, a Jewish female landowner, dated from 94 to 132 CE and written in Aramaic and Greek. Philip Esler claims, "Because of this archive we can say without fear of contradiction that we know more about her than we do about any other Jewish woman in antiquity" (Esler, 2017a–b). The documents were found in a waterskin near a pair of sandals, a mirror, thread, perfume, cosmetics, and other items. Among the documents were the deed to a palm grove, Babatha's marriage contract to her second husband (Yehudah), a document recording her loan of three hundred denarii to Yehudah (P.Yad. 17), and a petition for her to become the sole guardian of "Yeshua [Jesus] son of Yeshua, my orphan son." Yet another document accuses Judah's other wife, Mariam, of plundering "everything in the house of Judah son of Eleazer Khthusion, my husband and yours."

The story these legal documents tell is complicated, illuminating, and at points subject to differing interpretations. The setting is the area around the Dead Sea: Ein-Gedi, on the west side; and Maḥoza, on the southern shore and just across the border from Judea, in Nabatea, in the period leading up to the Bar Kokhba revolt (132–135 CE). In 99 CE, Shim'on ben Menahem, Babatha's father, bought a date-palm orchard in Maḥoza with the help of Archelaus, the provincial governor. The earliest of the documents (from 94–99 CE) relate to this purchase and are written in Nabatean Aramaic. Around 120 CE, Babatha, who would probably have been about fifteen years old, married Yeshua son of Yeshua son of Joseph Zaboudos, of Maḥoza. As a dowry, her father apparently gave her the date orchard he had purchased twenty years earlier because in 120 Shim'on gave the rest of his property to his wife, and the date orchard is not listed in this bequest. Within four years Babatha's husband died, leaving her with an infant son, also named Yeshua. In an action that reflects Babatha's powerlessness as a widow, the council at Petra assigned two guardians for the child, one Jewish and one Nabatean. The guardians gave Babatha the meager sum of two denarii (two days' wages) a month from Shim'on's estate. In 124, Babatha filed a petition to have the allowance increased, but apparently her petition was denied. In 127, for the provincial census, Babatha declared ownership of four date-palm orchards in Maḥoza, keeping a copy of the document, written in Greek, to confirm her title to the property. It is unclear whether she received the other three orchards from her husband, Yeshua; purchased them; or divided the original orchard.

Babatha also possessed a number of receipts for money on deposit: for example, the following receipt from her first husband's brother:

> . . . thirteenth of Daisios, in the consulship of Marcus Salvidienus Orfitus and Quintus Peducaeus Priscinus [110 CE], and, of the foundation of the province year the fifth, in Maoza of the Zoara dist[r]ict, I, Joseph son of Joseph surnamed Zaboudos, inhabitant of Maoza, acknowledge to Jesus son of my brother Jesus, of the same place, that you have with me a thousand and a hundred twenty "blacks" of silver as a deposit. . . . (P.Yad. 5, quoted from Lewis, Yadin, and Greenfield, 39; Hanson and Oakman, 123).

The editors speculate that the "black" coins were silver minas and that the Greek *m-l-n* (black) is a corruption of *m-n* (mina), but "blacks" also appear in other documents, where it appears to equal between one and two denarii (Broshi 1992, 237).

The story continues. By 128, Babatha remarried, this time to Yehudah son of El'azar Khthousion from Ein-Gedi. The marriage contract, written by Yehudah in Aramaic, declares that he took Babatha as his wife, "according to the law of Moses and the Judeans." Babatha contributed a dowry of 400 denarii. She also loaned Yehudah 300 denarii for his daughter's (Shelamzion, "Peace of Zion") wedding, from which (apparently) Yehudah provided Shelamzion a dowry of 200 denarii. The loan was recorded and would have had to be repaid (Sivertsev, 241). In another financial entanglement, Yehudah had borrowed 60 denarii from a Roman centurion in Ein-Gedi at the standard rate of interest, 12 percent per year.

Now the story gets complicated. Shortly thereafter, by June 130, Yehudah died, leaving his now-married daughter, Shelamzion, and two orphaned sons by his first wife, Miriam. A dispute arose between the sons and Shelamzion over ownership of a courtyard in Ein-Gedi that Yehudah had given her. Shelamzion won this case. Interestingly, both Shelamzion's marriage contract and the record of her case over the courtyard were among Babatha's documents. To regain her dowry and her loan to Yehudah, Babatha seized his orchards in Maḥoza. Miriam filed for an injunction to prevent Babatha from seizing Judah's house (presumably in Ein-Gedi), and Babatha charged that Miriam had removed items to which she was not entitled. In P.Yadin 26, dated July 131, Babatha charged Miriam with having seized "everything in the house of Yehudah, my and your deceased husband." Most scholars (Lewis, Yadin, and Greenfield, 22–24) interpret this phrase as meaning that both women were married to Yehudah at the same time, with Yehudah maintaining two households, one in Ein-Gedi and one in Maḥoza, which was permitted by Jewish law. In response, Ranon Katzoff (1995) argues that it is more likely a case of serial monogamy; Yehudah could have divorced Miriam, although there is no reference to a divorce in the archive; both women could have been claiming provisions made in their respective marriage contracts. If Yehudah divorced Miriam before marrying Babatha in 128, however, two or three years would have passed before Miriam's seizure of Yehudah's things. It is also more likely that Miriam would have said "my and your deceased husband" than that Babatha would have acknowledged their relationship in this way if Yehuda and Miriam were divorced for at least two years prior to his death. The outcome of these disputes, if they had been decided, is unknown.

Sometime in late 134 or 135, near the end of the Bar Kokhba revolt, Babatha apparently fled En-Gedi; took refuge in the cave along with others, perhaps including Shelamzion; and hid her documents in a crevice. Since the skeletal remains of some twenty persons, including eight women, were found in the cave, it is likely that Babatha was among those who perished there. At the end of a short and tumultuous life, she pre-served her memory for future generations by hiding her documents in that cave.

Babatha's marriage contract for her second marriage shows how Jewish practice regarding dowries and ketubbot varied and were changing, and how rabbinic legislation may not have been followed in practice (see Sivertsev, 241–43; Satlow, 204–13). Three Aramaic and three Greek marriage con-tracts (ketubbot) have been recovered in the Judaean desert (Yadin, Green-field, and Yardeni, 83–84; Ilan 1995, 92). Of these, the best preserved of the Aramaic ketubbot, P.Yadin 10, pertains to Babatha's second marriage, to Yehudah: it is written by the groom, who was a "practiced, experienced writer" although not a professional scribe (Yadin, Greenfield, and Yard-eni, 77). The marriage contract specifies a ketubah (in this case, proba-bly her dowry) of 400 *zuz* (denarii), which would revert to her if Yehudah divorced her or died (Satlow, 202–16; Cohick, 117, 120–21). In rabbinic sources, this is the specified amount for a virgin (m. Ketub. 1:5). The 400 *zuz* was therefore "an unusual increase of the standard (100), demanded by Babatha because of her social standing. She was a rather wealthy woman who 'belonged, both by birth and marriage, to the affluent stratum of local Jewish society'" (Lewis, Yadin, and Greenfield, 22, 24). Friedman recon-structs the opening of the document, the marriage proposal, as reading, "I Yehudah son of El'azar from Ein-Gedi, dwelling in Maḥoza, have declared and requested willingly to take you Babatha daughter of Shim'on from Maḥoza, dwelling in Maḥoza, to be my wife, according to the law of Moses and the Jews" (62; cf. Tob 7:12). The proposal is followed by the promise to give the bride her due. The original editors translated it thus: "and I will feed you and clothe you and I will bring you [into my house] by means of your *ketubba*" (Yadin, Greenfield, and Yardeni, 87). That is, Yehuda will draw upon Babatha's dowry to support her. Friedman explains, "Babatha's social status . . . may have enabled her to insist not only that the bride money be quadrupled, but also that she be entitled to collect it on demand, while retaining rights for support" (67).

The Mishnah records a story with striking affinities to Babatha's ketubah, which it ascribes to R. Akiba, the most famous rabbi of Babatha's time.

It once happened that a man vowed to have no benefit from his wife, whose *Ketubah* was 400 *denars*. She came before R. Akiba and he declared him liable to pay her her *Ketubah*. He said, "Rabbi, my father left but 800 *denars*, and my brother took 400 *denars* and I took 400; is it not enough that she should take 200 *denars* and I 200?" R. Akiba said to him, "Even if thou must sell the hair of thy head that shalt pay her her *Ketubah*." The husband answered, "Had I known that this was so, I [would not have] made my vow." And R. Akiba released him from his vow. (m. Ned. 9:5)

Following Yehudah's death, Babatha seized orchards belonging to him, "in lieu of my dowry and debt [owed me]" (P.Yad. 21; Lewis, Yadin, and Greenfield, 96). The next clause in the ketubah, which resembles an exposition of Exodus 21:10 attributed to a second-century rabbi (R. Yoshia), specifies further the bride's right to "your food, and your clothes, and your bed [that is, her conjugal rights], provision fitting for a free woman" (Friedman, 67). Regarding the latter, Noam Zion affirms that although the rabbis often disagree, "they all legislate that wives have an irrevocable right to regularly scheduled intercourse in marriage" (3, 10–27). The ketubah is therefore based on "customary law" (Friedman, 68). Mandatory clauses (cf. m. Ketub. 4:7–12) follow the promises to the bride: (a) the ketubah itself, the amount due to the wife in case of divorce or the husband's death; (b) the pledge of surety for the ketubah from the husband's property; (c) the ransom clause, in which the groom promises to ransom his wife, if she is taken captive, and take her back even if she had been defiled during her captivity—a significant issue, since if she were captured it would be assumed that she had been violated (Josephus, *Ag. Ap.* 1.35; *Ant.* 3.276); (d) provision for male heirs, declaring that if the husband predeceases the wife, their male children will inherit the bride's ketubah along with their share of the inheritance; (e) a clause promising support for female daughters until they marry; and (f) a clause declaring that his widow may dwell in his house and draw support from his estate, if the husband predeceases her (Yadin, Greenfield, and Yardeni, 92). Mishnah Ketubbot 4:12 states that the Galileans did not permit the heirs to terminate the widow's support, while the Judeans (as in Babatha's ketubah) promised support only as long as the widow did not remarry or until his heirs paid her the debt specified in the marriage contract. The last line of the contract acknowledges the groom's responsibility for its contents, and seven signatures are appended on the reverse side of the document.

The Babatha papyri shed light on relations between Jews and gentiles in that era and region, Roman provincial administration, appeals to law and gentile judges, agriculture by the Dead Sea, the status of even a wealthy widow, literacy and illiteracy, the roles of Aramaic and Greek, marriage contracts, and polygamy among Jews (see further Satlow, 97–99; Esler 2017a; Goodman 1991; Katzoff 1995, 2000; Lewis, Yadin, and Greenfield).

7.9 Reflections

This survey of the status and lives of Jewish women in the first century illustrates the differences in our sources (fictional stories that elevate certain ideals and virtues, interpretations of Jewish laws, and archaeological evidence) and differences according to a woman's social and marital status. Nevertheless, women typically managed households and engaged in various types of work, especially child-rearing, preparation of food (gathering, grinding, and cooking), and spinning and weaving, as well as other agricultural, business, social, and communal tasks.

The women of Jesus' parables lived in this world. Two women grinding grain (Matt 24:41//Luke 17:35) was a common scene. The woman who "hid" leaven in a large lump of dough (Matt 13:33//Luke 13:20–21) was engaged in the daily task of baking bread, although the quantity of dough far exceeded what could be consumed by a single household. A family who received an unexpected guest (Luke 11:5–8) would have known who had been baking that day and might have bread left over. The woman who lost a coin (Luke 15:8–10) lit a lamp because houses had no windows and were dark. She swept the floor because it was a dirt floor. The ten coins were either her own money or money she needed for managing the household. A drachma was a silver coin of significant value. With it she could buy a sheep (see BDAG, 261; see below, 9.6).

Women traveled, often together, to visit family members, especially for births and deaths (Huebner, 95–98). Weddings were major family and community events, with set customs and expectations: betrothal, a marriage contract, a procession to the groom's home, and a week of feasting (Tob 11:18; cf. Matt 22:1–14; 25:1–12; John 2:1–12). Women could also be patrons and benefactors, like the women who traveled with Jesus and supported him (Luke 8:1–3). Professional mourners were typically women (Matt 9:23// Mark 5:38). Midwives were women (Exod 1:15–21), and women often anointed the dead (Mark 16:1). Women could also be prophets (Anna: Luke 2:36–38; Philip's daughters: Acts 21:8–9).

Wives were divorced by their husbands, apparently all too frequently, since Jesus echoed Malachi's prophetic condemnation of divorce: "For I hate divorce, says the Lord, the God of Israel" (Mal 2:16; Collins, 122–27). "It was because you were so hard-hearted that Moses allowed you to divorce your wives" (Matt 19:8). "Therefore what God has joined together, let no one separate" (Matt 19:6//Mark 10:9).

Wives and mothers also experienced the death of their husbands and children with tragic frequency (Anna, Luke 2:36–38; the widow at Nain, Luke 7:12). Widows could be prosperous (Judith, Babatha), though usually destitute (Mark 12:40–44). Even those who were landowners, however, were subject to legal limitations and restrictions and appealed to judges for justice (Luke 18:1–5), as Babatha's documents illustrate. In short, women were more vital to the lives of their families and communities and worked in a wider range of activities than modern interpreters have often recognized.

Works Cited in Chapter 7

Amaru, Betsy Halpern. 1988. "Portraits of Biblical Women in Josephus' *Antiquities*." *JJS* 39:143–70.

Aviam, Mordechai. 2013. "People, Land, Economy, and Belief in First-Century Galilee and Its Origins: A Comprehensive Archaeological Synthesis." Pages 5–48 in *The Galilean Economy in the Time of Jesus*. Edited by David A. Fiensy and Ralph K. Hawkins. ECL 11. Atlanta: Society of Biblical Literature.

Baker, Cynthia M. 2004. "Imagined Households." Pages 113–28 in Edwards.

Bar-Ilan, Meir. 1998. *Some Jewish Women in Antiquity*. Atlanta: Scholars Press.

Brooten, Bernadette J. 1982. *Women Leaders in the Ancient Synagogue: Inscriptional Evidence and Background Issues*. BJS 36. Chico, CA: Scholars Press.

Broshi, Magen. 1992. "Agriculture and Economy in Roman Palestine: Seven Notes on the Babatha Archive." *IEJ* 42.3/4:230–40.

———. 2010. "Diet in Palestine." *EDEJ*, 542–43.

Cohick, Lynn H. 2009. *Women in the World of the Earliest Christians: Illuminating Ancient Ways of Life*. Grand Rapids: Baker Academic.

Collins, John J., et al. 1997. *Families in Ancient Israel*. Louisville: Westminster John Knox.

Corley, Kathleen E. 2010. *Maranatha: Women's Funerary Rituals and Christian Origins*. Minneapolis: Fortress.

Crossan, John Dominic. 1986. *Sayings Parallels: A Workbook for the Jesus Tradition*. Philadelphia: Fortress.

Edwards, Douglas R., ed. 2004. *Religion and Society in Roman Palestine: Old Questions, New Approaches*. New York: Routledge.

Esler, Philip F. 2017a. *Babatha's Orchard: The Yadin Papyri and an Ancient Jewish Family Tale Retold*. Oxford: Oxford University Press.

———. 2017b. "Babatha: The Ancient Jewish Woman about Whom We Know Most." https://bibleinterp.arizona.edu/articles/2017/03/esl418021.

Fitzmyer, Joseph A., and Daniel J. Harrington. 1978. *A Manual of Palestinian Aramaic Texts*. Rome: Biblical Institute.

Frankel, Rafael. 2003. "The Olynthus Mill, Its Origin, and Diffusion: Typology and Distribution." *AJA* 107:1–21.

———. 2013. "Corn, Oil, and Wine Production." Pages 233–44 in *The Oxford Encyclopedia of the Bible and Archaeology*. Edited by Daniel M. Master. New York: Oxford University Press.

Friedman, Mordechai A. 1996. "Babatha's Ketubba: Some Preliminary Observations." *IEJ* 46:55–76.

García Martínez. *See* Bibliography of Ancient Sources and Translations

Godwin, John, ed. 1995. *Catullus: Poems 61–68*. Warminster, UK: Aris & Philipps.

Goodman, Martin. 1991. "Babatha's Story: Review of Y. Yadin, *The Documents from the Bar Kokbha Period in the Cave of Letters: Greek Papyri.*" *JRS* 81:169–75.

Hanson, K. C. 1989. "The Herodians and Mediterranean Kinship, Part 2, Marriage and Divorce." *BTB* 19:142–51.

Hanson, K. C., and Douglas E. Oakman. 1998. *Palestine in the Time of Jesus: Social Structures and Social Conflicts.* Minneapolis: Fortress.

Hezser, Catherine, ed. 2010. *The Oxford Handbook of Jewish Daily Life in Roman Palestine.* Oxford: Oxford University Press.

Huebner, Sabine R. 2019. *Papyri and the Social World of the New Testament.* Cambridge: Cambridge University Press.

Hylen, Susan E. 2019. *Women in the New Testament World.* Oxford: Oxford University Press.

Ilan, Tal. 1995. *Jewish Women in Greco-Roman Palestine.* Peabody, MA: Hendrickson.

———. 1999. *Integrating Jewish Women into Second Temple History.* Peabody, MA: Hendrickson.

———. 2010. "Gendered Issues in Daily Life." Pages 48–68 in Hezser.

Jeremias, Joachim. 1963. *The Parables of Jesus*. Rev. ed. Translated by S. H. Hooke. New York: Scribner's Sons.

———. 1967. "*nymphē.*" *TDNT* 4:1099–1106.

Katzoff, Ranon. 1995. "Polygamy in *P. Yadin?*" *ZPE* 109:128–32.

———. 2000. "Babatha." Pages 73–75 in *Encyclopedia of the Dead Sea Scrolls.* Edited by Lawrence H. Schiffman and James C. VanderKam. Oxford: Oxford University Press.

Kihlstrom Timpte, Katherine Joy. 2022. *The Transformational Role of Discipleship in Mark 10:13–16: Passage towards Childhood.* LNTS 650. London: T&T Clark.

Kraemer, Ross, S. 1998. "Jewish Women in the Diaspora World of Late Antiquity." Pages 46–72 in *Jewish Women in Historical Perspective.* Edited by Judith Baskin. Detroit: Wayne State University Press.

———. 2020. "Jewish Mothers and Daughters in the Greco-Roman World." Pages 89–112 in *The Jewish Family in Antiquity.* Edited by Shaye J. D. Cohen. Providence: Brown Judaic Studies. https://doi.org/10.2307/j.ctvzgb9cp.

Leibner, Uzi. 2010. "Arts and Crafts, Manufacture and Production." Pages 264–96 in Hezser.

Lewis, Naphtali, Yigael Yadin, and Jonas C. Greenfield, eds. 1989. *The Documents from the Bar-Kokhba Period in the Cave of Letters: Greek Papyri (P. Yadin).* Jerusalem: Israel Exploration Society.

Marks, Susan. 2012. "Present and Absent: Women at Greco-Roman Wedding Meals." Pages 123–48 in *Meals in the Early Christian World: Social Formation, Experimentation, and Conflict at the Table.* Edited by Dennis E. Smith and Hal E. Taussig. New York: Palgrave Macmillan.

Mathew, Susan. 2013. *Women in the Greetings of Romans 16.1–16.* LNTS 471. London: Bloomsbury.

Meyers, Carol. 1999. "'Women of the Neighborhood' (Ruth 4:17): Informal Female Networks in Ancient Israel." Pages 110–27 in *Ruth and Esther: A Feminist Companion to the Bible (Second Series).* Edited by A. Brenner. Sheffield: Sheffield Academic Press.

———. 2008. "Grinding to a Halt: Gender and the Changing Technology of Flour Production in Roman Galilee." Pages 65–74 in *Engendering Social Dynamics: The Archaeology of Maintenance Activities.* Edited by S. Montón-Subías and M. Sanchez-Romero. Oxford: ArchaeoPress.

———. 2013. *Rediscovering Eve: Ancient Israelite Women in Context.* Oxford: Oxford University Press.

Meyers, Eric, James F. Strange, and Carol Meyers. 1981. *Excavations at Ancient Meiron, Upper Galilee, Israel, 1971–72, 1974–75, 1977.* Cambridge, MA: American Schools of Oriental Research.

Myers, Alicia D. 2017. *Blessed among Women? Mothers and Motherhood in the New Testament.* New York: Oxford University Press.

Netzer, Ehud. 1991. *Masada.* Vol. 3, *Yigael Yadin Excavations 1963–1965: Final Reports, the Buildings Stratigraphy, and Architecture.* Jerusalem: Israel Exploration Society and Hebrew University.

Peskowitz, Miriam. 2004. "Gender, Difference, and Everyday Life: The Case of Weaving and Its Tools." Pages 129–45 in Edwards.

Pfann, Stephen J. 2000. *Qumran Cave 4: Cryptic Texts: Miscellanea,* Part 1. Edited by Philip Alexander et al. DJD 36. Oxford: Oxford University Press.

Reed, Jonathan L. 2003. "Stone Vessels and Gospel Texts. Purity and Socio-Economics in John 2." Pages 381–401 in *Zeichen aus Text und Stein: Studien auf dem Weg zu einer Archäologie des Neuen Testaments.* Edited by S. Alkier and J. K. Zangenberg. TANZ 42. Tübingen: Francke.

Safrai, Shmuel, and Menahem Stern, eds. 1987. *The Jewish People in the First Century: Historical Geography, Political History, Social, Cultural and Religious Life and Institutions.* Vol. 2. Assen: Van Gorcum.

Satlow, Michael L. 2001. *Jewish Marriage in Antiquity.* Princeton: Princeton University Press.

Sivertsev, Alexei. 2010. "The Household Economy." Pages 229–45 in Hezser.

Weingarten, Susan. 2005. "'Magiros,' 'nahtom' and Women at Home: Cooks in the Talmud." *JJS* 56.2:284–97.

Yadin, Yigael, Jonas C. Greenfield, and Ada Yardeni. 1994. "Babatha's *Ketubba.*" *IEJ* 44:75–101.

Zion, Noam Sachs. 2021. *Sanctified Sex: The Two-Thousand-Year Jewish Debate on Marital Intimacy.* Philadelphia: Jewish Publication Society.

Chapter 8

Meals

Wedding Feast (Matt 22:2–13//Luke 14:15–24)
Choice Places at the Table (Luke 14:7–11)
Rich Man and Lazarus (Luke 16:19–31)

Several of Jesus' parables assume social customs related to meals, especially celebratory meals. A man prepares a great dinner (Luke), or a king prepares a wedding feast for his son (Matthew), then sends his servant to call those who have been invited. When the invited guests would not come, offering various excuses (Luke), he sends his servant out again to announce, "Look, I have prepared my dinner, my oxen and my fat calves have been slaughtered, and everything is ready; come to the wedding banquet" (Matt 22:4). When they still will not come, he sends his servant out again: "Go out into the roads and lanes, and compel people to come in, so that my house may be filled" (Luke 14:23; see Matt 22:9–10). Jesus also alludes to the practice of inviting friends, relatives, and rich neighbors (Luke 14:12–14); the proper attire for a king's wedding feast (Matt 22:11–12); and proverbial wisdom regarding where one should sit at such a meal (Luke 14:7–11).

The parable of the rich man and Lazarus contrasts the two in terms of their dress and diet: "There was a rich man who was dressed in purple and fine linen and who feasted sumptuously every day. And at his gate lay a poor man named Lazarus, covered with sores, who longed to satisfy his hunger with what fell from the rich man's table" (Luke 16:19–21). Like the king in Matthew's parable of the wedding feast, the prodigal son's father kills the fatted calf when his son returns home, saying, "Let us eat and celebrate." The elder brother grumbles, "You have never given me even a young goat so that I might celebrate with my friends" (Luke 15:23, 29). These parables reflect the significance of meals in the first century and assume that those who hear the parables understand the customs surrounding such occasions.

While meals are important in all the Gospels, they are especially prominent in Luke, where Jesus eats with tax collectors and sinners, Pharisees,
the crowd, and his disciples. Robert Karris reports someone's quip: "Jesus
is either going to a meal, at a meal, or coming from a meal" (47). Given
the role of meals in defining identities and boundaries, it is no surprise that
Jesus defines the kingdom of God and its coming by his inclusive table fellowship, challenging the practices of the Pharisees and evoking controversy.
When Jesus eats with tax collectors and sinners (Matt 9:10–11; 11:19; Mark
2:15–16; Luke 5:30; 7:34; 15:1; "tax collectors and prostitutes," Matt 21:31–
32), the Pharisees find it scandalous and call him "a glutton and a drunkard"
(Matt 11:19//Luke 7:34). When a Pharisee hosts Jesus, as in Luke 7:36, 39;
11:37–38; 14:1, the host takes exception to Jesus' lack of regard for issues
of purity (being touched by a sinful woman, failing to wash before eating).
When the Pharisees note that Jesus and his disciples violate the "tradition of
the elders" by not washing before they eat (Matt 15:2//Mark 7:2–3), Jesus
says, "It is not what goes into the mouth that defiles a person, but it is what
comes out of the mouth that defiles" (Matt 15:11//Mark 7:15). Mark adds,
"Thus he declared all foods clean" (7:19).

So significant are Jesus' teachings and practices related to meals that
scholars have found them essential for understanding the historical Jesus.
John Dominic Crossan, for example, observed that for Jesus "commensality was not just a strategy for supporting the mission. . . . Commensality
was, rather, a strategy for building or rebuilding peasant community on rad-
ically different principles from those of honor and shame, patronage and
clientage" (344). Given the importance of meals in ancient culture—Greek,
Roman, and Jewish, as well as in Jesus' teachings and ministry—examination of meal practices may shed light on first-century Galilee as well. As
with other topics, the challenge is to identify the ancient references most
pertinent to Galilee. What did Galileans eat, how were meals socially and
religiously significant, and what customs characterized their meals?

8.1 Food in First-Century Galilee

Sirach, in the second century BCE, said, "The basic necessities of human
life are water and fire and iron and salt and wheat flour and milk and honey,
the blood of the grape and oil and clothing" (39:26). Cereals, vines, and
olives—or bread, wine, and olive oil—have been called "the Mediterranean
Triad." Cereals encompass a whole group of seed crops: wheat and barley as well as millets, rye, and oats. Olives require a dry season and a cool
winter, but they do not tolerate frost or thrive above an elevation of 800

meters (Garnsey, 14). Peas, beans, and lentils (pulses) were also common. The promised land was a land of "milk and honey" (Exod 3:8; Lev 20:24; Num 14:8; 16:13–14). "Honey" designated both bee honey and the syrup from fruits (Pilch, 233). Milk came from sheep and goats, and honey was used for sweetening (Prov 24:13; 25:16, 27). Chicken eggs (Luke 11:12) were prized, and grasshoppers ("locusts," Matt 3:4//Mark 1:6) were delicacies (Broshi, 137–38). Salt was important as a preservative and for seasoning (Ep Jer 28; 1 Esd 6:30; 8:20; Matt 5:13; Mark 9:50).

Describing the Jewish diet in more detail, the Mishnah declares: "If a husband maintained his wife at the hands of a third person, he may not grant her less than two *kabs* of wheat or four *kabs* of barley [every week]. . . . He must also give her half a *kab* of pulse and half *log* of oil and a *kab* of dried figs or a *mina* of fig-cake; and if he has none of these he must provide her with other produce in their stead" (m. Ketub. 5:8–9). This description is less informative than it appears, however, because it is prescriptive rather than descriptive, it sets a minimum standard, there is no agreement regarding the modern equivalent of the rabbinic measures (*kab, log,* and *mina*), and we do not know how representative it may have been for first-century Galileans (D. Kraemer 2010, 404). Nevertheless, the diet is built around bread made from wheat or barley, which was probably like today's pita bread or small loaves. Bread was dipped in olive oil or served with olives or legumes. Barley required less water to grow than wheat, is lower in gluten content, and was regarded as inferior (Philo, *Spec. Laws* 2.175). Barley therefore was cheaper than wheat and was a staple of the poor, slaves, and animals (see 1 Kgs 4:28; 2 Kgs 4:42; 7:16, 18; John 6:9, 13; Rev 6:6). Wheat was more common in Galilee, where there was more rain. Summer cereals, rice and perhaps sorghum, appeared in Palestine by the Hellenistic period, but rice requires heavy irrigation.

Legumes—especially lentils, beans, peas, and chickpeas, "the poor man's meat"—were also common, added nutritional value, and could be dried and stored. Olive presses at Galilean sites (especially Gamla and Yodefat) confirm that the production of olive oil was important to both the diet and the economy (Josephus, *J.W.* 2.590–592). Mordechai Aviam suggests that the Hasmoneans subsidized large olive groves and olive presses in Galilee:

The mass production of olive oil did not gain its place of importance in the rural life of the Galilee until the Hasmonaean period (in earlier periods, production was limited mainly to the domestic level). The growing of grapes and production of wine was of greater importance. The Hasmonaeans repopulated Galilee with Jewish inhabitants, among them Judaeans, who probably brought with them the knowledge of olive cultivation and the new technology of the mechanized oil press. (56)

This large-scale olive production contributed to the prosperity of Galilee during the reign of Herod Antipas.

The fourth item specified in Mishnah Ketubbot 5:8–9 is dried figs or some other dried fruit. Deuteronomy 8:8–9 describes the land of Israel, perhaps with some hyperbole, as "a land of wheat and barley, of vines and fig trees and pomegranates, a land of olive trees and honey, a land where you may eat bread without scarcity." Fig trees were so prevalent that peace and prosperity could be characterized as a time when Israelites could live under their vines and fig trees (1 Kgs 4:25; Mic 4:4; 1 Macc 14:11–12); the king of Assyria deceptively promised, "Every one of you will eat from your own vine and your own fig tree, and drink water from your own cistern" (2 Kgs 18:31). In contrast, war and locusts destroyed vines and fig trees (Ps 105:33; Jer 5:17; Hos 2:12). Pliny the Elder reports that pistachio nuts, figs, and plums grew in Syria (*Nat.* 13.51). Date palms were grown around the Dead Sea because they tolerated heat and salinity but were also cultivated upriver in the Bet She'an Valley. Carob pods were used as animal fodder but could be eaten in times of famine (see Luke 15:16; m. Ma'aś. 3:4; m. Shabb. 24:2).

Vegetables, wild and cultivated; nuts; and dairy products, especially cheese (Job 10:10; goat's milk and cheese, Deut 14:21; 2 Sam 17:29; Prov 27:27; cow's milk, 1 Sam 6:10) supplemented the diet. The Israelites remembered "the fish we used to eat in Egypt for nothing, the cucumbers, the melons, the leeks, the onions, and the garlic" (Num 11:5). The rabbis referred to Jews (and Samaritans) as "them that eat garlic" (m. Ned. 3:10). Leafy vegetables (cabbage and kale) were common (Broshi, 131).

Deuteronomy 28:51 lists the triad of "grain, wine, and oil" as "the fruit of your ground" without which the Israelites would perish. Palestine and Syria were famous for the wine they produced. In the third century BCE, the Macedonians in Egypt judged that the wine from a vineyard in Beth-Anath in Galilee "was so excellent that it was indistinguishable from the wine of the Aegean (Chios)" (Hengel, 1:39; Kloppenborg, 285, 368). Wine, usually mixed two parts water to one part wine (m. Nid. 2:7), was a staple food: "Eat of my bread and drink of the wine I have mixed" (Prov 9:5). "Wine mixed with water is sweet and delicious and enhances one's enjoyment" (2 Macc 15:39).

Meat was not a staple, even for the elite, but the frequency with which it was consumed is debated. The common understanding is that "in antiquity the average person could not afford to eat meat, except on special occasions" (Lev-Tov, 427). Arable land was so limited that it was not economical to use it to raise livestock. The grazing potential of the land indicates that it could not have supplied abundant meat (Broshi, 132). Moreover,

oxen were used for plowing (Prov 14:4; Isa 30:24; Sir 38:25) and threshing (1 Cor 9:9). "Under these conditions, then, cattle-raising on a large-
scale was ruled out. There were oxen, but they were work animals, kept
neither for meat nor for dairy products. Sheep and goats were numerous,
but were raised primarily for wool (or hair), secondarily for cheese (and
skins)" (Garnsey, 16–17; see below, ch. 12).

Appealing to the emerging specialty of zooarchaeology, which focuses
on "how humans used or manipulated animals," Lev-Tov responds, "Period
diets included plenty of flesh, mainly from domestic animals raised in order
to supply meat" (422, 427). He continues: "The archaeological evidence
from animal bones, human bone chemistry, agricultural economics, and
even ceramic analysis strongly suggest that the Hellenistic and Roman
period populations of Palestine ate meat on a regular basis" (429). Nevertheless, when the host in Jesus' parable says, "My oxen and my fat calves
have been slaughtered" (Matt 22:4; see Isa 22:13; Jdt 2:17), it means his
feast will be a lavish occasion. Only the elites ate meat regularly; most of
the population ate meat only on special occasions.

The presence of pig bones in the Carmel and Galilee regions, which were
heavily Jewish in the Roman era, might be explained in various ways, but Lev-
Tov contends, "It would seem a simpler explanation to suggest that pig bones
are present at Jewish settlements because they ate pork" (431). This view is
so contrary to prevailing views that Lev-Tov's argument merits quotation:

> It is poor scientific reasoning to think we can determine Jewish ethnicity
> by the amount of pig bones present. This assumes, in a circular argu-
> ment, that Jews would not have consumed pork, such that pig bones must
> represent meals consumed by non-Jews. The argument then completes
> its circle, concluding that therefore the Jewish populations adhered to
> religious restrictions and their ethnic identity. Pigs and other nonko-
> sher animals are present at not only a variety of Hellenistic and Roman
> settlements in Palestine, but also at sites dating from all periods after the
> Israelite conquest. Thus the presence of these species over such a long
> period of time demonstrates that, most likely, at least some portion of
> the native population regularly ate such animals. (439)

Lev-Tov concludes, "Available bone evidence from sites in Palestine indicates that, as in preceding times, the population ate mainly sheep and goats,
along with minor dietary contributions from a variety of domesticated and
non-domesticated species. These other species included cattle, pigs, chickens, and a variety of Mediterranean fish" (Lev-Tov, 433; see also Horwitz,
518). Even if Lev-Tov is right about the significance of the presence of
pig bones, the *absence* of pig bones, when coupled with other markers of

Jewish identity and concern for purity, still points to a Jewish population concerned to maintain its distinctiveness.

Fish bones are found in Palestine in all time periods but become more abundant in the Roman era (Lev-Tov, 435, 439). Saltwater fish and shell-fish, as well as freshwater species—especially tilapia and catfish, which were common but not abundant in the Sea of Galilee and Jordan River (Broshi, 134–35)—were prepared and shipped to Sepphoris and other inland markets. Taricheae (see below, 11.5)—perhaps synonymous with Magdala, on the western shore of the Sea of Galilee—meant "the place of salting" or "factories for salting fish" (LSJ, 1758; Schrader and Tay-lor). Strabo (64/63 BCE–at least 21 CE) said, "At the place called Tari-cheae, the lake supplies the best fish for curing" (*Geogr.* 16.2.45). Fish were prepared and consumed in various ways, as reflected in the Mishnaic rulings on vows. *Konam* was the usual term introducing a vow to abstain from something: "[If he said, '*Konam!*] if I taste of fish or fishes,' he is forbidden them, large or small, salted or unsalted, raw or cooked, but he is permitted pickled chopped fish and brine" (m. Ned. 6:2). The increase in consumption of fish in this period may be due to various economic as well as social factors, one of which may have been the prominence of fish in Greek and Roman diets: "Rather than the widespread abandonment of the traditional Near Eastern diet[,] which emphasized sheep and goats, we have the situation that dishes featuring Mediterranean fish complemented the pre-existing cuisine" (Lev-Tov, 439).

Galilean Jews ate two meals a day. Breakfast was a simple meal, usu-ally bread with dried fruit, olives, cheese, or eggs. The evening meal, the main meal of the day, could begin mid-afternoon or closer to sundown (Smith, 21).

8.2 The Social and Religious Significance of Meals

Meals, especially meals on special occasions, were about much more than just eating. As Hal Taussig put it, "The meal was a construction site for iden-tity in the Hellenistic Mediterranean" (182). Banquets, communal meals, and festive meals created community while defining boundaries between Jews and non-Jews as well as between Jews. They also defined one's social status (Neyrey 1991). Although Jewish meals developed their own distinc-tive characteristics, Dennis Smith and Matthias Klinghardt have indepen-dently demonstrated that they shared the common elements of banquets or communal meals in the ancient world (Smith and Taussig, 1–33). In the Mediterranean culture, honor and shame drove many social patterns: who gave a banquet, who was invited, who was present, what was served, and where one sat or reclined—all defined one's status.

The wealthy hosted banquets in their own homes: Zacchaeus (Luke 19:5–7), a leader of the Pharisees (14:1), Levi (Mark 2:15), Simon the leper (14:3), and Mary and Martha (Luke 10:38–40). According to Taussig (35), "The semi-private character of these meals" and "the porous boundaries of the meal attendance" allowed the larger society to observe what occurred within them. Banquets were also held in temples and rented locations, like the upper room (Mark 14:12–16 par.). Those of lesser means and status hosted less lavish meals; associations, clubs, and schools also held meals. Birthdays, weddings, religious festivals, and gatherings with friends and clients required festive meals. Those of modest means in the Galilean towns and villages ate with relatives and neighbors on such occasions, as well as on the Sabbath, gathering in their courtyards or outdoors. Communal meals were also held in the ancillary rooms around synagogues and sanctuaries (Josephus, *Ant.* 14.214–215; Ezek 40:17; Levine, 140–42; Catto, 143–49). As Lynn Cohick observed, "Dining in the Greco-Roman world was a key cultural channel for social engagement, status reinforcement, religious expression, and entertainment" (87).

8.2.1 Defining Boundaries between Jews and Non-Jews at Meals

During the Second Temple period (515 BCE–70 CE), and especially from the Maccabean Revolt onward, the Mosaic laws related to food, especially meat, became a means of social separation between Jews and others (D. Kraemer 2007, 26–30). Daniel resolved not to "defile himself with the royal rations of food and wine," requesting instead, "Let us be given vegetables to eat and water to drink" (Dan 1:8, 12). Similarly, Tobit did not eat gentile foods, although his brothers did (1:10–11), and Judith did not dine with Holofernes but prepared her own food (Jdt 12:2, 9, 17–19).

Leviticus 11 prohibits the Israelites from eating unclean animals, certain birds, fish, insects, and reptiles. Unclean is "every animal that has divided hoofs but is not cleft-footed or does not chew the cud" (11:26) as well as all that walk on their paws. Camels, rock badgers, hares, and pigs are specifically forbidden (11:4–7). The Maccabean literature, in which the prohibition against pork appears for the first time in isolation from other animals, dramatically portrays the centrality of dietary laws for Jewish self-definition. When the temple was defiled under Antiochus Epiphanes, "The altar was covered with abominable offerings that were forbidden by the laws" (2 Macc 6:5). Yet Jews were forced to partake of these sacrifices (6:7). When Eleazar, one of the scribes, was forced to eat swine's flesh (6:18),

"Those who were in charge of that unlawful sacrifice took the man aside because of their long acquaintance with him, and privately urged him to bring meat of his own providing, proper for him to use, and to pretend that he was eating the flesh of the sacrificial meal that had been commanded by the king" (6:21). But Eleazar refused because such pretense might lead the young astray. Not only Eleazar but also the mother and her seven sons chose death instead of eating the sacrifices (2 Macc 7, esp. 7:42). Many others also "stood firm and were resolved in their hearts not to eat unclean food. They chose to die rather than to be defiled by food or to profane the holy covenant; and they did die" (1 Macc 1:62–63).

Observing the Mosaic food laws became an important mark of Jewish identity (D. Kraemer 2007, 33–37). Jubilees (161–140 BCE) attributes the following words to Abraham: "You also, my son, Jacob, remember my words, and keep the commandments of Abraham, our father. Separate yourself from the gentiles, and do not eat with them" (22.16). The Letter of Aristeas (150–100 BCE) explains the reason the Jews ate separately:

> In his wisdom, the legislator [Moses] . . . being endowed by God for the knowledge of universal truths, surrounded us with unbroken palisades and iron walls to prevent our mixing with any of the other peoples in any matter, being thus kept pure in body and soul, preserved from false beliefs and worshiping the only God omnipotent over all creation. . . . So, to prevent our being perverted by contact with others or by mixing with bad influences, he hedged us in on all sides with strict observance connected with meat and drink and touch and hearing and sight, after the manner of the Law. (139, 142)

Philo also sought to explain the distinction between meat that was allowed and meat that was forbidden as well as the laws regarding preparation of meat and dairy products (*Spec. Laws* 4.106–108; *Virt.* 142–144). The significance of these texts is underscored by Jordan Rosenblum: "The *Letter of Aristeas* and Philo represent a pivotal moment in the history of Jewish food. . . . They understand these biblical regulations as binding, but they seek to explain *why* these particular rules were commanded" (353). Similarly, Philip Esler observes, "Eating with outsiders carried the risk of being offered food prohibited by the food laws. . . . Commensality [also] involved a most serious dereliction from the fundamental objective of preserving the separate identity of the Jewish people" (76). The same restrictions appear also in Joseph and Aseneth (100 BCE–117 CE). When Joseph was entertained at the house of Aseneth's parents, "They set a table before him by itself, because Joseph never ate with the Egyptians, for this was an abomination to him" (7.1). Then, when Aseneth repents of her idolatry, she protects even her dogs from her idolatrous food: "And Aseneth took her royal dinner and the fatlings and the fish and the flesh of the heifer and all the sacrifices of her gods and the vessels of their wine of libation and threw everything through the window looking north, and gave everything to the strange dogs. For Aseneth said to herself, 'By no means must my dogs eat from my dinner and from the sacrifice of the idols, but let the strange dogs eat those'" (10.13). Separation from non-Jews at the table was the major issue of the Jerusalem conference recounted in Acts 15 (cf. Gal 2:11–14), but the practice continued in some Christian communities. The author of the Clementine Homilies (3rd c. CE) declares, "Nor do we take our food from the same table as Gentiles, inasmuch as we cannot eat along with them, because they live impurely" (13.4, *ANF* 8:300).

By the first century BCE, gentile authors begin to criticize the Jews for their refusal to engage in table fellowship with others (Esler, 76–86). Diodorus Siculus (ca. 60–30 BCE) wrote that the Jews "alone of all nations avoided dealings with any other people and looked upon all men as their enemies," and hence they did not "break bread with any other race" (*Hist.* fragments of book 34; 35.1–2). Tacitus (2nd c. CE) likewise wrote, "They sit apart at meals, and they sleep apart" (*Hist.* 5.5.2). Philostratus (2–3 c. CE) adds, "The Jews cut themselves off long ago, not only from the Romans, but [also] from all mankind," and "devised an unsociable way of life, with no meals, libations, prayers, or sacrifices in common with other men" (*Vit. Apoll.* 5.33.4).

Many of these references are promotional or polemical, Jews exhorting other Jews to maintain their separation, identity, and purity in their foods and meal practices, and gentiles condemning Jews for doing so. The extent to which first-century Galilean Jews observed the dietary laws and refrained from eating pork or eating with non-Jews probably varied, with some being more observant than others. Still, it is significant that the Gospels do not describe meals at which Jesus ate with gentiles—"tax collectors and sinners," yes, but not gentiles. Mark 7:19 comments that Jesus "declared all foods clean," a comment that may represent Mark's agenda more than Jesus'. Matthew omits it. Mark may also construct the feeding of the 4,000 (8:1–9) as a gentile feeding "in the region of the Decapolis" (7:31). In Matthew, Jesus encounters gentiles only twice in his ministry (the gentile centurion in Capernaum, 8:5–13; and the Canaanite woman in the region of Tyre and Sidon, 15:21–28), not counting his encounter with Pilate during his trial. In both passages, Jesus resists their requests. The correct reading of Matthew 8:7 is probably not as a statement (NRSV) but as a skeptical question: "And *I* should come and heal him?" Matthias Konradt explains: "Understanding the text requires the central insight that v. 7 is not an indicative statement signaling Jesus' readiness to go with the centurion. . . . Jesus thus reacts to the centurion with a question, which expresses not only amazement, but [also] unwillingness" (131; see Culpepper 2021a, 168–69). In John 18:28, the Jewish leaders who led Jesus to Pilate's Praetorium will not enter it because to do so would mean that they were defiled and could not eat the Passover meal that evening. While in Mark and Luke the Pharisees are consistently critical of Jesus for not maintaining purity, Luke mentions two occasions when Pharisees invited Jesus to dine with them (7:39; 11:37). Both may be true. Meals not only defined boundaries between Jews and gentiles but also between Jews, and different hosts had different standards.

8.2.2 Defining Social Status at Meals

Identity and social status among Jews were also defined at meals. By hosting a banquet, the host identified his or her status. Receiving an invitation to a meal was an honor and a sign of social standing. Associations, *haburoth*, were formed, possibly by the Pharisees, to maintain ritual purity. Members of these associations, *haberim*, ate with other *haberim*, and Pharisees ate with others who also observed their standards of purity. The relationship between *haburoth* and the Pharisees has long been debated: "There is no scholarly consensus as to whether the *haberim* and the Pharisees were two distinct entities or rather two different names for the same group of people" (Kobel, 132, 132–41; see Sanders, 692–96; and ch. 17 below).

Whether one sat or reclined, and where one did so, was also a marker of status (Smith, 17, 33–34; see below, 8.3.3). Perhaps for this reason, Luke moves Jesus' teaching on greatness (cf. Mark 10:41–45//Luke 22:24–27) to the Last Supper, where "a dispute also arose among them [the disciples] as to which one of them was to be regarded as the greatest" (Luke 22:24).

What guests were served could also differ according to their status. Pliny the Younger (a Roman magistrate, 61–ca. 113 CE) describes the common practice at a Roman banquet: the host and his favored guests were served the best food and wine, while others were served cheap fare. In an unexpected twist, when one of the guests remarked about this practice, Pliny the Younger responded that he did not approve of it but treated his guests equally. Surprised, his companion remarked that it must be expensive to serve everyone equally, but Pliny said, "No," adding, "My freedmen do not drink the sort of wine I do, but I drink theirs" (*Ep.* 2.6).

At Qumran, one's rank in the community, which was reviewed annually (1QS V, 23–24), determined one's place at meals.

And all the chiefs of the cl[ans of the congre]gation with the wise [men and the learned] shall sit before them, each one according to his dignity. And [when] they gather at the table of community [or to drink] the new wine, and the table of community is prepared [and] the new wine [is mixed] for drinking, [no-one should stretch out] his hand to the first-fruit of the bread and of the [new wine] before the priest, for [he is the one who bl]esses the first-fruit of bread and of the new wine [and stretches out] his hand towards the bread before them. Afterwards, the Messiah of Israel shall stretch out his hand towards the bread. [And after, he shall] bless all the congregation of the community, each [one according to] his dignity. And in accordance with this regulation they shall act at each me[al, when] at least ten m[en are gat]hered. (1QSa II, 16–22, García Martínez, 127–28; see also 1QS VI, 2–11)

Philo describes the lavish and excessive banqueting practices of the time, complete with luxurious appointments, comely slaves, "the flesh of every creature that land, sea and rivers or air produce," gluttony, and "flute girls, dancers, jugglers, [and] fun-makers," practices he says are "now prevalent everywhere" (*Contempl. Life* 48–63). In contrast to such banquets, Philo describes those of the Therapeutae, an ascetic community near Alexandria. Philo's knowledge of this group is open to question, however, and his account of their practices may be "a product of Philo's literary imagination" (Walsh, 129; R. Kraemer, 66) or a "utopian fantasy done for a serious purpose" (Engberg-Pedersen, 43).

Philo's Therapeutae were dedicated to "the contemplation of the verities of nature, following the truly sacred instruction of the prophet Moses" (*Contempl. Life* 64). On the fiftieth day (after seven weeks of seven days), they file in, clad in white robes, cheerful, and with "the utmost seriousness." With eyes and hands lifted to heaven, they pray that their feasting may be acceptable to God. Thereafter, the Therapeutae recline, "according to the order of their admission" to the community (67), on common plank beds, men on the right and women on the left. Most of the women were aged virgins who had kept their chastity, devoting themselves to the pursuit of wisdom. They had no slaves since they considered slavery "entirely against nature" (70). Outstanding young members of the association serve the diners. No wine is drunk, only water; and no animal flesh is served, only bread with salt and sometimes hyssop as a relish (73, 81). After these preliminaries, the president discusses at length an issue or question from the Scriptures (75). When he finishes, "The president rises and sings a hymn composed as an address to God, either a new one of his own composition or an old one by the poets of an earlier day" (80). Then all the others "in proper order" sing, with the diners joining in to "chant the closing lines or refrains," men and women alike (80). The servers then bring in the tables and food. The priests, however, ate the simplest and purest food: unleavened and unsalted bread. Following the meal, they form two choirs, one of men and one of women, singing hymns to God before forming a single choir, like the choir of Israelites at the Red Sea (85). Continuing in this way until dawn, they greet the rising sun with hands outstretched.

The reference to women at the banquets of the Therapeutae raises the question of the presence and status of women at banquets generally. For the Greeks, the dining room was the man's room and the banquet a gathering of influential men. If women were present, they were the flute girls, dancers, courtesans, or prostitutes. Judith assumes this stereotype:

> On the fourth day Holofernes held a banquet for his personal attendants only, and did not invite any of his officers. He said to Bagoas, the eunuch who had charge of his personal affairs, "Go and persuade the Hebrew woman who is in your care to join us and to eat and drink with us. For it would be a disgrace if we let such a woman go without having intercourse with her. If we do not seduce her, she will laugh at us." So Bagoas left the presence of Holofernes, and approached her and said, "Let this pretty girl not hesitate to come to my lord to be honored in his presence, and to enjoy drinking wine with us, and to become today like one of the Assyrian women who serve in the palace of Nebuchadnezzar." (Jdt 12:10–13)

By the Hellenistic period, respectable women were more visible in public and participated in symposia more frequently (Smith, 42–43). Aristocratic women hosted banquets (cf. the woman Herais below, 8.3.1), and Sirach presumes that women will be at meals when he admonishes his students, "Never dine with another man's wife, or revel with her at wine; or your heart may turn aside to her, and in blood you may be plunged into destruction" (9:9). By the first century, wives were present at some banquets, either sitting at their husband's feet or reclining with them. Plutarch counseled grooms to eat with their wives. "Men who do not like to see their wives eat in their company are thus teaching them to stuff themselves when alone. So those who are not cheerful in the company of their wives, nor join with them in sportiveness and laughter, are thus teaching them to seek their own pleasures apart from their husbands" (*Conj. praec.* 15). Kathleen Corley offers the following crisp summary of the pertinent texts: "From this sort of evidence it is difficult to determine the everyday meal practice of Jews in first-century Palestine and the Diaspora; nonetheless, it seems that Jewish men expected to find married women at a banquet, that women were required to recline next to their husbands at the Passover Seder, and that certain wealthy Jewish women participated in the communal meals of an ascetic Jewish community in Alexandria" (71).

In light of this survey, details in the Gospel accounts of women at meals with Jesus take on new significance (Elliott). When Jesus dines in the homes of his followers, women often serve the meal. There is no mention of slaves or other servers. In Mark, for example, Peter's mother-in-law serves (1:30–31). In Luke, Martha prepares a meal for Jesus while her sister, Mary, sits at his feet, listening to his teachings (10:38–42). In John, in the home of Lazarus, Martha again serves, while Mary anoints Jesus' feet (12:1–8). When Jesus eats with tax collectors and sinners (Matt 9:10–13//Mark 2:15–17), women are not mentioned. In the same pericope, Luke seems to clarify that Jesus ate with "tax collectors and others," while some *Pharisees* say that Jesus eats with "tax collectors and sinners" (5:29–32). Were the "sinners" women? Perhaps echoing the formulaic phrase, "tax collectors and sinners," Jesus explains the parable of the man with two sons, adding, "For John came to you in the way of righteousness and you did not believe him, but the tax collectors and the prostitutes believed him; and even after you saw it, you did not change your minds and believe him" (Matt 21:32); but here the reference is to prostitutes responding to John's preaching, not Jesus'. Again, in Luke 7:36–50, at the home of a Pharisee, the woman who weeps at Jesus' feet is identified as "a sinner," perhaps meaning that she was a harlot. Clearly, she was not invited to the dinner by the Pharisee, and she was not reclining with Jesus. Given the semiprivate/public nature of such a dinner, she came to witness the occasion, perhaps after hearing Jesus. The Pharisee was scandalized. Women may have been at meals where Jesus was the guest of honor, but they were not there as courtesans or prostitutes in the manner of licentious Greco-Roman banquets (Cohick, 90–91).

8.3 Meal Customs

The condemnation of the lavish meals of the rich in Amos, one of the oldest literary testimonies to reclining on couches at meals (cf. Esth 1:6), shows that many of the elements of such meals remained constant across the centuries.

> Alas for those who lie on beds of ivory, and lounge on their couches, and eat lambs from the flock, and calves from the stall; who sing idle songs to the sound of the harp, and like David improvise on instruments of music; who drink wine from bowls, and anoint themselves with the finest oils, but are not grieved over the ruin of Joseph! Therefore they shall now be

the first to go into exile, and the revelry of the loungers shall pass away.
(Amos 6:4–6)

Likewise, Jeremiah was forbidden to "go into the house of feasting to sit
with them, to eat and drink" (Jer 16:8). The sources most relevant to meal
customs in Galilee generally follow the customs documented across the
Greco-Roman world. Drawing on materials closest to our subject, we can
sketch a picture of banquet customs one might have found in first-century
Galilee.

8.3.1 Invitations

Invitations were sent out in advance, in writing for lavish gatherings, orally
for most meals. Second- and third-century papyri from Oxyrhynchus (P.Coll.
Youtie 51–55) contain invitations to a banquet in honor of Sarapis. Each follows a common form, such as this: "Herais asks you to dine in the (dining-)
room of the Sarapeion at a banquet of the Lord Sarapis tomorrow, namely
the 11th, from the 9th hour [3:00 p.m.]" (Horsley, 5). In this case, the host
is a woman (Herais), probably a widow. Presumably invitations had been
extended orally, so the written invitation is merely a reminder. Jesus' parable of the great banquet presumes a double invitation to guests who live in
the vicinity. Invitations were extended and accepted in advance. When the
banquet was ready, a servant called the guests to come.

The practice of double invitations is attested in Esther (5:8; 6:14), Roman
sources (Terence, *Haut.* 169–170; Apuleius, *Metam.* 3.12), and a later rabbinic text: "Why were they [men of Jerusalem] precious? There was not one
of them who went to a feast unless he was summoned for a second time"
(Lam. Rab. on Lam 4.2; Davies and Allison, 196, n. 16).

Philo alludes to the practice in the context of his argument concerning creation: "Just as givers of a banquet, then, do not send out the sum-
monses to supper till they have put everything in readiness for the feast,
. . . exactly in the same way the Ruler of all things, like some provider of
contests or of a banquet, when about to invite man to the enjoyment of a
feast and a great spectacle, made ready beforehand the material for both"
(*Creation* 78). Herais's banquet will begin at the customary hour (3:00
p.m.) in the banquet room (*klinē*) of the Sarapeion. In an age of sundi-
als and sand clocks, the times would have been only approximate. The
announcement "Everything is ready" is echoed by Akiba, "All is made
ready for the banquet" (m. Avot 3:17), to illustrate the point that "all is
given against a pledge": that is, a host prepares a banquet in trust that
those who are invited will come.

A parable strikingly similar to Jesus' parable of the wise and foolish maidens is attributed to the late first-century rabbi Johanan b. Zakkai.

> This may be compared to a king who summoned his servants to a banquet without appointing a time. The wise ones adorned themselves and sat at the door of the palace. ["For,"] said they, "is anything lacking in a royal palace?" The fools went about their work, saying, "Can there be a banquet without preparations"? Suddenly the king desired [the presence of] his servants: the wise entered adorned, while the fools entered soiled. The king rejoiced at the wise but was angry with the fools. "Those who adorned themselves for the banquet," ordered he, "let them sit, eat and drink. But those who did not adorn themselves for the banquet, let them stand and watch." (b. Shabb. 153a, Soncino)

The practice of double invitations would have allowed the invited guests to confirm that other guests of status would be attending also—and make excuses (as in the parable) if that were not the case.

8.3.2 Washing and Anointing

In Luke 7:44–46, Jesus' response to his host, Simon the Pharisee, refers to the acts of hospitality that a guest might expect: "I entered your house; you gave me no water for my feet, but she has bathed my feet with her tears and dried them with her hair. You gave me no kiss, but from the time I came in she has not stopped kissing my feet. You did not anoint my head with oil, but she has anointed my feet with ointment." Each of these gracious gestures is attested elsewhere.

Removing sandals and washing a traveler's dusty feet, following Abraham's example (Gen 18:4; T. Ab. 3.7–9; Coloe, 131–34; see below, 13.5), were ancient acts of hospitality, normally performed by slaves, children, wives (1 Sam 25:41; b. Ketub. 61a), or pupils. Yet John the Baptist declares that he was not worthy to unloose the sandal of the one coming after him (John 1:27). When Jesus washes the feet of his disciples, Peter, shocked, protests, "You will never wash my feet" (John 13:6, 8). Showing hospitality and washing the feet of "the saints" attested to a widow's virtue, according to 1 Timothy 5:10.

Footwashing is also attested in Joseph and Aseneth. When Joseph enters the house of Aseneth's family, "they washed his feet and set a table before him" (7.1). Aseneth's washing of Joseph's feet before their wedding is charged with conjugal overtones and described in extraordinary detail. "She brought water to wash his feet. And Joseph said, 'Let one of the virgins come and wash my feet.' And Aseneth said to him, 'No, my Lord, because you are my lord from now on, and your feet another [woman] will never wash.' And she urged him and washed his feet. . . . And after this Joseph grasped her right hand and kissed it, and Aseneth kissed his head and sat at his right hand" (Jos. Asen. 20.2–4). Here the second act of hospitality is also mentioned, greeting the guest with a kiss, which was common in ancient cultures (Herodotus, *Hist.* 1.134; Strabo, *Geogr.* 15.3.20; see Stählin, 121). Judas's kiss in the act of betraying Jesus demonstrated such egregious treachery that, in time, it became a cipher for his betrayal (Luke 22:48).

Kissing or refusing to kiss another could also be a boundary marker (Luz, 417). Jews probably did not kiss non-Jews unless they were family members (Exod 18:7; Ruth 1:9, 14), as Joseph and Aseneth illustrates:

> And as Aseneth went up to kiss Joseph, Joseph stretched his right hand out and put it on her chest. . . . And Joseph said, "It is not fitting for a man who worships God, who will bless with his mouth the living God, . . . to kiss a strange woman who will bless with her mouth dead and dumb idols and eat from their table . . . and anoint herself with ointment of destruction. . . . Likewise, for a woman who worships God it is not fitting to kiss a strange man, because this is an abomination before the Lord God." (8.4–7)

In the Pauline churches, "a holy kiss" was the common greeting (Rom 16:16; 1 Cor 16:20; 2 Cor 13:12; 1 Thess 5:26; cf. 1 Pet 5:14).

Anointing one's head or a guest's head with oil was also an ancient practice (Deut 28:40; Ruth 3:3; Ps 23:5; Amos 6:6; Mic 6:15) associated with consecration, purification, and hospitality. Anointing oil could also be a boundary marker, as it is in these Psalm texts: "How very good and pleasant it is when kindred live together in unity! It is like the precious oil on the head, running down upon the beard, on the beard of Aaron, running down over the collar of his robes" (133:1–2). "Never let the oil of the wicked anoint my head, for my prayer is continually against their wicked deeds" (141:5). The same distinction between the anointing of the righteous and the wicked appears in Joseph and Aseneth (8.5; 15.4; quoted above) and Ahiqar (Arabic): "O my son! Let the wise man beat thee with a rod, but let not the fool anoint thee with sweet salve" (2.61; Charles, 2:737).

Other oils and perfumes were also used for anointing. In Esther, women chosen for the king's harem completed a year of cosmetic treatment: "six months with oil of myrrh and six months with perfumes and cosmetics for women" (2:12; see also Ps 45:8; Prov 7:17; Song 1:13; 3:6; Sir 24:15). In an incredibly extravagant act, the woman who anointed Jesus broke a flask of pure nard. This costly ointment, prepared from the roots and stems of an aromatic Indian herb, is also mentioned in Song 1:12; 4:13–14. Pliny the

Elder says that the best ointment was preserved in alabaster (*Nat.* 13.3.19). Breaking the flask meant that none of the ointment would be held back for a later occasion. Mark expresses the value of the fragrance with three descriptions, each progressively more specific: "pure" (*pistikēs*), which can mean "genuine, unadulterated" or describe a specific kind of nard, *pistakia*, from a pistachio tree (BDAG 818); "expensive" (*polytelous*); and "worth more than three hundred denarii" (14:3, 5), about the annual income of a day laborer.

8.3.3 Sitting and Reclining

In the New Testament, *klinē* is used for a bed (e.g., Matt 9:2; Mark 4:21) rather than a dining couch, but several verbs are used for reclining at meals (*anakeimai*, Matt 9:10; 22:10, 11; 26:7, 20; Luke 22:7; John 12:2; 13:23; *katakeimai*, Mark 2:15; 14:3; Luke 5:29; 7:37; 1 Cor 8:10; *anaklinō*, Matt 8:11; 14:19; Mark 6:39; Luke 12:37; 13:29; and *kataklinō,* only in Luke 7:36; 14:8; 24:30; in 9:14–15 it may mean lie or sit). Although these verbs denote reclining, generally to eat, modern translations often render them as "sit" in keeping with modern practice. Whereas in ancient Israel diners sat up, reclining was the common practice in the Greek world (see also m. Ber. 6:6, where both are mentioned). These same verbs, however, are used for reclining to eat in the Septuagint (*anakeimai*, 1 Esd 4:10; Tob 9:6; *katakeimai*, Jdt 13:15; *anaklinō*, 3 Macc 5:16; *kataklinō*, Jdt 12:15). A dining room was called a *triclinium* because it had three dining couches that typically accommodated nine diners (Smith, 14–18). First Corinthians 10:7, which quotes Exodus 32:6, is the only New Testament reference to sitting (*kathizō*) for a meal. Amos condemns those who "lie on beds of ivory, and lounge on their couches, and eat lambs from the flock, and calves from the stall" (Amos 6:4; see Tob 9:6).

Tables (*trapeza*) for dining appear in the Gospels only in Matthew 15:27// Mark 7:28; and Luke 16:21; 22:21; 22:30. Other occurrences refer to the tables of moneychangers. Peasants reclined on the floor or outdoors; only the elite reclined on couches: "*Reclining* is the definitive word for Hellenistic meals and, indeed, the definitive behavior. . . . Reclining signified both leisure and status. To recline was an indication of privilege" (Taussig, 45). Elite women also reclined at banquets, their status overruling their gender (Cohick, 89–90).

Roman aristocracy transformed the four-sided arrangement of the Greeks into the three-sided *triclinium* that reflected hierarchical status more clearly (Dunbabin). The guest of honor reclined on his left elbow at the bottom left corner of the square-sided "U." A "broad room" used for banqueting first appears in a mansion in Palestine in the Late Hellenistic period (late second/

early first century BCE) at Tel Anafa in upper Galilee. Others have been found in the Hasmonean palace at Jericho, Herod's palaces in Jericho and at Masada, a Nabatean villa at Petra, and the palatial mansion in Jerusalem (1st c. CE; Keddie, 69–70). Three *triclinia* with masonry benches have been found in Palestine, one in an outdoor area of the Hasmonean palaces at Jericho, another at a late Hasmonean (75–50 BCE) mansion outside Jericho, and a third at a mansion in Idumea. In contrast to Herod's extravagance, however, the Hasmonean palaces, dining facilities, and meals were deliberately modest. Banquets may not have been common, since relatively few drinking vessels have been found in the palaces; those that have been found are plain and locally produced, suggesting that the Hasmoneans sought to show that they were "fellow Jews" (*ḥeber hayehudim*) in contrast to Seleucid kings (Regev, 261, 263–65).

Partially excavated mansions with decorative elements typical of those with *triclinia* have also been found at Sepphoris and Tiberias and may have belonged to Herod Antipas or Jewish elites (Jensen, 142–43; Keddie, 72–73). A banqueting hall with two identical rooms (22 BCE–mid-1st c. CE), no doubt used by Jewish elites, was located about twenty-five meters from the Western Wall of the temple in Jerusalem (Keddie, 73). Anthony Keddie argues further that apocalyptic texts from the period interpret *triclinia* and their banqueting couches as emblematic of the wickedness, excess, and idolatry of the kings and their "great men," who exploited the righteous (1 En. 46:4–7; T. Mos. 7.3–10; Keddie, 74–81). Given this lack of evidence for widespread use of couches (*klinē*) and *triclinia* in Jewish homes, the use of verbs for reclining in the Gospels need not signal the adoption of "a Greek style of dining" in first-century Palestine (contra Horsley, 9).

8.4 Meal and Symposium

That people ate from bowls and plates is confirmed by Judith's order for her maid to pack her dishes (10:5) and the discovery of small plates and bowls both at Qumran and among Babatha's belongings (D. Kraemer 2010, 409–10). Diners wiped their hands on bread, and dogs were often present to eat the bread crumbs and other scraps (Matt 7:6; 15:26–27; Luke 16:21; Taussig, 26). Sirach instructs his students on good manners at a banquet, which are consistent with those of the Greeks and Romans:

> Do not reach out your hand for everything you see, and do not crowd your neighbor at the dish. Judge your neighbor's feelings by your own, and in every matter be thoughtful. Eat what is set before you like a well

brought-up person, and do not chew greedily, or you will give offense. Be the first to stop, as befits good manners, and do not be insatiable, or you will give offense. If you are seated among many persons, do not help yourself before they do. . . . (31:14–18)

Do not try to prove your strength by wine-drinking, for wine has destroyed many. . . . (31:25)

If they make you master of the feast, do not exalt yourself; be among them as one of their number. Take care of them first and then sit down. . . . (32:1)

Where there is entertainment, do not pour out talk; do not display your cleverness at the wrong time. . . . (32:4)

Speak, you who are young, if you are obliged to, but no more than twice, and only if asked. Be brief; say much in few words; be as one who knows and can still hold his tongue. Among the great do not act as their equal; and when another is speaking, do not babble. . . . (32:7–9)

Leave in good time and do not be the last; go home quickly and do not linger. (32:11)

The common pattern of Greco-Roman meals distinguished between the meal (*deipnon*) and the symposium. After the meal, the tables were removed, the wine was mixed, a libation of wine was poured out or drunk, and the diners sang a hymn in preparation for the symposium (Athenaeus, *Deipn.* 11.462c–d; Plato, *Symp.* 176A; Xenophon, *Symp.* 2.1). Sirach waxes eloquent about music at a banquet: "A ruby seal in a setting of gold is a concert of music at a banquet of wine. A seal of emerald in a rich setting of gold is the melody of music with good wine" (32:5–6).

The entertainment that followed could be as raucous as Herod Antipas's birthday feast (Mark 6:21–28) or the *symposia* condemned by Philo (quoted above), as cultured as philosophical discussions, or as devout as exposition and discussion of the Mosaic law (Smith and Taussig, 30–31). The latter is attested in Sirach (9:15–16), at Qumran (1QS VI, 6–8), in Philo's description of the Therapeutae (also quoted above), and in the Mishnah: "If three have eaten at one table and have spoken over it words of the Law, it is as if they have eaten from the table of God" (m. 'Abot 3:3). These traditions probably influenced both the Jewish Passover meal and the Christian Eucharist.

8.5 The Passover Meal

Special occasions called for banquets: birthdays, weddings, and funerals (funerary meals: 2 Sam 12:17; m. Sanh. 2:1; m. Mo'ed Qaṭ. 3:7). Fish and fish imagery were commonly associated in Greco-Roman culture with ceremonial, religious, and funerary meals (Neyrey 1996, 163–64; Standhartinger, 99; Culpepper 2021b, 547–53). The Sabbath (Philo, *Contempl. Life* 36; Josephus, *Life* 279), Sukkot, and Passover were also observed with special meals. Josephus declares, "There is not one city, Greek or barbarian, nor a single nation, to which our custom of abstaining from work on the seventh day has not spread, and where the fasts and the lighting of lamps and many of our prohibitions in the matter of food are not observed" (*Ag. Ap.* 2.282).

At Sukkot, following Leviticus 23:34–36, 39–43 (esp. 23:42), Jews lived for a week in a temporary shelter (*Sukkah*, booth). The rabbis debated how many meals had to be eaten in the *Sukkah*, fourteen, or only on the first day of the feast (m. Sukkah 3:6).

The Passover meal was eaten annually, in the spring, on the evening of Nisan 14/15, after sunset (Exod 12:6–49). Ostraca and a papyrus text from Elephantine in Egypt dating to the late fifth century BCE refer to "Passover" but do not describe what the celebration entailed (Adler, 151–55). Two Jewish writings generally ascribed to the second century BCE command the observance of Passover. Ezekiel the Tragedian says the observance shall be called "Passover" (184) and commands both the Paschal sacrifice (157) and the seven-day feast of unleavened bread (169–171, 189). Jubilees devotes chapter 49 to the command to keep the Passover, repeatedly prescribing the date and time, "the fourteenth of the first month [Nisan] between the evenings" (49.10). The command is "an eternal decree" (49.8), and one who fails to observe the Passover "shall be uprooted" (49.9). Only those over the age of twenty can eat the Passover (49.17; cf. 11QTemple XVII, 8). Moreover, the Passover can only be observed in the temple:

> And in the days when the house is built in the name of the Lord in the land of their inheritance, they shall go there and they shall sacrifice the Passover at evening when the sun is setting on the third (part) of the day. And they shall offer up its blood on the threshold of the altar. . . . And they shall not be able to observe the Passover in their cities or in any district except before the tabernacle of the Lord or before his house in which his name dwells. (Jub. 49.19–21)

The classic description of this observance, in Mishnah Pesaḥim 10:1–9, from around 200 CE, is a formal liturgy for Jewish families; it specifies sitting at a table and consuming no less than four cups of wine during the meal. The houses of Hillel and Shammai debated various points of the ritual, which essentially proceeded as follows:

The first cup
The benediction over the first cup and over the day
The food is brought.
The breaking of bread (unleavened), eaten with bitter herbs dipped into
    nuts and fruit, pounded together and mixed with vinegar
The second cup
The son asks the father, "Why is this night different from other nights?"
The father instructs him, "A wandering Aramean was my father [Deut
    26:5] . . ." through the exodus story.
Reciting the first part of the Hallel (Pss 113–118)
The third cup
The benediction over the meal
The fourth cup
The rest of the Hallel
The benediction over song
After midnight, the Passover offering

Rosenblum (351) observes, "The structure of this most rabbinic meal is clearly indebted to that of the Greek and Roman symposium": the meal, wine, discussion, and singing. Similarly, t. Berakhot 4:8, an early rabbinic text, prescribes the order for an elaborate meal with washings, benedictions, the first course, second course, and desserts (Rosenblum, 350). But how much of this liturgy reflects first-century practices? Were the rabbis following the pattern of the symposium or defining the Passover Seder in opposition to the symposium? It appears to draw on the symposium pattern, departing at the point of the benedictions and rabbinic formulae.

David Kraemer summarizes the current state of research, claiming,

There are two things upon which virtually everyone would agree: (1) the Passover celebration in the time before the destruction of the Temple in 70 CE differed significantly from the later rabbinic ritual, and was most assuredly not a symposium [Bokser, 14–28], and (2) whether constructing a symposium or an anti-symposium, the rabbis, in formulating their ritual, were employing and/or referencing a uniquely Hellenistic-Roman cultural vocabulary. (2010, 414–15)

David Kraemer observes further that "the seder, as such, is an invention of the rabbis" (414), attested nowhere before the Mishnah. On the other hand, the similarities between the seder and the symposium are evident in the Mishnaic text quoted above, while the differences "also highlight the symposium-like quality of the rabbinic ritual, for they make sense as negations or adaptations only in relationship to the ritual-vocabulary of the symposium" (415).

Philo's description of Passover and the seven-day feast of unleavened bread (*Spec. Laws* 2.145–175), written in the first century, does not contain the rabbinic liturgy for the meal.

> On this day every dwelling-house is invested with the outward semblance and dignity of a temple. The victim is then slaughtered and dressed for the festal meal which befits the occasion. The guests assembled for the banquet have been cleansed by purificatory lustrations, and are there not as in other festive gatherings, to indulge the belly with wine and viands, but to fulfil with prayers and hymns the custom handed down by their fathers. (*Spec. Laws* 2.148)

Note Philo's insistence that the guests assembled "not as in other festive gatherings, to indulge the belly with wine," but in fulfillment of their ancient traditions.

8.6 Reflections

Most Galileans ate a simple diet of grains, olives and olive oil, fruit, vegetables, herbs, and wine. Fish and meat were generally consumed on special occasions. Communal meals followed the pattern of Greco-Roman banquets with invitations, double invitations, gestures of hospitality (kissing, footwashing, and anointing), reclining, the meal, then drinking, entertainment, and conversation. The elite might hold a banquet in their dining room (*triclinium*), but peasants and artisans gathered in their courtyard, outdoors, or rented space. Such meals defined both boundaries and status based on purity, wealth, and honor: who was invited, what was served, what standards of purity were observed, and where one sat or reclined. Relatively little is recorded about the communal meals of the non-elites.

Both Jesus' parables and the Gospel meal scenes fit this setting. Jesus, an itinerant teacher and prophet, is the honored guest on several occasions, eating both with tax collectors and Pharisees. Debates about washing, purity, gestures of hospitality, and social boundaries appear often in connection with meals. Somewhat surprisingly, the only account of Jesus eating with his disciples on a special occasion is the Last Supper, at Passover in Jerusalem. According to John, Jesus washed the disciples' feet, the Beloved Disciple reclined closest to Jesus, and an extended period of discussion and teaching followed the meal. In the Synoptics, Jesus blessed and broke bread, then gave the wine, and they sang a hymn before they went out to the Mount of Olives.

Because the Gospel of Luke places Jesus at table more frequently than the other Gospels and at the same time regularly warns against the dangers of wealth, the connections between wealth, banquets, and reclining on couches are especially suggestive for interpreting the parables cited at the beginning of this chapter. Jesus' parable of the rich man who filled his table with "the poor, the crippled, the blind, and the lame" when the elite refused his invitation (Luke 14:15–24) sharply condemns the wealthy elite. At the same time, Luke reports that Jesus dined in the homes of Pharisees (7:36, 39; 11:37–38; 14:1) and advises his followers to take the lowest place at the table (Luke 14:7–11)—wise counsel in the spirit of Sirach, assuming that they too will be invited to tables where status matters. Here the influence of different settings in the development of the tradition of Jesus' teachings and the composition of the Gospels calls for further study.

Works Cited in Chapter 8

Adler, Yonatan. 2022. *The Origins of Judaism: An Archaeological-Historical Reappraisal*. AYBRL. New Haven: Yale University Press.

Aviam, Mordechai. 2004. *Jews, Pagans and Christians in the Galilee: 25 Years of Archaeological Excavations and Surveys, Hellenistic to Byzantine Periods*. Rochester, NY: University of Rochester Press.

Bokser, Baruch M. 1984. *The Origins of the Seder: The Passover Rite and Early Rabbinic Judaism*. Berkeley: University of California Press.

Broshi, Magen. 2001. *Bread, Wine, Walls and Scrolls*. JSPSup 36. Sheffield: Sheffield Academic Press.

Catto, Stephen K. 2007. *Reconstructing the First-Century Synagogue: A Critical Analysis of Current Research*. LNTS 363. London: T&T Clark.

Cohick, Lynn H. 2009. *Women in the World of the Earliest Christians: Illuminating Ancient Ways of Life*. Grand Rapids: Baker Academic.

Coloe, Mary L. 2007. *Dwelling in the Household of God: Johannine Ecclesiology and Spirituality*. Collegeville, MN: Liturgical Press.

Corley, Kathleen E. 1993. *Private Women, Public Meals: Social Conflict in the Synoptic Tradition*. Peabody, MA: Hendrickson.

Crossan, John Dominic. 1991. *The Historical Jesus: The Life of a Mediterranean Jewish Peasant*. New York: HarperSanFrancisco.

Culpepper, R. Alan. 2021a. *Matthew: A Commentary*. Louisville: Westminster John Knox.

———. 2021b. *Designs for the Church in the Gospel of John: Collected Essays, 1980–2020*. WUNT 465. Tübingen: Mohr Siebeck.

Davies, W. D., and Dale C. Allison Jr. 1997. *Matthew 19–28*. ICC. London: Bloomsbury.

Dunbabin, Katherine M. D. 1991. "Triclinium and Stibadium." Pages 121–48 in *Dining in a Classical Context*. Edited by William J. Slater. Ann Arbor: University of Michigan Press.

Elliott, John. 1991. "Household and Meals versus the Temple Purity System: Patterns of Replication in Luke-Acts." *HvTSt* 47.2:386–99.

Engberg-Pedersen, Troels. 1999. "Philo's *De Vita Contemplativa* as a Philosopher's Dream." *JSJ* 30:40–64.

Esler, Philip F. 1987. *Community and Gospel in Luke-Acts*. SNTSMS 57. Cambridge: Cambridge University Press.

García Martínez. *See* Bibliography of Ancient Sources and Translations

Garnsey, Peter. 1999. *Food and Society in Classical Antiquity*. Cambridge: Cambridge University Press.

Hengel, Martin. 1974. *Judaism and Hellenism: Studies in the Encounter in Palestine during the Early Hellenistic Period*. 2 vols. Translated by John Bowden. Philadelphia: Fortress.

Horsley, G. H. R. 1981. *New Documents Illustrating Early Christianity*. Vol. 1. Macquarie University, NSW: The Ancient History Documentary Research Centre.

Horwitz, Liora K. 2000. "The Animal Economy of Horvat 'Eleq." Pages 511–28 in *Ramat Hanadiv Excavations: Final Report of the 1984–1998 Seasons*. Edited by Yizhar Hirschfeld. Jerusalem: The Israel Exploration Society.

Jensen, Morten Hørning. 2006. *Herod Antipas in Galilee*. WUNT 215. Tübingen: Mohr Siebeck.

Karris, Robert J. 1985. *Luke: Artist and Theologian, Luke's Passion Account as Literature*. New York: Paulist.

Keddie, G. Anthony. 2020. "Triclinium Trialectics: The Triclinium as Contested Space in Early Roman Palestine." *HTR* 113:63–88.

Kloppenborg, John S. 2006. *The Tenants in the Vineyard: Ideology, Economics and Agrarian Conflict in Jewish Palestine*. WUNT 195. Tübingen: Mohr Siebeck.

Kobel, Esther. 2011. *Dining with John: Communal Meals and Identity Formation in the Fourth Gospel and Its Historical and Cultural Context*. BibInt 109. Leiden: Brill.

Konradt, Matthias. 2020. *The Gospel according to Matthew: A Commentary*. Translated by M. Eugene Boring. Waco, TX: Baylor University Press.

Kraemer, David. 2007. *Jewish Eating and Identity through the Ages*. New York: Routledge.

———. 2010. "Food, Eating, and Meals." Pages 403–19 in *The Oxford Handbook of Jewish Daily Life in Roman Palestine*. Edited by Catherine Hezser. Oxford: Oxford University Press.

Kraemer, Ross Shepard. 2011. *Unreliable Witnesses: Religion, Gender, and History in the Greco-Roman Mediterranean*. New York: Oxford University Press.

Levine, Lee I. 2005. *The Ancient Synagogue: The First Thousand Years*. 2nd ed. New Haven: Yale University Press.

Lev-Tov, Justin. 2003. "'Upon What Meat Doth This Our Caesar Feed . . . ?' A Dietary Perspective on Hellenistic and Roman Influence in Palestine." Pages 420–46 in *Zeichen aus Text und Stein: Studien auf dem Weg zu einer Archäologie des Neuen Testaments*. Edited by S. Alkier and J. K. Zangenberg. TANZ 42. Tübingen: Francke.

Luz, Ulrich. 2005. *Matthew 21–28*. Translated by James E. Crouch. Hermeneia. Minneapolis: Fortress.

Neyrey, Jerome H. 1991. "Ceremonies in Luke-Acts: The Case of Meals and Table Fellowship." Pages 361–87 in *The Social World of Luke-Acts: Models for Interpretation*. Edited by Jerome H. Neyrey. Peabody, MA: Hendrickson.

———. 1996. "Meals, Food, and Table Fellowship." Pages 159–82 in *The Social Sciences and New Testament Interpretation*. Edited by Richard L. Rohrbaugh. Peabody, MA: Hendrickson.

Pilch, John. 1993. "The Necessities of Life: Drinking and Eating." *TBT* 31:231–37.

Regev, Eyal. 2013. *The Hasmoneans: Ideology, Archaeology, Identity*. Göttingen: Vandenhoeck & Ruprecht.

Rosenblum, Jordan D. 2015. "Jewish Meals in Antiquity." Pages 348–56 in *A Companion to Food in the Ancient World*. Edited by John Wilkins and Robin Nadeau. Oxford: Wiley Blackwell.

Sanders, E. P. 2016. *Judaism: Practice and Belief, 63 BCE–66 CE*. Minneapolis: Fortress.

Schrader, Elizabeth, and Joan E. Taylor. 2021. "The Meaning of 'Magdalene': A Review of Literary Evidence." *JBL* 140:751–73.

Smith, Dennis E. 2003. *From Symposium to Eucharist: The Banquet in the Early Christian World*. Minneapolis: Fortress.

Smith, Dennis E., and Hal Taussig, eds. 2012. *Meals in the Early Christian World: Social Formation, Experimentation, and Conflict at the Table*. New York: Palgrave Macmillan.

Stählin, Gustav. "*phileō*." *TDNT* 9:113–71.

Standhartinger, Angela. 2012. "Women in Early Christian Meal Gatherings." Pages 87–108 in *Meals in the Early Christian World: Social Formation, Experimentation, and Conflict at the Table*. New York: Palgrave Macmillan.

Taussig, Hal E. 2009. *In the Beginning Was the Meal: Social Experimentation and Early Christian Identity*. Minneapolis: Fortress.

Walsh, Robyn Faith. 2021. *The Origins of Early Christian Literature: Contextualizing the New Testament within Greco-Roman Literary Culture*. Cambridge: Cambridge University Press.

Part III

Galilean Society

Chapter 9

Landowners, Tenants, Stewards, Day Laborers, and Debtors

Planted Weeds (Matt 13:24–30)
Unmerciful Servant (Matt 18:23–34)
Vineyard Laborers (Matt 20:1–15)
Tenants (Matt 21:33–43)
Wise and Wicked Servant (Matt 24:45–51)
Talents (Matt 25:14–30)
Rich Farmer (Luke 12:16b–20)
Tower Builder (Luke 14:28–30)
Unjust Steward (Luke 16:1–7)

*J*esus' parables feature occupations and roles that were common in first-century Galilee. Since Galilee was predominantly rural and agrarian, in this chapter we will start with the landowners and those they employed, then farmers and fishermen in following chapters.

The parables tell us a great deal about Galilean society, but they also presume knowledge of a society and an economy about which we have only fragmentary and tantalizing data. Landowners might own grain-fields as well as olive groves and vineyards (Deut 8:8). Jesus tells stories about all three, although olives and olive oil appear in the Gospels only in the parable of the unjust steward (Luke 16:6) and references to the Mount of Olives. The principal agricultural activities of sowing and reaping, "seedtime and harvest" (Gen 8:22), will be treated in detail in the next chapter. Here our interest focuses on the householder who has an enemy (Matt 13:24–30), the vineyard owner who leases his vineyard to tenants (21:33–43), and the vineyard owner who employs day laborers (20:1–15). Landowners often employed a steward or manager (an *epitropos*, Matt 20:8; or *oikonomos*, Luke 16:1) to manage their fields and vineyards. These parables tease us to learn more about the status, roles, and attitudes toward each of these common figures in Galilean society: the landowners, stewards, day laborers, and slaves. The last are treated in chapter 14 (below).

Were the landowners Galileans or foreigners? How did they get to be landowners? What contractual arrangements did they make with tenants? Why did some landowners engage tenants, while others had slaves? And what characterized the relationships between the laborers and the landowners? To address these specific questions, some understanding of Galilean economy, the production and marketing of goods, is essential.

9.1 Galilee's Agrarian Economy

By the first century, the Galilean economy was a mix of household and village subsistence, village and city networks, and Herodian administration and taxation. The basic units were households, most of which struggled to provide for their basic needs at a subsistence level. The villages, the diversity of crops and trades, and the village ethic all provided "safety valves" in times of drought or crisis (Moreland). Households and extended families collaborated. If they owned a small parcel of land, they struggled to maintain it, producing their own food, making their tools, and weaving their clothes, while paying their taxes and debts and setting aside seed for the next year. Many of these households could not make it without another source of income, so they worked as tenants or day laborers, especially in harvest season. They lived in the villages and tended the nearby fields, groves, and vineyards. Artisans (masons, carpenters, potters, and weavers) and merchants supplied items the households could not produce themselves.

Under Herod Antipas (4 BCE–39 CE), Galilee was relatively prosperous. Excavations in Yodefat, Gamla, Cana, and elsewhere give evidence of social stratigraphy and local industries (olive pressing, wine making, pottery, and weaving). Clusters of the better houses of the local elite have been found, for example, at Capernaum (Mattila, 244–45), Yodefat (Aviam 2015, 114–15), Cana (McCollough, 137–38), and Magdala (Fiensy 2020, 67). Villages were largely self-sufficient (Oakman 2008, 101), while specializing in diverse products that would be sold in surrounding towns and cities: wheat from Arbela, Kefar Hittaia (Village of Wheat), and Huqoq; pottery production from Kefar Hananya, Shikhin, and Nahaf; pottery and olive oil production at Yodefat (Aviam 2013, 26–28); and fish processing at Magdala (Taricheae; see below, 11.5). The density of villages in Galilee allowed one to reach as many as forty of them in a day's travel (Strange, 42). Locally produced pottery was sold throughout upper and lower Galilee. In short, "there was a highly developed, local trade network in Galilee upon which the citizens of Galilee transported goods and services from village to village, to town, to cities, and vice-versa" (Strange, 39–41).

Most of the trade and commerce in Galilee was local; yet grain, olive oil, wine, and salted fish were transported to the coast (Acts 12:20; Josephus, *J.W.* 2.591–592; *Life* 74–76; see Harland, 518–20; Root, 21–22). The export of olive oil was an important element in Galilee's economy. In return, Galilee imported Egyptian grain in times of famine (Josephus, *Ant.* 20.51–52; as in 46/47 CE) as well as glazed pottery, fine linens, and metals.

Nevertheless, prosperity was not uniform: the structures of landownership (tending toward latifundia in certain areas; see below, 9.3), heavy taxation, and debt ensured that wealth was extracted from the farmers and artisans and flowed into the hands of the elite. Josephus recalls the envoy of Jews who petitioned Caesar to end the rule of the Herodians. They charged that Herod

> had not ceased to adorn neighboring cities that were inhabited by foreigners although this led to the ruin and disappearance of cities [villages] located in his own kingdom. He had indeed reduced the entire nation to helpless poverty after taking it over in as flourishing a condition as few ever know, and he was wont to kill members of the nobility upon absurd pretexts and then take their property for himself. . . . In addition to the collecting of tribute that was imposed on everyone each year, lavish contributions had to be made to him and his household and friends and those of his slaves who were sent out to collect the tribute because there was no immunity at all from outrage unless bribes were paid. (Ant. 17.306, 308)

Given these conditions, about 90 percent of the population of Galilee lived at or near subsistence level, with the dominant economy stacked against them (Fiensy 1991, 155–70; Harland, 515; Magness, 13–14).

9.2 Friesen's Poverty Scale

In 2004, as a contribution to scholarship on the Pauline churches, Steven Friesen (341) proposed the following "poverty scale [PS]," with seven levels (PS 1–7) for urban centers in the Roman Empire.

Figure 2

PS1 Imperial elites	imperial dynasty, Roman senatorial families, a few retainers, local royalty, a few freedpersons
PS2 Regional or provincial elites	equestrian [one rank below senators] families, provincial officials, some retainers, some decurial [military officers over a unit of ten] families, some freedpersons, some retired military officers
PS3 Municipal elites	most decurial families, wealthy men and women who do not hold office, some freedpersons, some retainers, some veterans, some merchants
PS4 Moderate surplus resources	some merchants, some traders, some freedpersons, some artisans (especially those who employ others), and military veterans
PS5 Stable near subsistence level	many merchants and traders, regular wage earners, artisans (with reasonable hope of large shop owners), freedpersons, some farm families remaining above the minimum level to sustain life
PS6 At subsistence level (and often below minimum level to sustain life)	small farm families, laborers (skilled and unskilled), artisans (esp. those employed by others), wage earners, most merchants and traders, small shop/tavern owners
PS7 Below subsistence level	some farm families, unattached widows, orphans, beggars, disabled, unskilled day laborers, prisoners

Friesen (347) estimates the following distribution in Roman cities, recognizing that the estimates for PS4 and PS5 are speculative.

Figure 3

PS1	Imperial elites	0.04%
PS2	Regional elites	1.00%
PS3	Municipal elites	1.76%
PS4	Moderate surplus	7%?
PS5	Stable near subsistence	22%?
PS6	At subsistence	40%
PS7	Below subsistence	28%

Friesen's poverty scale can be adapted for our purposes, but some changes are necessary. Based on the archaeological data, Fiensy advises that "the extreme distance between the elites and the lower class, found elsewhere in the Roman Empire and even in Jerusalem, was diminished in Galilee" (2020, 44). The agrarian base of the Galilean economy, the olive oil and other industries, and the predominance of villages over cities in the region meant that "the standard of living was undoubtedly much higher than has been generally assumed" (Safrai 1994, 126). Safrai's judgment probably assumes closer connections to the land and to one's family in villages. Some landowners (such as Babatha; see 7.8 above) were relatively wealthy (Esler, 80–82).

Early first-century Galilee had few if any imperial elites (PS1) beyond the Herodian household, and they would have been clustered in Sepphoris and later in Tiberias. Among the regional elites (PS2), we can identify the "high officials and military commanders and the leading men of Galilee" (Mark 6:21 NIV) who were invited to Herod Antipas's birthday celebration. Josephus dined with "the chief men of Galilee" (*Life* 220; see also 266, 305). Municipal elites (PS 3) lived in the fine houses in Sepphoris, Tiberias, Magdala, and Yodefat. Friesen's estimates of about 3 percent for the top three levels and 7 percent for PS 4, households with "moderate surplus resources," seem about right for Galilee, although there may have been more PS 4 households in Galilee than in the urban centers of the Roman Empire as a whole. Patronage, practiced at least among the elite, conveyed status to the patron and benefits to the client. Perhaps as a result, there were no major class conflicts in Galilee during this period: "Instead of turning on the upper classes, the Galilean masses backed their local elites fiercely" (Root, 33; cf. Overman).

Most households in rural Roman Palestine maintained a subsistence-level existence (Killebrew, 200), subject to droughts, famines, and the constant pressure of taxes and debts. Even small landholders were vulnerable to the loss of their holdings. Since landownership was the key to wealth, loss of land often initiated one into the fellowship of the destitute. The majority of the population in Galilee, even if not as many as Friesen estimates, belonged to the bottom three levels. Distinctions in status were readily apparent. The rich had fine clothes and changes of clothing (Jas 2:2–4).

> Poor people, on the contrary, had a single set of cheaper clothing that they could shorten for work, since a long mantle and tunic would have impeded movement. Long tunics and ample mantles, which were normally made of high quality wool, sometimes linen, enhanced the social status of elites who didn't need to do physical work. . . . The absence of stripes [adornments] was characteristic of the clothing of slaves and people of menial occupations. (Hamel 2010, 318)

Poor people wore clothing that had not been dyed, black or brown clothing in its natural color: "The widow of Zarephath is also represented at Dura-Europos as wearing a brown *himation* [cloak]: this was perhaps the customary dress for widows; and it may have helped Elijah recognize her" (Hamel 1989, 87). A poor man's cloak was his most valuable possession. It may have been the only cloak in his household, which also served as a blanket at night for two people or a parent and small children (cf. Exod 22:26–27). Yet the cloak could be stolen by bandits or taken to pay a debt (Luke 10:30; m. B. Qam. 10:2; Hamel 1989, 71).

The economic realities become apparent when one begins to calculate the amount of land needed to sustain a person, which Oakman estimates to be 1.5 acres, with another 1.5 acres lying fallow each year, and an annual seed-to-yield ratio of 1:5 (see 10.2, below). On this basis, one-fifth of each harvest had to be put aside as seed for the next year. Years with low yields could have devastating consequences.

> If the yield was low, 1:3 for instance, one-third of the harvest would have to be put aside as seed for the following year and between one-quarter and one-third for various taxes, tolls, and tithes, leaving about one-third for subsistence. This also meant that a large part of the land and of human and animal energies were reserved simply to renew the seed. But if the average yield was higher, 1:8 for instance, the farmer had more possibilities: he could decrease the surfaces devoted to cereals or feed more people and more animals, which also meant more manure and more haulage power. (Hamel 1989, 134)

Some of the harvest would also have been needed for bartering and purchasing necessary goods, fodder for the livestock, and taxes (Oakman 1986, 61–66; Harland, 522). Rent owed to a landowner was typically a third to a half of the harvest after the payment of fees, seed, and other costs. Taxes can be calculated at 28 percent (see below on vineyard leases, 9.3 and 9.5; on taxation, ch. 15).

Martin Goodman (1987, 62) describes the situation of those struggling to survive: "The spark which set off each family's crisis came probably either from the effect of a bad year and the prospect of immediate starvation or from the death of the farm's owner and the prospect of dividing up the plot between his heirs, usually his sons." The new landowners in turn reduced the number of tenants to the smallest number to increase their own profits. The result was a grim struggle for subsistence, hard agrarian labor, heavy taxation, and recurring conflict between laborers and landlords.

The bottom echelon, those who could not maintain a subsistence level of "daily bread," had to rely on charity—an important element of Jewish piety. Harvest was left for the poor and the aliens along the edges of fields (Lev 19:9–10); part of the tithes were set aside for the Levites and the poor (Deut 14:27–29; Tob 1:3, 8; Sir 4:1, 8–10; 7:32; 29:9; Gal 2:10; see below, 15.2–3). Giving to the poor in Jerusalem at the religious festivals was especially meritorious (Mark 12:41–43; John 13:29). Synagogues provided charity (Ryan, 48; Levine, 144), and Sirach comments that one's acts of charity will be proclaimed in the synagogue (31:11). At least from later Roman and Byzantine periods, treasuries of small coins, no doubt intended for the poor, have been found in synagogues (Hamel 2010, 320). The Essenes also gave regularly to provide for the needy, including orphans, the elderly, vagabonds, prisoners, and girls and women with no protectors (CD XIV, 12–16).

9.3 Landowners

Conquered land passed from royal domains to army veterans and other beneficiaries. Although tenancy can be traced back to the Iron Age, the system of absentee landlords and stewards or managers spread in the time of the Ptolemies (see Kloppenborg, 290–95; Keddie, 73–75). Antiochus IV (ca. 215–163 BCE) converted Judea into royal settlements (*katoikiai*, 1 Macc 3:36). One of the first large estate owners in Galilee was the governor, or *strategos*, appointed by Antiochus III "the Great" (223–187 BCE), a man named Ptolemaios, who owned several villages and had jurisdiction over others (Keddie, 27). A set of Greek inscriptions discovered at Hefzibah in the Bet She'an Valley contains correspondence between Antiochus III and Ptolemaios, which Strange summarizes: "It seems that the villagers worked his land and lived upon it in villages[,] which he owned in fee simple" (46). Herod seized Hasmonean lands and gave land to his supporters, including high-priestly families, thereby increasing landownership among the Herodian elites (Fiensy 1991, 28–30; Keddie, 87–88, 92).

Villas with large dwellings on the estates of wealthy landowners are rare in Roman Palestine (Killebrew, 195; Keddie, 65–70). The extent of large estates (over 315 acres) in Galilee is debated (Applebaum, 633–38; Udoh, 382). Nevertheless, large estates occupied the best land (Jensen, 56), including the Plain of Esdraelon (Jezreel Valley), where Agrippa II's wife, Berenice, owned estates (Josephus, *Life* 118–119; Keddie, 92), and the Plain of Bet She'an (Fiensy 1991, 55–60; Fiensy 2012). Most of the royal estates, however, were in Judea, the coastal plain, Samaria, and around Jericho (Dar, 307–8). The number of winepresses found on the Plain of Esdraelon suggests that it was an area of large-scale wine production (Fiensy 2012, 138). Medium-sized estates (50–315 acres) have been identified in the Beit Netofa Valley, north of Nazareth. These estates were probably owned by the elite of Sepphoris, one of whom was Eleazar ben Harsom (1st c. CE), according to rabbinic sources (Lam. Rab. 2:2, y. Ta'an. 4.5, 69a). Luke 16:1–7 refers to debts of 100 measures of oil and 100 measures of wheat, which would have required a medium-sized estate to produce, comprising 160 olive trees and 40 acres of wheat (Fiensy 2012, 134, citing Herz).

The number of villages spread across Galilee confirms that land was still owned by villagers (Harland, 515; Killebrew, 201). Elite landowners typically owned scattered plots rather than large single holdings (Safrai 2010, 250) because this made it easier to recruit labor, while diminishing the risk of catastrophe from fires, droughts, and wars. Landowners were advised to divide their investments among the three principal crops—grain, olives, and grapes—so that a bad year for one would not ruin them (b. B. Meṣ. 107a). Most wealthy elites were landowners (Fiensy 2012, 134). Michael Wise (309–11) has correlated the literate signatories to the Babatha documents with the landowners. Scribes, Pharisees, and priests who were literate in Hebrew constituted a second level of elites. Landowners in Galilee no doubt included such professionals also.

The system of leasing and tenancy grew over the two centuries prior to the Common Era. The landless and small landholders found employment as tenants; estate holders could receive half or more of the harvest with minimal supervision or risk: "The landlord could not lose in such a system" (Kloppenborg, 306). Lease contracts provided stability for both parties since they were normally drawn up for two or three years or longer (307). While lease contracts have not been found in Galilee, Kloppenborg (355–549) collected fifty-eight papyrus texts dealing with vineyard leasing and operations. Not included in this collection is P.Yale 237, a contract for the lease of land in Egypt that can be dated to April 11, 184 BCE, in which Petebenetitis, a desert-guard, leases land to two tenants. The contract specifies the payment of grain and the consequences for failure to pay. The tenants, Agathokles and Herakles, will pay rents

> yearly at the end of the year or whenever the release of the crop is granted, as grain, new, clean, and unadulterated, by just measure and with just measurement, bringing it at their own expense to Kerkesoucha wherever Petebentetis shall decide, and if they do not pay the grain as it is written above, let Agathokles and Herakles pay to Petebentetis for each artab for which they do not pay [*X*] drachmas of bronze money or whatever is the greatest fine in . . . Petebentetis shall control the crop until he gets the rent. (Oates, Samuel, and Welles, 148)

The contracts Kloppenborg collected from Egyptian papyri prescribe various rates for splitting the harvest between the lessee and the lessor: (1) half and half: "sometimes for vineyards, more commonly for other crops"; (2) one-quarter to lessee, three-quarters to lessor: the least common rate, attested only once before the fifth century CE; (3) one-third to lessee, two-thirds to lessor: "a standard rental for vineyards" (Kloppenborg, 581, 292–94). Contrary to common exegesis of the parable of the tenants, Kloppenborg finds "no evidence at all" of foreign absentee vineyard owners (316). Most vineyard owners lived near their vineyards so that they could visit them when necessary. Josephus reports that Crispus, for example, lived in Tiberias and had estates in the Transjordan (*Life* 33).

Given the constant struggle for subsistence and the thin profit margins for laborers and small landholders, debt was a pervasive reality. Laborers commonly owed landholders not only the lessor's share of the harvest but also payment on their debt and interest. The standard rate of interest was 12 percent (P.Yad. 11 and 15; Broshi, 239–40), but P.Mur. 18 (55–56 CE) specifies a rate of 20 percent. If one died before repaying a loan, the debt passed to his descendants.

Yet, there was little commonly accepted warrant for such a system: "No ties of loyalty, no feudal oath, no sanction of long custom existed to coax the tenant into believing that his payment of rent to his supervisor was part of the natural order of things; on the contrary the peasant will have known that the divinely ordained ideal in the Torah required each man to own his own land as a free and equal citizen (cf. Micah 4:4, etc.)" (Goodman 1987, 67).

The distinction between landowners, tenants, and day laborers probably obscures the reality that many farmers of small plots could not live on the harvest they generated and therefore supplemented their income by working as artisans or as tenants or day laborers for large landowners. In addition, "It was not uncommon for landowners to lease some properties, or for tenants to own some land" (Keddie, 100). James F. Strange comments, "This fact of life appears to have forced a diversification in social role that remains largely unrecognized in modern scholarship" (46).

9.4 Managers

Managers (*oikonomoi* or *epitropoi*) appear in Jesus' parables as working harmoniously with the master (Matt 20:1–15 par.) and working surreptitiously for their own advantage in the parable of the unjust steward (Luke 16:1–7; see below, ch. 14). The wicked slave who beats his fellow slaves and eats and drinks with drunkards will be severely punished, but the slave who proves worthy will be put in charge of the master's household, "to give the other slaves their allowance of food at the proper time" (Matt 24:45).

Columella (1st c. CE) describes the qualifications he sought in a manager.

> A man should be chosen who has been hardened by farm work from his infancy, one who has been tested by experience. If, however, such a person is not available, let one be put in charge out of the number of those who have slaved patiently at hard labour; and he should already have passed beyond the time of young manhood but not yet have arrived at that of old age, that youth may not lessen his authority to command, seeing that older men think it beneath them to take orders from a mere stripling, and that old age may not break down under the heaviest labour. He should be, then, of middle age and of strong physique, skilled in farm operations or at least very painstaking, so that he may learn the more readily; for it is not in keeping with this business of ours for one man to give orders and another to give instructions, nor can a man properly exact work when he is being tutored by an underling as to what is to be done and in what way. Even an illiterate person, if only he [has] a retentive mind, can manage affairs well enough. Cornelius Celsus says that an overseer of this sort brings money to his master oftener than he does his [own] book, because, not knowing his letters, he is either less able to falsify accounts or is afraid to do so through a second party because that would make another aware of the deception. (*Rust.* 1.8.2–4)

Managers were usually slaves, probably even in Galilee, where large landowners generally employed local tenants and day laborers. The harvest saying in Luke 10:2 seems to have in view a large estate for which the "Lord of the harvest" may be either the owner or the manager (Howes,

60–62). Columella adds that the manager or overseer should be industrious, not given to "the voluptuous occupations of the city" (*Rust.* 1.8.1) and be circumspect around women. Preferably he should have a female companion. He should have "no acquaintance with the city or with the weekly market, except to make purchases and sales in connection with his duties" (1.8.6), which included care of the equipment and tools and keeping on hand twice as many tools as the number of workers so there would be no interruption in the work (1.8.8). The overseer should also "exercise authority without laxness and without cruelty," humoring the better hands and forbearing the lesser ones, "so that they may rather fear his sternness than detest his cruelty" (1.8.10). The overseer should not conduct any business of his own or invest the master's funds, as this would distract him from his duties and prevent him from balancing his accounts with the master (1.8.13).

Varro (116–27 BCE) benevolently cultivated and motivated his managers.

> The foremen are to be made more zealous by rewards, and care must be taken that they have a bit of property of their own, and mates from among their fellow-slaves to bear them children; for by this means they are made more steady and more attached to the place. . . . The good will of the foremen should be won by treating them with some degree of consideration; and those of the hands who excel the others should also be consulted as to the work to be done. (*Rust.* 1.17.5–6)

A third-century papyrus text provides another glimpse into the relationship between manager and landowner: "To my lord Theon, from Hebdomus, greetings. I am sending you a record of the daily account of expenses for your inspection. If it meets your approval, my lord, please send me money for the ongoing farming labors and other business for which I am responsible. Also, I do not see any culpability on my part concerning the wine collection about which you wrote me" (P.Oxy. 9.1220.1–12; Sterling and Paffenroth). Clearly, a landowner's life could be made easier by a good steward or complicated by a bad one!

9.5 Tenants

Most tenants were local villagers who could not support themselves by other means. The landowner provided the land, the necessary tools and equipment, and the draft animals. There were two kinds of leases: fixed-rent leases and crop-share leases (Keddie, 98–99). In the former, the tenant assumed greater risk in case of crop failure but stood to gain more in the event of a bountiful harvest, while the landowner accepted greater risks in the latter and therefore exercised closer supervision, especially at harvest-time (Kloppenborg, 292–94, 312). Jesus' parable in Mark 12:1–9 clearly assumes a crop-share agreement since the owner sends his agents to collect his share of the harvest. Tenants and landowners negotiated the obligations and risks of each partner, "including resources such as seed, labor, draft animals, farming tools and equipment, and labor, as well as whether to diversify crops to increase profit" (Keddie, 100).

Columella asserts that the ideal arrangement involves long-term, local tenants who are good farmers.

> Furthermore, I myself remember having heard Publius Volusius, an old man who had been consul and was very wealthy, declare that estate most fortunate which had as tenants natives of the place, and held them, by reason of long association, even from the cradle, as if born on their own father's property. So I am decidedly of the opinion that repeated letting of a place is a bad thing, but that a worse thing is the farmer who lives in town and prefers to till the land through his slaves rather than by his own hand. Saserna used to say that from a man of this sort the return was usually a lawsuit instead of revenue, and that for this reason we should take pains to keep with us tenants who are country-bred and at the same time diligent farmers, when we are not at liberty to till the land ourselves or when it is not feasible to cultivate it with our own servants. (*Rust.* 1.7.3–4)

Free farmers are better than slaves and slave overseers, who are less likely to care for the land and the animals and more likely to cheat and steal from the owner.

> On far distant estates, however, which it is not easy for the owner to visit, it is better for every kind of land to be under free farmers than under slave overseers, but this is particularly true of grain land. To such land a tenant farmer can do no great harm, as he can to plantations of vines and trees, while slaves do it tremendous damage: they let out oxen for hire, and keep them and other animals poorly fed; they do not plough the ground carefully, and they charge up the sowing of far more seed than they have actually sown; what they have committed to the earth they do not so foster that it will make the proper growth; and when they have brought it to the threshing-floor, every day during the threshing they lessen the amount either by trickery or by carelessness. For they themselves steal it and do not guard against the thieving of others, and even when it is stored away they do not enter it honestly in their accounts. (Columella, *Rust.* 1.7.6–7)

Clearly, a lot depended on the quality of laborers a landowner could hire.

9.6 Day Laborers

Day laborers constituted the most exposed and dependent stratum of the agrarian labor force, hoping for work each day. They were also assigned harder labor than slaves, who were a valuable commodity (Varro, *Rust.* 1.17.3; Howes, 71). Generally, there was a constant need for laborers for "periodic tasks such as clearing brushwood, weeding, burning weeds, hoeing and pruning." "Viticulture was the most labour-intensive of ancient agricultural pursuits, requiring three times as many workers as olive cultivation and four times as many workers as cereal and vegetable crops" (Kloppenborg, 287–88). The demand for laborers doubled during the harvest season. As Jesus observed, "The harvest is plentiful, but the laborers are few" (Matt 9:37). Nevertheless, agricultural work was physically demanding (Sir 38:24–26), and the specter of unemployment was never far away (Josephus, *Ant.* 20.219–220).

Laborers contracted for the work they would do (Howes, 64) and were paid at the end of the day, so they would be able to feed their families that day (Lev 19:13; Deut 24:14–15). The parable in Matthew 20:1–16 records that the day laborers were paid a denarius (see Tob 5:15), a silver Roman coin bearing the image of the emperor. Douglas Oakman calculated the value of a denarius by collecting references to the prices of various food items. A denarius would buy around four and one-half pounds of wheat (.375 bushels), which would feed an average person for about ten days. One denarius might also purchase four liters of wine, two to forty liters of olive oil, or 190–640 figs (depending upon whether these items were plentiful or scarce). A denarius would feed a family of two adults with probably a minimum of four children for three to six days (Oakman 2008, 43–44; Fiensy 2020, 172–75). Of course, part of a day's wage would go to pay the laborer's taxes and debt.

Life was hard for day laborers, and it took its toll even on their bones. The hands and feet of a man who only lived to be twenty-two, buried at Qumran, are thick and gnarled, reflecting a life of walking barefoot and doing heavy labor. Another skeleton recovered at Qumran has deformities of the shoulders and legs, probably caused by carrying heavy loads (Fiensy 2020, 191). For them, Jesus' invitation, "Come to me, all you that are weary and are carrying heavy burdens, and I will give you rest" (Matt 11:28), would have been scarcely imaginable.

9.7 Debtors

Debtors and the effects of debt are considered here not because they are limited to day laborers or the poor but because they are closely associated with wealthy lenders, who were usually landowners; many tenants and day laborers were also debtors. Those of moderate wealth were often debtors also. As Clifton Black observed, in the first century, indebtedness "was serious for many, incendiary for a few" (175).

The attention given to debt in the Mosaic law suggests its pervasiveness and its potential for social disruption. Early Israelite law imposed limitations on the purchase of a Hebrew slave and the sale of one's daughter (Exod 21:2–11). One could lend money to a fellow Israelite, but not at interest (22:25); if one took another's cloak as security, he had to return it by sundown (22:26). Nehemiah addressed the effects of debt during a famine. Some complained, "We are having to pledge our fields, our vineyards, and our houses in order to get grain during the famine"; others said, "We are having to borrow money on our fields and vineyards to pay the king's tax" (Neh 5:3–4). Lenders charged interest, forced debtors to sell their sons and daughters into slavery, and confiscated the debtors' fields and vineyards (Neh 5:5, 7; Ezek 18:16–18). The prophets railed against such outrages. Some Israelites even took infants as a pledge (Job 24:9). The needy were sold for a pair of sandals, young girls were ravished, and garments taken from the poor were deposited in sanctuaries (Amos 2:6–8). As a result, measures were adopted to address these abuses. Debts had to be remitted every seventh year (Deut 15:1–2); a Hebrew slave had to be freed in the seventh year and compensated generously (15:12–14). Israelites were forbidden to charge interest to other Israelites (Exod 22:25; Lev 25:36–37; Deut 23:19, 30). Anyone who embraced the law had to be generous to the needy and cancel debts in the seventh year (4 Macc 2:8).

We do not know how many Jews observed the Year of Jubilee in canceling debts. The Sabbatical Year appears to have been "largely ignored" (Fiensy 1991, 6; Safrai 2003, 107; cf. Lev 26:34–35; 2 Chr 36:21; 1 Esd 1:58). Nevertheless, to make it easier for borrowers to secure loans, Hillel (1st c. BCE) established the *prozbul*, a legal declaration that a loan will not be canceled during the seventh year, the Sabbatical Year, when he saw that lenders refrained from giving loans and borrowers defrauded lenders (m. Sheb. 10:3–4). At the same time, the *prozbul* effectively annulled the Deuteronomic law that periodically relieved the poor of their debts, ensuring that the lenders would be repaid (see Oakman 2008, 139). A contract of indebtedness found at Wadi Muraba'at (P.Mur. 18, dated 56 CE) declares, "I will reimburse you with (interest of) a fifth and will settle in en[tirety], even if this is the Year of Release" (Fitzmyer and Harrington, 139).

Debt was common even among the prosperous; when debtors could not repay their debt, the creditor could seize the debtor's property. The elites also encroached on small landowners and seized land by intimidation and violence (Fiensy 1991, 78–79). In 43 CE, two Judeans were indebted to one 'Isimilk son of 'Abdai for the equivalent of 1600 denarii, with interest. When they could not repay the loan, 'Isimilk seized property equivalent to their debt. Years later, their heir, 'Ele'azar, repaid the loan and recovered the land (P.XHev/Se Nab 1, also known as Papyrus Starcky; Yardeni, 126–28; Esler, 81).

When Babatha's second husband died, owing her 700 denarii, she seized some of his date orchards to recoup that loan (P.Yad. 21 and 22). Babatha also sued her son's guardians, complaining that they were only paying her 6 percent per annum when she could earn 9 percent. Moreover, her second husband had borrowed 60 denarii from a Roman centurion (P.Yad. 11) at the maximum rate allowed by Roman law: 12 percent (Esler, 85).

When the harvest was lean and laborers could not pay their debts, landowners faced the alternative of exacting payment and thereby displacing their laborers or abating the debts. Because the latter "ensured for landowners the grateful return of labour," the most profitable course was one of "steep rents, indebtedness, and enlightened benevolence" (Hamel 2010, 314). Pliny the Younger illustrates this dynamic: "The farms I own in the district bring in more than 400,000 sesterces, and I cannot postpone letting them, especially as the new tenants should be there to see to the pruning of the vines, and this must be done soon. Moreover, the series of bad harvests we have had are forcing me to consider reducing rents, and I cannot calculate these unless I am on the spot" (*Ep.* 10.8). Pliny judged each debtor according to how much of their debt they had repaid: "I thought it most unfair to treat them all with the same generosity in granting a rebate when they had not been equally conscientious in discharging their debts. . . . This seemed a suitable way both of expressing my gratitude, to each individual according to his past merits, and of encouraging them all not only to buy from me in the future but also to pay their debts. My system—or my good nature—has cost me a lot, but it has been worth it" (*Ep.* 8.2.7–8).

In another letter, Pliny laments, "The last owner on more than one occasion sold the tenants' possessions, so that he temporarily reduced their arrears but weakened their resources for the future, and consequently their debts mounted up again" (*Ep.* 3.19; see also m. B. Meṣ. 5:8; Goodrich, 555–59). Columella, a first-century farmer, also counseled restraint and benevolence, saying that the master "should be civil in dealing with his tenants, should show himself affable, and should be more exacting in the matter of work than of payments, as this gives less offence yet is, generally speaking, more profitable" (*Rust.* 1.7.1). Goodrich argues that the unjust steward in Jesus' parable (Luke 16:1–13) shrewdly and with no dishonesty grants partial remission of debts, exercising his power as a steward, and thereby fosters praise from his master and hospitality for himself should he need it (563–65).

Some estate owners were not so accommodating. Citing rabbinic sources (t. B. Meṣ 6.15; b. B. Bat. 87a), Fiensy (1991, 87) says, "There is good evidence that the workers were defrauded at every opportunity." Over time, more small holders lost their land. Landlessness grew, while landownership was concentrated in the hands of fewer and fewer landowners (Oakman 2008, 24–25). Conditions were similar in Egypt, where papyri reveal that a peasant named Kronion (ca. 100 CE) "and his likes were chronically short of cash and constantly going into short-term debt. It is thus no accident that nineteen of the sixty-nine documents in the Kronion archive relate to loans" (Lewis, 71, cited by Hanson and Oakman, 112).

Taxes placed a further burden on the Galilean villagers (see ch. 15 below) and periodically fueled outbreaks of violence. Seleucid taxation, the underlying reason for Antiochus IV's demand for idolatrous sacrifices as demonstrations of loyalty, led to the Maccabean Revolt (167–164 BCE). Roman taxation was imposed by Pompey (63 BCE), which contributed to the revolt of Judas the Galilean (6 CE) and ultimately the Jewish Revolt of 66–70 (Goodman 1982; Goodman 1987; Richardson and Edwards). The economy in Roman Palestine was therefore stacked against the Galilean farmer and artisans. The increase in monetization, suggested by the number of coins recovered from the Hasmonean period, made the collection of taxes easier, contributed to hoarding, and aggravated the situation of the poor, while it invigorated commerce (Keddie, 32). Debt and taxes added to the often-unmanageable burden on subsistence farmers, while wealth was extracted by the elite landowners, the high priests in Jerusalem, the Romans, and their Herodian vassals. No one missed the point of Jesus' proverb, "I tell you, to all those who have, more will be given, but from those who have nothing, even what they have will be taken away" (Mark 4:25//Luke 19:26).

In such circumstances, paradise meant sufficient sustenance without work or worry. Loss of paradise meant painful work (Gen 3:17, 23). Regaining paradise would mean deliverance from worry about sustenance (Hamel 1989, 161–62). "Therefore I tell you, do not worry about your life, what you will eat or what you will drink, or about your body, what you will wear. Is not life more than food, and the body more than clothing? Look at the birds of the air; they neither sow nor reap nor gather into barns, and yet your heavenly Father feeds them. Are you not of more value than they?" (Matt 6:25–26).

9.8 Reflections

The sheer number of parables that feature the economic conditions and the familiar roles we have surveyed in this chapter show that Jesus exposed the political and economic system to prophetic criticism, while announcing the coming of divine justice and judgment in the kingdom of God. Wealth was closely tied to owning land. Local elites collected plots of land and employed tenants to farm them and return the lion's share of the yield to the landowner. Tenants and small farmers struggled to produce enough to sustain their families while letting half of their land lie fallow each year to ensure that it was not depleted, putting aside seed for the coming year, feeding their livestock, and paying their tithe(s), rent, and debts. Those who could not make it eventually lost their land, and their situation became even more desperate.

Assigning the characters of Jesus' parables to one of the categories in Friesen's poverty scale (discussed above, 9.2) is admittedly an exercise in generalizing and recognizing stereotypes. Nevertheless, this exercise highlights their social and economic status. The characters generally play their expected roles, but sometimes with a twist that calls the audience to reassess the prevailing economic system. Although the imbalance of wealth and poverty in the parables reflects Jesus' setting, it also provides context for Jesus' critique of the economic practices of his day. The parables represent identities, roles, and actions that hearers could identify, not the composition of Jesus' audiences. The following assignments also reflect the judgment that Galilean villagers were often better off than the majority of the (landless) poor in the Roman urban settings that Friesen studied. Many of the assignments can slide up or down a category.

In this analysis the imperial elites (PS1) may be represented by kings, who dispense a form of justice. The king in the parable of the unforgiving servant is initially merciful but then imposes a stern judgment. The king in the parable of the wedding banquet similarly excludes those who rebuff his invitation and throws out the guest without a wedding garment. The king who judges the sheep and the goats, a Davidic shepherd king, also imposes judgment for what his people have done and what they have failed to do. The king going to war prudently calculates what he needs to do.

The regional and municipal elites (PS2 and PS3) have resources to assign. The king in Matthew 18:23–34 lends his servant the enormous sum of ten thousand talents, and the servant lends a hundred denarii to a fellow servant. Similarly, the master in the parable of the talents assigns one, two, and five talents to his servants. The parable of the unjust steward envisions a landowner who owns whole villages (Oakman 2008, 28–29, 266–72).

The vineyard owners may be considered either regional elites (PS2) or municipal elites (PS3), landowners who lived near their estates. Yet the parables do not imply any animosity toward them. The vineyard owner in the parable of the laborers is generous, giving even those who worked only one hour at the end of the day a full day's wage. The owner in the parable of the wicked tenants is mistreated by the tenants but does not evict them until they have killed his son. Fig trees were subsistence crops rather than cash crops, but the owner of the fig tree has a gardener (Luke 13:6–9) and hence is probably a municipal elite. Unlike the vineyard owner, however, the owner of the fig tree takes a harsher stance than does his gardener.

The municipal elites (PS3) include a master with servants, the first invited to the king's wedding feast for his son, and the host of a banquet and his guest. Others are wealthy: a master with servants (Mark 13:34–36), a rich farmer who plans to build bigger barns, a tower builder, the father of the prodigal son, the rich man at whose gate Lazarus lies, and probably the servants assigned talents. Two others are municipal elites by virtue of their occupations: the unjust judge and the tax collector.

Friesen admits that it is difficult to determine the number of those who enjoyed a moderate surplus (PS4). Candidates for this category in Jesus' parables might be the man who found a treasure and bought the field, the pearl merchant, and the Pharisee in Luke 18:11–12, about whom we know nothing more than his haughty attitude.

Again, the line between PS4 and PS5 (stable near subsistence) is vague at best. Here I have assigned the householders, the sower (presumably a farmer), the farmer or vintner in John 15:1, the stewards in Matthew 20:1–15 and Luke 16:1–9, and the king's servants in Matthew 22:2–13. Also probably belonging to PS5 (or higher on the scale), we may place the debtors in the parable of the unjust steward and the characters in the parable of the good Samaritan: the traveler who is beaten and robbed, the Levite and priest, the good Samaritan, and the innkeeper.

The rather large contingent of characters living at subsistence level (PS6) include farmers and agricultural workers: sowers and reapers, day laborers, gardeners, and tenants. Others who live at or near subsistence may include servants, the woman baking bread, the woman with ten coins, shepherds, fishermen, and the debtors in Luke 16:1–7. Debtors also appear in Matthew 5:25//Luke 12:58.

Those living below subsistence (PS7) are the poor, crippled, blind, and lame suffering outside the city in "the streets and lanes of the town" (Luke 14:21); the hungry, thirsty, stranger, naked, sick, and imprisoned; Lazarus, the beggar; the widow pleading with an unjust judge; and the hireling thief in John 10:1–5. Many of the assignments can be debated; I have refrained from assigning the ten maidens waiting for the bridegroom, the father, the traveler, and the neighbor at midnight.

Even this rough exercise illustrates the range of characters and the focus on the lower three poverty levels, which suggests that Jesus was speaking to the poor *about* the rich rather than directly to the rich. Jesus' audiences would have recognized themselves and their exploitation by the powerful and the wealthy. This contrast is especially characteristic of Luke's parables. "A paradigmatic character of parables in Luke is a relatively affluent proprietor, who owns slaves, fields, and livestock, employs hired labour to work his fields, and occasionally presides at Roman[-]style banquets for his landowning peers (Luke 12:36–38, 42–48; 13:6–9; 14:16–24)" (Sivertsev, 234; cf. Sherwin-White, 139–40; Freyne 1980, 165). Kloppenborg concurs. In its original form, the parable of the tenants "is a piece of realistic fiction which functioned first to invoke certain 'normal' aspects of life in Jewish Palestine . . . the middling rich and their pursuit of wealth, the prevalence of absenteeism, and ubiquitous resorts to status displays, . . . and then to challenge the values underlying these 'normalcies' by means of the clever turn of its narrative" (Kloppenborg, 349).

Not only do the characters in Jesus' parables and sayings reflect his rural, agrarian Galilean setting, but the prominence of the needy and the struggling, debt, lending, and debt forgiveness also point to his compassion for the poor and his outrage at the economic system that exploited them. He warned against trying to "serve God *and* mammon" (Matt 6:24 KJV; "wealth," NRSV), declared that God desired mercy rather than sacrifices (Matt 9:13; 12:7; Hos 6:6), and taught that God only forgives us our debts when we forgive others (Matt 6:12, 14–15; Mark 11:25; Luke 11:4). For Jesus' audiences, debt forgiveness was a familiar, if not common, practice: they could readily identify with the plea, "Forgive us our debts!" (Matt 6:12).

Rather than a revolt against Rome, Jesus called his fellow Jews to live out the solidarity with the poor, the widow, the orphan, and the stranger that lay at the foundation of Israel's constitution as the people of God (Exod 22:21–24; Deut 10:18; Ps 68:5; Isa 1:17; Jer 7:5–7; 22:3; Zech 7:10; Jas 1:27). The holy people of a holy God will be marked not by their purity but by their compassion and their care for the least among them.

Works Cited in Chapter 9

Applebaum, Shimon. 1987. "Economic Life in Palestine." Pages 631–700 in *The Jewish People in the First Century: Historical Geography, Political History, Social, Cultural and Religious Life and Institutions.* Vol. 2. Edited by S. Safrai and M. Stern. Philadelphia: Fortress.

Aviam, Mordechai. 2013. "People, Land, Economy, and Belief in First-Century Galilee and Its Origins: A Comprehensive Archaeological Synthesis." Pages 5–48 in *The Galilean Economy in the Time of Jesus.* Edited by David A. Fiensy and Ralph K. Hawkins. ECL 11. Atlanta: Society of Biblical Literature.

————. 2015. "Yodefat-Jotapata: A Jewish Galilean Town at the End of the Second Temple Period." Pages 109–26 in vol. 2 of Fiensy and Strange.

Black, C. Clifton. 2018. *The Lord's Prayer*. Louisville: Westminster John Knox.

Blasi, A. J., J. Duhaime, and P.-A. Turcotte, eds. *Handbook of Early Christianity: Social Science Approaches*. Walnut Creek, CA: AltaMira.

Broshi, Magen. 1992. "Agriculture and Economy in Roman Palestine: Seven Notes on the Babatha Archive." *IEJ* 42.3/4:230–40.

Dar, Shimon. 2007. "The Agrarian Economy in the Herodian Period." Pages 305–11 in *The World of the Herods*. Edited by Nikos Kokkinos. OeO 14. Stuttgart: Steiner.

Edwards, Douglas R., and C. Thomas McCollough, eds. 1997. *Archaeology and the Galilee: Texts and Contexts in the Graeco-Roman and Byzantine Periods*. Atlanta: Scholars Press.

Esler, Philip F. 2017. *Babatha's Orchard: The Yadin Papyri and an Ancient Jewish Family Tale Retold*. Oxford: Oxford University Press.

Fiensy, David A. 1991. *The Social History of Palestine in the Herodian Period: The Land Is Mine*. Lewiston, NY: Mellon.

————. 2012. "Did Large Estates Exist in Lower Galilee in the First Half of the First Century CE?" *JSHJ* 10:133–53.

————. 2020. *The Archaeology of Daily Life: Ordinary Persons in Later Second Temple Israel*. Eugene, OR: Cascade.

Fiensy, David A., and James R. Strange, eds. 2014–15. *Galilee in the Late Second Temple and Mishnaic Periods*. 2 vols. Minneapolis: Fortress.

Fitzmyer, Joseph A., and Daniel J. Harrington. 1978. *A Manual of Palestinian Aramaic Texts*. Rome: Biblical Institute.

Freyne, Séan. 1980. *Galilee from Alexander the Great to Hadrian, 323 B.C.E. to 135 C.E.: A Study of Second Temple Judaism*. Wilmington, DE: Glazier.

Friesen, Steven J. 2004. "Poverty in Pauline Studies: Beyond the So-Called New Consensus." *JSNT* 26:323–61.

Goodman, Martin. 1982. "The First Jewish Revolt: Social Conflict and the Problem of Debt." *JJS* 33:417–27.

————. 1987. *The Ruling Class of Judaea: The Origins of the Jewish Revolt against Rome (A.D. 66–70)*. Cambridge: Cambridge University Press.

Goodrich, John K. 2012. "Debt Remission and the Parable of the Unjust Steward (Luke 16:1–13)." *JBL* 131:547–66.

Hamel, Gildas H. 1989. *Poverty and Charity in Roman Palestine, First Three Centuries C.E.* University of California Publications: Near Eastern Studies 23. Berkeley: University of California Press.

————. 2010. "Poverty and Charity." Pages 308–24 in Hezser.

Hanson, K. C., and Douglas E. Oakman. 1998. *Palestine in the Time of Jesus: Social Structures and Social Conflicts*. Minneapolis: Fortress.

Harland, Philip A. 2002. "The Economy of First-Century Palestine: State of Scholarly Discussion." Pages 511–72 in Blasi, Duhaime, and Turcotte.

Herz, Johannes. 1928. "Grossgrundbesitz in Palästina im Zeitalter Jesu." *PJ* 24:98–113.

Hezser, Catherine, ed. 2010. *The Oxford Handbook of Jewish Daily Life in Roman Palestine*. Oxford: Oxford University Press.

Howes, Llewellyn. 2022. "The Agricultural Background of the Harvest Logion in Matthew 9.37–8 and Luke (Q) 10.2." *NTS* 69:57–75.

Jensen, Morten Hørning. 2012. "Rural Galilee and Rapid Changes: An Investigation of the Socio-Economic Dynamics and Developments in Roman Galilee." *Bib* 93.1:43–67.

Keddie, G. Anthony. 2019. *Class and Power in Roman Palestine: The Socioeconomic Setting of Judaism and Christian Origins.* Cambridge: Cambridge University Press.

Killebrew, Anne E. 2010. "Village and Countryside." Pages 189–209 in Hezser.

Kloppenborg, John S. 2006. *The Tenants in the Vineyard: Ideology, Economics, and Agrarian Conflict in Jewish Palestine.* WUNT 195. Tübingen: Mohr Siebeck.

Levine, Lee I. 2005. *The Ancient Synagogue: The First Thousand Years.* 2nd ed. New Haven: Yale University Press.

Lewis, Naphtali. 1983. *Life in Egypt under Roman Rule.* Oxford: Clarendon.

Magness, Jodi. 2011. *Stone and Dung, Oil and Spit: Jewish Daily Life in the Time of Jesus.* Grand Rapids: Eerdmans.

Mattila, Sharon Lea. 2015. "Capernaum, Village of Naḥum, from Hellenistic to Byzantine Times." Pages 217–57 in Fiensy and Strange, vol. 2.

McCollough, C. Thomas. 2015. "Khirbet Qana." Pages 127–45 in Fiensy and Strange, vol. 2.

Moreland, Milton. 2004. "The Galilean Response to Earliest Christianity: A Cross-Cultural Study of the Subsistence Ethic." Pages 37–48 in *Religion and Society in Roman Palestine: Old Questions, New Approaches.* Edited by Douglas R. Edwards. New York: Routledge.

Oakman, Douglas E. 1986. *Jesus and the Economic Questions of His Day.* SBEC8. Lewiston: Mellen.

———. 2008. *Jesus and the Peasants.* Eugene, OR: Cascade.

Oates, John F., Alan E. Samuel, and C. Bradford Welles, eds. 1967. *Yale Papyri in the Beinecke Rare Book and Manuscript Library.* Vol. I. ASP 2. New Haven: American Society of Papyrologists.

Overman, J. Andrew. 1997. "Jesus of Galilee and the Historical Peasant." Pages 67–73 in Edwards and McCollough.

Richardson, Peter, and Douglas Edwards. 2002. "Jesus and Palestinian Social Protest: Archaeological and Literary Perspectives." Pages 247–67 in Blasi, Duhaime, and Turcotte.

Root, Bradley W. 2014. *First-Century Galilee: A Fresh Examination of the Sources.* WUNT 378. Tübingen: Mohr Siebeck.

Ryan, Jordan J. 2017. *The Role of the Synagogue in the Aims of Jesus.* Minneapolis: Fortress.

Safrai, Ze'ev. 1994. *The Economy of Roman Palestine.* London: Routledge.

———. 2003. "The Agrarian Structure in Palestine in the Time of the Second Temple, Mishnah, and Talmud." Pages 105–25 in *The Rural Landscape of Ancient Israel.* Edited by Aren M. Maeir, Shimon Dar, and Ze'ev Safrai. BAR International Series 1121. Oxford: Archaeopress.

———. 2010. "Agriculture and Farming." Pages 246–63 in Hezser.

Sherwin-White, A. N. 1963. *Roman Society and Roman Law in the New Testament.* Oxford: Clarendon.

Sivertsev, Alexei. 2010. "The Household Economy." Pages 229–45 in Hezser.

Sterling, Gregory E., and Kim Paffenroth. 2021. "*ergon.*" Contexticon of New Testament Language. Edited by Richard M. Harley. contexticon.com.

Strange, James F. 1997. "First-Century Galilee from Archaeology and from the Texts." Pages 39–48 in Edwards and McCollough.

Udoh, Fabian. 2014. "Taxation and Other Sources of Government Income in the Galilee of Herod and Antipas." Pages 366–87 in Fiensy and Strange, vol. 1.

Wise, Michael Owen. 2015. *Language and Literacy in Roman Judaea: A Study of the Bar Kokhba Documents.* New Haven: Yale University Press.

Yardeni, Ada. 2001. "The Decipherment and Restoration of Legal Texts from the Judaean Desert: A Reexamination of *Papyrus Starcky (P.Yadin 36).*" *SCI* 20:121–37.

Chapter 10

Farmers

Sower (Matt 13:3–8; Mark 4:3–8; Luke 8:5–8)
Planted Weeds (Matt 13:24–30)
Mustard Seed (Matt 13:31–32; Mark 4:30–32; Luke 13:18–19)
Seed Growing Secretly (Mark 4:26–29)
Barren Fig Tree (Luke 13:6–9)
Sower and Reaper (John 4:35–38)
Vine and Vinedresser (John 15:1–8)

*B*ecause the Galilean economy was primarily agrarian and Jesus taught in the villages and countryside, it is not surprising that so many of his parables feature the agricultural cycle: plowing, planting, weeding, pruning, harvesting, and threshing. Jesus appeals to the natural processes to tease his hearers' imaginations into insights into the mystery of God's workings and the coming kingdom. For example, the sower sows his seed in the customary way, loses most of it to birds, rocky soil, scorching heat, and weeds, yet reaps a magnificent harvest. The tiny mustard seed, a common weed, grows to be the largest of the shrubs. Miraculously, seeds grow, even while the farmer sleeps. Yet, while the farmer sleeps, weeds grow also, as though they were planted by the farmer's enemy. Still, he lets the weeds grow along with the wheat until harvesttime. What about the unproductive plants? The gardener appeals to the vineyard owner to let the unproductive fig tree have another year, while he fertilizes it. In the Johannine parable, the vine grower removes the unproductive branches and burns them. The harvest, the climax of the agricultural cycle, demands intense labor; but when it is done, the "sower and reaper may rejoice together" (John 4:36).

10.1 Farming in Galilee

The Bible and other ancient sources were written by the elite, who seldom had reason to describe a farmer's work. Sirach's attitude was typical: "The wisdom of the scribe depends on the opportunity of leisure; only the one who has little business can become wise. How can one become wise who handles the plow, and who glories in the shaft of a goad, who drives oxen and is occupied with their work, and whose talk is about bulls? He sets his heart on plowing furrows, and he is careful about fodder for the heifers" (38:24–26). Then he describes the artisans' work, adding, "But they maintain the fabric of the world, and their concern is for the exercise of their trade" (38:34a). He makes his point: "How different the one who devotes himself to the study of the law of the Most High!" (38:34b).

Jewish writers took pride in the productivity of their land. The Letter of Aristeas describes Palestine without distinguishing regions. "In fact their land is thickly covered with large numbers of olive trees and corn [cereal] crops and pulse, and moreover with vines and abundant honey. As for the fruit trees and date palms which they have, no number can be given" (112). Fruit trees, including date palms, grew around Jericho and the Dead Sea (Ein-Gedi, Maḥoza). Galilee was the breadbasket of Palestine, however, and Josephus praised its fertility: "The land is everywhere so rich in soil and pasturage and produces such variety of trees, that even the most indolent are tempted by these facilities to devote themselves to agriculture. In fact, every inch of the soil has been cultivated by the inhabitants; there is not a parcel of waste land" (*J.W.* 3.42–43). And again, "Skirting the lake of Gennesar, and also bearing that name, lies a region whose natural properties and beauty are very remarkable. There is not a plant which its fertile soil refuses to produce, and its cultivators in fact grow every species; the air is so well-tempered that it suits the most opposite varieties" (*J.W.* 3.516).

As we saw in the previous chapter, most of the agricultural work in Galilee was done by small landholders who lived in the towns and villages scattered across Galilee and worked their own land, probably 6 to 12 acres (Fiensy 1991, 93–94; Oakman 2008, 52), in the nearby fields. Half the field lay fallow each year. Farmers consumed most of what they produced. The rest they stored, bartered, or sold locally. A smallholder might have owned a donkey but not an ox; donkeys were expensive, oxen prohibitively costly (Safrai 2010, 258; see below, 13.4).

The work was relentless. Exodus refers to "all kinds of field work" (1:14 NAB), and the Mishnah details thirty-nine classes of work, including "sowing, ploughing, reaping, binding sheaves, threshing, winnowing, cleansing crops," followed by "grinding, sifting, kneading, baking" (m. Shabb. 7:2). The Gezer Calendar, inscribed on a limestone tablet around 925 BCE, describes the work required in each season. This calendar may have been a school exercise that lists the months by their agricultural tasks (Hopkins, 151).

> two months of ingathering [olives] harvest
>   two months of sowing [cereals]
>   two months of late sowing [vegetables]
>   a month of hoeing weeds [for hay]
>   a month of harvesting barley
>   a month of harvesting [wheat] and measuring [grain]
>   two months of grape harvesting
>   a month of ingathering summer fruit.
>   (Borowski, *ABD* 1:97; cf. Albright in Pritchard, 287)

Neither the seasons nor the farmer's work changed in a thousand years. Unlike the Jewish year, which began in the spring with the month of Nisan, the Gezer Calendar begins with the olive harvest in the fall. November to February was the busiest time of the year. The olives had to be gathered and crushed; as soon as the rains softened the earth, it had to be plowed in preparation for sowing the grain (Fiensy 2020, 167–69). The rainy season lasted from October/November until March/April; droughts could bring on famines.

Religious festivals marked the major events in the agricultural cycle (Borowski 1987, 31–44). Harvesting barley began at the Passover festival (end of March). The Festival of Firstfruits/Harvest (Exod 23:16), also called the Festival of Weeks (*Shavu'ot*, Pentecost), marks the end of the wheat harvest, seven weeks after the offering of the first sheaf of barley (Deut 16:9). The Festival of Booths (Tabernacles, *Sukkot*), the major pilgrimage festival, comes at the end of the year, after the fruit harvest and before sowing the next year's crop (Borowski 1992, 1:98; Falk, 638–41). As we have seen (ch. 8 above), the primary crops were wheat, olives, and grapes (Deut 8:8; Hos 2:8), and the demands of each were different. Wheat grew in the plains, olives and grapes on the hills, and especially in upper Galilee (Avi-Yonah, 201–4).

10.2 Wheat and Barley

Although the book of Ruth is set in the time of the judges, it offers a reflection of Palestinian agriculture, especially during the harvest. Famine drove Elimelech and Naomi from Bethlehem to Moab, where their two sons married Moabite women, Orpah and Ruth. First Elimelech died. Then, after they had been there ten years, both of Naomi's sons died. Parenthetically, their deaths reflect the mortality patterns traced in chapter 4 (above). Naomi and Ruth returned to Bethlehem at the beginning of the barley harvest (Ruth 1:22), which preceded the wheat harvest. Ruth volunteered to go into the fields to glean what she could behind the reapers and perhaps attract the attention of a prospective husband (2:1–3). "As it happened" (2:3), she chose to go to the field of Elimelech's kinsman, Boaz, who came that day to supervise the work. When Boaz asked the servant in charge of the reapers who Ruth was, he reported that she was a Moabite who had asked to "'glean . . . among the sheaves behind the reapers.' So she came, and she has been on her feet from early this morning until now, without resting even for a moment" (2:7). Boaz ordered the reapers not to bother Ruth, told Ruth to stay close to his "young women," then invited her to drink water and eat bread and roasted grain with the workers (2:14). He instructed the reapers to let her glean among the standing sheaves and to pluck some out for her (2:15–16). That evening she beat out the grain she had gathered, enough for her to share with Naomi. She continued "gleaning until the end of the barley and wheat harvests" (2:23). Knowing that Boaz was winnowing barley one evening, Naomi instructed Ruth to wash and anoint herself, put on her best clothes, wait until he had finished eating and drinking, and then lie down beside him. Like other landowners, Boaz would have slept by the harvest to protect it from thieves. The rest is history: the ancestry of David (4:22) and of Jesus (Matt 1:5–6).

Cultivation of the grains began with clearing and plowing the field, which had to wait until the winter rains softened the soil. Interpreters have toiled over Jesus' description of the farmer sowing seed that fell by the road or path and on rocky soil. Was he a careless farmer, wasting seed? Some interpreters suggest that the custom was to sow before plowing, as some references imply (Jeremias, 12; White, 301–2; Payne, 123–29; Scott, 353): "And Prince Mastema sent crows and birds so that they might eat the seed which was being sown in the earth in order to spoil the earth so that they might rob mankind of their labors. Before they plowed in the seed, the crows picked it off the surface of the earth" (Jub. 11.11). According to tradition, Abraham invented a device that allowed farmers to plant the seed *as* they plowed:

Abram taught those who were making the implements for oxen, the skilled carpenters. And they made implements above the ground facing the handle of the plow so that they might place seed upon it. And the seed would go down from within it onto the point of the plow, and it would be hidden in the earth. And therefore they were not afraid of the crows. And they did likewise with all of the plow handles above the ground. And they sowed and tilled all of the earth just as Abram commanded them. And therefore they were not afraid of the birds. (Jub. 11.23–24)

At least in Judea, two plowings were the norm. The first plowing allowed the soil to soak up more rain and uprooted weeds. The second plowing prepared the soil for sowing. Isaiah 28:24 refers to pulverizing and smoothing, while Job 39:10 describes following the furrow, "the valleys," cut by the first plowing (Hopkins, 152–53). Tree trunks or branches, sometimes bent to grow in the desired shape, were used for the wooden parts of the plow, and the metal plowshare was symmetrical, digging a furrow by forcing the dirt to both sides (Frankel 2013, 234). A draft animal or yoke of oxen pulled a wooden plow through the earth, or one with a bronze or iron point (1 Sam 13:20–21). With one hand the plowman grasped the handle of the plow and with the other the ox goad—a stick with an iron fork at the end, used to spur the animals and break up clods of dirt. Even under ideal conditions, the work was exhausting for both the farmer and the oxen.

While not as exhausting as plowing, sowing the seed by hand, casting it broadly and evenly over the field, required practiced skill, and the conditions had to be right: "Whoever observes the wind will not sow; and whoever regards the clouds will not reap" (Eccl 11:4). The seed could be covered by a third plowing or, if conditions were right, by dragging a bundle of sticks over the field. Alternatively, a helper could walk behind the plow, dropping seed into the furrows so that it could be covered by the soil when the next row was plowed. The quotation from Jubilees 11 (above) describes a "seed trumpet," or funnel, that dropped seeds onto the ground just ahead of the plow. The rate of seeding varied with the crop and the condition of the soil. "Given the weakness of composting and soil preparation, a lighter hand would not have meant a significantly higher yield per seed ratio but almost surely a lower yield per acre, with smaller heaps on the threshing floor. . . . 'The one who sows sparingly will also reap sparingly, and the one who sows bountifully will also reap bountifully' (2 Cor 9:6; cf. 2 Esd 4:32; 3 Bar 15; 4 Ezra [2 Esd] 9.17)" (Hamel 1989, 135–36). Wheat was sown more thickly than barley, lentils much more sparsely. Regardless of how it was done, casting or dropping the precious seed on the ground was a time of risk and hope. If the seed did not grow, people and animals would go hungry.

The seed shrivels under the clods, the storehouses are desolate; the grana-ries are ruined because the grain has failed. How the animals groan! The herds of cattle wander about because there is no pasture for them; even the flocks of sheep are dazed. To you, O LORD, I cry. For fire has devoured the pastures of the wilderness, and flames have burned all the trees of the field. Even the wild animals cry to you because the watercourses are dried up, and fire has devoured the pastures of the wilderness. (Joel 1:17–20)

To reduce the risk of unpredictable rain patterns and crop failure, ancient farmers practiced "staggered sowing," sowing their fields at different times during the planting season (Hopkins, 155).

Jesus' parables draw on the farmer's bane of weeds growing up with the crop. Weeds consumed precious water and nutrients, complicated the harvest, added weight to the bundles that had to be moved to the threshing floor, and slowed the process of winnowing. Any weed seeds that remained in the grain had to be removed before it could be ground into flour. Dar-nel seeds (*Lolium temulentum*), also called "false wheat" or "poison dar-nel," were especially troublesome because they resembled cereal grains but were often infected by a fungus and hence toxic (Hos 10:4; cf. Matt 13:24–30). For this reason, they were often allowed to grow until the har-vest approached, when they could be identified more easily. Weeding was often done by women and children, using a hoe or handpicking the weeds (Hopkins, 156–57).

The psalmist promises, "Those who go out weeping, bearing the seed for sowing, shall come home with shouts of joy, carrying their sheaves" (126:6). Harvesting required the greatest amount of labor yet had to be com-pleted in a short span of time. Families and villages worked together, cut-ting or uprooting the grain. Tenant farmers hired workers (*ergatas*, Luke 10:2) for the harvest (Howes, 60). The stalks were cut with a sickle, like the one found with Babatha's possessions (see above, 7.8). Straw could be left in the field for the animals or harvested for thatch roofs. Hopkins describes the process.

> In pre-modern Palestine, the village men consolidated the cuttings into sheaves, while the women collected the sheaves and transported them to the threshing ground. Numbers of harvesters no doubt worked in a coor-dinated effort, forming a line across a field to ensure its thorough and efficient cutting. Hands and limbs of all suffered abrasion as they came into contact with prickly awn fragments. Adding to the intensity and sheer strain of harvest labor were the conditions under which it occurred: the hottest, driest months of the year, when noontime temperatures turned the open fields into ovens. (Hopkins, 158; cf. Howes, 70–71)

Despite the drudgery, the harvest was normally a time of joy, but it could also be an image for reckoning or judgment. John the Baptist echoed the prophets when he warned the people, "His winnowing fork is in his hand, and he will clear his threshing floor and will gather his wheat into the granary; but the chaff he will burn with unquenchable fire" (Matt 3:12; see Jer 51:33).

The reapers, using donkeys if they could, carried the sheaves to the threshing ground, which had to be prepared, smoothed, and swept clean (Ruth 3:2). Threshing floors were often communal, located near the fields, yet open to the wind. Using a threshing sledge made of boards with stone or metal teeth on the bottom side (2 Sam 24:22; Isa 28:27–28; 41:15) and pulled by donkeys or oxen (Deut 25:4; 1 Cor 9:9), they separated the ears of grain from the stalks. Alternately, oxen could thresh the grain by walking circles without a sledge, while the workers turned the pile with forks (Isa 30:24), raked off the straw, and swept the spikelets to one side (Varro, *Rust.* 1.52). This process continued through the harvest period.

Winnowing required tossing the piles of spikelets and straw into the air so that the lighter straw could be blown away (Job 21:18; Pss 1:4; 83:13; Jer 13:24), while the grain fell back to the threshing floor (Luke 3:17). Both the grain and the chaff or straw were then collected. The latter was used as fodder or mixed in building material (Exod 5:7–18; Isa 25:10) and potter's clay. The spikelets, remaining pieces of straw, and weed seeds were then sifted through a series of sieves (Amos 9:9; Isa 30:28; Luke 22:31). At the end of the process, the spikelets were collected and put in storage, ready for the women's daily labor of the final cleaning and grinding of flour (Hopkins, 158–61).

Grain was grown every other year, letting the field lie fallow or growing other crops, such as lentils, in the odd year (Safrai 2010, 252). Hanson and Oakman estimate that ancient farmers could expect at best a yield of 10 to 15 times the grain seed sown (104; cf. Jeremias, 150, n. 84). Others accept a more modest rate of 1:5 (Oakman 1986, 63; Fiensy 1991, 94; Harland, 522; Hamel 2010, 310–11). Once the farmer set aside seed for the next year and paid taxes, rent, and debts, the yield left to feed the family supported a marginal subsistence at best.

10.3 Olives

Large landholders preferred the relatively less labor-intensive and more transportable yields of olive oil and wine production. Olive oil was used for a variety of purposes, making it a valued commodity: for dipping bread

(John 13:26), food preparation (Num 11:8; Ezek 16:13), fuel for lamps (Exod 27:20; Matt 25:3, 8), anointing (1 Sam 10:1; 2 Kgs 9:3; Ps 89:20; Ezek 16:9; Mic 6:15), salve for wounds (Isa 1:6; Luke 10:34), healing (Mark 6:13; Jas 5:14), cosmetics (Esth 2:12), perfume, and even as sunscreen (Amos 6:6; Pss 23:5; 133:2; Josephus, *J.W.* 2.123; cf. Pilch, 235; Frankel 2013, 242; Welch, 118–19). Donkeys were used for most of the heavy work required for cultivating olives: hauling olives to the press, rotating the mill, carting manure, and so on (Hyland, 231).

Establishing an orchard or vineyard, however, required both labor and expertise. Isaiah's song of the vineyard (5:1–7) lists some of the steps, omitting others. "A very fertile hill" had to be secured, "dug," and terraced, clearing it of stones. A "hedge" was put around it. "Choice vines" were planted and staked. A "watchtower" was constructed, apparently for protection of the crop (Isa 21:8; Mark 12:1) and also to provide a place where the workers could sleep, store tools, and ferment the wine (Fiensy 1991, 31–34; Keddie, 97 n. 104; Kloppenborg, 321). Then, an olive press had to be built or a wine vat hewed out.

Josephus commented that "figs and olives . . . require a milder atmosphere" (*J.W.* 3.517), therefore "Galilee is a special home of the olive" (*J.W.* 2.592). Pliny the Elder commented that while the Egyptian olives produce a scant amount of oil, the small olives of the Decapolis "have an attractive flesh" and were imported to Italy (*Nat.* 15.4.15–16). Through the Hellenistic period, oil cultivation was limited to domestic production. Exporting olive oil began in the Hasmonean period and flourished in the Byzantine period (Aviam 2004, 51–58; Leibner 2010, 285). Oil processing centers have been found at Meiron, Gamla, Sepphoris, Yodefat, and elsewhere. It appears, therefore, that the Judeans who moved to Galilee under the Hasmoneans brought with them the knowledge required to cultivate olives along with mechanized olive presses: "In their attempts to resettle the Galilee and to establish a large, economically strong and wealthy community, the Hasmonaean rulers probably subsidized the planting of large olive groves and the erection of the new mass-producing oil presses" (Aviam 2004, 56). To establish olive groves, ovules (bulges on top of the roots of a mature tree) are cut and planted in the orchard. Once the rootstock grew to four or five feet, branches from the desired species could be grafted onto it (see Rom 11:17, 24). In time, each limb developed its own independent contact with the roots and hence could survive even when the trunk was hollowed out (Singer, 34–35). Olive production required a long-term investment. While vines produced grapes in three to five years and fig trees in twice that time, "the lag time for the olive was twice again as long, climbing to upwards of twenty years. The slow growth of the olive was matched, however, by incredible longevity, spanning centuries. . . .

Given human life spans, one planted an olive orchard for the next generation (Ps. 128.3)" (Hopkins, 165). The most ancient trees today, such as those
at Gethsemane, may date back to the Roman period (Singer, 31). Periodic
pruning spurred new growth.

Pliny the Elder (23/24–79 CE), who passes on the contemporary "best
practices" for olive cultivation and processing from Theophrastus (ca. 370–
288/5 BCE) and Cato (*Agr.*, ca. 160 BCE), says, "Making olive-oil requires
even more science than making wine, as the same olive-tree produces a variety of oils" (*Nat.* 15.2.5). Olive trees "like the ground to be raked between
them" (15.2.5), presumably to provide the trees as much moisture as possible. One of the decisions the farmer had to make was when to harvest the
olives. Pliny advises, "The best age for picking olives, as between quantity
and flavour, is when the berry is beginning to turn black" (15.2.6). Farmers beat the tree branches with sticks (Deut 24:20; Isa 17:6; 24:13), pruned
branches to reach the inaccessible olives, picked them, and gathered fallen
fruit from the ground (Hopkins, 167). Again, Pliny advises caution for those
who compromise between hiring pickers and collecting the fallen fruit:

> Those who compromise on a middle course in this matter knock the fruit
> down with poles, so injuring the trees and causing loss in the following
> year; in fact there is a very old regulation for the olive harvest: "Neither
> strip nor beat an olive-tree." Those who proceed most carefully use a reed
> and strike the branches with a light sideway blow; but even this method
> causes the tree to produce fruit only every other year, as the buds get
> knocked off, and this is no less the case if people wait for the olives to
> fall off, for by remaining attached to the branches beyond their proper
> time they use up the nourishment for the coming crop and occupy its
> space. (*Nat.* 15.3.11–12)

Olives need to be eaten, pickled, or pressed immediately after harvesting:
"The best olive-oil is made from the bitterest olive obtainable; for the rest
the olives should be collected off the ground as soon as possible, and washed
if they are dirty; it is enough to leave them to dry for three days, and if the
weather is cold and frosty they must be pressed on the fourth day, and when
pressed they should be sprinkled with salt" (*Nat.* 15.5.21). Another common
mistake was "keeping the olives when gathered on wooden shelves and not
crushing them till they sweat out juice, inasmuch as all delay diminishes the
yield of oil and increases the quantity of lees" (*Nat.* 15.4.14). Olives were
commonly divided into three grades: "The first grade of olives was taken
straight from the tree to the press, the second was stored on the roof before
pressing and the third was stored indoors and then dried on the roof before
pressing. The explanation is apparently that the olives were often picked

faster than they were pressed and had to be stored, their quality deteriorating during storage" (Frankel 2009, 12; see m. Menaḥ. 8:4–5).

Following Cato, Pliny recommended heating the installation with a stove to keep it as warm as possible. Olive cultivators had learned

> to wash the olives in absolutely boiling water, and at once put them whole into the press—for that method crushes out the lees—and then to crush them in oil-mills and put them under the press a second time. People do not approve of pressing more than a hundred pecks of olives at a time: this is called a "batch," and what is squeezed out first after the millstone is called the "flower." It is a fair amount for three batches to be pressed in twenty-four hours by gangs of four men using a double holder [the part of the press in which the olives were laid]. (*Nat.* 15.6.23)

Pickling olives to ameliorate their bitter taste emerged during the Hellenistic period (Hopkins, 167), but olives were used mainly for oil, which was extracted in three steps. First, the olives were crushed. Rotary crushers, large circular vats in which a round, wheel-like stone was rotated, appeared in the Hellenistic period (Frankel 2009, 4; Hopkins, 168; Frankel, 240–42; see: https://www.123rf.com/photo_41187582_ancient-olive-oil-production-machinery-stone-mill-and-mechanical-press-oil-mill-for-olives.html). The oil collected at this point was the purest.

Second, the crushed olives were collected in sacks, which were placed under weights. From the Iron Age through the Roman period (Frankel 2009, 4–5; Leibner, 283), the beam or lever-and-weight presses were used to exert a much greater force on the sacks of crushed olives. A beam was attached to the wall (the fulcrum), and heavy weights were hung over the other end of the beam (see: https://www.123rf.com/photo_62654740_ancient-olive-oil-press-beit-guvrin-israel.html). The sacks of crushed olives were placed under the beam near the fulcrum to press as much oil as possible from the olives. Vitruvius (ca. 25 BCE) stipulates that the press, if it is worked by levers and a press-beam, should be not less than forty feet long and the room not less than sixteen feet wide (*Archi.* 6.6.3). Although lever-and-screw presses and direct-pressure screw presses were already in use in Italy in the first century (Pliny the Elder, *Nat.* 18.74.317), and many of these presses have been found in Israel, "none of the first and very few of the second type can be dated to the Roman period with certainty" (Leibner, 284). Pliny continues: "The first oil of all is obtained from the raw olive and when it has not yet begun to ripen—this has the best flavour; moreover, its first issue from the press is the richest, and so on by diminishing stages, whether the olives are crushed in wicker sieves or by enclosing the spray in narrow-meshed strainers, a method recently invented" (*Nat.* 15.2.6).

The oil was channeled into a collecting vat. This process produced a mixture of olive oil and water. The third step was skimming the lighter oil from the watery lees and transferring it to ceramic vessels. Olives consist of oil (20%), solid waste (40%), and watery lees (40%; Frankel 2009, 8). At this point, Pliny advises, "The actual oil can be guarded against the defect of thickening by the addition of salt" (*Nat.* 15.4.18). Unlike wine, olive oil needs to be used quickly.

Figuring that the ancients planted eleven or twelve olive trees per dunam (1/4 acre) and that each dunam yielded 132 kilograms of olives or 26.4 liters of oil per year, and that the trees produce olives every other year, Safrai calculates that a family would need to cultivate 4.9 to 9.8 dunams of olives to generate enough income to provide their food for a year (1994, 122–23). Olives were eaten raw, dipped in salt, or pickled.

The prevalence of *miqva'ot* (washing pools) and stone vessels in Judea and Galilee signals the heightened concern for ritual purity among Jews in the late Second Temple period. Liquids, especially, transmitted uncleanness. Grain and fruits were not milled or washed before they were taken to market and were therefore not susceptible to uncleanness, but grapes and olives were susceptible to uncleanness transmitted by the laborers (m. Ṭehar. 10:1; cf. 10:2–3). Consequently, Jews avoided olive oil produced by gentiles, preferring locally produced olive oil. In upper Galilee, John of Gischala exported locally produced olive oil to Caesarea Philippi, where he sold it for eight times as much as he had paid for it (Josephus, *J.W.* 2.591–592; *Life* 74–76). The oil production facilities at Yodefat and Gamla were equipped with *miqva'ot* (Adler; Aviam 2009; Aviam 2013, 26; Wagner, 303–4) so that the workers could bathe before handling the olives. Such *miqva'ot* were found exclusively in Second Temple period contexts, however, and rabbinic sources imply the gradual disappearance of stringencies regarding purity of oil (Leibner, 284).

10.4 Grapevines

Grapes in Galilee were predominantly red, giving rise to the association of wine with blood: "the blood of the grape" (Sir 39:26). White (green) grapes did not appear in the region until the Hellenistic period (Walsh, 132). Josephus praised Galilee for its productive climate: "For ten months without intermission it supplies those kings of the fruits, the grape and the fig" (*J.W.* 3.519). The process for establishing a vineyard, summarized in Isaiah 5:1–7, was much the same as that for an olive orchard: acquiring a suitable site, clearing it of stones, terracing, constructing a perimeter wall to keep out animals that might damage the vines, hewing out a winepress, and constructing storage facilities and water collection installations (Hopkins, 163). A winepress could be created wherever there was a large flat stone ledge or where such a surface could be quarried from the rock. Still, "a vineyard required outlays for vine supports, the construction of fences and water wheels, the excavation of a treading floor, catch basins, and storage tanks, the construction of a press and room to store amphorae, and the purchase of iron tools and draft animals" (Kloppenborg, 296, citing Cato's list of the equipment required for a vineyard, *Agr.* 11.2–13.2). Only the wealthy could create a vineyard, but vineyards were more profitable than grainfields (Duncan-Jones, 35, 59). Vineyards also required constant attention, hoeing and weeding, pruning, desuckering, and replacing unhealthy vines to increase their productivity (Hopkins, 165; see John 15:1–8). As Isaiah says, "For before the harvest, when the blossom is over and the flower becomes a ripening grape, he will cut off the shoots with pruning hooks, and the spreading branches he will hew away" (Isa 18:5). The first harvest could be expected in three to five years.

Timing was critical. When the grapes were ready, the vineyard owner needed enough workers to bring in the grapes, then get them to market, dry them in the sun for raisins, or press them for wine. Grapes for wine or raisins had to be processed immediately, so a great deal of work had to be done quickly. The grape harvest was therefore "a time of urgency, communal collaboration, and public celebration" (Hopkins, 166). Treading the grapes was a social activity, marked by singing, shouting, and dancing (Judg 9:27; Isa 16:10), and the harvest was followed by "a banquet of wine" (Sir 32:5–6; 49:1; cf. Walsh, 133–36).

Harvesters cut the bunches of grapes, put them in a basket, and carried them to the treading basin, which was usually nearby. Isaiah appeals to the visceral experience of trampling to describe God's anger with Israel: "I have trodden the wine press alone, and from the peoples no one was with me; I trod them in my anger and trampled them in my wrath; their juice spattered on my garments, and stained all my robes" (Isa 63:3). Juice from the crushed grapes was collected as it ran off the pressing floor. Beam presses appear in Israel in the Iron Age (Frankel 2009, 4). The grape juice was fermented in a vat and decanted into jars, which were then stoppered. The jars of wine would be aged in a tower or in caves that were always cool, then sold in local markets. Although the production of wine required a greater initial investment and was more labor-intensive than either grain or olive oil production, it was also more profitable (Safrai 1994, 126; Safrai 2010, 253).

10.5 Figs

Moses lists fig trees among the seven crops of the "good land" (Deut 8:8). Figs were eaten fresh, dried in cakes (1 Sam 25:18; 30:12; Jdt 10:5), and used in wine and as a sweetener. The tree's large leaves provided shade and were woven into baskets, dishes, umbrellas, or even clothing (Gen 3:7). The fruit was also used as a laxative and made into a poultice for boils (2 Kgs 20:7; Isa 38:21; see also Pliny the Elder, *Nat.* 23.117–130).

Fig trees begin to produce fruit in six to eight years, but an ancient law with obscure origins forbade harvesting the fruit for three years. "When you come into the land and plant all kinds of trees for food, then you shall regard their fruit as forbidden; three years it shall be forbidden to you, it must not be eaten. In the fourth year all their fruit shall be set apart for rejoicing in the Lord. But in the fifth year you may eat of their fruit, that their yield may be increased for you: I am the Lord your God" (Lev 19:23–25). In the early spring, before they put forth leaves, fig trees produce "winter figs" (Rev 6:13) that are not edible. The "summer figs" (Isa 28:4; Jer 24:2–3; Hos 9:10; Mic 7:1; Nah 3:12; Mark 13:28) begin to ripen in June. The first fig of the season was especially prized (Isa 28:4; Hos 9:10; Mic 7:1; Nah 3:12). Commentators have struggled to explain why Jesus looked for figs on a barren fig tree at Passover, which as the Gospels say was not the season for figs (Mark 11:13). Mark "sandwiches" Jesus' prophetic condemnation of the temple (11:15–19) between Jesus' condemnation of the fig tree (11:12–14) and the disciples' amazement the next morning, when they saw that it had withered (11:20–25). Jesus' act recalls God's dismay over Israel's faithlessness in Jeremiah 8:13, "When I wanted to gather them, says the Lord, there are no grapes on the vine, nor figs on the fig tree; even the leaves are withered." By juxtaposing the two events, Mark makes Jesus' cursing of the fig tree, although it had leaves and appeared to be healthy, a warning of the coming destruction of the temple.

Fig trees often appear in figurative references. Grapevines and fig trees represented Israel's agriculture (Jer 5:17; Hos 2:12; Joel 1:7, 11–12; 2:22; Hab 3:17). Sitting under one's vine or fig tree was therefore a sign of peace (1 Kgs 4:25; 2 Kgs 18:31; Isa 36:16; Mic 4:4; Zech 3:10; 1 Macc 14:12). Israel's righteousness could also be likened to producing figs: "When I wanted to gather them, says the Lord, there are no grapes on the vine, nor figs on the fig tree; even the leaves are withered, and what I gave them has passed away from them" (Jer 8:13; cf. Amos 4:9; Isa 34:4). On the other hand, the withering of fig trees was a sign of judgment, and the destruction of its vines and fig trees meant Israel was destroyed (Jer 5:17; Hos 2:12).

Along with grapes, Josephus calls figs "the royal fruit" (*J.W.* 3.519; see

Judg 9:8–15). Figs were a common subsistence crop, and most small farmers had a few fig trees (see m. Kil. 6:5). Although figs were not as demanding as olives or grapes, farmers needed to check their trees every day during the two-month harvest season. Ripe figs were put in baskets (Jer 24:2; Amos 8:1). Drying the figs was the only processing needed. Palestine was self-sufficient in its production of figs, which were imported only when there was a famine. During the famine in 46 or 47 CE, for example, Queen Helena (of Adiabene, in Mesopotamia) procured a cargo of dried figs from Cyprus, which she distributed to the needy in Jerusalem (Josephus, *Ant.* 20.51).

10.6 Reflections

For those whose lives revolved around the annual agricultural cycle, Jesus' parables were stories of life as they knew it, with twists of amazing incongruity. Everyone knew that sowing the seed was the culmination of preparing the field, clearing stones, and plowing (twice!), before scattering the seed, knowing there was no more seed. Feeding their families and their animals, paying their debts and taxes, and having any seed for next year depended on the seed cast on the rocky soil—seed that was at the mercy of birds and weeds, uncertain rains, and the hot sun. And yet, the sower in Jesus' parable finds that his fields—or stalks—yielded thirty, sixty, and a hundredfold at the end of the season. There is the twist. The usual harvest was around fivefold. The only hundredfold harvest Jesus' hearers had ever heard about was from their sacred texts (Gen 26:12, the harvest God gave Isaac). Did they go away pondering how the everyday world of their own experience differed from the world they envisioned when they heard the Scriptures read and Jesus tell his stories? Which was the "real" world? The essence of trust and hope was to cast the only seed you had on the ground, trusting in God and hoping for a bountiful harvest.

The kingdom of God is like seed (Mark 4:3–8). Seed grew mysteriously, night and day, germinating, poking its shoot above the ground, growing taller, then bearing fruit (Mark 4:26–29). Weeds had to be removed and the soil hoed to receive the needed rain, yet the farmer in Jesus' parable was so concerned about uprooting the good plants that he let weeds stand until the harvest (Matt 13:28–30). A gardener pleaded with the landowner to let him tend an unproductive fig tree for another year (Luke 13:6–9). Galilean farmers knew it could take six to eight years for a fig tree to begin producing and that landowners could be impatient, looking for the firstfruits. At the harvest, the grain, the olives, and the grapes were gathered, while the weeds, the chaff, and the pruned branches were burned. Jesus even compared the kingdom of God to a roadside weed, a mustard plant (Matt 13:31–32; Oakman 2008, 111–17).

Modern readers, most of whom have never worked the land, can easily underestimate the toil involved in sowing, weeding, and harvesting; the precariousness of life lived on a subsistence economy at the mercy of nature; and the joy of a good harvest. For those who labor, Jesus promises rest and an easy yoke. God's kingdom will come, and the harvest will be more wonderful than they can imagine.

Works Cited in Chapter 10

Adler, Yonatan. 2008. "Second Temple Period Ritual Baths Adjacent to Agricultural Installations: The Archaeological Evidence in Light of the Halakhic Sources." *JJS* 59:62–72.

Aviam, Mordechai. 2004. "The Beginning of Mass Production of Olive Oil in Galilee." Pages 51–59 in Aviam, *Jews, Pagans, and Christians in the Galilee.* Rochester, NY: University of Rochester Press.

———. 2009. "An Early Roman Oil Press in a Cave at Yodefat." Pages 97–98 in Ayalon, Frankel, and Kloner.

———. 2013. "People, Land, Economy, and Belief in First-Century Galilee and Its Origins: A Comprehensive Archaeological Synthesis." Pages 5–48 in *The Galilean Economy in the Time of Jesus.* Edited by David A. Fiensy and Ralph K. Hawkins. ECL 11. Atlanta: Society of Biblical Literature.

Avi-Yonah, Michael. 2002. *The Holy Land from the Persian to the Arab Conquest (536 B.C.–A.D. 640): A Historical Geography.* Rev. ed. Jerusalem: Carta.

Ayalon, Etan, Rafael Frankel, and Amos Kloner, eds. 2009. *Oil and Wine Presses in Israel from the Hellenistic, Roman and Byzantine Periods.* BAR International Series 1972. Oxford: Archaeopress.

Borowski, Oded. 1987. *Agriculture in Iron Age Israel.* Winona Lake, IN: Eisenbrauns.

———. 1992. "Agriculture." *ABD* 1:95–98.

Duncan-Jones, Richard. 1982. *The Economy of the Roman Empire: Quantitative Studies.* 2nd ed. Cambridge: Cambridge University Press.

Eitam, David, and Michael Heltzer, eds. 1996. *Olive Oil in Antiquity: Israel and Neighbouring Countries from the Neolithic to the Early Arab Periods.* History of the Ancient Near East/Studies 7. Padova, Italy: Sargon.

Falk, Daniel K. 2010. "Festivals and Holy Days." *EDEJ*, 636–45.

Fiensy, David A. 1991. *The Social History of Palestine in the Herodian Period: The Land Is Mine.* Lewiston, NY: Mellen.

———. 2020. *The Archaeology of Daily Life: Ordinary Persons in Later Second Temple Israel.* Eugene, OR: Cascade.

Frankel, Rafael. 2009. "Introduction." Pages 1–18 in Ayalon, Frankel, and Kloner.

———. 2013. "Corn, Oil, and Wine Production." Pages 233–44 in *The Oxford Encyclopedia of the Bible and Archaeology.* Edited by Daniel M. Master. New York: Oxford University Press.

Fu, Janling, Cynthia Shafer-Elliott, and Carol Meyers, eds. 2022. *T&T Clark Handbook of Food in the Hebrew Bible and Ancient Israel.* New York: Bloomsbury.

Hamel, Gildas H. 1989. *Poverty and Charity in Roman Palestine, First Three Centuries C.E.* University of California Publications: Near Eastern Studies 23. Berkeley: University of California Press.

———. 2010. "Poverty and Charity." Pages 308–24 in Hezser.

Hanson, K. C., and Douglas E. Oakman. 1998. *Palestine in the Time of Jesus: Social Structures and Social Conflicts.* Minneapolis: Fortress.

Harland, Philip A. 2002. "The Economy of First-Century Palestine: State of the Scholarly Discussion." Pages 511–27 in *Handbook of Early Christianity: Social Science Approaches.* Edited by Anthony J. Blasi, Jean Duhaime, and Paul-André Turcotte. Walnut Creek, CA: AltaMira.

Hezser, Catherine, ed. 2010. *The Oxford Handbook of Jewish Daily Life in Roman Palestine.* Oxford: Oxford University Press.

Hopkins, David C. 2007. "'All Sorts of Field Work': Agricultural Labor in Ancient Palestine." Pages 149–72 in *To Break Every Yoke: Essays in Honor of Marvin L. Chaney.* Edited by Robert B. Coote and Norman K. Gottwald. Sheffield: Sheffield Phoenix.

Howes, Llewellyn. 2022. "The Agricultural Background of the Harvest Logion in Matthew 9.37–[3]8 and Luke (Q) 10.2." *NTS* 69:57–75.

Hyland, Ann. 1990. *Equus: The Horse in the Roman World.* London: Basford.

Jeremias, Joachim. 1963. *The Parables of Jesus.* Rev. ed. Translated by S. H. Hooke. New York: Scribner's Sons.

Keddie, G. Anthony. 2019. *Class and Power in Roman Palestine: The Socioeconomic Setting of Judaism and Christian Origins.* Cambridge: Cambridge University Press.

Kloppenborg, John S. 2006. *The Tenants in the Vineyard: Ideology, Economics and Agrarian Conflict in Jewish Palestine.* WUNT 195. Tübingen: Mohr Siebeck.

Leibner, Uzi. 2010. "Arts and Crafts, Manufacture and Production." Pages 264–96 in Hezser.

Oakman, Douglas E. 1986. *Jesus and the Economic Questions of His Day.* SBEC 8. Lewiston: Mellen.

———. 2008. *Jesus and the Peasants.* Eugene, OR: Cascade.

Payne, Philip B. 1978–79. "The Order of Sowing and Ploughing in the Parable of the Sower." *NTS* 25:123–29.

Pilch, John. 1993. "The Necessities of Life: Drinking and Eating." *TBT* 31:231–37.

Pritchard, James B., ed. 2011. *The Ancient Near East: An Anthology of Texts and Pictures.* Princeton: Princeton University Press.

Safrai, Ze'ev. 1994. *The Economy of Roman Palestine.* London: Routledge.

———. 2010. "Agriculture and Farming." Pages 246–63 in Hezser.

Scott, Bernard Brandon. 1989. *Hear Then the Parable.* Minneapolis: Fortress.

Singer, Avraham. 1996. "The Traditional Cultivation of the Olive Tree." Pages 29–39 in Eitam and Heltzer.

Wagner, David. 1996. "Oil Production at Gamla." Pages 301–6 in Eitam and Heltzer.

Walsh, Carey Ellen. 2022. "Grapes and Wine." Pages 125–38 in Fu, Shafer-Elliott, and Meyers.

Welch, Eric Lee. 2022. "Olives and Olive Oil." Pages 113–23 in Fu, Shafer-Elliott, and Meyers.

White, Kenneth D. 1964. "The Parable of the Sower." *JTS* 15:300–307.

Chapter 11

Fishermen

Fishnet (Matt 13:47–48)

*A*lthough only one of Jesus' parables features fishermen, the region in which most of his ministry occurred, the west side of the Sea of Galilee, was the heart of the Galilean fishing industry. Four of Jesus' disciples were fishermen. Jesus taught from their boats and traveled around and across the lake by boat. He fed multitudes with loaves and fish (Mark 6:35–44 par.; Mark 8:1–10 par.), and the risen Jesus prepared a shore breakfast of bread and fish for his disciples (John 21:9–14). Jesus also frequented the centers of the fishing industry (Capernaum, Magdala [Migdal], and Kursi [on the northeast shore of the Sea of Galilee; Dalmanutha?]). Following Jesus' instructions, the disciples let down their nets and enclosed a great catch of fish (Luke 5:1–10; John 21:1–8); also, Jesus tells Peter to cast a fishhook into the lake, open the mouth of the first fish he caught, and he would find a silver coin (a *statēr*) with which he could pay the temple tax (Matt 17:24–27). A hungry boy might ask his father for fish (Matt 7:10//Luke 11:11) or carry a lunch of bread and fish (Mark 6:38; John 6:9). The parable of the fishnet likens the kingdom of God to a dragnet that "was thrown into the sea and caught fish of every kind; when it was full, they drew it ashore, sat down, and put the good into baskets but threw out the bad" (Matt 13:47–48). Only recently, however, have scholars recognized the significance of the fishing industry in Galilee for understanding Jesus' ministry and teaching (Wuellner 1967; Hanson 1997; Hakola 2017; Bauckham 2018).

The Sea of Galilee (Kinneret, Num 34:11; Josh 13:27; Gennesaret, Luke 5:1; or Tiberias, John 21:1) is an inland lake fed by the Jordan River. This pear-shaped lake is thirteen miles long (north to south) and eight miles across at its greatest width. The waters around its north and south shores are relatively shallow, with its greatest depths, around 150 feet, at its center. Josephus provides the following description:

The lake of Gennesaret takes its name from the adjacent territory. . . . Notwithstanding its extent, its water is sweet to the taste and excellent to drink: clearer than marsh water with its thick sediment. It is perfectly pure, the lake everywhere ending in pebbly or sandy beaches. Moreover, when drawn it has an agreeable temperature, more pleasant than that of river or spring water, yet invariably cooler than the expanse of the lake would lead one to expect. . . . The lake contains species of fish different, both in taste and appearance, from those found elsewhere. (*J.W.* 3.508)

11.1 Fish

Four of the nineteen species of fish in the Sea of Galilee in antiquity were eaten: freshwater sardines, tilapia, barbels, and catfish (Bauckham 2018, 186–87). The warm springs at Tabgha (southwest of Capernaum) and the nutrients flowing into the lake at the mouth of the Jordan River (near Bethsaida) at the north end of the lake attract the tilapia (De Luca, 172). The area around Kursi also provided good fishing. The schools of sardines and tilapia (*musht*, Saint Peter's fish) can be caught most easily in winter, until late March or early April. The *Tilapia galilaea* is Palestine's most common freshwater fish. The barbel (carp) can be eaten, but it is bony. Although the dietary laws forbade eating catfish (because it does not have scales; Lev 11:9–12; Deut 14:9–10), catfish bones have been found at both et-Tell and Sepphoris (Bauckham 2018, 188). Actually, following the pentateuchal references, these prohibitions do not appear again until the Roman period (Philo, *Spec. Laws* 4.101, 110–112; cf. 4 Macc 1:34; Adler and Lernau, 7–8). The lake also contained a raven-black fish that resembled an eel, leading some Galileans to imagine that the Sea of Galilee was a branch of the Nile, "from its producing a fish resembling the *coracin* found in the lake of Alexandria [Lake Mareotis]" (Josephus, *J.W.* 3.520). The Nile catfish (*Clarias gariepinus*), which grows to about forty inches long, is the largest of the fish in the Jordan River system (Fradkin, 112; Driesch and Boessneck, 99). Since any of these species might be caught in their nets, the fishermen had to sort their catch before taking it to market (Matt 13:47–50).

Excavations at Sepphoris and Tell Hesban (in Jordan) give some indication of the quantity and varieties of fish that were consumed. These finds also confirm a lively trade in fish from the Mediterranean and the Sea of Galilee, especially in the Hellenistic and Roman eras, with more saltwater fish than freshwater (Driesch and Boessneck, 99; Hakola, 118–19; Bauckham 2018, 262). At Sepphoris, the majority of the fish and mollusks came from the Mediterranean, although others came from the Sea of Galilee, the

Jordan River, and as far away as the Nile River (Fradkin, 107–8, 112–13).
Only a limited number of fish bones from the Roman period have been
found in the Jerusalem city dump (Adler and Lernau, 18), but among these
are bones of carp, cichlids, and catfish, which may have been imported
from Magdala (Luff, 174).

The varieties of fish became a rubric for characterizing students of the
rabbis:

> On the subject of disciples Rabban Gamaliel the Elder [ca. 10–80 CE]
> spoke of FOUR kinds: An unclean fish, a clean fish, a fish from the
> Jordan, a fish from the Great Sea. An unclean fish: who is that? A poor
> youth who studies Scripture and Mishnah, Halakha and Agada, and is
> without understanding. A clean fish: who is that? That's a rich youth who
> studies Scripture and Mishnah, Halakha and Agada, and has understand-
> ing. A fish from the Jordan: who is that? That's a scholar who studies
> Scripture and Mishnah, Midrash, Halakha, and Agada, and is without the
> talent for give and take. A fish from the Great Sea: who is that? That's
> a scholar who studies Scripture and Mishnah, Midrash, Halakha, and
> Agada, and has the talent for give and take. (Goldin, ARN 40)

11.2 Galilean Fishermen

The status of Galilean fishermen has been the subject of considerable debate.
James and John (the sons of Zebedee) and Peter and Andrew (the sons of
Jonah) were members of fishing families (Matt 16:17; Mark 1:16–20). Did
they organize cooperatives (*koinōnoi*) like their counterparts in Egypt and
elsewhere? Did they have to lease rights to fish in the Sea of Galilee? Did
they own their own boats? Were they relatively secure economically, or
were they the lowest rank within the Galilean fishing industry?

Some level of cooperation or partnership is suggested by the Gospels,
especially the following reference in Luke:

> [Jesus] saw two boats there at the shore of the lake; the fishermen had
> gone out of them and were washing their nets. He got into one of the
> boats, the one belonging to Simon, and asked him to put out a little way
> from the shore. Then he sat down and taught the crowds from the boat.
> When he had finished speaking, he said to Simon, "Put out into the deep
> water and let down your nets for a catch." Simon answered, "Master, we
> have worked all night long but have caught nothing. Yet if you say so, I
> will let down the nets." When they had done this, they caught so many
> fish that their nets were beginning to break. So they signaled their part-
> ners [*metochois*] in the other boat to come and help them. (5:2–7)

A few verses later, James and John, the sons of Zebedee, are called Simon Peter's "partners" (*koinōnoi*, 5:10). Based on the systems in Egypt and Syria, Wuellner (23–25) proposed that Galilean fishermen formed cooperatives to bid for fishing contracts and leases. Hanson disputes Wuellner's conclusion that the Jonah-Zebedee cooperative were "professional middle[-]class fish catcher[s] and fish trader[s]" because they owned the boats. On the contrary,

> the boats were actually owned by the brokers and used by the coopera-
> tive. . . . I see no reason to conclude that they were in a different "social
> class" than the fishing families who owned boats. We see both working
> alongside each other in the gospels (e.g., Mark 1:20). I conclude that both
> of these groups were "peasants" in the broad sense, since they both live
> from their work in the boats. (Hanson, 104)

Responding to Wuellner's conclusion that the fishermen were "middle class," while assuming that the Galilean economy was "a highly regulated, taxed, and hierarchical political-economy," Hanson rightly observes that they were "certainly not 'middle-class,' as many authors have contended, since the whole conceptualization of a middle-class is anachronistic relative to Roman Palestine" (Hanson, 108; see the discussion of Friesen's poverty scale above, 9.2). The hired laborers were "manning the oars and sails, mending nets, sorting fish. . . . These laborers represent the bottom of the social scale in the fishing sub-system" (Hanson, 106).

Caution is in order regarding importing evidence for organizations and administrative patterns from elsewhere in the eastern Mediterranean. From the Egyptian and Syrian patterns, Hanson (103) argues that fishermen were indebted to local brokers for fishing leases. He further suggests, "The location of Levi's toll office in Capernaum—an important fishing locale—probably identifies him as just such a contractor of royal fishing rights" (Matt 9:9//Mark 2:13–14; cf. Wuellner, 43–44; Hanson and Oakman, 106–10). While it is possible that Herod Antipas sought to establish a royal monopoly on fishing in the Sea of Galilee, it is more likely that no centralized authority controlled the cities around the lake (Bauckham 2018, 264–65). Hakola suggests, "In a situation like this, it is probable that fishermen, Jews as well as non-Jews, from different administrative areas were able to practice their profession on the lake without the intrusion of patrolling officials. It is not likely that any kind of central authority would have issued fishing licenses and then tried to control where Galilean fishermen from various cities or towns around the lake laid their nets" (124). Instead of leases, customs dues or taxes were paid on fish brought to the harbor and sold in markets.

Associations of fishermen are attested in first- and second-century papyri from Egypt (P.Oxy. 3495; PSI 8.901; P.Corn. 46) and an inscription from

Ephesus (*IEph* 20, 54–59 CE; Bauckham 2018, 234–44). While there is no direct evidence of such associations in Galilee, Luke's references to the fishermen as "partners" suggest that they were fellow members of an association. Although the extent to which the documents from Egypt are reflective of arrangements in Galilee is debated (Bauckham 2018, 263–65), the fishermen probably owned their own boats. Josephus claims he collected all the boats he could find on the lake, 230 boats, for a ruse by which he duped Tiberias into surrendering without a fight (*J.W.* 2.635). From this number, Safrai calculated that "almost every extended family (7–8 persons or 4 males) possessed a fishing boat" (164).

11.3 Boats

Josephus describes the Jews' "skiffs" as being "small and built for piracy" (*J.W.* 3.523). They took a crew of five and could carry ten others (*J.W.* 2.639; *Life* 168). Thanks to the vigilance of amateur archaeologists in the region, an example of this class of boat was discovered in January 1986 when drought reduced the water level of the lake. The shell of the boat—26.5 feet long, 7.5 feet wide, and 4.5 feet high—was mostly buried in the mud near the edge of the Sea of Galilee between Kibbutz Ginnosar and Migdal. Initially there was speculation that the boat may have been used in the Battle of Migdal (67 CE). Josephus reports that the Jews "were sent to the bottom with their skiffs" and "the beaches were strewn with wrecks" (*J.W.* 3.525, 530). Further study, however, revealed that the boat underwent numerous repairs before it was stripped of reusable parts and pushed out into the lake. The mast block, stempost, and sternpost had been removed. The shell was made by a master craftsman using cedar planking and oak frames held together by mortise-and-tenon joints, a construction technique found in other Mediterranean vessels. A carbon-14 test indicated that the wood used for the boat dated to 40 BCE, plus or minus 80 years; hence, 120 BCE to 40 CE. It is uncertain, however, how long the boat was in use before it was scuttled. By all accounts, it appears to have been a typical fishing vessel used during the period of Jesus and the disciples (Wachsmann; Bauckham 2018, 218–24).

A similar vessel is depicted in a first-century mosaic found in the floor of a villa in Migdal (https://commons.wikimedia.org/wiki/File:Boat_from_Magdala_Mosaic.jpg). Like the boat recovered from the lake, the boat depicted in the mosaic could be rowed or sailed. It was designed for a crew with four rowers and a helmsman, who would have stood on a large stern platform. The mosaic is a symbolic representation of a small-to-medium-sized vessel designed to transport cargo or passengers: "The Migdal Ship may have been used as an auxiliary vessel in the navy stationed on the shores of the Sea of Galilee (patrolling or transporting . . . supplies and warriors). This ship also could be engaged in maritime trade on the Sea of Galilee or even fishing" (Freidman, 53). Josephus's report that Vespasian ordered the construction of rafts at Taricheae—and that, "with an abundance of wood and of workmen, the flotilla was soon ready" (*J.W.* 3.505)—implies a boatyard near Magdala where craftsmen and the wood for making rafts were available (Bauckham 2018, 220).

11.4 Nets

Line fishing, either with bait or to snag fish, was not sufficiently productive for commercial purposes, but especially the wealthy may have fished for recreation: "A fine bronze fishhook was found in an Early Roman context in the fountain house" at Magdala (Bauckham 2018, 213). No Galilean nets have survived the centuries, but lead sinkers, specifically net sinkers (larger than those used for line fishing) have been recovered at et-Tell and el-Araj (Aviam, personal communication), Hippos, Tabgha, and Magdala (Bauckham 2018, 208–11). Oppian (late 2nd or early 3rd c. CE) lists eight types of nets in his treatise on fishing but allows for "innumerable" others (*Hal.* 3.79–84). Some of these can no longer be identified.

The Gospels contain three terms for nets. The cast net (*amphiblēstron*, Matt 4:18) was a circular net up to twenty feet across, with weights around the circumference. The fisherman waded out, watched for signs of fish, cast the net so that it fanned out in a circle, and drew it in by means of a center cord that pulled cords attached to the circumference of the net so that fish beneath the net would be entrapped in it. Mark 1:16 says Jesus saw Simon and Andrew, probably wading near the shore, casting their nets (*amphiballontas*) into the lake. Jesus' parable describes the use of a dragnet or large seine, a *sagēnē*, which could be several hundred yards long (Hab 1:15; Eccl 9:12; Ezek 26:5; 47:10; Matt 13:47–48). The net is set out by boat in a large semicircle, with the two ends near the shore. The top of the net is held up by floats, while the bottom is anchored with weights. Men on the shore then draw the net in by means of ropes attached to the upper and lower corners, keeping the net in constant motion while it is being retrieved. These fishing operations were often carried out near the shore. In John 21:7, Peter is stripped, ready to jump into the lake to free the net when it catches on the bottom. The Gospels also use the general term when the fishermen were washing and mending their "nets" (*diktya*; Matt 4:21//Mark 1:19; Luke 5:2). Jesus' command to "let down" the nets may imply that they were using trammel nets, although the use of such nets in the first century has not been confirmed. Bauckham disputes the interpretation of the plural reference to "nets" in Mark 1:19 and Luke 5:1–7 as evidence that the disciples used trammel nets: "As far as I can tell, there is no good evidence of the use of the trammel net in antiquity" (2018, 196–97). He therefore postulates that they used seines or dragnets from their boats (202). Trammel nets consisted of three to five nets combined to form a barrier with which to encircle schools of fish. Like the drag net, the trammel nets were held up by floats and anchored by weights. Fish could swim through the outer nets, which had a wide mesh, and become trapped by a net with fine mesh. The verbs used to describe the great catch of fish do not conclusively settle the question of the type of nets used. Luke 5:6 uses *synkleiō*, which means "to catch by enclosing, close up together, hem in, enclose" (BDAG, 952); John 21:6 says that when they "cast" (*ebalon*) their net they were no longer able to "draw" it up (*helkysai*, which John uses elsewhere [6:44; 12:32]). After surveying the available literary and archaeological evidence, Bauckham judiciously concludes, "Cast nets, beach seines, and boat seines were certainly used, and gill nets may well have been used. There was also some line fishing" (2018, 214–15).

11.5 Harbors

The lack of natural harbors, apart from two small bays which lie northeast and southwest of Capernaum, created the need for man-made shelters, especially during the winter months. Remains of stone harbors exist at New Testament sites—Capernaum, Gennesar, Magdala (Taricheae), Gadara, Gergasa, and elsewhere (Hanson, 103; De Luca and Lena, 325–26; Bauckham 2018, 225). Correlating the elevations of these harbors and mooring stones with first-century roads and floor levels of buildings near the lake establishes that the water level was around 209.5 meters below sea level in the early Roman period and fell to 212 meters below sea level in the Byzantine period. Most of the stone remains of harbors correlate with the water level during the Byzantine era. Only the harbors at Magdala, Kursi (on the east side of the lake, which may have been the otherwise unknown place called Dalmanutha in Mark 8:10; Bauckham 2017), and possibly Tiberias date to the early Roman period. These were important centers for the fish trade located near good fishing waters. Other harbors, wooden, must have been built near the fishing villages at the shallow, north end of the lake, but these have not survived (Bauckham 2018, 224–31).

Strabo, who had never been to Galilee, writes, "At the place called Taricheae the lake supplies excellent fish for pickling" (*Geogr.* 16.2.45). The identification of Taricheae with Magdala/Migdal, also designated Migdal Tsebayya (the Tower of Dryers) and Migdal Nuniyya (the Tower of Fish) in later rabbinic literature, is generally accepted (De Luca and Lena, 280–83; Bauckham 2018, 360; but disputed by Taylor and by Schrader and Taylor); the archaeological evidence confirms that Magdala was a center of the fish-processing industry. Vats probably used for fish processing have been discovered there.

Magdala was founded in the first century BCE by the Hasmoneans, sacked and partly abandoned in 67 CE, but continued to exist until the fourth century. The harbor was extended in the first century CE, when the fishing industry in the area flourished, suggesting that "the founding of Tiberias can be seen as part of Antipas' attempts to get the already thriving trade, including the fishing business, under his control" (Hakola, 114; see also Udoh, 380). The custom house in Capernaum (where Levi/Matthew worked) and the local "clerk of the market" (*agoranomos*) at Magdala are probably further evidence of Herod Antipas's efforts to regulate and tax the local fishing industry (Hakola, 126–28; Chancey, 88; see above, 5.4). Although Magdala was more prosperous than Capernaum, a fine set of glassware and a high-grade mausoleum from the early Roman period were found in Capernaum (Mattila 2013, 90–95; Mattila 2015, 245), suggesting that some "were able to benefit from the Galilean fishing economy and gain a moderate livelihood from their profession" (Hakola, 129; see Mattila 2013, 130).

Fishing at night provided fresh fish for the markets the next day. Fish not sold fresh were dried on racks or salted either commercially or by individual families. The fish in the feeding stories in the Gospels are probably dried fish. Salt was brought to Magdala from the Dead Sea (Zwickel, 172). Before salting, the fish were split, cleaned, rinsed thoroughly, and soaked in brine. They were then placed in a vat or large vessel with salt added between each layer of fish. Heavy weights were placed over the top layer of salt to press liquid out of the fish and salt into it. The liquid could be drained from the salted fish and consumed as a fish sauce (*garum*) or paste (*allec*). The fish could also be left in the preserving brine and transported in an amphora (a large jar with handles). When it was removed from the brine, the fish were dried. Pickled fish had to be soaked in water to remove some of the salt before it was eaten (Bauckham 2018, 248–49). Garum and allec were byproducts of curing fish, and garum was commonly used as a seasoning in place of salt. Processed fish were loaded on donkeys, transported to towns in lower Galilee and beyond, and sold in the markets. However, because the species of fish preserved in a briny fish sauce could not be determined, such fish could not be bought from non-Jews (m. ʿAbod. Zar. 2:6; see m. Ter. 10:8).

11.6 Reflections: Fish Iconography in the Early Church

Jesus called Galilean fishermen to follow him. Then he taught them by using metaphors and images drawn from their trade. Jesus said, "Follow me, and I will make you fishers of men." The missionary activity of the church is deliberately prefigured in this call story. In the Greek philosophical literature, fishing was a metaphor for teaching, learning, and rhetoric. Like the angler, the sophist seeks to persuade (Plato, *Soph.* 218d–222d). In Jewish literature, fish and fishing were associated with judgment, defeat, and captivity (Amos 4:2; Hab 1:14–15; 1QH V, 8). In Jeremiah 16:15–18, following a reference to Israel's idolatry and exile, Jeremiah records three related words of the Lord: (1) "I will bring them back to their own land"; (2) "I am now sending for many fishermen, . . . and they shall catch them"; and (3) "I will doubly repay their iniquity and their sin." The role of the fishermen in this context is presumably to find the Israelites and bring them back for judgment. Jindřich Manek (139) proposed an allegorical interpretation: "To fish out a man means to rescue him from the kingdom of darkness." The metaphor is found in the Jewish literature before it was adopted by the early church: "And by his beauty he caught me, and by his wisdom he grasped me like a fish on a hook" (Jos. Asen. 21.21).

John's account of the miraculous catch of fish reflects ecclesiastical interpretation of the tradition. The catch is so great that the disciples are unable to draw it in (21:6); they drag it to shore, where the risen Lord has prepared a charcoal fire (21:9; cf. 18:18) on which lay fish and bread. Responding to the Lord's command, Peter hauls the net ashore, "full of large fish, a hundred fifty-three of them; and though there were so many, the net was not torn" (21:11). Assuming that the number must have some significance, interpreters have spared no effort to find a symbolic meaning by factoring it as the sum of 100, 50, and 3; noting that it is the sum of the numbers one to 17 (10 plus 7 or 12 plus 5), which can be arranged as a pyramid; using gematria to find phrases whose letters total 153; or appealing to biblical references where names equal 17 and 153 (Ezek 47:10; see further Culpepper, 536–47). Jerome (Migne, PL 25, 474C, translation in Hoskyns, 554) cites writers, among them the poet Oppianus Cilix, who claimed there were 153 different kinds of fish, which provides the appealing symbolism that the disciples caught one of each species. After writing his commentary on this reference, Raymond Brown quipped at a professional meeting (at which the author was present) that he had a recurring dream that when he got to heaven, he would ask the apostle John why he wrote that there were 153 fish, and every night the apostle gave the same answer: "because that's how many there were."

The comment that the net "was not torn" (*ouk eschisthē*; lit., "had no schism") repeats John's emphasis on the unity of the church (10:16; 11:52; 17:11, 21–23; 19:23) and confirms that John interprets the catch of fish as prefiguring the risen Lord's guiding presence with the church as it fulfills its mission to "draw all people" to the Lord (see 12:32).

Early Christian iconography incorporated fish imagery, probably because it was already in wide use in pagan culture and associated with death and new life. Günther Bornkamm (55) followed Tertullian (*Bapt.* 12) in seeing the boat as an image of "the little ship of the Church." Ulrich Luz (21) suggests that the metaphor of the storm and the transparency of the disciples as the church in Matthew's account of the stilling of the storm (8:23–27) led to the metaphor of the church as a ship. At least it is clear that the boat became a symbol for the church by the end of the second century (cf., similarly, Noah's ark in 1 Pet 3:20).

By this time, the early church was interpreting Christ and believers as fish: "But we, little fishes, after the example of our IXΘΥΣ Jesus Christ, are born in water, nor have we safety in any other way than by permanently abiding in water" (Tertullian, *Bapt.* 1; *ANF* 3:669; see also Sib. Or. 8.217–250). An inscription on the grave monument of Avercius, bishop of Hieropolis, is dated between 192/193 and 212 CE and describes the fish as "a symbol that was understood by all Christians *everywhere*" (Kant, 347). Origen refers to unbelievers as irrational fish (*Hom. Jer.* 16.1), and the Pseudo-Clementine *Recognitions* contain a story about Peter being so lost in thought that he did not realize he had a large fish on his line (2.62–63).

Tertullian claims that the followers of Marcion considered fish "the more sacred diet" (*Marc.* 1.14; *ANF* 3:281). Meals of fish and bread are a common subject in the catacomb iconography of the second to the fourth centuries and in the bas-reliefs of sarcophagi belonging to the fourth and fifth centuries. Lawrence Kant provides the following synopsis of the evidence: "In general, a single large, long, and undivided fish is placed on one or more oval platters. In all the relevant paintings of CatPM [Catacomb of Peter and Marcellinus in Rome] and in some sarcophagi, these platters rest on round three-legged tables; . . . in all other paintings and in many sarcophagi, they rest directly on the ground" (519–20). Kant comments: "The fish is here a symbolic representation of a cultic practice in which Christians ingested the body of Christ in the form of bread and wine. . . . In other words, the eucharist did not actually involve fish as part of the menu, but fish symbolically represented the eucharist" (375). By the time of Augustine, the association of the roasted fish with the suffering Christ had become formulaic: *"Piscis assus, Christus est passus"* ("The roasted fish is the suffering Christ"; Augustine, *Trac. Ev. Jo.* 123.2; Kant, 485, 719).

Robin Jensen cites the discovery of a mid-third-century banquet hall beside a complex of pagan and Christian catacombs and mausoleums dating from the second century, under the church of San Sebastiano in Rome. From this he concludes, "The Christian banquet paintings portray a combination of the post-resurrectional meal described in John 21, a meal in Paradise granted to the baptized, and an actual funerary banquet held in honor of the deceased" (Jensen, 48). The fish on the fire in John 21:9, therefore, can represent the Eucharist, Christ, who nourishes the believer, or a meal in which Christians ate bread and fish, with or without the Eucharist (Culpepper, 550–53).

In this way, the historical context of Jesus' ministry in the heart of the fishing industry around the Sea of Galilee has suggested fish imagery that tapped ordinary meals of fish and bread, associations in the Hebrew Scriptures, and Greco-Roman ceremonial, religious, and funerary meals.

Works Cited in Chapter 11

Adler, Yonatan, and Omri Lernau. 2021. "The Pentateuchal Dietary Prescription against Finless and Scaleless Aquatic Species in Light of Ancient Fish Remains." *Tel Aviv* 48:5–26.

Bauckham, Richard. 2017. "Where Was Dalmanutha? Mark 8:10." Pages 23–29 in *Texts and Contexts: Gospels and Pauline Studies.* Edited by Todd D. Still. Waco, TX: Baylor University Press.

———. 2018. *Magdala of Galilee: A Jewish City in the Hellenistic and Roman Period.* Waco, TX: Baylor University Press.

Bornkamm, Günther. 1963. "The Stilling of the Storm in Matthew." Pages 52–57 in Günther Bornkamm, Gerhard Barth, and Heinz Joachim Held, *Tradition and Interpretation in Matthew.* Translated by Percy Scott. NTL. Philadelphia: Westminster.

Chancey, Mark A. 2005. *Greco-Roman Culture and the Galilee of Jesus.* SNTSMS 134. Cambridge: Cambridge University Press.

Culpepper, R. Alan. 2021. *Designs for the Church in the Gospel of John: Collected Essays, 1980–2020.* WUNT 465. Tübingen: Mohr Siebeck.

De Luca, Stefano. 2013. "Capernaum." Pages 168–80 in vol. 1 of *The Oxford Encyclopedia of the Bible and Archaeology.* 2 vols. Edited by Daniel M. Master. Oxford: Oxford University Press.

De Luca, Stefano, and Anna Lena. 2015. "Magdala/Taricheae." Pages 280–342 in vol. 2 of Fiensy and Strange.

Driesch, Angela von den, and Joachim Boessneck. 1995. "Final Report on the Zooarchaeological Investigation of Animal Bone Finds from Tell Hesban, Jordan." Pages 65–108 in

Faunal Remains: Taphonomical and Zooarhaeological Studies of the Animal Remains from Tell Hesban and Vicinity. Edited by Øystein Sakala LaBianca and Angela von den Driesch. Hesban 13. Berrien Springs, MI: Andrews University Press.

Fiensy, David A., and James R. Strange, eds. 2014–15. *Galilee in the Late Second Temple and Mishnaic Periods.* 2 vols. Minneapolis: Fortress.

Fradkin, Arlene. 1997. "Long-Distance Trade in the Lower Galilee: New Evidence from Sepphoris." Pages 107–16 in *Archaeology and the Galilee: Texts and Contexts in the Graeco-Roman and Byzantine Periods.* Edited by Douglas R. Edwards and C. Thomas McCollough. Atlanta: Scholars Press.

Freidman [*sic*], Zaraza. 2008. "The Ship Depicted in a Mosaic from Migdal, ISRAEL." *JMR* 1–2:45–54.

Hakola, Raimo. 2017. "The Production and Trade of Fish as Source of Economic Growth in the First Century CE Galilee: Galilean Economy Reconsidered." *NovT* 59:111–30.

Hanson, Kenneth C. 1997. "The Galilean Fishing Economy and the Jesus Tradition." *BTB* 27:99–111.

Hanson, Kenneth C., and Douglas E. Oakman. 1998. *Palestine in the Time of Jesus: Social Structures and Social Conflicts.* Minneapolis: Fortress.

Hoskyns, Edwin C. 1947. *The Fourth Gospel.* Edited by F. N. Davey. London: Faber & Faber.

Jensen, Robin A. 1998. "Dining in Heaven: The Earliest Christian Visions of Paradise." *BRev* 14:32–39.

Kant, Laurence H. 1993. "The Interpretation of Religious Symbols in the Graeco-Roman World: A Case Study of Early Christian Fish Symbolism." 3 vols. in 2. PhD diss., Yale University.

Luff, Rosemary Margaret. 2019. *The Impact of Jesus in First-Century Palestine: Textual and Archaeological Evidence for Long-Standing Discontent.* Cambridge: Cambridge University Press.

Luz, Ulrich. 2001. *Matthew.* Vol. 2. Translated by James E. Crouch. Hermeneia. Minneapolis: Fortress.

Manek, Jindřich. 1957. "Fishers of Men." *NovT* 2:138–41.

Mattila, Sharon Lea. 2013. "Revisiting Jesus' Capernaum: A Village of Only Subsistence-Level Fishers and Farmers?" Pages 75–138 in *The Galilean Economy in the Time of Jesus.* Edited by David A. Fiensy and Ralph K. Hawkins. Atlanta: Society of Biblical Literature.

———. 2015. "Capernaum, Village of Naḥum, from Hellenistic to Byzantine Times." Pages 217–57 in vol. 2 of Fiensy and Strange.

Safrai, Ze'ev. 1994. *The Economy of Roman Palestine.* London: Routledge.

Schrader, Elizabeth, and Joan E. Taylor. 2021. "The Meaning of 'Magdalene': A Review of Literary Evidence." *JBL* 140:751–73.

Taylor, Joan E. 2014. "Missing Magdala and the Name of Mary 'Magdalene.'" *PEQ* 146:205–23.

Udoh, Fabian. 2014. "Taxation and Other Sources of Government Income." Pages 366–87 in vol. 1 of Fiensy and Strange.

Wachsmann, Shelley. 1988. "The Galilee Boat—2,000 Year-Old Hull Recovered Intact." *BAR* 14.5:18–33.

Wuellner, Wilhelm. 1967. *The Meaning of "Fishers of Men."* NTL. Philadelphia: Westminster.

Zwickel, Wolfgang. 2013. "Der See Gennesaret in hellenistischer und frührömischer Zeit." *ZNW* 104:153–76.

Chapter 12

Shepherds

Lost Sheep (Matt 18:12–13//Luke 15:4–6)
Sheep and Goats (Matt 25:31–46)
Good Shepherd (John 10:1–5)

Shepherds did not leave scrolls or inscriptions for archaeologists to recover, but this humble occupation left a larger-than-life legacy in Israel's traditions and Scripture. Two Synoptic parables and a Johannine discourse feature shepherds. The parable of the lost sheep focuses on the predilection of sheep to wander, the shepherd's duty to safeguard every sheep in his care, and his joy in recovering a stray sheep. The parable of the sheep and the goats likens the judgment on the nations to a shepherd separating sheep from goats at the end of the day. The discourse on the Good Shepherd in John 10 adopts several features from sheepherding: the distinction between a shepherd and a hireling, the threat of wolves and thieves, and entering the sheepfold through a gate. The good shepherd lays down his life for the sheep, and his sheep respond to his voice. The hireling abandons the sheep in time of danger, and the sheep will not come when he calls them. Jesus' teachings, therefore, evoke the daily work of a shepherd, but they also resonate with the shepherds in Israel's Scriptures (Abel, Jacob, Moses, and David) and the characterization of shepherds in the psalms (Ps 23) and the prophets (Ezek 34). Commenting on the prominence of shepherding in Israel's Scriptures, Philo writes, "For the men of the nation are noted particularly as graziers and stock-breeders, and keep flocks and herds of goats and oxen and sheep and of every kind of animal in vast numbers" (*Spec. Laws* 1.136)

By gathering clues to the role of shepherds in first-century Galilee, then surveying the development of the shepherd-king motif, we can set Jesus' parables in context and better understand how they may have been heard by rural Galileans.

12.1 Shepherds and Sheepherding in Galilee

While many Galilean farmers probably kept a few sheep and goats, sheep-herding was not an important part of their economy. The available land was limited, and it was more profitable to cultivate the land than to graze sheep on it, particularly in lower Galilee. In Judea and southern Palestine, which were more arid, sheep could be grazed in the desert throughout the year or grazed in the summer (from Passover until the first rain) and returned to the settlement during the winter (Safrai 1994, 165). Feeding livestock in the winter was such a problem that owners resorted to whatever was available: "straw, branches, young shoots, hay, rice-stalks, unripe corn-stalks, carobs and gourds, and the pods of peas and lentils" (Applebaum, 656).

The Mishnah distinguishes between "domestic animals," which may be watered or slaughtered during a festival; and "desert animals," which may not (m. Beṣah 5:7; b. Beṣah 40a). Parenthetically, watering and slaughtering are mentioned together because if the animal was watered, it was easier to skin after it was slaughtered. Sheepherder settlements near the desert, such as Anab-a-Kabir (13 miles southwest of Hebron), had sheep pens with a room for the herder and courtyards for the sheep (Safrai 1994, 165). In Galilee, especially in lower Galilee, the average farmer may have kept only a few sheep for their wool and contracted with a shepherd to graze and tend his sheep (m. Beṣah 5:3; m. B. Qam. 6:2; Safrai 1994, 165–67, 170). Flocks were often mingled, having sheep from various owners (Kloppen-borg, 59). Because of the nature of the terrain, sheep grazing was probably more common in the upper Galilee (Safrai 1994, 168).

One could either milk the sheep or raise lambs, but not both. Therefore, goats generally provided milk, while sheep were raised for their wool (b. B. Meṣ. 64a). One sheep would produce enough wool each year for one small garment, while a garment for an adult required three times as much wool (Safrai 1994, 171). Consequently, sheep were slaughtered for food only for special occasions. Shearing the sheep was an annual ritual. Genesis 38 records Judah's sin with Tamar when he went to Timnah (in the southern hill country), "to his sheepshearers" (38:12), and Tobit says, "I would hurry off to Jerusalem with the first fruits of the crops and the firstlings of the flock, the tithes of the cattle, and the first shearings of the sheep" (1:6).

Because Galilean farmers kept only a few sheep while they worked their own lands and at times hired out as tenant farmers to survive, there was a niche in the economy for the "hired" shepherd. Recent study of papyri from Egypt sheds light on shepherding during the New Testament period (Kloppenborg; Huebner, 115–34, esp. 124–26). Shepherds were expected to lead the sheep to pasture, keep the flock together, search out and return lost sheep, protect them from harm and theft, pen them securely at night, and care for weak, pregnant, or injured animals (Huebner, 127).

Shepherds typically came from poor, landless families, often the teen-age son of a local farmer (Huebner, 125). Shepherds moved from place to place. They were unsupervised, armed, and poorly paid, so some turned to banditry (Kloppenborg, 60–62; Huebner, 132–33). Philo's description of a shepherd, even if it is a caricature, may have rung true: "See, there is a shepherd, a goatherd, a cowherd leading flocks of sheep and goats, and herds of kine. They are men not even strong and lusty in body, unlikely, so far as healthy vigour goes, to create consternation in those who see them" (*Creation* 85). Elsewhere, Philo characterizes "the care of literal goats and sheep": "Such pursuits are held mean and inglorious" (*Agr.* 61). Similarly, Josephus relates the story of Athronges, "merely a shepherd," who never-theless "had the temerity to aspire to the kingship" (*Ant.* 17.278). Never-theless, Philo credits shepherds with the virtues of loyalty and a sense of duty; a "keeper of the sheep" or "cattle-rearer" is indifferent to the flock, while "a good and faithful one is called a shepherd" (*Agr.* 29; Harris, 58).

A shepherd would be held liable for any sheep lost on his watch and was required to return the same number and type of the animals entrusted to him (Huebner, 130). While a shepherd was paid only sixteen drachmae (silver coins worth about a denarius) per month, a sheep could sell for 11.5 drachmae or more (Kloppenborg, 63). Of course, a shepherd would go to seek a lost sheep! Head counts of the flocks were also required for tax pur-poses and lease payments for grazing rights.

The flock sizes recorded in the Egyptian papyri are congruent with the size of the flock in Jesus' parable, around eighty to a hundred. Where large landowners might own several hundred to several thousand sheep, the size of flocks was limited to avoid the risk of an epidemic. Around a hundred was also the maximum one shepherd could manage. Flocks of sheep usually included at least one goat, but sometimes as many as a quarter of the flock were goats (Huebner, 126). Apparently, the more curious and aggressive goats reduce the agitation and stress among the timid sheep. In the parable of the sheep and the goats, the shepherd-king does what shepherds have done since the time of Jacob and Laban: he divides the flock at the end of the day (Gen 30:32; Matt 25:32–33).

Hostilities between farmers and sheepherders were as common then as now, yet each needed the other. Sheep provided wool, meat, milk, cheese, and manure. Farmers provided fodder during the dry summer months; while the sheep and goats grazed on the stubble, their manure fertilized the land. Herds could also be enclosed, and the manure collected and carried to other fields. If the fields were not fertilized, the yield would be low; in times of drought, animals would be underfed. It was a vicious cycle. Gildas Hamel describes the problem:

Most certainly, Jewish farmers wished to have well-fed animals that would allow a deeper and more regular plowing. . . . "Abundant crops come by the strength of the ox" (Prov 14:4). This was the desirable state of affairs, but it was not often the case in ancient Palestine. Cows, oxen, and donkeys were often malnourished and tired. It was, therefore, difficult to make them work day after day. The fact that the animals were ill-fed implied a low level of fertilization and traction, which in turn meant that crops could not be very large. (122)

Conflicts arose when the animals grazed where they were not supposed to, especially when they were moved from one field to another (see Gen 13:7; Hamel, 118). Hired shepherds introduced a host of financial and legal issues. What responsibilities and liabilities fell to the hired shepherd? Philo comments on Exodus 22:5, which requires restitution for damages caused by grazing on another's land: "So if anyone in charge of sheep or goats or a herd of any kind feeds and pastures his beasts in the fields of another and does nothing to spare the fruits or the trees, he must recoup the owner in kind by property of equal value" (*Spec. Laws* 4.21–22; cf. 4.25). Some of the judgments codified by the rabbis no doubt reflect standing practices. Legally, "the herdsman stands in the place of the owner" (m. B. Qam. 6:2). What about the damage that stray sheep might cause to crops? "If a man brought his flock into a fold and shut it in properly and it nevertheless came out and caused damage, he is not culpable. If he had not shut it in properly and it came out and caused damage, he is culpable. If the fold was broken through in the night, or if robbers broke into it, and the flock came out and caused damage, he is not culpable. If the robbers brought out the flock the robbers are culpable" (m. B. Qam. 6:1).

Moreover, "None may buy wool or milk from herdsmen" (m. B. Qam. 10:9) because of suspicion that they may have taken it from the flocks in their care. The Talmud further interprets this ruling.

Our Rabbis taught: It is not right to buy from shepherds either goats or kids or fleeces or torn pieces of wool, though it is allowed to buy from them made-up garments, as these are certainly theirs. It is similarly allowed to buy from them milk and cheese in the wilderness though not in inhabited places. It is [also] allowed to buy from them four or five sheep, four or five fleeces, but neither two sheep nor two fleeces. R. Judah says: Domesticated animals may be bought from them but pasture animals may not be bought from them. The general principle is that anything the absence of which, if it is sold by the shepherd, would be noticed by the proprietor, may be bought from the former, but if the proprietor would not notice it, it may not be bought from him. (b. B. Qam. 118b, Soncino)

Later rabbis also included shepherds in their list of despised trades: "A man should not teach his son to be an ass-driver or a camel-driver, or a barber or a sailor, or a herdsman or a shopkeeper, for their craft is the craft of robbers" (m. Qidd. 4:14). The rabbis sanctioned this judgment. According to Joachim Jeremias, "[Shepherds] were *de jure* and officially deprived of rights and ostracized. Anyone engaging in such trades could never be a judge, and his inadmissibility as a witness put him on the same footing as a gentile slave [m. Rosh. Hash. 1:8]. In other words he was deprived of civil and political rights to which every Israelite had claim" (311–12). Such descriptions and judgments stand in sharp contrast to the lofty image of shepherds in many ancient cultures.

12.2 Reflections on the Shepherd-King

The ideal of the shepherd-king was widespread in antiquity, including Assyria, Babylonia, and Egypt. Jennifer Freeman surveys the development of the shepherd tradition and its functions, documenting how, "over the three millennia leading up to the time of Jesus, the shepherd [image] took on connotations of divinity, political authority, and cultic power even as it sometimes functioned to romanticize the nomadic and pre-urban age" (12). The epilogue of the Code of King Hammurabi of Babylon (1792–1750 BCE), for example, reads,

> I am Hammurabi, noble king. I have not been careless or negligent toward humankind, granted to my care by the god Enlil, and with whose shepherding the god Marduk charged me. I have sought for them peaceful places, I removed serious difficulties, I spread light over them. . . . I annihilated enemies everywhere, I put an end to wars, I enhanced the well-being of the land, I made the people of all settlements lie in safe pastures, I did not tolerate anyone intimidating them. The great gods have chosen me; I am indeed the shepherd who brings peace, whose scepter is just. (Freeman, 20, citing Roth, Hoffner, and Michalowski, 133)

Also in Egyptian artifacts, primarily in funerary contexts, the divine and human shepherd-king rules and guides his people into the afterlife (Freeman, 37).

Israel's patriarchs are all portrayed as shepherds. Abraham was "very rich in livestock" (Gen 13:2); Isaac "had possessions of flocks and herds, and a great household, so that the Philistines envied him" (26:14); Jacob bred speckled, spotted, and black sheep and goats in Laban's flock (30:31–43); at seventeen, Joseph "was shepherding the flock with his brothers" (37:2; see Freeman, 37). Even God is imaged as a shepherd.

> YHWH as the ideal shepherd is one who leads and guides his flock [Exod 15:13–17; Pss 5:8; 23:2–3; 31:3; 78:52–55; Isa 49:9–13; Mic 7:14], doing so with gentleness and sensitivity so as not to overburden them [Ps 28:9; Isa 40:11]; he searches for strays [Ezek 34:4, 11–12, 16], gathers his sheep together [Isa 40:11; Jer 31:8–10; Mic 2:12–13], and provides them with pasture [Ezek 34:13–15]; he protects and rescues his flock from danger [Gen 48:15–16; Ezek 34:10], and heals the wounds of the injured [Ezek 34:4, 16]. (Baxter 2009, 213)

In contrast, Israel's leaders are described as false shepherds, especially in the exilic and postexilic prophetic writings (Ezek 34; Jer 23:1–3; Zech 11:4–17). Ezekiel's oracle charges that Israel's leaders feed themselves rather than the sheep (Ezek 34:2, 8) and scatter the flock (Jer 23:1–3). They do not heal the sick, bind up the injured, or search for the lost (Ezek 34:4; Zech 11:16). They rule harshly (Ezek 34:4). Therefore, the sheep were scattered, with no one to search for them (34:6).

In postbiblical Jewish literature the shepherd is associated with qualities of leadership, especially compassion and teaching. For Sirach, "YHWH as a shepherd represents the embodiment of compassion" (Baxter 2012, 70), especially for those who accept his precepts:

> The compassion of human beings is for their neighbors,
> But the compassion of the Lord is for every living thing.
> He rebukes and trains and teaches them,
> And turns them back, as a shepherd his flock.
> He has compassion on those who accept his discipline
> And who are eager for his precepts.
> (Sir 18:13–14; cf. 2 Bar. 77.13–16)

The Psalms of Solomon extend the metaphor to the expected Davidic Messiah: "Faithfully and righteously shepherding the Lord's flock, he will not let any of them stumble in their pasture. He will lead them in all holiness and there will be no arrogance among them, that any should be oppressed" (17.40–41). The Damascus Document speaks of the *Mebaqqer* (Overseer, Instructor, Examiner) as a shepherd: "He shall have pity on them like a

father on his sons, and will heal all the strays [?] like a shepherd his flock"
(CD XIII, 9; García Martínez, 43).

Philo reflects on the association of shepherding and kingship in the biblical tradition, contending that "the shepherd's business is a training-ground
and a preliminary exercise in kingship for one who is destined to command
the herd of mankind" (*Moses* 1.60). "Therefore," he adds,

> kings are called "shepherds of their people," not as a term of reproach
> but as the highest honour. And my opinion, based not on the opinions
> of the multitude but on my own inquiry into the truth of the matter, is
> that the only perfect king (let him laugh who will) is one who is skilled
> in the knowledge of shepherding, one who has been trained by manage-
> ment of the inferior creatures to manage the superior. (*Moses* 1.61–62;
> see also *Agr.* 41; *Joseph* 2)

Shepherds appear only incidentally in Roman literature; Roman authors
"held shepherds in low regard; and this critical attitude towards shepherds
would likely explain why they never use 'shepherd' for Roman emperors: it would have been offensive" (Baxter 2012, 96). While Vergil's *Eco-
logues* paint a bucolic picture, Ramsay MacMullen warns that the reality
was far different: "Rustic swains had indeed nothing to sing about. Their
world was as poverty-stricken and ignored as it was dangerous" (3–4). Livy
portrays shepherds as "semi-violent, unprincipled rabble-rousers" (Baxter
2012, 92, citing Livy, *Ab urbe* 1.4.9; 5.7; 5.53; 8–9). Among the peasants,
"only the goatherds and shepherds constitute a separate and lower class"
(MacMullen, 15).

Nevertheless, there are exceptions to this pattern that illustrate the natural affinities of the shepherd metaphor to the qualities of a leader. Xenophon explains the use of the metaphor in Homer [*Il.* 2.243]:

> For what purpose do you think Homer addressed Agamemnon as "Shep-
> herd of the people"? Isn't it because, just as shepherds should attend to it
> that the ewes will be safe and have their provisions and that the purpose
> for which they are sustained will be achieved, so also the general must
> attend to it that the soldiers will be safe and have their provisions and
> that the purpose for which they go on campaign will be achieved? And
> they go on campaign so that through overpowering their enemies they'll
> be happier. (*Mem.* 3.2.1)

The role of shepherds in ancient cultural tradition and memory was therefore oddly contradictory: noble, romantic, and idealistic, yet also demean-
ing and punitive. Despite the latter, the former view of shepherds persisted.

Assuming that Tertullian is referring to ordinary Roman pottery, a passing remark testifies to the idealization of shepherds in the Greco-Roman world. Commenting on the parable of the lost sheep, Tertullian notes the conventional cultural image of a shepherd carrying a sheep or a goat on his shoulders (probably the *Hermes kriophoros*, the representation of a shepherd carrying a small ram): "Let the very paintings upon your cups come forward to show whether even in them the figurative meaning of that sheep will shine through" (*Pud.* 7.1–4; *ANF* 4:80).

Just as the Hebrew Scriptures image God as a shepherd, so the Gospels also appropriate that image for Jesus. The Gospel writers, especially Matthew (2:6; 9:36; 10:6; 18:12–14; 25:32–33; 26:31) and John 10, characterize Jesus as the ideal shepherd: leading, caring, teaching, protecting, and rescuing. Jesus also fulfills the role of the most imminent shepherds: Moses, the deliverer of his people and mediator of God's law; and David, Israel's preeminent king. On the other hand, the lowly shepherds, "keeping watch over their flock by night" (Luke 2:8), see the heavenly host and bear witness to the birth of the Christ child.

Works Cited in Chapter 12

Applebaum, Shimon. 1987. "Economic Life in Palestine." Pages 631–700 in vol. 2 of *The Jewish People in the First Century: Historical Geography, Political History, Social, Cultural and Religious Life and Institutions.* Edited by S. Safrai and M. Stern. Philadelphia: Fortress.

Baxter, Wayne. 2009. "From Ruler to Teacher: The Extending of the Shepherd Metaphor in Early Jewish and Christian Writings." Pages 208–24 in *Early Christian Literature and Intertextuality.* Edited by C. A. Evans and D. Zacharias. LNTS 391. London: T&T Clark.

———. 2012. *Israel's Only Shepherd: Matthew's Shepherd Motif and His Social Setting.* LNTS 457. London: T&T Clark.

Freeman, Jennifer Awes. 2021. *The Good Shepherd: Image, Meaning, and Power.* Waco, TX: Baylor University Press.

García Martínez. *See* Bibliography of Ancient Sources and Translations

Hamel, Gildas H. 1989. *Poverty and Charity in Roman Palestine, First Three Centuries C.E.* University of California Publications: Near Eastern Studies 23. Berkeley: University of California Press.

Harris, Sarah. 2016. *The Davidic Shepherd King in the Lukan Narrative.* LNTS 558. London: Bloomsbury.

Huebner, Sabine R. 2019. *Papyri and the Social World of the New Testament.* Cambridge: Cambridge University Press.

Jeremias, Joachim. 1969. *Jerusalem in the Time of Jesus: An Investigation into Economic and Social Conditions during the New Testament Period.* Translated by F. H. and C. H. Cave. Philadelphia: Fortress.

Kloppenborg, John S. 2010. "Pastoralism, Papyri, and the Parable of the Shepherd." Pages 47–70 in *Light from the East: Papyrologische Kommentare zum Neuen Testament*. Edited by Peter Arzt-Grabner and Christina M. Kreineker. Wiesbaden: Harrassowitz.

MacMullen, Ramsay. 1974. *Roman Social Relations: 50 B.C to A.D. 284*. New Haven: Yale University Press.

Roth, Martha Tobi, Harry A. Hoffner, and Piotr Michalowski, eds. 1995. *Law Collections from Mesopotamia and Asia Minor*. WAW 6. Atlanta: Society of Biblical Literature.

Safrai, Ze'ev. 1994. *The Economy of Roman Palestine*. London: Routledge.

Chapter 13

Merchants, Travelers, and Innkeepers

Treasure in a Field (Matt 13:44)
Pearl (Matt 13:45–46)
Good Samaritan (Luke 10:30–35)
Friend at Night (Luke 11:5–8)

*A*nother facet of the Galilean economy appears in these parables: merchants, travel, and the infrastructure that supported travel and commerce. In the first parable, a farmer finds a treasure in a field; in the second, a merchant finds a magnificent pearl. Both the businessman and the farmer sell all they have and buy the great prize. The focus is on the incomparable treasure of the kingdom Jesus heralds and the urgency of sacrificing everything to acquire it. The parable of the Good Samaritan does not say *why* the man was going down the steep descent (from 2500 to –900 feet elevation) to Jericho, but it illustrates the danger of travel and incidentally the place of inns and innkeepers. Behind these parables lie the roads in first-century Palestine, the nature of travel in antiquity, markets, and merchants.

13.1 Roads

"The way of the sea," the main coastal road, dates back at least to the time of Isaiah: "In the latter time he will make glorious the way of the sea, the land beyond the Jordan [viewed from the east], Galilee of the nations" (Isa 9:1). Towns and villages were connected by "footpaths, donkey caravan paths, trails, cart tracks, and 'roads' of the time" (Strange 2014, 266; see Fiensy and Strange 2014, Maps 4A–D). These trails intersected, forming a network that was "the imprint of everyday travel in the Galilee for trade" (Strange 2014, 269). Vespasian found the road to Yodefat to be only "a mountain track, difficult for infantry and quite impracticable for mounted

troops" (*J.W.* 3.141). Although there were no imperial roads in Galilee in
the Second Temple period, the major west-to-east artery ran from Ptolemais, past Sepphoris, and to Tiberias (Aviam, 136–37; see Map of Galilee). Josephus mentions a road from Tiberias to Magdala (*J.W.* 3.539; *Life*
276; Bonnie, 27), and smaller, regional routes have been identified around
Khirbet Qana and Beth She'arim (Edwards 2002, 101–2; Safrai, 282–87).
The later Roman roads appear to have followed earlier routes.

Eventually, an extensive network of roads linked the cities, towns, and
villages of Galilee, facilitating travel and the transport of goods (Dorsey).
North-south roads ran along the coast, through the high country past
Shechem to Jerusalem (Luke 9:51–56; John 4), and in the Jordan River
valley. These roads were intersected by three major east-west roads, one
from Ptolemais to Bethsaida, one from Ptolemais to Tiberias, and one from
Legio (near Megiddo) to Bet She'an-Scythopolis. Secondary roads linked
the towns and villages. Late in the first century some paved, Roman roads
began to appear, built by the Roman army primarily for its use. Construction
of Roman roads, therefore, followed the establishment of military installations. Although Jesus meets a centurion (Matt 8:5–13//Luke 7:1–10), there
is no evidence of a Roman military colony in Galilee during Jesus' time.
Vitellius, legate of Syria (35–37 CE), marched his army from Antioch to
Ptolemais and from Ptolemais southeast through the Valley of Jezreel to
Scythopolis and on to Petra. The first military colony was settled at Ptolemais in the mid-fifties of the first century or a few years earlier. Mark
Chancey notes its significance: "Soon after the colony's foundation, the
road connecting Ptolemais to Antioch was paved in the Roman fashion, as
shown by a milestone dating to 56 CE. This was not only the first Roman
road in Palestine; it was also the earliest anywhere in the Near East" (58;
see also Isaac and Roll, 7–9; Isaac, 147–59). After sacking Jewish strongholds in Galilee, Vespasian left troops from the X Fretensis legion behind to
build a paved Roman road. A milestone along the road from Scythopolis to
Legio is dated 69 CE. This road was quite wide, 2 to 4 lanes, 9 to 10 meters
(Hezser 2011, 69). It facilitated travel and communication between Caesarea
and Scythopolis and eventually extended to Pella and Gerasa. Other milestones carry second-century dates, when a more intricate system of roads
was built in Galilee and Judea. The milestones ensured that everyone knew
whose road it was (Rome's! Avi-Yonah, 181–87; Chancey, 66; Hezser 2011,
74–75; see Bonnie, 26, 28, for a list of the roads and milestones).

The nascent urbanization of Galilee—especially Magdala, Sepphoris,
and Tiberias—spurred local trade: the roads allowed farmers and artisans to
transport their harvest and their products to markets, boosting the economy
(Edwards 1992, 54–60). They also facilitated communication and cultural

influences. Local pottery spread across lower Galilee: villages such as Shikhin, Kefar Hananya, and Nahaf could devote themselves to the production of pottery, while others produced wheat (the plain of Arbela [as distinct from Arbel], Kefar Hittaia [Village of Wheat], and Huqoq), olive oil, and wine (Strange 1997, 39–42). The parable-famed Jericho road carried fruit grown around Jericho to the Holy City and provided access to necessary goods for which Jerusalem was not self-sufficient. It also connected Jerusalem with the caravan routes to the east (see below, 20.4).

Goods from the caravan routes (especially perfumes and spices from the east) flowed from Damascus and Nabatea through Capernaum and Bet She'an to Sepphoris and on to the coast (Ptolemais and Caesarea). In general, however, Galilee engaged in relatively little interregional trade in the first century. Josephus brags, exaggerating the Jews' lack of foreign trade: "Well, ours is not a maritime country, neither commerce nor the intercourse which it provides with the outside world has any attraction for us. Our cities are built inland, remote from the sea; and we devote ourselves to the cultivation of the productive country with which we are blessed" (*Ag. Ap.* 1.60). Palestinian wine amphorae found in shipwrecks confirm that wine export flourished during the Byzantine period (Kingsley, 50–51, 86–92; Hezser 2010, 40–41). In addition, Galileans probably traveled to Phoenicia and the Decapolis for business (Root, 122). Trade between Galilee and Judea certainly flourished under the Hasmoneans and Herod, as attested by the number of Herodian lamps made in Jerusalem and found in Galilee (Jensen 2012, 61; Jensen 2013, 21–22); but "there is no evidence of trade between Galilee and Samaria in this period" (Root, 123).

13.2 Markets

While Herod the Great ushered in "a major spurt in the development of Palestinian trade" (Pastor, 300), most of the trade was local. Towns had a permanent marketplace, villages did not, and satellite settlements did not have stores (Safrai, 231). Farmers kept some or most of their harvest and sold the rest at the market (m. Ma'aś. 1:5; m. Demai 5:7). Products such as pottery, glassware, and woven garments were sold to shopkeepers and merchants or directly to customers. The following Mishnaic ruling gives us a glimpse of village life: "A man may protest against [another that opens] a shop within the courtyard and say to him, 'I cannot sleep because of the noise of them that go in and out.' He that makes utensils should go outside and sell them in the market. But none may protest against another and say, 'I cannot sleep because of the noise of the hammer' or 'because of the noise of the mill-stones' or 'because of the noise of the children'" (m. B. Bat. 2:3). Because the courtyard belongs to all the residents adjoining it, they could protest if a neighbor opened it to the public. Stores and shops were therefore normally accessed directly from the street.

Only cities such as Tiberias (Josephus, *Ant.* 18.149) had permanent markets (Gk. *agorai*). Towns and villages might have periodic markets, usually once a week and in the village square (m. B. Qam. 2:2) or an open area, where the villagers, farmers, artisans, traveling merchants, and peddlers hawked their goods. As Rosenfeld and Menirav report, "Residents of nearby villages would bring their agricultural produce to the city, and in exchange would purchase work tools that were either manufactured in the city or manufactured elsewhere and brought into the region via the city" (36–37). Land, mules, oxen, horses, and slaves were auctioned (Rosenfeld and Menirav, 34; cf. Rev 18:11–13). Laborers found work, and landowners found laborers. Market days also became the time for social and religious activities and court proceedings. News, gossip, and rumors flowed from city to village and village to village.

13.3 Merchants

Satellite settlements surrounded larger towns and villages. Farmers traveled to cities and towns to sell their produce, while merchants and traveling salesmen (*rochelim*) traveled to the satellite settlements (Safrai, 77–81). Traveling salesmen bought and sold goods in the offshoot settlements and returned home in the evening. The rabbis distinguished the *rochel* from a merchant, who was not required to set aside tithes until he reached his destination. "If a man brought up produce from Galilee to Judea or if he went up to Jerusalem, he may eat of it [without tithing] until he reaches his journey's end; and so too, if he went back again. . . . Pedlars that go around from town to town may make a [chance] meal [of untithed produce that they have received] until they come to the place where they will spend the night" (m. Ma'aś. 2:3). The Palestinian Talmud adds: "What is a place to sleep? His own house. R. Simeon b. Lakish stated in the name of R. Hoshaiah—like those [*rochelim*] of Kefar Hananiah who go out and sell in four or five villages and come and sleep in their [own] houses" (y. Ma'aś. 2:49b). *Rochelim* dealt especially in spices and perfumes, which were easily transportable. The peddler's accoutrements are also mentioned in the Mishnah: a peddler's box (*kuppah*) or basket (m. Shabb. 9:7), a funnel used to pour oils and perfumes (m. Kelim 2:4), and hooks for carrying the box on a long pole on his shoulder (m. Kelim 12:2). Evidently drawing on common experience, the rabbis debated whether donkey drivers who carried produce from town to town could be considered trustworthy: "If ass-drivers entered a city and the one said, 'My produce is new and that of my fellow is old,' or 'My produce is not duly tithed but that of my fellow is duly tithed,' they may not be believed" (m. Demai 4:7).

13.4 Travel

Mobility and travel increased significantly in the Roman period, with the result that more Galileans traveled within and outside of Galilee in the first part of the first century than in earlier times. Based on the frequency of travel reflected in the Egyptian papyri, Huebner confidently asserts that "travel in ancient times was not the sole preserve of members of the social elite" (113). People moved from one place to another for trade and the transport of goods (Huebner, 89). "Public officials, businessmen, and landowners will have been the most mobile members of society" (Hezser 2010, 215). People also traveled to visit family members. At the same time, travel to Jerusalem for the pilgrimage festivals (Passover, Shavuot, and Sukkot; Deut 16:16; Josephus, *Ant.* 17.213–214; *J.W.* 2.10; 6.423) increased dramatically with Herod's construction of the temple (Goodman; Hezser 2010, 221), as we see in the Gospels. Herod and the high priests no doubt promoted this practice. As a result, there was more travel to Jerusalem for the festivals in the first century than at any other time in antiquity.

From scattered sources we can gather insights into what travel involved for non-elites, who did not have state privileges or share social networks with other elites. People accustomed to walking could cover as much as 20 to 25 miles in a day, depending on the terrain and how much they were carrying (Hezser 2011, 83). Greeting fellow travelers was apparently expected etiquette (Ruth 2:4; Matt 5:47; 10:12–13).

Only the elites had horses. Everyone else either walked or rode a donkey, and donkeys were not cheap. An Egyptian papyrus from 141 CE (P.Bas. II.19) sets the price of a donkey at 148 drachmas, the equivalent of half a year's wages (Huebner, 100; Hezser 2011, 132). Still, donkeys were cheaper than mules or horses and cost less to maintain. Mules could carry heavier loads than donkeys but rented for twice as much (Josephus, *Life* 127; *J.W.* 3.90, 95, 121; Hyland, 231–32; Hezser 2011, 148–50). Probably for that reason, Shimon bar Kokhba sent donkeys to bring supplies to Ein Gedi (P.Yad. 57; Hezser 2011, 147). Horses were owned only by the military, royalty, and the wealthy (Jos. Asen. 5.4; 17.7–8; 1 Macc 10:81–83; Josephus, *Life* 115–117, 402). Horses could also be difficult to control (Jas 3:2–3; Philo,

Alleg. Interp. 3.223). While less common in Galilee, camels were also used (Josephus, *Life* 119). The earliest attested public transport, involving mules, donkeys, and carts, was authorized by the legate Sotidius, in the region of Pisidia, in 18–19 CE (Horsley, 42–44). There is no evidence, however, of such public transportation in first-century Galilee.

The *Metamorphoses* by Apuleius (2nd c. CE) offers insights into travel during the Roman *pax Augusta*. Horace describes traveling from Rome to Brundisium in 37 BCE, meeting along the way "stingy tavern-keepers" (*Sat.* 1.5.4), "cursed gnats" (1.5.14), and "a bustling host" (1.5.71). Finding food and water was a common struggle. At one point, he had a stomach illness, "owing to the water, for it was villainous" (1.5.7), and at another he reports, "Here water, nature's cheapest product, is sold, but the bread is [by] far the best to be had, so that the knowing traveller is wont to shoulder a load for stages beyond" (1.5.89–91).

The fictional book of Tobit also describes a journey. When Tobit sends his son to reclaim ten talents he left in trust in Media, Tobias complains that he does not know the roads. Tobit instructs him to find a trustworthy man to go with him (Tob 4:20–5:3). Tobias meets the angel Raphael, who assures Tobias that he has been to Media many times, knows the roads, is a fellow Israelite, and has stayed with their kinsman, Gabael (5:4–10). Tobit agrees to pay Raphael a drachma a day plus expenses and add something to it. A dog joins them for the journey (6:2; 11:4; cf. Odysseus's dog in Homer, *Od.* 17.290–327). The first night they camp by the Tigris River and catch a fish, which they roast (6:1–6). In Ecbatana, they stay with Tobias's relative, Raguel; Tobias eventually marries Raguel's daughter.

The Gospels report women traveling as well as men. Mary traveled to meet her kinswoman Elizabeth (Luke 1:39–40), then to Bethlehem with Joseph (2:5), where there was no place for them in the inn (2:7). Women and children were among the crowds that followed Jesus in Galilee, even to remote places (Mark 6:32–44 par.). Women traveled with Jesus and his disciples in Galilee (Luke 8:1–4) and followed him to Jerusalem (Matt 27:55// Mark 15:40–41; Luke 23:55).

The discoveries at Nahal Hever document that Babatha traveled between Maḥoza and Ein-Gedi and to Petra for her court appeals. Egyptian papyri also "reveal that women were able to move around much more freely than is commonly assumed" (Huebner, 95). Still, it is unlikely that women traveled very far without their husbands (Hezser 2011, 390–99). When women traveled, it was often to prepare for the birth of a child, to assist a mother, to see an ill family member, or following a death in the family. Rabban Gamaliel the Elder (late 1st c.) permitted a midwife to travel on the Sabbath to assist a woman giving birth (m. Rosh. Hash. 2:5; m. Shabb. 18:3).

Therefore, "The sight of a heavily pregnant woman riding a donkey—as the Evangelist Luke depicts Mary [actually, Prot. Jas. 17; cf. Ps.-Mt. 18.1]— would not have been unusual at the time" (Huebner, 96). It is also true, however, that there are few references to peasant women traveling: "The poorer the woman, the less she traveled away from home" (Cohick, 225). Because travel could be hazardous, people, and especially pregnant women, usually did not travel alone: "A woman named Serapias . . . writes to her son-in-law to request that he bring her pregnant daughter home to her so she can give birth in her parents' house. She assures him in her letter that she will bear the cost of (renting) a donkey" (P.Oxf. 19, after 208 CE; Huebner, 96).

In parts of the empire, Roman officials could use the state-run transport system, the *cursus publicus*, which provided relay stations every six to nine miles, to change horses and pack animals; and guest houses ("mansions," Greek *monai*; John 14:2) at intervals of 22 to 25 miles (Huebner, 88); but relatively little is known about how ordinary people found accommodations and food.

13.5 Neighbors and Guests

Whenever possible, travelers stayed with family or friends, camped at oases (1QapGen XX, 34–XXI, 1 on Gen 13:3), found a cave for shelter, or stayed at an inn (Gk. *pandokeion*, Luke 10:34). Most travelers in Galilee probably relied on the hospitality of kin, friends, or associates (Arterbury, 91; Hezser 2011, 110–12).

Abraham was the model for Jewish hospitality: the story that Abraham and Sarah "entertained angels unawares" (Gen 18:1–16; Heb 13:2 KJV) was retold and embellished by Philo (*Abr.* 107–118), Josephus (*Ant.* 1.191–198), and the Testament of Abraham (esp. 1–6). The story "functioned prescriptively for the later generations" (Arterbury, 59). The Testament of Abraham claims that Abraham "pitched his tent at the crossroads of the oak of Mamre and welcomed everyone . . . [all] on equal terms" (1); it ends with the admonition, "Let us too, my beloved brothers, imitate the hospitality of the patriarch Abraham" (20.15, Recension A). The protocol for gracious hospitality included compelling the travelers to stay in one's home, moving swiftly, washing the guests' feet or providing water from them to wash, preparing a lavish feast, and gift giving (Arterbury, 71, 91). In the parables (Luke 15:11–32), the waiting father follows this protocol in detail. He sees his son at a distance (Gen 18:2; 43:16; Judg 19:3, 17), runs to greet him (Gen 18:2; 24:29; 33:4; Judg 19:3), moves quickly (Gen 18:6–8; Jos. Asen. 3.4; 18.2; 19:1–2; Philo, *Abr.* 109), gives gifts (Gen 33:11; 1 Kgs

13:7), and provides an extravagant feast (Gen 18:5–7; Judg 13:15; 19:6; 1 Sam 9:24; 2 Sam 12:4; 2 Kgs 4:8; Ps 23:5; Tob 7:9; Jos. Asen. 7.1; cf. Arterbury, 91–92).

In this context, we may note how Josephus embroiders Abraham's servant's negotiation for hospitality in Rebecca's home. "He [Abraham's servant] also besought that he might lodge with them, night prohibiting him from journeying farther, and . . . he said that he could not entrust himself to safer hosts than such as he had found her to be, . . . nor would he be burdensome to them, but would pay a price for their gracious hospitality and live at his own expense. . . . But she upbraided him for suspecting them of meanness, for he should have everything free of cost" (*Ant.* 1.250–251). In other stories, Joseph sent a message to the priest, Pentephres in Heliopolis, saying he would lodge in his home, have lunch, and rest there (Jos. Asen. 3.2). According to the Testament of Job, in his piety Job ordered that the four doors of his home be open for those in need. He had tables spread at all hours for strangers and required that they be fed at his table before he gave them alms (9.7–10.4).

Apparently, not everyone followed Abraham's example. The sage Sirach (2nd c. BCE) found it necessary to teach neighborliness and what was expected of guests as well as hosts.

> Assist your neighbor to the best of your ability. . . . Be content with little or much, and you will hear no reproach for being a guest. It is a miserable life to go from house to house; as a guest you should not open your mouth; you will play the host and provide drink without being thanked, and besides this you will hear rude words like these: "Come here, stranger, prepare the table; let me eat what you have there." "Be off, stranger, for an honored guest is here; my brother has come for a visit, and I need the guest-room." It is hard for a sensible person to bear scolding about lodging and the insults of the moneylender. (Sir 29:20, 23–28; cf. Wis 19:14–17)

Sirach also warned his students about the danger of extending hospitality: "Receive strangers into your home and they will stir up trouble for you, and will make you a stranger to your own family" (11:34).

According to Josephus, Essenes could be found in every town; whenever Essene travelers arrived, "all the resources of the community were put at their disposal, just as if they were their own; and they enter the houses of men whom they have never seen before as though they were their most intimate friends" (*J.W.* 2.125).

Jesus too instructed his disciples to depend on hospitality wherever they went, bless those who received them, and "shake off the dust from [their] feet" where they were rejected (Matt 10:11–15). The mission of the church depended upon itinerant preachers and evangelists finding hospitality: "If the one who comes is simply passing through, help him as much as you can" (Did. 12.2). The traveling emissaries from John the Elder "began their journey for the sake of Christ, accepting no support from non-believers" (3 John 7). Yet, when itinerant evangelists abused the hospitality, the early church responded with the rule that true prophets never stayed for more than three days, never asked for money, and took nothing except bread when they left (Did. 11.5–6; Culpepper 2021, 200).

13.6 Inns and Innkeepers

Travelers in need of cheap hot meals and a place to spend the night could find inns along the main roads and the outskirts of cities and larger villages (Huebner, 111; Oakman, 175–77), but there is no archaeological evidence of inns in Roman Palestine (Hezser 2011, 94). The Theodotos Inscription (above, 3.2; Hezser 2011, 96–100) confirms that some synagogues accommodated travelers.

While we do not know about the availability or quality of inns in Galilee, Polybius praises the inns in northern Italy: "Travelers in this country who put up in inns do not bargain for each separate article they require, but ask what is the charge per diem for one person. The innkeepers, as a rule, agree to receive guests, providing them with enough of all they require for half an *as* per diem, *i.e.*[,] the fourth part of an obol, the charge being very seldom higher" (*Hist.* 2.15.5). Similarly, when Epictetus chides his students not to become so captivated with eloquence or logic that they fail to go on to moral perfection, he likens these way points in the students' journey to an inn: "Men act like a traveler on the way to his own country who stops at an excellent inn, and since the inn pleases him, he stays there" (*Diatr.* 2.23.36).

Inns, especially those owned by gentiles, suffered ill repute among the rabbis, who would not allow "a woman [to] remain alone with them since they are suspected of lewdness" (m. 'Abod. Zar. 2:1; see also m. Qidd. 4:12). Similarly, in the Pseudo-Clementine Recognitions, a homeowner protests Peter's intention to stay at an inn: "It is base and wicked that such and so great men should stay in a hostelry" (9.38, *ANF* 8:192). Strabo recounts that when a brothel-keeper lodged in the inns at a village along the Meander River with many women, an earthquake struck the place (*Geogr.* 12.8.17). Josephus illustrates the heightened purity demanded of priests by noting that they were forbidden to marry a harlot, a slave, a prisoner of war (m. Ketub. 2:9), a hawker or innkeeper (since a female innkeeper might be assumed to be a harlot), or a woman who had been separated from a former husband for any reason (*Ant.* 3.276). Parenthetically, the Loeb translator,

H. St. J. Thackeray, adds the observation that the Aramaic targum on Josh 2:1 translates the Hebrew *zonah* (harlot) with the Greek word *pyndokita*, which is derived from the verb *pandokeuein* (to keep an inn). Therefore, "The 'inn-keeper' of Josephus has been evolved out of the 'harlot' of the Bible through the medium of current Aramaic exegesis" (LCL 242:451). On the contrary, a virtuous mistress of an inn buried a Levite who died at her inn and gave his staff, bag, and scroll of the law to his companions when they asked about him (m. Yebam. 16:7).

Inns were often filthy. The apocryphal Acts of John (60–61) contains a popular story about the apostle John's encounter with bedbugs at an inn on his journey from Laodicea to Ephesus. Troubled by the insects, the apostle commanded, "Behave yourselves, one and all; you must leave your home for tonight and be quiet in one place and keep your distance from the servants of God" (Hennecke, 193)—and they did! (Culpepper 1994, 197–98).

The hardships for ordinary travelers, who did not have the privileges or social networks of the elite, are also suggested by Pseudo-Matthew's embellishments of Matthew's account of Joseph and Mary's flight to Egypt: "When they came to a cave and wished to rest in it" (18.1), dragons came out of the cave. On the third day, Mary, wearied by the heat, rested in the shade of a palm tree, while Joseph worried about their lack of water for themselves and their animals (20.1). When they entered an Egyptian city, they knew no one there whom they could ask for hospitality (22.2; Schneemelcher, 463–64; see further Huebner, 87–114).

13.7 Reflections: Lost Treasure and Pearls

The parables of the Hidden Treasure and the Pearl are similar yet different. Hidden treasure excited the imagination and spurred the production of many stories in antiquity (see Crossan). The Copper Scroll from Qumran (3Q15), for example, describes sixty-four treasures hidden in that area. Horace expresses this common fantasy: "O that some lucky strike would disclose to me a pot of money, like the man who, having found a treasure-trove, bought and ploughed the self-same ground he used to work on hire, enriched by favour of Hercules" (*Sat.* 2.6.10–13).

In the parables, both the businessman and the farmer sell all they have and buy the great prize. The focus is on the incomparable treasure of the kingdom and the urgency of sacrificing everything to acquire it. The act of hiding the treasure allows the man to do what he must to acquire it—a shrewd and not necessarily dishonest act. In Roman law, the buyer of a field acquired any treasure buried in it as long as the previous owner did not know of it (Luz, 277, n. 19, citing Paulus in *Dig.* 41.2; 3.3).

The rabbis wrestled with the moral obligations of one who finds a treasure (m. Ketub. 4:1, 4; 6:1). Regarding a field, the terms of the sale could specify whether the buyer was entitled to its stones, cane, or crop (m. B. Bat. 4:8). If a man gives a field as a gift, "he gives everything that is in it. If brothers who divided [a heritage] came into possession of a field, they come into possession of everything that is in it"; and if someone has secured title to "the property of a proselyte and secured title to a field, he secures title to everything that is in it" (m. B. Bat. 4:9).

The merchant—presumably a wealthy businessman, not a poor peddler—was seeking beautiful pearls. Pliny the Elder says that pearls held "the topmost rank among all things of price," and pearls from the Indian Ocean and the Persian Gulf were especially prized (*Nat.* 9.106). A lengthy description follows: "Their whole value lies in their brilliance, size, roundness, smoothness and weight, qualities of such rarity that no two pearls are found that are exactly alike: this is doubtless the reason why Roman luxury has given them the name of 'unique gems.' . . . Women glory in hanging these on their fingers and using two or three for a single-earring, . . . and now-a-days even poor people covet them" (9.112–114; cf. T. Jud. 13.5).

A famous rabbinic story combines the motifs of lost treasure and a fine pearl. When the students of Simeon ben Shetah (ca. 120–40 BCE) bought a donkey for him from an Ishmaelite, they found a pearl entangled in its neck. Because the seller did not know about the pearl, Simeon ordered them to return it. The students protested, "Even those who say that cheating a Gentile is forbidden nevertheless admit that an article lost by the Gentile may be kept." But Simeon replied, "What do you think, that Simeon ben Shetah is a barbarian? Simeon ben Shetah would rather hear 'Blessed be the God of the Jews' than gain any profit in this entire world" (y. B. Meṣ. 2.5, 8c; Bialik and Ravnitzky, 659, no. 196).

Works Cited in Chapter 13

Arterbury, Andrew E. 2005. *Entertaining Angels: Early Christian Hospitality in Its Mediterranean Setting*. Sheffield: Sheffield Phoenix.

Aviam, Mordechai. 2004. *Jews, Pagans and Christians in Galilee*. Rochester, NY: University of Rochester Press.

Avi-Yonah, Michael. 2002. *The Holy Land from the Persian to the Arab Conquest (536 B.C.–A.D. 640): A Historical Geography*. Rev. ed. Jerusalem: Carta.

Bialik, Hayim Nahman, and Yehoshua Hana Ravnitzky, eds. 1992. *The Book of Legends, Sefer Ha-Aggadah: Legends from the Talmud and Midrash*. Translated by William G. Braude. New York: Schocken Books.

Bonnie, Rick. 2019. *Being Jewish in Galilee, 100–200 CE*. Studies in Eastern Mediterranean Archaeology 11. Turnhout, Belgium: Brepols.

Chancey, Mark A. 2005. *Greco-Roman Culture and the Galilee of Jesus*. SNTSMS 134. Cambridge: Cambridge University Press.

Cohick, Lynn H. 2009. *Women in the World of the Earliest Christians: Illuminating Ancient Ways of Life*. Grand Rapids: Baker Academic.

Crossan, John Dominic. 1979. *Finding Is the First Act: Trove Folktales and Jesus' Treasure Parable*. Philadelphia: Fortress.

Culpepper, R. Alan. 1994. *John the Son of Zebedee: The Life of a Legend*. Columbia: University of South Carolina Press.

———. 2021. *Matthew*. NTL. Louisville: Westminster John Knox.

Dorsey, David A. 1991. *The Roads and Highways of Ancient Israel*. Baltimore: Johns Hopkins University Press.

Edwards, Douglas R. 1992. "The Socio-Economic and Cultural Ethos of the Lower Galilee in the First Century: Implications for the Nascent Jesus Movement." Pages 53–73 in *The Galilee in Late Antiquity*. Edited by Lee I. Levine. New York: Jewish Theological Seminary of America.

———. 2002. "Khirbet Qana: From Jewish Village to Christian Pilgrim Site." Pages 101–32 in vol. 3 of *The Roman and Byzantine Near East*. Edited by J. D. Humphrey. JRASup 49. Portsmouth, RI: Journal of Roman Archaeology.

Fiensy, David A., and James R. Strange, eds. 2014. *The Archaeological Record from Cities, Towns, and Villages*. Vol. 1 of *Galilee in the Late Second Temple and Mishnaic Periods*. Minneapolis: Fortress.

Goodman, Martin. 1999. "The Pilgrimage Economy of Jerusalem in the Second Temple Period." Pages 69–76 in *Jerusalem: Its Sanctity and Centrality to Judaism, Christianity, and Islam*. Edited by Lee I. Levine. New York: Continuum.

Hennecke, Edgar. 1992. *New Testament Apocrypha*. Vol. 2. Edited by Wilhelm Schneemelcher. Translated by R. McL. Wilson. Louisville: Westminster John Knox.

Hezser, Catherine, ed. 2010. *The Oxford Handbook of Jewish Daily Life in Roman Palestine*. Oxford: Oxford University Press.

———. 2011. *Jewish Travel in Antiquity*. TSAJ 144. Tübingen: Mohr Siebeck.

Horsley, G. H. R. 1981. *New Documents Illustrating Early Christianity*. Macquarie University, NSW: The Ancient History Documentary Research Centre.

Huebner, Sabine R. 2019. *Papyri and the Social World of the New Testament*. Cambridge: Cambridge University Press.

Hyland, Ann. 1990. *Equus: The Horse in the Roman World*. London: Basford.

Isaac, Benjamin. 2010. "Infrastructure." Pages 145–64 in Hezser.

Isaac, Benjamin, and Israel Roll. 1982. *Roman Roads in Judaea I: The Legio-Scythopolis Road*. British Archaeological Reports International Series 141. Oxford: B.A.R.

Jensen, Morten Hørning. 2012. "Rural Galilee and Rapid Changes: An Investigation of the Socio-Economic Dynamics and Developments in Roman Galilee." *Bib* 93.1:43–67.

———. 2013. "Purity and Politics in Herod Antipas' Galilee: The Case for Religious Motivation." *JSHJ* 11:3–34.

Kingsley, Sean A. 2004. *Shipwreck Archaeology of the Holy Land: Processes and Parameters*. London: Duckworth.

Luz, Ulrich. 2001. *Matthew 8–20*. Edited by Helmut Koester. Translated by James E. Crouch. Hermeneia. Minneapolis: Fortress.

Oakman, Douglas. 2008. *Jesus and the Peasants*. Eugene, OR: Cascade.

Pastor, Jack. 2010. "Trade, Commerce, and Consumption." Pages 297–307 in Hezser.

Root, Bradley W. 2014. *First-Century Galilee: A Fresh Examination of the Sources*. WUNT 378. Tübingen: Mohr Siebeck.

Rosenfeld, Ben-Zion, and Joseph Menirav. 2005. *Markets and Marketing in Roman Palestine*. JSJSup 99. Leiden: Brill.

Safrai, Ze'ev. 1994. *The Economy of Roman Palestine*. London: Routledge.

Schneemelcher, Wilhelm, ed. 1991. *New Testament Apocrypha*. Vol. 1. Translated by R. McL. Wilson. Louisville: Westminster John Knox.

Strange, James F. 1997. "First-Century Galilee from Archaeology and from the Texts." Pages 39–48 in *Archaeology and the Galilee: Texts and Contexts in the Graeco-Roman and Byzantine Periods*. Edited by Douglas R. Edwards and C. Thomas McCollough. Atlanta: Scholars Press.

———. 2014. "The Galilean Road System." Pages 263–71 in Fiensy and Strange.

Chapter 14

Masters and Slaves

*T*he relationship between masters and subordinates is one of the stock themes of Jesus' parables. John Dominic Crossan identified nine parables that have two axes: "[1] a master-servant relationship or superior-subordinate relationship and [2] a moment of critical reckoning between them. Servant parables are those whose central story line concerns such a relationship at some instance of critical confrontation between master and servant" (19). The common term *doulos* can mean either "slave" or "servant." Due to its frequency in the parables, the term *doulos* occurs more often in Matthew and Luke than anywhere else in the New Testament. *Doulos* regularly appears in juxtaposition to *eleutheros* ("free"):

When you were slaves of sin, you were free in regard to righteousness. (Rom 6:20)

For in the one Spirit we were all baptized into one body—Jews or Greeks, slaves or free—and we were all made to drink of one Spirit. (1 Cor 12:13; cf. 7:21–22)

There is no longer Jew or Greek, there is no longer slave or free, there is no longer male and female; for all of you are one in Christ Jesus. (Gal 3:28)

Whatever good we do, we will receive the same again from the Lord, whether we are slaves or free. (Eph 6:8)

198

In that renewal there is no longer Greek and Jew, circumcised and uncircumcised, barbarian, Scythian, slave and free; but Christ is all and in all! (Col 3:11)

Everyone, slave and free, hid in the caves and among the rocks of the mountains. (Rev 6:15; see 13:16; 19:18)

In the parables, *doulos* invariably designates a slave rather than a free person paid to be a servant. Slaves could be good or bad, faithful, prudent and wise, honest or dishonest, and they could be assigned various duties, but they were enslaved to their master.

The "moment of critical reckoning" (Crossan, 19) in the parables is precipitated either by the master's return, an accounting of entrusted property, or a demand for repayment of debts. The slave's actions are tested, resulting in reward or punishment. The parable of the doorkeeper develops the theme of watchfulness. Each slave has his duty; one of them (in Mark) is to watch for the master's return. Jesus admonishes his disciples to be "dressed for action" and, as in the parable of the wise and foolish maidens, "have your lamps lit" (Luke 12:35): "Blessed are those slaves whom the master finds alert [watching, awake] when he comes" (12:37). The parable's exaggerated element occurs in its description of the master's reward for the obedient, alert slave. Their roles will be reversed. The master will dress for action, "fasten his belt," invite them to sit down to eat, and serve them (12:37).

In the parable of the wise and wicked servant, the master puts his manager in charge of the other slaves, to feed them at the proper time. If he finds the manager at work when he comes, he will put him in charge of all his possessions; if the manager beats the other slaves, eats, drinks, and gets drunk, he will "cut him in pieces" (12:46; see 1 Sam 15:33; Heb 11:37; Mart. Isa. 5.1, where Manasseh sawed Isaiah in half with a wood saw). Is this also an exaggerated element?

The master going on a journey in the parable of the talents entrusts his wealth to slaves, five talents, two, and one (*minas* in Luke 19:13 NIV). When he returns, he rewards the two who used the entrusted wealth to earn more for their master and punishes the one who hid his talent rather than invest it.

The parable of the servant's reward challenges the presumption that the faithful slave will be rewarded. Could any of Jesus' hearers imagine that a master would say to his servant returning from plowing or tending sheep, "Come here at once and take your place at the table" (Luke 17:7)? Would the master not say, "Prepare supper for me, put on your apron and serve me while I eat and drink" (17:8)?

The parable of the unmerciful servant (or the two debtors) envisions two fellow slaves (Matt 18:28), one of whom is forgiven an enormous debt of 10,000 talents but refuses to forgive his fellow slave a small debt of 100 denarii. When the master heard of this, he handed the slave over to "the merciless jailers" (BDAG, 168) until he repaid everything he owed.

Clearly, these parables assume not only that wealthy elites have slaves but also that they have various conventions regarding the work assigned to slaves, what might be entrusted to them, expectations regarding their performance of their duties or failure to do so, and rewards or punishments a master might mete out to slaves. What do we know about slaves in the Roman world and especially in first-century Galilee? The answer is both "a great deal" and yet, regarding slavery in Galilee, "not enough." Although she wrote a 439–page monograph on *Jewish Slavery in Antiquity*, Catherine Hezser cautions, "What needs to be emphasized here is that we are unable to reconstruct a historically accurate picture of slavery in ancient Jewish society" (380).

14.1 Slavery in Second-Temple Sources

The problem of sources is much the same as in earlier chapters. Our understanding of slavery in first-century Galilee depends on literary sources, with little support from archaeology or inscriptions. There are no census or tax records that record the number, distribution, origin, or monetary value of slaves in Galilee. The Hebrew Scriptures contain laws regarding Israelite and non-Israelite slaves (Exod 21:2; Deut 15:13–18; 21:10–14), but this distinction does not seem to have made any difference in the purchase, treatment, or manumission of slaves in the first century: "The Mishnah's framers spoke of Hebrew and Canaanite slaves only in order to remain true to the scriptural categories and not because those categories reflected any actual social structures of their own time" (Martin 2020, 116). In ancient Israel, impoverished Hebrews might sell themselves, but their Israelite owners should treat them as hired laborers, not slaves (Lev 25:39–40). Manumission of Israelite slaves in the seventh, Jubilee Year "seems to have been an ideal rather than reality" (Hezser, 387; so also, Fiensy 1991, 5–6, 91–92). Nor can we be sure how much of the Mishnaic traditions reflect first-century practices in Galilee. While there is a relative abundance of material regarding slavery in Greece and Italy, Greco-Roman sources are little help for understanding slavery in Galilee. Furthermore, "no sources formulated or written from the viewpoint of slaves themselves have come down to us" (Hezser, 13).

More promising, as in earlier chapters, are the glimpses of slavery in Second Temple Jewish sources: the Apocrypha (esp. Judith and Tobit); Josephus, who traveled in Galilee early in the First Jewish Revolt; the Gospels themselves; and potentially early traditions in the Mishnah. These sources suggest the extent of slavery in this period and give glimpses into slaves' status and roles. Although the extent of slavery in Palestine during this period is debated, these sources confirm that "the upper classes employed slaves both on their estates and as domestics" (Hezser, 320). For the later rabbis, the ownership of at least one slave was expected for even poor people to preserve their honor (y. Pe'ah 8.8, 21a; Hezser, 175).

14.1.1 The Apocrypha

The elite Judean Sirach instructs his privileged pupils in the prudent management of slaves: provide for them, do not let them be idle, and discipline them harshly when necessary.

> Fodder and a stick and burdens for a donkey; bread and discipline and work for a slave. Set your slave to work, and you will find rest; leave his hands idle, and he will seek liberty. Yoke and thong will bow the neck, and for a wicked slave there are racks and tortures. Put him to work, in order that he may not be idle, for idleness teaches much evil. Set him to work, as is fitting for him, and if he does not obey, make his fetters heavy. Do not be overbearing toward anyone, and do nothing unjust. If you have but one slave, treat him like yourself, because you have bought him with blood. If you have but one slave, treat him like a brother, for you will need him as you need your life. If you ill-treat him, and he leaves you and runs away, which way will you go to seek him? (Sir 33:25–33; see also 7:20–21; 42:5)

Similarly elitist, Tobit mentions the presence of slaves in the household as a matter of course. Sarah's maidservant(s) blamed Sarah for the fate of her seven husbands on their wedding night: "So the maid said to her, 'You are the one who kills your husbands! See, you have already been married to seven husbands and have not borne the name of a single one of them. Why do you beat us? Because your husbands are dead? Go with them! May we never see a son or daughter of yours!' (Tob 3:8–9). On Tobias and Sarah's wedding night, her father ordered his slaves to dig a grave for Tobias, assuming that he, too, would be killed by the demon. Then he sent Sarah's maid into the bridal chamber to check on them. When she reported that they were sleeping peacefully, he ordered his slaves to fill in the grave before morning (8:9–18). The next day, Tobias ordered Raphael to take four slaves and two camels, travel to Rages, and bring back the money Gabael held in trust for his father, Tobit (9:2–5; 1:14). When Tobias insisted on returning to his father after their two-week-long wedding celebration, Sarah's father gave Tobias her dowry: "half of all his property: male and female slaves, oxen and sheep, donkeys and camels, clothing, money, and household goods" (10:10).

Elsewhere, Esther was assisted by two maids (Add Esth 15:2–4), and Susanna was accosted in the garden while her maidservants were away (Sus 15–19). The Jews as a people were considered "natural slaves" by their enemies. Summarizing the book of Esther, Josephus says that Haman was outraged when he learned that Mordecai was a Jew: "this man who was a slave" (*Ant.* 11.211).

The heroine Judith was also assisted by her maidservant. When Holofernes, Nebuchadnezzar's general, plundered Israel, "Every man of Israel cried out to God with great fervor, and they humbled themselves with much fasting. They and their wives and their children and their cattle and every resident alien and hired laborer and purchased slave—they all put sackcloth around their waists" (Jdt 4:9–10). Judith was also a woman of some means because her husband, who had died of a heat stroke during the barley harvest (Jdt 8:2–3; cf. Ruth 2:21), "had left her gold and silver, men and women slaves, livestock, and fields; and she maintained this estate" (8:7). Judith's maidservant, whom Judith took with her into Holofernes's camp, was "in charge of all she possessed" (8:10). Because Judith did not plan to eat with the gentile soldiers, "she gave her maid a skin of wine and a flask of oil, and filled a bag with roasted grain, dried fig cakes, and fine bread; then she wrapped up all her dishes and gave them to her to carry" (10:5). Following her duplicitous plan, Judith presented herself to Holofernes as his slave and his servant (11:5, 16). On the fateful night she murdered Nebuchadnezzar's general, she sent her maid to spread lambskins on the ground for her to recline on (12:15); then she "ate and drank" "what her maid had prepared" (12:19) and sent "her maid to stand outside the bedchamber" (13:3). After cutting off the general's head, Judith gave it to her maid, who put "it in her food bag" and carried it back to the Israelites (13:9–10). Emboldened by Judith's assassination of Holofernes, the Jews streamed out of the city to drive away the Assyrians. Holofernes's officers went immediately to his tent to wake him up, "for the slaves have been so bold as to come down against us" (14:13). When they found their general dead, they went out saying, "The slaves have tricked us!" (14:18). In the end, Judith granted her maid freedom for her assistance in this heroic assassination, which delivered Israel from its enemy (16:23).

The inhabitants of Jerusalem were threatened in a similar way when Antiochus Epiphanes sent his generals to sack the city. "Antiochus sent Apollonius, the captain of the Mysians, with an army of twenty-two thousand, and commanded him to kill all the grown men and to sell the women and boys as slaves" (2 Macc 5:24). Ptolemy, governor of Coele-Syria (southern Syria, Hollow-Syria, between mountain ranges, at times including Israel) and Phoenicia, then sent Nicanor to aid Antiochus's forces. "Nicanor determined to make up for the king the tribute due to the Romans, two thousand talents, by selling captured Jews into slavery. So he immediately sent to the towns on the seacoast, inviting them to buy Jewish slaves and promising to hand over ninety slaves for a talent" (= ca. 16 years of labor; 2 Macc 8:10–11). The low total price confirms that the market was flooded: Jewish slaves were being sold for a ridiculously low price. When Judas Maccabeus routed Nicanor's army, however, "the thrice-accursed Nicanor, who had brought the thousand merchants to buy the Jews, having been humbled with the help of the Lord by opponents whom he regarded as of the least account, took off his splendid uniform and made his way alone like a runaway slave across the country" to Antioch (2 Macc 8:34–35).

14.1.2 The Essenes

According to Philo and Josephus, the Essenes considered slavery "entirely against nature" (Philo, *Contempl. Life* 70), "outraging the law of equality" (Philo, *Good Person* 12.79), and contributing to injustice (Josephus, *Ant.* 18.21). Nevertheless, the Damascus Document contains instructions concerning slaves: "The wet-nurse should not lift the baby to go out or come in on the Sabbath. [blank] And if he should press his servant or his maidservant or his employee on the Sabbath [blank]" (CD XI, 11–12; 4QD^e fr. 10 col. V, 16–17; trans. García Martínez, 42, 66). Moreover, a piece of pottery with Hebrew lettering (an ostracon) from Qumran that dates to the mid-first century records that one Honi, who was in the process of joining the community, deeded all his property, including the slave Hisday, to Eleazar ben Nachmani, who was probably the community bursar (Pfann, 497–507). Donating one's property to the community was part of the initiation process (1QS VI, 18–23); but if the Qumran community inherited slaves from its members, there is no record of what it did with these slaves: "They may have sold them and deposited the money in the common treasury or used them for communal purposes" (Hezser, 292).

14.1.3 Josephus

Josephus, who provides especially relevant information for first-century Galilee, makes frequent reference to slaves of the royal families. Pheroras, a treacherous member of Herod's court, rejected Herod's offer for him to marry Herod's eldest daughter, marrying a slave girl instead (*J.W.* 1.484). Alexander, Herod's son, tried to enlist in his conspiracy three of Herod's most favored slaves, eunuchs who poured his wine, served his supper, put him to bed, and slept in his chamber (*J.W.* 1.488). Women in Herod's family had slave girls, whom Herod tortured for information about a conspiracy against him (*J.W.* 1.584–586; cf. 1:641–643). At Herod's death, five hundred of his domestics and freedmen carried spices for the interment at the Herodium (*J.W.* 1.673). Following Herod's death, Simon, formerly one of Herod's slaves, sought to usurp the crown (*J.W.* 2.57–59; *Ant.* 17.273).

Josephus also provides occasional references to others who owned slaves. The high priests not only had slaves but even sent them to collect tithes at the threshing floors (*Ant.* 20.181, 206–207). Josephus's mother confided in her handmaidens (*J.W.* 5.545), while he himself had a eunuch who served as his son's tutor (*Life* 429). Furthermore, reporting his activities in Galilee during the Jewish revolt, Josephus relates that Philip, King Agrippa's lieutenant, sent messages by his freedmen (*Life* 48, 51). Justus, a native of Tiberias, had a domestic slave (*oiketēs*) who was killed in battle (*Life* 341; Martin 2020, 126). In Judea, the rebel leader Simon Bar Giora sought to build his forces: "By proclaiming liberty for slaves and rewards for the free, he gathered around him the villains from every quarter" (*J.W.* 4.508).

While these roughly contemporary writings show clearly that slavery was widespread among the Jewish elite in this period, they tell us little about the extent of slavery in Galilee. Dale Martin synthesizes the data:

> Finally, Josephus's statement that the Essenes did not keep wives or slaves is evidence that what was considered remarkable was not that there were Jews who had slaves but that there was a group of them who, as a matter of principle, did not (*Ant.* 18.21). The evidence seems clear: definitely from the time of the Tobiads, when Arion served as slave *oikonomos* for Joseph the Tobiad in Alexandria [*Ant.* 12.200–204; ca. 185 BCE], through the Jewish War [66–70 CE] the slave structures of Jews in Palestine were not discernably different from the slave structures of other provincials in the eastern Mediterranean. It was mainly the upper[-]class families who had slaves and freedpersons, and large slave *familiae* were maintained by those Jews whose economic and social position enabled them to do so. (Martin 2020, 127)

By exploring the status and functions of slaves, we may be able to understand the situation in Galilee more clearly.

14.2 The Status of a Slave

The status of slaves is notoriously ambiguous since they were regarded as both property and persons. Moses Finley identifies "two qualities in which the slave was unique as property: first, slave women could and did produce children sired by free men; second, slaves were human in the eyes of the gods, at least to the extent that their murder required some form of purification and that they were themselves involved in ritual acts, such as baptism" (62). To the latter point we might add "and circumcision" (see below). Although they were legally chattel, slaves were also deemed responsible for their own actions (Hezser, 68). Unlike an ox or ass, or an underage child, slaves "have understanding" and hence are responsible for damage they may do (m. Yad. 4:7; m. B. Meṣ. 7:6).

The place of slaves in ancient Roman society is made even more complex because slaves gained power and status by education, skills, and association with high-ranking elites (Martin 1990, 22–26, 47–48). As Martin observes, "Subservience to a powerful patron was the surest route to power for oneself" (1990, 29). Managers (*oikonomoi*) of the slave owners' business affairs and estates were commonly slaves. In this capacity they could acquire wealth and property and enjoy a status higher than a poor free person. This "status inconsistency" and social mobility in a society that saw little upward mobility generated anxiety among the elite and resentment among those who saw slaves gaining in status while they, who formally held a higher rank, were not (Martin 1990, 42–44).

Still, the formal distinction between slave and free was sharply drawn, as the New Testament references above indicate. Widely diverse writers reiterate the fear of being enslaved. Dio Chrysostom (ca. 40–115 CE) observed, "Men desire above all things to be free and say that freedom is the greatest of blessings, while slavery is the most shameful and wretched of states" (*Or.* 14.1). The Testament of Judah warns Judah's descendants that their temple will be consumed by fire, their land made desolate, and they will be enslaved by the gentiles (23.3–5; cf. Jdt 4:12).

Agrippa sought to dissuade the Jews from rebelling against the Romans, saying, "If your object is to have your revenge for injustice, what good is it to extol liberty? If, on the other hand, it is servitude which you find intolerable, to complain of your rulers is superfluous;

were they the most considerate of men, servitude would be equally dis-
graceful" (*J.W.* 2.348–349). Continuing, Agrippa acknowledges that it
is just (*dikaios*) to strive to avoid servitude; but once enslaved, if one
then seeks freedom, he is a rebellious slave (2.356). When the Romans
attacked Jerusalem, some Jews cried out that "they would never be
slaves of the Romans, so long as they might die free men" (*J.W.* 5.321).
While some held that enslavement is preferable to death (Jdt 7:26–27;
Esth 7:4), others chose death (*J.W.* 5.458). At Masada, Eleazar encouraged the Zealots, "We have in our power to die nobly and in freedom"
(7.325; cf. 7.334, 336, 382).

The Mosaic law distinguishes between Israelite and non-Israelite
slaves, allowing harsh treatment only for gentile slaves (Lev 25:46). Yet
even distinctions between Jewish and gentile slaves could not be maintained. Slaves, many of whom were war captives sold into slavery, were
stripped of their identity and carried off from their people, land, and families: "During the period of their enslavement[,] they were seen as blank
slates whose identity was determined by the masters whose extensions
they were. If their masters were committed Jews, they will have required
their gentile slaves to accommodate to their Jewish lifestyle" (Hezser,
53). Jews circumcised non-Jewish slaves, following Genesis 17:12–13
and Exodus 12:44, until this practice was prohibited at the end of the
third century CE (Hezser, 41, who cites Paulus, in *Dig.* 48.8.11; Paulus, *Sent.* 5.22.3–4). Circumcision was necessary because the presence
of a gentile slave within the house rendered the house unclean. By the
rabbinic period, Hezser explains, "The biblical differentiation between
Hebrew and Canaanite slaves was of limited value only. Since by their
time Jewish owners would customarily circumcise (and immerse) their
non-Jewish slaves, and since enslaved Jews were not considered proper
Jews anyway, distinctions between these two categories of slaves were
blurred" (47). Slaves were also given a new name, often a slave name, a
nickname based on a physical attribute, or their master's name, indicat-
ing to whom they belonged (Hezser, 47).

Egyptian papyri document Jewish slave owners:

> In Edfu, on January 10, 162, Rufus, freedman of a woman named Sarra,
> pays the wine tax; Sarra is probably Jewish. Other documents record
> payment of the "Jewish tax" by slaves. In the years 75 and 80 freed-
> men of another Sarra payed the tax. This woman seems to have been
> a Roman citizen as well as Jewish, since her freedman has the name
> Akyntas Kaikillias (Quintus Caecilius). In the year 107, Sporos, slave
> of Aninios, payed the tax, and in 116, Thermouthos, slave of a centurion
> named Aninios, did so. (Martin 2020, 123)

If such papyri had survived in Galilee, they might have documented comparable tax payments for Jewish slaves: "Jews both had slaves and freedpersons and were slaves and freedpersons" (Martin 2020, 113).

Slaves were a relatively cheap source of labor: "Slaves had certain advantages over other types of labour: they were always available; they could be used for any task and any type of work; their annual maintenance costs were lower than the hire of day labourers; they might reproduce themselves; once they were old or sick they could easily be dismissed" (Hezser, 383). Generally, slaves could not marry, and they could not own property. Whereas children produced by unions between master and slave were considered members of the family at an earlier time, by the first century desire to protect one's estate led to denying such children any inheritance (Jos. Asen. 24.8–9; cf. m. Qidd. 3:12–14; m. Ker. 2:2–4).

Wisdom teachers instructed their students that slaves require harsh discipline: "By mere words servants are not disciplined, for though they understand, they will not give heed" (Prov 29:19; cf. Sir 42:5; Ahiqar 83). But there were limitations. A slave owner could be punished for causing a slave's death or maiming the slave (Exod 21:20–21, 26–27; cf. Philo, *Spec. Laws* 3.195; m. B. Qam. 8:3, 5). The Mosaic law gave special consideration to Israelite slaves. Those who became so impoverished that they sold themselves into slavery should not be made to "serve as slaves" or be treated harshly (Lev 25:39, 43). There was wisdom in leniency, for the slave would then serve better (Sir 7:20–21; Philo, *Spec. Laws* 2.83; Ps.-Phoc. 223–227).

Slaves generally wore the same simple, ragged clothes worn by the lower strata of society. Those who held elevated positions, serving royalty or conducting business for a wealthy landowner, wore finer clothes (T. Jos. 11.3; Hezser, 88). The Testament of Job says that Job's wife, wearing ragged clothes after Job lost everything, fell at the feet of his friends, saying, "Do you remember me, Eliphas, you and your two friends—what sort of person I used to be among you and how I used to dress? But now look at my appearance and my attire" (39.1–5).

In some situations, especially when one had only a few slaves or a slave who became a manager, adviser, or confidant, close relationships developed between master and slave. A famous case is that of Rabbi Gamliel's regard for Tabi: "And when his slave Tabi died he accepted condolence because of him. [His students] said to him, 'Master, didst thou not teach us that men may not accept condolence because of slaves?' He replied, 'My slave Tabi was not like other slaves: he was a worthy man'" (m. Ber. 2:7; cf. m. Sukkah 2:1). Monuments and inscriptions set up by masters for their slaves or by slaves or freedmen for their masters also testify to close relationships between master and slave. A third-century inscription from Tiberias proclaims, "For the honour of our deceased lord Sirikios we, your *threptoi*, set up [this monument]" (Hezser, 165). *Threptoi* were abandoned children or children of a slave who were taken in and raised in one's house.

14.3 How One Became Enslaved

One could become a slave in three ways: being taken as a prisoner of war and sold into slavery, selling oneself or being sold into debt slavery, or being born a slave. War captives were the most common source of slaves, as reported by Josephus (e.g., *J.W.* 1.65; 2:68). When the Roman general Cassius captured Taricheae in 52 BCE, "He reduced thirty thousand Jews to slavery" (1.180). The people of Gophna, Emmaus, Lyda, and Thamma followed in 44 BCE (*Ant.* 14.275; *J.W.* 1.222). Sepphoris was also sacked and its inhabitants sold into slavery (67–68 CE; *J.W.* 2.68). When the Romans sacked Yodefat (67 CE), they sold the infants along with the women into slavery (3.304; cf. 4.488). When they took Taricheae (67 CE), they sent six thousand youths to work on the canal at the isthmus of Corinth (3.540) and sold the rest (3.541). When Jerusalem fell in 70 CE, rebels in arms were killed; the rest were taken prisoner (6.414). The most handsome young men were taken for the triumph in Rome. Of the rest, "those over seventeen years of age he [Titus] sent in chains to the works in Egypt, while the multitudes were presented by Titus to the various provinces, to be destroyed in the theatres by the sword or by wild beasts; those under seventeen were sold" (6.418; cf. 7.208). Thousands of captive Jews, 97,000 according to Josephus (6.420), were sold into slavery throughout the Mediterranean, driving down the price of slaves. Although there is no ancient evidence that Jewish slaves were used to construct the Colosseum in Rome, it would have been "quite possible and commensurate with Roman practice" (Elkins, 23).

In addition to the threat that one might be seized in an attack on one's city, ancient travelers risked being kidnapped by bandits and sold into slavery (Deut 24:7; Jos. Asen. 4.10; T. Jos. 12.2–3). Strabo describes the threat of piracy on the coast of Cilicia.

> The exportation of slaves induced them [pirates] most of all to engage in their evil business, since it proved most profitable; for not only were they easily captured, but the market, which was large and rich in property, was not extremely far away, I mean Delos, which could both admit and send away ten thousand slaves on the same day. . . . The Romans, having become rich after the destruction of Carthage and Corinth, used

many slaves; and the pirates, seeing the easy profit therein, bloomed forth in great numbers, themselves not only going in quest of booty but also trafficking in slaves. (*Geogr.* 14.5.2)

Those who were captured and sold in this way had little recourse or means by which to secure their freedom.

In desperation, impoverished parents abandoned infants (esp. gentiles; see above, 4.2) and sold their children. Abandoned children were often taken in and raised as slaves by others. When he encountered this problem in Bithynia early in the second century, Pliny the Younger requested guidance from the emperor Trajan, who responded, "The question you raise of free persons who were exposed at birth, but then brought up in slavery by those who rescued them, has often been discussed, but I can find nothing in the records of my predecessors which could have applied to all provinces" (*Ep.* 10.66). Trajan therefore expressed his opinion that such persons be allowed to claim emancipation and should not be required to purchase their freedom or refund the cost of their maintenance. Special consideration was given to women and children, such as women taken captive in war (Deut 21:10–14; Philo, *Virt.* 111–112) and daughters sold to be concubines (Exod 21:7–11; cf. m. Soṭah 3:8; m. Ketub. 3:8).

Debtors unable to pay their debts (see above, 9.7) either sold themselves into slavery or were put under bond to their creditors until they could pay their debt (2 Kgs 4:1; Neh 5:1–5; Prov 22:7; Amos 2:6; Matt 18:24–34). Leviticus (25:39–41) directs that Israelites in this situation should not be treated as slaves but as "hired or bound laborers" and released in the Jubilee Year (see the discussion of the *prozbul* above, 9.7). Philo admonishes that the Levitical law be observed: "Creditors are not to exact interest from their fellow-nationals but to be content with recovering what they provided. Masters are to treat their purchased slaves as their hired servants, not as their slaves by nature, and give them secure access to liberty on the spot if they can provide their ransom, or in the case of the needy at a later time" (*Spec. Laws* 2.122; cf. 2.82; *Virt.* 122–123). Similarly, thieves could be sold into slavery if they could not repay the stolen property four times over (see Exod 22:1). The rabbis agreed, however, that a woman could not be sold for thievery (m. Soṭah 3:8), presumably because female slaves were commonly violated. Children born to a slave belonged to the master, which led to the practice of slave breeding. Columella (1st c. CE), for example, advised Roman landowners to reward prolific mothers: "To women, too, who are unusually prolific, and who ought to be rewarded for the bearing of a certain number of offspring, I have granted exemption from work and sometimes even freedom after they had reared many children. For to a mother of three sons exemption from work was granted; to a mother of more her freedom as well. Such justice and consideration on the part of the master contributes greatly to the increase of his estate" (*Rust.* 1.8.19). When slaves were bought or sold, a deed was normally written. The Mishnah allows that slaves may be acquired through payment and a deed of sale, by piercing their ear, and by usucaption (undisputed possession over a length of time; m. Qidd. 1:2–3). Unfortunately for modern historians, no deeds of slave sales were found with Babatha's papyri; nor have any been found elsewhere in Roman Palestine. "This does not necessarily mean, however, that Jews never used such contracts or that they never sold or purchased slaves" (Hezser, 272). Aulus Gellius (ca. 130–180) cites an edict that reads, "See to it that the sale ticket of each slave be so written that it can be known exactly what disease or defect each one has, which one is a runaway or a vagabond, or is still under condemnation for some offence" (*Noct. att.* 4.2.1).

What evidence survives regarding prices paid for slaves suggests that the elite could easily afford slaves, while the poor could not. "At the high end, well-educated slaves or a famous prostitute cost 100,000 sesterces [a sesterce = ¼ denarius] in Rome. Normal prices, however, were much lower: 2,700 for a cook at Rome (first century CE), 2,500 for an adult female at Ravenna (second century CE), 725 each for two boys at Pompeii (61 CE), 600 for a girl at Herculaneum (mid-first century CE)" (Friesen, 345–46, citing Duncan-Jones, 343–44). While the prices of slaves varied by supply and demand, gender, age, and abilities, Hezser concludes, "The average price for unskilled adult slaves seems to have been 500–600 denarii" (248). Children were cheaper. Small landholders in Galilee did not have the means to acquire a slave and managed without one.

14.4 Slave Work

Jesus' parables portray a spectrum of both masters and slaves. Some masters are kings; others have several or many slaves; some paint a more modest picture of a master with only one or a few slaves. The slaves are engaged in various tasks. One works in the fields, plowing and tending sheep, and serves meals (Luke 17:7–10). An *oikonomos* manages the master's accounts (16:1–8). A vineyard owner has a manager (*epitropos*, cf. 8:3), probably a slave, who pays the hired workers at the end of the day (Matt 20:8). Another vineyard owner sends his slave to collect the owner's share from the tenants (Mark 12:2). The farmer who has weeds growing in his field has slaves who offer to gather the weeds (Matt 13:28). The father of the prodigal son has slaves who prepare the celebration while the elder brother is coming in from the fields (Luke 15:22–26). These parables fit a context in which slaves do agricultural tasks for landowners whose fields and vineyards are worked by his sons, hired workers, and slaves. Also, slaves managed the master's accounts and supervised other slaves (Matt 24:45–51//Luke 12:42–46; see Martin 1990, 15–22; Martin 2020, 128). The parable of the talents (Matt 25:14–30//Luke 19:12–27) and the parable of the unmerciful servant (Matt 18:24–34) envision high-ranking elites with vast resources: one, five, ten talents, ten thousand talents! The parables with slaves engaged in agricultural work are as good as any other evidence for slaves working on Galilean farms in the first century, not just on royal estates but also on the land of elites living in towns and cities.

Beyond the New Testament, direct evidence for slaves in first-century Galilee is limited. According to Ramsay MacMullen, "In the Levant of the Principate [beginning with Augustus], while commerce in slaves is amply attested along with large households of them in Palestine, there is otherwise nothing known; but for the period after 350 and especially in and around Antioch, the sources are exceptionally rich and the picture exceptionally clear: slaves were abundant in the city, very rare in the countryside" (238–39). Catherine Hezser follows MacMullen, concluding that slaves would have been more common in cities than in the countryside; at least in post-70 times, household slaves would have been more prevalent than agricultural slaves (122; see also Keddie, 93).

In addition to agricultural labor, serving as managers, and performing household chores, slaves were often craftsmen and shopkeepers. Slave girls worked at the loom (Josephus, *J.W.* 1.479), nursed and took care of children (Prov 17:2), and served elite women (Judith, Susanna, Josephus's mother; see above). Slaves could perform a variety of tasks for their mistress or the owner's wife (m. Ketub. 5:5). Male slaves represented their master in business transactions, bought and sold goods, extended invitations (Luke 14:17), and managed their master's house and property while he was away (12:42). Slaves accompanied their master in public, displaying his or her elevated status, and generally performed tasks that allowed their owner to live a life of ease and luxury (Hezser, 212). Slaves could be hired out, and a slave could serve two (human) masters, although that situation must have been rare (m. Giṭ. 4:5; Betz, 456; Hezser, 106–8).

14.5 Manumission and Freed Persons

The philosopher Epictetus, a former slave, said, "It is the slave's prayer that he be set free immediately" (*Diatr.* 4.1.33). But then he proceeds to describe the challenges a freed slave faced that would lead him to yearn for his slavery again. Hardworking slaves might be manumitted for their faithful service, inspiring other slaves to work hard; old slaves might be released, so that the master did not have to maintain them; or sold, so the master could buy a younger slave. Often, slaves were freed at the master's death.

The Mosaic law provides that Hebrew slaves be released after seven years or in the Jubilee Year (Exod 21:2–3; Lev 25:41–42; Deut 15:13–14). Whether this humanitarian law was ever practiced is unclear, however. Non-Israelite slaves had no such protection but could be passed on to one's children (Lev 25:46). To secure a family's estate, Ezekiel declares that the prince's gift to a son becomes part of the son's inheritance, while a gift to a slave reverted to the master in "the year of liberty" because "only his sons may keep a gift from his inheritance" (46:16–17). The Mishnah allows that a non-Israelite slave might buy freedom with money given by a third party (m. Qidd. 1:3). Alternatively, slaves could become free if their master bequeathed his property to them (m. Pe'ah 3:8; Hezser, 166–67).

A slave who did business for a Roman master was given a peculium, working capital. Proceeds from investment of the peculium belonged to the master, but "as an incentive to conduct their business well[,] some masters would give slaves the possibility of eventually purchasing their freedom with the help of the peculium. Once freed, slaves could receive a legacy of their peculium and take the whole or parts of it with them into freedom" (Hezser, 277). Rabbinic sources never mention this Roman practice, however; neither Roman nor rabbinic law allowed a slave to make a gift from his peculium to a third party, who might in turn use it to purchase the slave's freedom (Hezser, 280).

Acts 6:9 refers to the "synagogue of Freedmen," which may have been established for Jewish freedmen who returned to Jerusalem after gaining their freedom. An inscription on the ossuary of Theodotos (Nathanael in Hebrew) in Jericho testifies that he was a freedman of Agrippina the Younger (15–59 CE), the wife of Claudius and mother of Nero, and a Roman citizen (Martin 2020, 122). The family of another first-century Jewish freedman, also named Theodotos, established a synagogue as a meeting place and hostel in Jerusalem (Hezser, 50; see above, 3.2).

Runaway slaves appear occasionally in the texts. When two slaves of Shimei ran away to King Achish of Gath, Shimei rode to Gath on a donkey and brought them back (1 Kgs 2:39–40). After Onesimus ran away from Philemon, he sought the help of the apostle Paul, who sent Onesimus back to Philemon, asking him to welcome Onesimus back as "a beloved brother" (Phlm 16), while suggesting that Philemon might let him stay with Paul to serve him "in your place during my imprisonment for the gospel" (Phlm 13). The rabbis, however, exhorted their followers not to help slaves escape, "for the general good" or "for the good order of the world" (m. Giṭ. 4:6). Likewise, "for the general good," captives should not be ransomed for more than their value, so as not to encourage slave traders to capture others.

14.6 Effects of Slavery

Finally, the corrosive effects of slavery must be recognized, and they were pervasive: "In the first and second century CE[,] Jewish slavery was at its height both in Roman Palestine and in Roman Italy" (Hezser, 382). But slavery did not originate with the Romans. The Pentateuch assumes that Israelites both were slaves and had slaves in the patriarchal period. By the Roman period, there was a well-developed culture of power, privilege, luxury, and prestige built on slave ownership. Yet, slavery dehumanized both slaves and owners. Slaves were treated as chattel and cut off from their family, often from their home country, language, and religion. They could not marry. They were disciplined harshly (the stick), while the hope of manumission (the carrot) served as an incentive to loyalty and hard work.

Slavery also corrupted slave-owning families. Children witnessed brutality from an early age. Slaves were ever present and knew all the family's secrets. Susanna's maids accompanied her to her bath (Sus 17). Judith's maid managed her possessions, prepared her food, and stood outside the bedchamber (Jdt 8:10; 10:5; 12:15, 19; 13:3, 9). As we have seen, Sarah's maids accuse Sarah of beating them and killing (strangling) her bridegrooms. Then they vow, "May we never see a son or daughter of yours!" (Tob 3:8–9). Her maids could enter her bridal chamber (8:12–14). The Testament of Gad warns, "If the hater is a slave, he conspires against his master, and whenever difficulty arises, [the slave] plots how [the master] might be killed" (4.4). A recurring motif in Josephus is that slaves could easily be bribed to conspire against their masters, with the predictable result that they were distrusted. Aeme, a Jewish slave belonging to Caesar's wife, Julia, wrote a letter to Herod alleging that Salome was plotting against Herod; this slave did so because she had been bribed by Antipater (Herod's son), who was conspiring against his father and his aunt (*Ant.* 17.141).

Female slaves were available to their masters or anyone he might give access to them. The relationship between husbands and wives was therefore polluted because wives naturally resented their husband's sexual relations with his slaves. Hillel therefore had good reason when he observed, "The more female slaves the more unchastity, the more male slaves the more theft" (m. Avot 2:7; trans. Hezser, 151).

14.7 Reflections

Because slavery is so offensive to modern readers, its presence throughout the ancient and biblical materials has often been minimized and glossed over. Mary Ann Beavis called out this failing in New Testament scholarship:

> NT scholars have tended to overlook or to gloss over the servile status of the *douloi*, although they are stock characters. As mentioned above, biblical interpreters well know that, in NT Greek, *doulos* almost invariably means "slave" as opposed to "hired servant"; nevertheless, they characteristically translate this word as "servant" (*Knecht, serviteur*) when it occurs in a parable (words with the *doul-* stem occur seventy-two times in the Synoptic Gospels). (Beavis, 40)

The sad truth is that the Bible accepts the institution of slavery, nowhere challenging its legitimacy. As far as we can tell, slavery seems to have been so deeply embedded in ancient economies that its beneficiaries were effectively blind to its intrinsic evil. At best, the Bible calls for humane treatment of slaves. Ephesians, for example, exhorts slaves and masters to fulfill their roles honorably, knowing that in God's sight they are equal:

> Slaves, obey your earthly masters with fear and trembling, in singleness of heart, as you obey Christ; not only while being watched, and in order to please them, but as slaves of Christ, doing the will of God from the heart. Render service with enthusiasm, as to the Lord and not to men and women, knowing that whatever good we do, we will receive the same again from the Lord, whether we are slaves or free. And, masters, do the same to them. Stop threatening them, for you know that both of you have the same Master in heaven, and with him there is no partiality. (6:5–9)

While masters are admonished to avoid "threatening" their slaves, most of the attention in these verses is directed toward encouraging slaves to obey their masters and render good service.

Jesus' parables employ recognizable masters and slaves, at times narrating actions that violate expectations. Masters never served their slaves, regardless of how hard the slave had been working: "Who among you would say to your slave who has just come in from plowing or tending sheep in the field, 'Come here at once and take your place at the table'?" (Luke 17:7). No one! "Do you thank the slave for doing what was commanded?" (17:9). No! The parable assumes a small farmer with one slave, who does both the fieldwork and the household chores. "The point of the parable," Beavis emphasizes, "is not that the *doulos* is an outstandingly good or faithful one, but merely that he does what is expected of a slave in Greco-Roman society: he attends to his master's needs without question" (41). In its Lukan context, this parable follows Jesus' instructions to forgive one's brother or sister seven times a day (17:4). The parable achieves its effect by shifting the point of view from the master to the slave. No slave would be commended or thanked for doing what was required. Having accepted this premise, the disciples (and Luke's readers) are then challenged to see that they are God's slaves. Therefore, even when they do all that is required, they have done nothing for which they might be rewarded, even if they forgive seven times a day. Jesus accepts the practice of slavery as a given but challenges his hearers to see themselves as slaves and God as their master. Regardless of their obedience, they have no claim on God.

The parable of the wise and wicked slave cuts in the opposite direction in both Matthew (24:45–50) and Luke (12:42–48). The good slave, who does what he is commanded and is at work when his master returns, will be rewarded. The wicked slave—who acts as a master, beating the other slaves, eating, and getting drunk (Luke 12:45)—will be cut into pieces. The slave who knew what was expected and did not do it will receive a heavy beating; the slave who did not know what was expected will receive a light beating. Obviously, lessons on the coming judgment and lessons on leadership in the church show through the veneer of the parable (see Culpepper 1995, 263–64). The warning to disciples, as to slaves, is clear: work hard, be diligent; the master is coming. At the same time, there are proportional responsibilities and degrees of reward and punishment: "To whom much is given, much will be required" (Luke 12:48). The parable of the talents extends this lesson: To the one who is faithful, more will be given; yet even what a person has will be taken from the one who fails with the little that has been received (Matt 25:14–30).

The parable of the dishonest manager (*oikonomos*, Luke 16:1–9) seems to presuppose the practice of giving a slave manager a peculium with which to do business for the master. The slave has been profiting from accounts with the master's clients. When the master hears what the manager is doing, he resolves to take the position away from his slave. Before the master does so, the slave obligates the master's clients to reward him by encouraging them to write false receipts for grain and olive oil, reducing what they owe. The shocking reversal comes when "his master commended the dishonest manager because he acted shrewdly" (16:8). The Lukan Jesus might well have asked, "Who among you would reward a dishonest manager?"

The slave parables, therefore, are based on what first-century audiences expect of slaves and masters, whether they narrate expected actions and responses or dramatically depart from them for effect. Nevertheless, "the slave parables . . . do not directly attack the institution of slavery," even if, as Beavis observed, "their tendency to suggest that owner identify with his/her human property might have been perceived as radical social teaching by ancient audiences" (54).

Although the New Testament does not call for the abolition of slavery, even in the teachings of Jesus, Jesus offers hope for an end of slavery in the promise of the coming of God's kingdom. At Nazareth, echoing Isaiah 61:1, Jesus declares, "The Spirit of the Lord is upon me, because he has anointed me to bring good news to the poor. He has sent me to proclaim release to the captives and recovery of sight to the blind, to let the oppressed go free" (Luke 4:18). For this declaration, the people of his hometown attempt to stone him.

Works Cited in Chapter 14

Beavis, Mary Ann. 1992. "Ancient Slavery as an Interpretive Context for the New Testament Servant Parables with Special Reference to the Unjust Steward (Luke 16:1–8)." *JBL* 111:37–54.

Betz, Hans Dieter. 1995. *The Sermon on the Mount.* Edited by Adela Yarbro Collins. Hermeneia. Minneapolis: Fortress.

Crossan, John Dominic. 1974. "The Servant Parables of Jesus." *Semeia* 1:17–62.

Culpepper, R. Alan. 1995. "The Gospel of Luke." Pages 1–490 in vol. 9 of *NIB*. Nashville: Abingdon.

Duncan-Jones, Richard. 1982. *The Economy of the Roman Empire: Quantitative Studies.* Cambridge: Cambridge University Press.

Elkins, Nathan T. 2019. *The Monument to Dynasty and Death: The Story of Rome's Colosseum and the Emperors Who Built It.* Baltimore: Johns Hopkins University Press.

Fiensy, David A. 1991. *The Social History of Palestine in the Herodian Period: The Land Is Mine.* Lewiston, NY: Mellon.

———. 2020. *The Archaeology of Daily Life: Ordinary Persons in Later Second Temple Israel.* Eugene, OR: Cascade.

Finley, Moses I. 1999. *The Ancient Economy.* Updated ed. Berkeley: University of California Press.

Friesen, Steven J. 2004. "Poverty in Pauline Studies: Beyond the So-Called New Consensus." *JSNT* 26:323–61.

García Martínez. *See* Bibliography of Ancient Sources and Translations

Hezser, Catherine. 2005. *Jewish Slavery in Antiquity.* Oxford: Oxford University Press.

Keddie, G. Anthony. 2019. *Class and Power in Roman Palestine: The Socioeconomic Setting of Judaism and Christian Origins.* Cambridge: Cambridge University Press.

MacMullen, Ramsay. 1990. *Changes in the Roman Empire: Essays in the Ordinary.* Princeton: Princeton University Press.

Martin, Dale B. 1990. *Slavery as Salvation: The Metaphor of Slavery in Pauline Christianity*. New Haven: Yale University Press.

————. 2020. "Slavery and the Ancient Jewish Family." Pages 113–30 in *The Jewish Family in Antiquity*. Edited by Shaye J. D. Cohen. Atlanta: Scholars Press.

Pfann, Stephen J. 2000. *Qumran Cave 4.XXVI: Cryptic Texts: Miscellanea, Part 1*. Edited by Philip Alexander et al. DJD 36. Oxford: Oxford University Press.

Part IV

Officials

Chapter 15

Tax Collectors

Pharisee and Tax Collector (Luke 18:10–13)

A tax collector features in only one of Jesus' parables. A Pharisee and a tax collector go up to the temple to pray. The Pharisee asks nothing of God but boasts of his righteousness; his fasting and tithing are ample evidence of his piety. The tax collector boasts of nothing before God. Instead, his prayer echoes the opening words of Psalm 51, "Have mercy on me, O God." The crucial addition to the words of the Psalm is the tax collector's self-designation: "a sinner." Nothing more is reported of the tax collector's prayer. It is complete as it stands, and nothing more needs to be said of his character (Culpepper, 342). The parable concludes with Jesus' comment, "I tell you, this man [the tax collector] went down to his home justified rather than the other; for all who exalt themselves will be humbled, but all who humble themselves will be exalted" (18:14). This lesson on prayer has parallels in the immediate context in Luke, where the tax collector may be compared with the humble but persistent widow in 18:1–8 and the little children in 18:15–17. Jesus' audience would likely have agreed with the tax collector's self-characterization, "a sinner," and been shocked by Jesus' declaration that he "went down to his home justified."

Tax collectors appear in all three Synoptic Gospels. Jesus calls Matthew/ Levi while he is sitting at the toll booth in Capernaum, and a banquet follows "in the house," presumably Matthew's house, where Jesus eats with "many tax collectors and sinners" (Matt 9:10–11//Mark 2:14–16//Luke 5:27–30). Because of this, Jesus was accused of being "a friend of tax collectors and sinners" (Matt 11:19//Luke 7:34). Yet even tax collectors love those who love them (Matt 5:46). If a church member refuses to be reconciled, "let such a one be to you as a Gentile and a tax collector" (Matt 18:17). On the other hand, tax collectors came to John the Baptist to be baptized (Matt 21:32; Luke 3:12; 7:29) and came to hear Jesus' teachings, which scandalized the Pharisees and scribes (Luke 15:1–2). Jesus warns the chief priests and elders, "Truly I tell you, the tax collectors and the prostitutes are going into the kingdom of God ahead of you" (Matt 21:31). When Zacchaeus, a chief tax collector, declares, "Look, half of my possessions, Lord, I will give to the poor; and if I have defrauded anyone of anything, I will pay back four times as much," Jesus says, "Today salvation has come to this house, because he too is a son of Abraham" (Luke 19:8–9). Behind the Gospel references to tax collectors lies a fascinating scene of imperial power, privilege, corruption, and extortion, but Bible commentaries seldom take us very far into this world.

15.1 Roman Taxation

The obstacles to understanding the role of tax collectors are multiple and complicated. Our sources, especially for tax collection in Galilee, are quite limited. The other complicating factor is "the amazing divergence between the provinces and even between cities in the same province" (Broshi, 236). Roman taxation varied by region and province and changed over time, complicating the matter of who paid what to whom, for what purposes, and by what means.

Specialists continue to gather and correlate data from the literary, epigraphical, papyrological, and numismatic sources (Günther). Generalizations about Roman taxation, therefore, will not take us very far, and they are often misleading. As in other chapters, we must ask specifically about the evidence for the situation in Galilee in the time of Herod Antipas. Finally, the Latin terminology for the various Roman taxes can discourage all but the most determined student of the Gospels. The approach taken here will be to introduce the development of Roman taxation in its various forms, giving special attention to developments in the period of Caesar Augustus and Tiberius, before turning specifically to taxation in Judea and Galilee under Herod the Great and Herod Antipas.

Roman conquests expanded the empire, generated new resources and wealth, and secured its frontiers. Keith Hopkins insightfully observed that during the first two centuries CE, the Roman Empire comprised two rings around Italy and its capital: an outer ring of frontier provinces and defensive outposts; and an inner ring of tax- and resource-generating provinces that supported both the city of Rome and its armies on the frontiers (101). As we will see, Palestine served as a defensive outpost protecting the eastern provinces from the Parthians. Herod and his sons were charged with securing their territory, pacifying it, and maintaining its loyalty to Rome, while also collecting taxes.

As Julius Caesar himself said, Roman conquest was maintained by "soldiers and money," and "these two were dependent upon each other" (Dio Cassius, *Hist.* 42.49.4). A common pattern developed: conquest of a region; pacification; assessment of its wealth and resources, at times by means of a census; extraction of wealth by various means; protest by rebels; and harsh reprisals (MacMullen, 35). Roman occupation of Palestine followed this pattern precisely. Conquered territories were placed under the authority of local rulers or Roman governors, who in turn sold, leased, or gave property to local elites, thereby creating patron-client relationships and generating support for the local authority, who made gifts, paid leases, and collected taxes and tolls. Still, "no attempt was made to impose a uniform tax system" (Garnsey and Saller, 229).

The frequency and regularity of censuses has been a matter of great debate because Luke says, "A decree went out from Caesar Augustus that all the world should be registered" (2:1 NRSVue), adding, "This was the first registration and was taken while Quirinius was governor of Syria" (2:2). P. A. Brunt first argued that the lack of evidence for censuses is because taking a census was so common that it was unremarkable, but he later revised his view (Brunt 1981, 163–67; Brunt 1990, 533). There is no evidence elsewhere for an empire-wide census, but there were censuses in Egypt, Arabia, and Nabatea during this period: the administration of the census and documents recording what was registered varied from province to province (Keddie, 73–76). Cestius, legate of Syria (63–67 CE), ordered a census in Jerusalem (Josephus, *J.W.* 6.423). A fragmentary document from Nahal Se'elim (P.Jud.Des.Misc. 4; Keddie, 77–78) preserves a census list from early in the second century CE. Whether by census or other means, direct as well as indirect taxes, tolls, levies, and other extractions of wealth were imposed.

Sven Günther clarifies the Latin terminology. The so-called direct taxes, *tributa* or *stipendia*, were based on a census or tax list. *Stipendia* were paid to the Roman garrison by the province's population. Calculations, rates, and immunities varied by province: Rome typically accommodated existing practices and circumstances. After 167 BCE, *tributa* were collected only from inhabitants of Roman provinces, though not from Roman citizens except in emergency situations, thus enforcing their status as conquered provincials. *Tributa* included land tax (*tributum soli*) and poll tax (*tributum capitis*). The *fiscus Judaicus* was a specific tribute imposed on Jews after the war of 66–70 CE (see below). The *tributa* were collected by tax collectors (*publicani*).

As Rome extended its territory, the *publicani* formed associations (*societates publicanorum*) that maintained paid staffs to conduct tax collection and construction of public works, as well as venturesome speculation and usury (Youtie, 10–12). Julius Caesar first and then Augustus sought to control the power of the *publicani*. Nero instituted broad reforms to control extortion by the tax collectors. The collection of *tributa* and *stipendia* was taken from them and delegated to cities and local authorities, who sold contracts for direct taxes to local elites, who in turn relied on their agents, clients, slaves, or freedmen to carry out the actual task of collecting taxes or customs fees (van Nijf, 285–86). Again, the situation was fluid and varied by region; in some locations *publicani* continued to be active through the second century. The government set the amount each town had to pay (Strabo, *Geogr.* 10.5.3; 14.2.19; Brunt 1981, 168), and therefore the government could grant a remission of tribute following natural disasters or wars (Tacitus, *Ann.* 2.47; 12.63). Local authorities set the value of each property. Consequently, "we should expect there to have been substantial differences between (a) what peasants paid in tax and (b) what rich landowners paid on similar land; and between (c) what tax-collectors gathered and (d) what they transmitted to the central government" (Hopkins, 121). Peasants paid a disproportionate share of the taxes: "The saying that 'unto every one that hath shall be given, and he shall have abundance, but from him that hath not shall be taken away even that which he hath' made good sense in the Roman world" (Brunt 1981, 162; Matt 25:29 KJV). Wealth flowed upward from the poor to the elites and on to the governors or kings and ultimately to Rome (Hanson and Oakman, 257). The issue of taxes was raw—often a flashpoint for rebellion. When the Roman governor Florus raided the treasury in the temple and took seventeen talents, allegedly for "imperial service" (lit. "for Caesar's needs," *eis tas Kaisaros chreias*), violence broke out in Caesarea and quickly escalated into the revolt of 66–70 CE (Josephus, *J.W.* 2.293–296).

Vectigalia, so-called indirect taxes, were based on goods bought and sold and were paid by citizens and noncitizens alike, and here we meet the "tax collectors" of the Gospels (see below). *Vectigalia* included both empire-wide and local taxes and varied under different emperors. The inheritance tax (5 percent) was introduced by Augustus in 6 CE to help fund a military treasury to pay his veterans (Woolf, 196–97). Wills had to be opened and recorded by an official, and the inheritance tax had to be paid. Small inheritances were exempt. The manumission tax (5 percent) may have been used for imperial slaves and freedmen. Augustus required that to gain citizenship, a slave had to be manumitted before a Roman official, who collected the tax. Slaves could also buy their freedom and pay the tax from their peculium (see above, 14.5). Ancient Rome also administered a sales tax, implemented after the civil wars between Octavian and Marc Antony, to fund the military treasury: a 1 percent flat rate that was applied across the empire but limited to public auctions and leases. The sales tax was reduced to 0.5 percent in 17 CE (Tacitus, *Ann.* 2.42.4), then canceled by Caligula in 38 CE (Suetonius, *Cal.* 16.3; Günther). A tax on the sale of slaves (4 percent) was also established in 7 CE by Augustus.

Portoria (custom duties or tariffs) were another form of the indirect taxes (Schürer, 1:373–76). These tariffs were paid in cash at customs stations (*telōnia*) at the outer borders (where the rate could range from 12.5 to 25 percent) and internally, where the rate was much lower (1 to 5 percent). The customs house was where the staff worked, searching transported goods, assigning and collecting tariffs, writing receipts, and keeping records. The officials may also have lived there (van Nijf, 288–91).

There was ample opportunity for skimming and malpractice (Brunt 1981, 170). Merchants and shippers sought to hide goods or bypass customs stations, while the tax collectors sent out scouts to catch them. In Chariton's novel, *Chaeras and Callirhoe*, for example, "A merchant who had a beautiful girl for sale approached me. Because of the custom officials he had anchored his boat outside the city" (2.1.3). Quantities were estimated, and tariffs were assigned, no doubt to the advantage of the tax collector, who in turn may not always have entered true figures in the official records (van Nijf, 291–94). Augustus changed the system, replacing the payment of a lump sum up front with a percentage system, so the tax farmers worked on commission (van Nijf, 295–97).

The Romans collected taxes in three ways: "(1) payment in cash; (2) payment in kind of agricultural produce grown by the farmer himself; (3) payment in kind of agricultural produce not produced by the farmer himself" (Safrai, 350). While direct tax on land was often paid in kind (a percentage of the harvest), indirect taxes were paid in cash. The requirement of cash for the payment of taxes had a measurable effect on the economy of the empire. In an influential article, Keith Hopkins proposed that "the Romans' imposition of taxes paid in money greatly increased the volume of trade in the Roman Empire (200 B.C.–A.D. 400)"; second, "in so far as money taxes were levied on conquered provinces and then spent in other provinces or in Italy, then the tax-exporting provinces had to earn money with which to pay their taxes by exporting goods of an equal value" (Hopkins, 101). Peasants had to sell a portion of their harvest in local markets to generate money to pay their taxes. In turn, "the food which they sold was consumed locally by artisans, who made goods of higher value and lower volume than staple foods (for example, textiles, leather goods, pots)" (Hopkins, 102). The result was an increase in production, division of labor, and increases in the number of artisans, the size of towns, local markets, and export of goods.

Changes in consumption followed: "Government employees, soldiers and officials received tax monies as pay and spent their money on food, services and artisan-made goods, some of which came from the distant provinces which paid the original money taxes" (Hopkins, 102). Nevertheless, the economy of the empire remained at a subsistence level, with the majority of its population producing what they consumed and consuming most of what they produced (Hopkins, 104). There was no protection for small landholders. If the harvest was lean, little would be left after portions were set aside for taxes, leases, and debts. In support of these propositions, Hopkins cites the increase in archaeological artifacts from this period, the peak in the number of shipwrecks in the Mediterranean that can be dated to the period 200 BCE to 200 CE, and the increase in the number of coins minted during this period (Hopkins, 110, 116).

With this broad sweep of Roman taxation in view, we can turn to the situation in Galilee.

15.2 Roman and Jewish Taxation in Galilee

Roman taxation in Galilee changed under various rulers. In 63 BCE, Pompey annexed the Hasmonean state to the province of Syria, where one of the companies of *publicani* collected tribute for Rome (Seeman, 275–76), but revolts disrupted regular payments. In 57 BCE, Gabinius, governor of Syria, divided Palestine into five districts to organize the collection of taxes, with centers in Jerusalem, Gadara, Amathus, Jericho, and Sepphoris (Josephus, *Ant.* 14.91; *J.W.* 3.54).

Julius Caesar brought a measure of order by issuing a series of decrees approved by the Senate that excluded the *publicani*, recognized Hyrcanus II as the high priest, imposed a land tax, but allowed the collection of tithes for the temple, as in the past (Seeman, 322–33). The land tax was to be delivered every other year (except the Sabbatical Year) at Sidon, apparently meaning that the tax on farmers was 12.5 percent per year, whether it was collected every year or every other year (Udoh 2020, 51; Fiensy, 99–100). Tax assessors determined the tax based on the estimated produce. The tax would be paid in kind and recorded at the village granary. Caesar also relieved the Jews of winter-quartering Roman troops (billeting) and demands for money or transportation by soldiers; neither was any official allowed to raise auxiliary troops in Jewish territories, probably so there would be no potentially rebellious military force (Josephus, *Ant.* 14.200–204).

After Caesar's assassination, the civil war temporarily disrupted this arrangement. The Roman general Cassius exacted a onetime tribute of 700 talents of silver from the Jewish state: Herod raised 100 talents from Galilee (*Ant.* 14.272–274). With Herod's appointment as king, Judea and Galilee were removed from the province of Syria and became a Roman client state. As a client state, the territory governed by Herod and his sons paid no tribute to Rome. Udoh stresses this point: "It is still worth emphasizing, however, that the manner in which Herod actually managed his realm leaves no trace of his kingdom's external tax obligations. He imposed and remitted taxes at will; he stipulated financial and tax obligations for the cities and colonies he founded, all without reference to any supposed debts to Rome" (2020, 144). In return, Rome expected Herod to subdue the rebels in Judea and Galilee, serve as a defensive frontier for Rome (Seeman, 252–54, 359–64), and maintain order and loyalty to Rome. Seen in this context, Herod Antipas's war with the Nabateans and the repeated disturbances in Jerusalem and elsewhere were causes for concern to the Herods—and Rome.

At the same time, Herod extracted large sums of money for his building projects, including Caesarea, Samaria, Jerusalem and the temple, and his palaces and fortresses (Josephus, *Ant.* 15.303). Herod collected a land tax and demonstrated his loyalty to Rome by making gifts to Antony and Octavian (Josephus, *Ant.* 15.189–190, 200; *J.W.* 1.388). Herod also levied taxes on "public purchases and sales," taxes "ruthlessly exacted" (*Ant.* 17.205). A delegation of Jews traveled to Rome to appeal for relief from Herod's oppressive rule, arguing that Herod

> had indeed reduced the entire nation to helpless poverty after taking it over in as flourishing a condition as few ever know, and he was wont to kill members of the nobility upon absurd pretexts and then take over their property for himself. . . . In addition to the collecting of the tribute [*phoros*] that was imposed on everyone each year, lavish contributions had to be made to him and his household and friends and those of his slaves who were sent out to collect the tribute because there was no immunity at all from outrage unless bribes were paid. (*Ant.* 17.306–308)

Tacitus adds that in 17 CE, "Syria and Judaea, exhausted by their burdens, were pressing for a diminution of the tribute" (*Ann.* 2.42; see Schürer, 1:373; Hamel, 144–48). On the other hand, Herod returned a great deal of wealth to the economy through his building projects, especially the construction of the temple, the jobs it created, and the influx of crowds it drew to Jerusalem (Sanders, 270–71).

The question regarding the poll tax (*tributum capitis*) in the Synoptic Gospels (Matt 22:15–22//Mark 12:13–17//Luke 20:20–26) is particularly fraught because it requires interpreters to deal with the related issues of the frequency and regularity of censuses, what was registered (land, property, or persons), and the relationship between the poll tax and the temple tax. In Matthew and Mark, the Pharisees and Herodians ask Jesus, "Is it lawful to pay taxes [*kēnson*] to the emperor?" Luke reads, "Is it lawful for us to pay taxes [*phoron*] to the emperor?" (20:22). Our lexicons offer little clarity. BDAG (542) renders *kēnsos* as "tax, poll tax," while LSJ (947) has (I) "census" and (II) "poll-tax," for which it cites only Matthew 17:25. Udoh explains: "The meaning of the word here [Mark 12:14//Matt 22:17] also is clearly 'census' or 'assessment' rather than 'tax.' Other attestations of the word are from the second century CE and later. There is, in any case, no instance in which the Greek word is used to mean 'tax' or 'tribute'" (2020, 227).

The poll tax was introduced by Augustus in Gaul, following a census in 27 BCE. In the legendary story in 3 Maccabees, Ptolemy IV Philopator imposes the poll tax on the Jews:

> He proposed to inflict public disgrace on the Jewish community, and he set up a stone on the tower in the courtyard with this inscription: "None of those who do not sacrifice shall enter their sanctuaries, and all Jews shall be subjected to a registration involving poll tax [*laographian*] and to the status of slaves. Those who object to this are to be taken by force and put to death; those who are registered are also to be branded on their bodies by fire with the ivy-leaf symbol of Dionysus, and they shall also be reduced to their former limited status." In order that he might not appear to be an enemy of all, he inscribed below: "But if any of them prefer to join those who have been initiated into the mysteries, they shall have equal citizenship with the Alexandrians." (3 Macc 2:27–30)

The entire phrase "a registration involving poll tax" translates the term *laographian*; there is no separate term for "poll tax." The Babatha papyri discussed above (7.8) make no reference to a poll tax; Babatha registered her property. Appian (*Hist. rom.* 11.50.253) refers to a poll tax paid by the Jews after the destruction of the temple. After sacking Jerusalem in 70 CE, Vespasian "imposed a poll-tax of two drachmas [ca. 2 denarii], to be paid annually into the Capitol as formerly contributed by them to the temple at Jerusalem" (Josephus, *J.W.* 7.218).

> Prior to 70 CE, when Vespasian converted the temple tax into a poll tax imposed on all Jews (Josephus, *J.W.* 7.218), the Jews in Palestine did not pay an annual "head tax." They did not pay it under John Hyrcanus II; they did not pay it under Herod, or in Galilee under Antipas, or in Judea (Archelaus's ethnarchy) after it was annexed in 6 CE. (Udoh 2014, 378; see further Udoh 2020, 220–38)

The Arsinoe papyrus from Egypt dated 73 CE (*CPJ* 421) shows that the discriminatory "Jewish tax was collected from both men *and* women starting *at age 3*" (Keddie, 80). The Gospels, especially Matthew and Mark, seem therefore to be adducing Jesus' response to a Roman tax imposed on Jews, not during Jesus' own lifetime, but rather during the period in which the Gospels were composed (Keddie, 81–86). This tax, the *fiscus Judaicus*, was all the more odious because it was used to rebuild the Temple of Jupiter Optimus Maximus in Rome (Dio Cassius, *Hist.* 65.7.2; Heemstra, 9–23).

By definition, a poll tax is based on a census, but the only known census in Judea at this time was that of Quirinius. The assumption that censuses were conducted regularly in Judea or Galilee (Jones, 165; Brunt 1981, 163–66) cannot be confirmed from our sources (Udoh 2020, 220–38), nor is there any record apart from Luke of a census at the time of Jesus' birth. When Caesar removed Archelaus from power in Judea in 6 CE, he annexed Judea to Syria and sent Quirinius, legate of Syria, to conduct a census in Judea and "make an assessment of the property of the Jews" (Josephus, *Ant.* 18.2; *ILS* 2683; cf. Luke 2:2). Josephus seems to indicate that the purpose of the census was to register property, not to secure a head count: "Although the Jews were at first shocked to hear of the registration of property, they gradually condescended" (*Ant.* 18.2). Judas the Galilean, however, led a rebellion, declaring, "The assessment carried with it a status amounting to downright slavery" (*Ant.* 18.4). He called his countrymen "cowards for consenting to pay tribute to the Romans" (*J.W.* 2.118; cf. Eusebius, *Hist. eccl.* 1.5.5).

The upshot of this sparse record is that land or property tax was generally paid in kind, while "indirect taxes" (tolls and customs duties) were paid in cash.

15.3 The Tithes

Julius Caesar further stipulated that the Jews "shall also pay tithes to Hyrcanus [II] and his sons, just as they paid to their forefathers" (Josephus, *Ant.* 14.203). Although "tithe" clearly means "tenth," the biblical law was complicated, fueling generations of efforts to clarify it. According to Deuteronomy, a tithe of agricultural produce (grain, wine, oil, firstlings) was to be taken to Jerusalem every year except the Sabbatical Year, consumed there or sold, and the money spent in Jerusalem (Deut 14:22–27). For the third and sixth years, the tithe was given to the local levites and the needy (resident aliens, orphans, widows: Deut 14:27–29).

According to Leviticus, tithes from the land (seed and fruit) are holy, as is "every tenth one that passes under the shepherd's staff" (Lev 27:30–33); that is, either it belonged to the priests, or it was to be eaten in purity. According to Numbers, it went to the Levites, who collected the tithe in the rural towns and then set apart a tithe of the tithe for the priests (Num 18:21–28; cf. Neh 10:37–39). Efforts to harmonize Deuteronomy with the other books led to an accounting of three tithes: the first for the Levites (every year except the seventh), the second to be spent in Jerusalem (every year except the seventh), and in the third and sixth years a third tithe for the needy—a total of fourteen tithes every seven years, or perhaps eighteen tithes, if the three were offered every year (cf. Tob 1:6–8; Jub. 32.10–15; Josephus, *Ant.* 4.69, 205, 240).

Later, the Mishnah prescribes twelve tithes: the first to the Levites, the second to be spent in Jerusalem, and the third for the needy replaced the second tithe in years 3 and 6 (Sanders, 243–48). In addition, the firstfruits and firstlings went to the priests, to feed them and their families (Num 18:13). The rabbis regarded the heave offering (Neh 10:37, 39; m. Ter.), a small offering of produce for the priests, as a separate offering (Sanders, 254–56). The Pharisees and rabbis also developed special rules for paying the tithe on food purchased from one who may not have paid the tithe on it: "demai," doubtfully tithed produce (Sanders, 675–78; Saldarini, 216–20). As this practice suggests, the rabbis suspected that some small farmers did not pay the first tithe.

The tithes supported the temple personnel and ensured its continued operation while the temple was standing. Two systems of collection are evident throughout the postexilic period. Tithes were collected both at the temple and locally by individual priests and Levites throughout Israel. As Udoh argues, it would have been impractical for pilgrims to carry the first tithes to Jerusalem, then make the priests and Levites carry them back to their towns and villages (2020, 274, 278). Furthermore, only a fraction of the temple personnel would have been in Jerusalem in any given week.

Josephus refers to the local collection of tithes in Galilee when he reports that his colleagues, the priests Joazar and Judas, "men of excellent character" (*Life* 29), "amassed a large sum of money from the tithes, which they accepted as their priestly due" (*Life* 63). Josephus himself refused "the tithes which were due to me as a priest" (*Life* 80).

15.4 Determining the Tax Burden

Emperor Tiberius is famously reported to have said, "I want my sheep shorn, not shaven" (Dio Cassius, *Hist.* 57.10), but the matter was surely perceived differently by the lambs who felt fleeced. Scholars assess the tax burden variously. Richard Horsley contends that oppressive taxation contributed to social unrest in Galilee, calculating that farmers were subject to taxes amounting to "well over 40 percent of their production" (56). James

D. G. Dunn (310–11) identifies the layers of Roman and Jewish taxation: (1) tithes due to the priests and the half-shekel temple tax, which together, he estimates, amounted to at least 15 percent; (2) levies (land tax and customs tolls) collected by Herod Antipas; and (3) the Roman tribute, 12.5 percent per year—altogether about one-third or more of all produce and income. Others reach estimates ranging from 20 to over 40 percent. E. P. Sanders (275–76) figures that the total of the first tithe (10 percent), the poor tithe, firstfruits, heave offering, and temple tax would be 15.2 percent, to which one must add the Roman taxes, which would have varied but for which he accepts the estimate of 12.5 percent, resulting in a total for most years of under 28 percent (see also Oakman, 68–72; Harland, 521–22; Broshi, 236–38). Safrai despairs, "It is basically impossible to determine how much taxes were paid by the inhabitants of Palestine and the percentage of those taxes that were paid in cash. It is also impossible to point out the various processes which were instrumental in shaping tax policy" (352).

Whether from exorbitant rates, the cumulative burden of taxes, the brutality with which they were collected, or simply the resentment at paying taxes to a foreign power, there were sporadic outbreaks. Nevertheless, "the general view that excessive taxation of the Jewish state in the early Roman period was the cause of observable economic depravity in the first century C.E. is not supported by the evidence" (Udoh 2020, 285). Galilee enjoyed a period of general tranquility, stability, and prosperity under Herod Antipas.

15.5 The Status of Tax Collectors

The various types of taxes collected in Galilee during Jesus' ministry required a variety of tax collectors: some received the land tax (*tributum soli*), generally paid in kind; toll collectors extracted the "indirect taxes," including tolls on transported goods and sales tax on public sales. Herod Antipas organized the collection of these taxes, sending out his slaves (as his father had: Josephus, *Ant.* 17.308, quoted above) or granting the right to collect taxes to local elites, "the leaders [great men, *megistanoi*] of Galilee" (Mark 6:21). Tax farmers could bid for the right to collect indirect taxes in their village, town, or area. They could keep any excess they collected, but they were still obligated if expected harvests fell short. The "tax collectors" of the Gospels are therefore "toll collectors" or men who worked for the toll collectors (Donahue, 48, 59).

The two named toll collectors in the Gospels are Jewish: Levi/Matthew (Matt 9:9–13//Mark 2:17//Luke 5:27–32) and Zacchaeus (Luke 19:1–10). Zacchaeus was a "chief tax collector" (*architelōnēs*), the head of a group or association of tax farmers at Jericho. Herbert Youtie draws attention to the significance of the term Zacchaeus uses (Luke 19:8), *esykophantēsa*, which is translated *harass, squeeze, shake down, blackmail* (BDAG, 955): "The word is of Athenian origin and means to play the part of an informer. Subsequently it designated the activity of a dishonest informer, and so meant to bring false charges. But for us the importance of the word lies in the implied subordination of the tax-farmer to government officials" (Youtie, 18). The chief tax collector in Jericho answered to the procurator in Judea. Josephus identifies a third toll collector, named John, as one of the leading Jews of Caesarea (*J.W.* 2.287, 292; Udoh 2020, 241). Tithes were collected by priests and Levites in the towns and villages where they lived. Although the tithes were largely voluntary, "The ability to collect such taxes would have reinforced the priestly families' legitimate authority over the Jewish people" (Root, 182). The high-priestly aristocracy also used their slaves (*douloi*) and servants (*oiketai*) to collect tithes (Josephus, *Ant.* 20.181, 206–207).

Perhaps it should be no surprise that it is difficult to ascertain an unbiased picture of toll collectors: "The tax farmer, when he appears in literature, is represented in a negative light as someone who is marked by excessive greed and lack of morality" (van Nijf, 285). As the frequency of the phrase "tax collectors and sinners" suggests, most folks assumed that tax collectors *were* sinners. Cicero declares, "First, those means of livelihood are rejected as undesirable which incur people's ill-will, as those of tax farmers and usurers" (*Off.* 1.42.150). Similarly, Dio Chrysostom asks, "[Is it permissible to do things that,] while they are not expressly forbidden by the laws, yet are regarded as base and unseemly by mankind? I mean, for example, collecting taxes, or keeping a brothel, or doing other such things" (*Or.* 14.14; van Nijf, 282).

Tax collectors are also the dull-witted victims of a sharp wit in this story from Philostratus's *Life of Apollonius of Tyana*:

> When they were about to cross to Mesopotamia, the tax collector [*telōnēs*] in charge of Zeugma took them to the notice board [*pinakion*] and asked them what they were exporting. "Prudence," replied Apollonius, "Justice, Virtue, Temperance, Courage, Perseverance," thus stringing out many nouns in the feminine. The official, immediately thinking of his own profit, said: "Well then, register your servants." "I cannot," retorted Apollonius, "since it is not my servants I am exporting, but my governesses." (1.20.1)

Van Nijf finds "only one source [that] purports to give the opinion of a tax collector, and he takes a defensive stance: the tax gatherer Diomedon said, 'If it is not shameful for you to sell the taxes, it is not shameful for us to buy them'" (Dionysius of Halicarnassus, *1 Amm.* 12; van Nijf, 284). Funerary and honorary inscriptions from Asia Minor offer a contrasting picture, again biased but more positive. In these inscriptions the tax farmers "represented themselves as worthy members of society, as family men and reliable officials" (van Nijf, 305–6).

15.6 Reflections

The findings in this chapter have significant implications for our understanding of the context of Jesus' ministry. The tax burden by itself was not exorbitant. Udoh's analysis stands as a corrective to earlier work that found Roman taxation to be a major factor in extracting wealth from Galilee. Nevertheless, for the largely agrarian Galilean population living at or near subsistence level, most of them in debt, and some paying leases, Roman taxation would have been an easy target for their desperation. In this context, Jesus' references to tax collectors are noteworthy both for what they say and what they do not say. Jesus did not foster anti-Roman sentiment. Instead, he taught, "Render to Caesar the things that are Caesar's" (Matt 22:21 NASB). Moreover, the tax collectors in Galilee would have been Jews, agents of Herod Antipas, local tax farmers, or slaves. Where criticism is more apparent, the targets of Jesus' opposition are the chief priests, temple authorities, and money changers. Nevertheless, in the one Gospel reference to the temple tax, Jesus instructs Peter to pay it, "so that we do not give offense to them" (Matt 17:27).

Jesus' admonition to treat one who would not receive fellow church members and be reconciled as "a gentile and a tax collector" (Matt 18:17) is certainly pejorative, echoing stereotypical aspersions. On the other hand, Jesus calls a tax collector to be one of his disciples, then scandalously eats with "tax collectors and sinners" (Matt 9:10–11; 11:19; Mark 2:15–16; Luke 5:30; 7:34; 15:1). "Tax collectors and the prostitutes" will enter the kingdom before the chief priests and elders in Jerusalem (Matt 21:31–32). Luke portrays the toll collectors in a more positive light than Matthew. Zacchaeus, a "chief tax collector" and a rich man, professes his immediate readiness to repay any he may have cheated, prompting Jesus to say, "Today salvation has come to this house" (Luke 19:1–10). Finally, when a tax collector does feature in one of Jesus' parables, he is the foil for the Pharisee's self-satisfaction and presumed righteousness (18:9–14). Standing far off, the tax collector "would not even look up to heaven, but was beating his breast and saying, 'God, be merciful to me, a sinner!'" (18:13). Jesus also ate with Pharisees, however (7:39; 11:37). In this way, Jesus associated with both the taxed and the tax collectors, demonstrating God's grace while he announced the coming judgment, vindication of the poor, and the urgency of repentance.

Works Cited in Chapter 15

Blanton, Thomas R., IV, Agnes Choi, and Jinyu Liu, eds. 2022. *Taxation, Economy, and Revolt in Ancient Rome, Galilee, and Egypt.* RMCS. London: Routledge.

Broshi, Magen. 1992. "Agriculture and Economy in Roman Palestine: Seven Notes on the Babatha Archive." *IEJ* 42.3/4:230–40.

Brunt, P. A. 1981. "The Revenues of Rome [a review of Lutz Neesen, *Untersuchungen zu den direkten Staatsabgaben de römischen Kaiserzeit (27 v. Chr.–284 n. Chr.).* [Bonn: Habelt, 1980]." *JRS* 71:161–72.

———. 1990. *Roman Imperial Themes.* Oxford: Clarendon.

Culpepper, R. Alan. 1995. "The Gospel of Luke." Pages 1–490 in vol. 9 of *NIB*. Nashville: Abingdon.

Donahue, John R. 1971. "Tax Collectors and Sinners: An Attempt at Identification." *CBQ* 33:39–61.

Dunn, James D. G. 2003. *Jesus Remembered.* Vol. 1 of *Christianity in the Making.* Grand Rapids: Eerdmans.

El Mansy, Aliyah. 2023. "Τελῶναι im Neuen Testament – Zwischen sozialer Realität und literarischem Stereotyp." Habilitationsschrift. In Τελῶναι im Neuen Testament – Zwischen sozialer Realität und literarischem Stereotyp. Novum Testamentum et Orbis Antiquus / Studien zur Umwelt des Neuen Testaments, vol. 129. Göttingen: Vandenhoeck & Ruprecht.

Fiensy, David A. 1991. *The Social History of Palestine in the Herodian Period: The Land Is Mine.* Lewiston, NY: Mellen.

Garnsey, Peter, Richard Saller, et al. 2014. *The Roman Empire: Economy, Society and Culture.* 2nd ed. Berkeley: University of California Press.

Günther, Sven. 2016. "Taxation in the Greco-Roman World: The Roman Principate." Oxford Handbooks Online: www.oxfordhandbooks.com. Oxford: Oxford University Press.

Hamel, Gildas H. 1989. *Poverty and Charity in Roman Palestine, First Three Centuries C.E.* University of California Publications: Near Eastern Studies 23. Berkeley: University of California Press.

Hanson, K. C., and Douglas E. Oakman. 1998. *Palestine in the Time of Jesus: Social Structures and Social Conflicts.* Minneapolis: Fortress.

Harland, Philip A. 2002. "The Economy of First-Century Palestine: State of the Scholarly Discussion." Pages 511–27 in *Handbook of Early Christianity: Social Science Approaches.* Edited by Anthony J. Blasi, Jean Duhaime, and Paul-André Turcotte. Walnut Creek, CA: AltaMira.

Heemstra, Marius. 2010. *The* Fiscus Judaicus *and the Parting of the Ways.* WUNT 277. Tübingen: Mohr Siebeck.

Hopkins, Keith. 1980. "Taxes and Trade in the Roman Empire." *JRS* 70:101–25.

Horsley, Richard A. 1987. *Jesus and the Spiral of Violence: Popular Jewish Resistance in Roman Palestine.* San Francisco: Harper & Row.

Jones, A. H. M. 1974. *The Roman Economy: Studies in Ancient Economic and Administrative History.* Oxford: Blackwell.

Keddie, G. Anthony. 2022. "Roman Provincial Censuses as Sociopolitical Regulation: Implications for Interpreting the Synoptic Gospels and Acts." Pages 72–91 in Blanton, Choi, and Liu.

MacMullen, Ramsay. 1974. *Roman Social Relations.* New Haven: Yale University Press.

Oakman, Douglas E. 1986. *Jesus and the Economic Questions of His Day.* SBEC 8. Lewiston, NY: Mellen.

Root, Bradley W. 2014. *First-Century Galilee: A Fresh Examination of the Sources.* WUNT 378. Tübingen: Mohr Siebeck.

Safrai, Ze'ev. 1994. *The Economy of Roman Palestine.* London: Routledge.

Saldarini, Anthony J. 1988. *Pharisees, Scribes and Sadducees in Palestinian Society: A Sociological Approach.* Grand Rapids: Eerdmans.

Sanders, E. P. 2016. *Judaism: Practice and Belief, 63 BCE–66 CE.* Minneapolis: Fortress.

Schürer, Emil. 1973. *The History of the Jewish People in the Age of Jesus Christ (175 B.C.–A.D. 135).* Revised and edited by Géza Vermès, Fergus Millar, M. Black, and P. Vermès. Vol. 1. Edinburgh: T&T Clark.

Seeman, Chris. 2013. *Rome and Judea in Transition: Hasmonean Relations with the Roman Republic and the Evolution of the High Priesthood.* New York: Lang.

Udoh, Fabian E. 2014. "Taxation and Other Sources of Government Income in the Galilee of Herod and Antipas." Pages 366–87 in *Life, Culture, and Society.* Vol. 1 of *Galilee in the Late Second Temple and Mishnaic Periods.* Edited by David A. Fiensy and James R. Strange. Minneapolis: Fortress.

———. 2020. *To Caesar What Is Caesar's: Tribute, Taxes, and Imperial Administration in Early Roman Palestine (63 B.C.E.–70 C.E.).* 2nd ed. BJS 343. Providence, RI: Brown University.

van Nijf, Onno. 2008. "The Social World of Tax Farmers and Their Personnel." Pages 279–311 in *The Customs Law of Asia.* Edited by M. Cottier et al. Oxford: Oxford University Press.

Woolf, Greg. 2012. *Rome: An Empire's Story.* Oxford: Oxford University Press.

Youtie, Herbert C. 1967. "Publicans and Sinners." *ZPE* 1:1–20.

Chapter 16

Judges

Unjust Judge (Luke 18:2–5)

*J*udges make only fleeting appearances in the Gospels. In the parable of the widow and the "unjust judge" (*ho kritēs tēs adikias*, Luke 18:6), the widow goes to a judge "in a certain city" who "neither feared God nor had respect for people" (Luke 18:2) and demands that he hear her case: "Grant me justice against my opponent." The judge himself confirms this damning characterization, saying to himself, "Though I have no fear of God and no respect for anyone, yet because this widow keeps bothering me, I will grant her justice, so that she may not wear me out by continually coming" (18:4– 5). The Hebrew Scriptures repeatedly admonish Israel to give widows and orphans special care (e.g., Exod 22:22; Deut 24:17; Jer 22:3; Zech 7:10), yet this judge grants the widow justice only because of her dogged persistence. In contrast, the Scriptures declare the commands of the Lord, "who is not partial and takes no bribe, who executes justice for the orphan and the widow" (Deut 10:17–18). The audience is not told anything else about the judge. Is he Jewish or gentile? Who appointed the judge? What is the widow requesting? While these questions are not germane to the point Jesus is making—"their need to pray always and not to lose heart" (Luke 18:1)— the audience would have heard this parable in the context of the judicial systems in Palestine, a context that is largely unknown to modern readers.

Similarly, in a parabolic saying in the Sermon on the Mount, Jesus says, "Come to terms quickly with your accuser while you are on the way to court with him, or your accuser may hand you over to the judge, and the judge to the guard, and you will be thrown into prison. Truly I tell you, you will never get out until you have paid the last penny" (Matt 5:25–26). The related logion in Luke 12:58 says, "When you go with your accuser before a magistrate [*archonta*], on the way make an effort to settle the case, or you may be dragged before the judge, and the judge [*kritēs*] hand you over to the officer, and the officer [*praktōr*] throw you in prison." Elsewhere, Jesus responds to a request that he arbitrate an issue of inheritance: "Friend, who set me to be a judge or arbitrator [*meristēs*] over you?" (Luke 12:14). The Epistle of James describes judges indirectly. If the assembly makes distinctions among people, especially between rich and poor, you have "become judges with evil thoughts" (2:4). "Whoever speaks evil against another or judges another, speaks evil against the law and judges the law; but if you judge the law, you are not a doer of the law but a judge. There is one lawgiver and judge who is able to save and to destroy. So who, then, are you to judge your neighbor?" (Jas 4:11–12).

Jesus' warning to his disciples, "They will hand you over to councils and flog you in their synagogues; and you will be dragged before governors and kings because of me, as a testimony to them and the Gentiles" (Matt 10:17–18; cf. Mark 13:9; Luke 12:11; 21:12), clearly references two judicial systems, one Jewish and one Roman (Scott, 184; Derrett, 180). As we have had to observe in other chapters, the evidence for how these two systems functioned in Galilee is so deficient that we can only approach it indirectly. First I summarize basic elements of Roman judicial practices in the provinces, then survey the role of judges in the Hebrew Scriptures on the assumption that the Jews perpetuated elements of this system in the first century, and finally piece together scattered references from Josephus and other sources that provide glimpses of the situation in first-century Galilee.

16.1 Roman Judges

Roman governors were charged with bringing order to their province. As the highest-ranking officials, they were also the highest court of appeal. Quirinius, for example, was dispatched to Syria to be the *dikaiodotēs*, literally, "the justice-giver," a rare term that emphasizes the regard in which the governor was held (Josephus, *Ant.* 18.1; cf. 17.91; *J.W.* 1.618, 622). Typically, a province was permitted "to use its own laws" (*utere suis legibus*) in regulating the affairs of its inhabitants (Ando, 284–85). In 7–6 BCE, in instructions to the proconsul of Cyrene, Augustus provided for the delegation of jurisdiction in lesser cases, while reserving to Roman authority the death penalty and matters of concern to the imperial authorities (Paulus, in *Dig.* 1.18.12; Josephus, *J.W.* 2.117; Sherwin-White, 1–23; Schürer, 1:368).

The Gospels and Acts provide evidence for both Roman and local legal systems. Pilate initially rebuffed the chief priests who brought Jesus to him, saying, "Take him yourselves and judge him according to your law." The Jews replied, "We are not permitted to put anyone to death" (John 18:31). When Paul is brought before Gallio in Corinth, the governor responds, "If it were a matter of crime or serious villainy, I would be justified in accepting the complaint of you Jews; but since it is a matter of questions about words and names and your own law, see to it yourselves; I do not wish to be a judge of these matters" (Acts 18:14–15). Later, when Paul appears before Felix, the governor, Paul says, "I cheerfully make my defense, knowing that for many years you have been a judge over this nation" (24:10). As a Roman citizen, Paul had legal rights that noncitizens did not have (Acts 22:25–29; 23:27; see Walton).

Although differences in procedural models appeared in the provinces, during the first century Roman law employed the formulary system, by which the two parties could resolve their dispute (Metzger 2013, 21–26). In this two-step process, a magistrate authorized a judge to conduct a civil trial by means of a written document; then the judge conducted the trial. The plaintiff and the defendant could choose a judge from an official list, but if they could not agree, the magistrate assigned a judge. The Babatha archive (P.Yad. 28–30; see above, 7.8) provides evidence for the currency of this system in the region. Provincial governors either appointed members of their own staff as judges or decided cases themselves (Rüfner, 261; Ando, 290). Epictetus asks the imperial bailiff, "How did you come to be a judge? Whose hand did you kiss? . . . In front of whose bedroom door did you sleep? To whom did you send presents?" (*Diatr.* 3.7.30–31).

In civil cases, the plaintiff had to bring the defendant to court, then prove the case. The plaintiff summoned the defendant to accompany him to meet the magistrate (*in ius vocare*, to call to court). By the first century, authorities began to issue written summons (Rüfner, 262). If the magistrate was not available or if the defendant was not prepared, the case could be postponed. The two parties might also settle the dispute among themselves without the magistrate. The plaintiff could not force the defendant to submit to a lawsuit, but he could wear him down by repeated meetings (Metzger 2005, 177).

Babatha's documents provide insight into how local provincials used this system. Beginning in 106 CE, her documents (petitions, summons, depositions, contracts of deposit, deeds of gift, and bequests) are dated by the tenure of Roman consuls (Lewis, Yadin, and Greenfield, 27–28). The legal documents are written in Roman style. Papyrus Yadin 12 contains minutes of the court at Petra in Greek, retaining the Latin term *acta* and transliterating "tribunal" (Harris, 96). In form, they are double documents: "The text was written twice, once on the top, which was folded to become the

inside, and a second time lower down, so that the document could be identified. Over time, the upper text was abbreviated, eventually becoming a
summary of the lower (Lewis, Yadin, and Greenfield, 7–10). Following the
formulary system, the plaintiff petitioned the Roman governor (P.Yad. 13,
33, 34), who identified the legal issue and appointed a local judge or adju-
dicator to hear the case. The plaintiff then summoned the defendant to court
(P.Yad. 14, 23, 25, 26). For example, Besas son of Jesus, one of the guardians of Babatha's sons, summons Babatha "to meet him before Haterius
Nepos, *legatus pro praetore*, in Petra or elsewhere in his province in the
matter of a date orchard devolving to the said orphans which you hold in
your possession by force, and, equally important, to attend every hour and
day until judgment" (P.Yad. 23.13–19; Lewis, Yadin, and Greenfield, 103–
4). Such summons and countersummons (P.Yad. 24–25, 26) could have a
coercive effect even if the case were never heard. As Jill Harris observes,
"Babatha's archive shows that even relatively obscure people could hope
to use, or manipulate, Roman justice in their interests, and that they were
scrupulous in compiling the documents required for them to do so" (98).

Despite its aspirations, Roman justice was not blind. Certain favors
might be granted "without harm to the law" (Saller, 152), including sched-
uling the trial quickly or in a nearby town. A speedy trial could also prevent the forgery of documents by one's accuser (Apuleius, *Apol.* 84.5).
Beyond such benefits, the status of the litigants and their patrons carried
great influence, sometimes more influence than the facts of the case (May,
58–59). Patrons and friends could provide access to legal proceedings or
block them. A slave had no rights, and a poor person no chance of success. Dale Martin explains, "A powerful patron provided, if not justice,
at least legal success. The importance of patronal connections in court
cases is demonstrated by the *commendation*, which was actually a letter
of recommendation admitted as evidence in court. The strength of the recommendation, however, derived not from any introduction of factual evidence or demonstration of the client's competence, but simply from the
exercise of influence" (23). The practice can be traced from Cicero (1st
c. BCE) to Fronto (2nd c. CE), who somewhat apologetically defends the
practice (Ste. Croix, 42–44):

> The custom of recommendation is said in the first instance to have sprung
> from good will, when every man wished to have his own friend made
> known to another friend and rendered intimate with him. Then the custom
> gradually grew up of giving such recommendations in the case of those
> persons even who were parties to a public or private trial, provided
> however that the case was not a flagrant one, to the actual judges or their

assessors on the bench: not[,] I take it, to undermine the fairness of the judge or to lead him aside from giving true judgment. (Fronto, LCL 112, 1:283–85)

When the commendation came from a friend of the judge, "the favor really requested may sometimes have been nothing less than a favorable verdict" (Saller, 152–53). Aulus Gellius [*Noct. att.* 1.3] concluded that protection of a friend by a judge should sometimes take priority over justice (Saller, 154).

Practical and political considerations made the use of local courts administering local laws an expedient approach to provincial administration. The Roman magistrates could then accept or reject the application of local law (Ando, 291–92). Although judges in administrative courts may well have been Jewish, they were constrained by the necessity of acquiescing to imperial authority (Derrett, 182).

16.2 Jewish Judges

The provision of judges in Israel is based in the Mosaic law. When Moses' father-in-law saw that Moses "sat as judge for the people, while the people stood around him from morning until evening" (Exod 18:13), he told Moses that he could not do this task alone. He should teach the people the statutes, then appoint "men who fear God, are trustworthy, and hate dishonest gain" (18:21); let them sit as judges to decide minor cases; and bring important cases to Moses (18:22, 25–26; cf. Deut 1:13). Moses charged the judges: "Give the members of your community a fair hearing, and judge rightly between one person and another, whether citizen or resident alien. You must not be partial in judging: hear out the small and the great alike; you shall not be intimidated by anyone, for the judgment is God's" (Deut 1:16–17). Moses complains to God that he cannot carry "all this people" alone (Num 11:14), so God tells Moses to appoint seventy elders (11:16–17) to share the burden. Judges and officials throughout the tribes, "in all your towns," will "render just decisions for the people" (Deut 16:18). Again, they are charged, "You must not distort justice; you must not show partiality; and you must not accept bribes, for a bribe blinds the eyes of the wise and subverts the cause of those who are in the right" (16:19). If a case involves different kinds of bloodshed or different rights, the judges are instructed to consult with the Levitical priests (17:8–9). Anyone who disobeys the priest or the judge shall die (17:12).

Elders heard cases at the city gate (Deut 21:19; 22:15; 25:7; Josh 20:4; Ruth 4:1–12; Jdt 10:6; 13:12). The gate at Tel Dan, for example, is an open, shaded space within the thick wall surrounding the city (Judg 18:29). Samuel made a circuit each year, judging cases in Bethel, Gilgal, and Mizpah before returning to his home in Ramah (1 Sam 7:15–17). Absalom stood near the gate and sought to undermine David's authority, claiming that if he were judge he would grant justice to all who came to him (2 Sam 15:2–4). According to 1 Chronicles 23:4, at the end of his reign David appointed "six thousand . . . officers and judges" over Israel. King Jehoshaphat appointed judges in all the fortified cities of Judah and "Levites and priests and heads of families" in Jerusalem, "to give judgment for the LORD and to decide disputed cases" (2 Chr 19:8). He admonished the judges that because they judged on behalf of the Lord, they could not show partiality or take bribes (19:5–7). Ezra too was instructed to appoint judges "who know the laws of your God" (7:25; cf. 10:14; Josephus, *Ant.* 11.129). Still, justice was perverted; Micah lamented: "The faithful have disappeared from the land, and there is no one left who is upright; . . . the official and the judge ask for a bribe, and the powerful dictate what they desire; thus they pervert justice" (7:2–3).

Scattered references (disregarding chronology) offer glimpses of how the judicial system worked.

> The court was open to the public (Exod 18:13; Ruth 4:1ff.). Each party presented his view of the case to the judge (Deut 1:16; 25:1). Possibly the accused appeared in court clad in mourning (Zech 3:3). The accuser stood on the right hand of the accused (Zech 3:1; Ps 109:6). . . . The only evidence considered by the court was that given by the witnesses. In criminal cases, not fewer than two witnesses were necessary (Num 35:30; Deut 17:6; 19:15). In cases other than criminal the oath was applied (Exod 22:11; cf. Heb 6:16). The lot was sometimes used (Josh 7:14–18), especially in private disputes (Prov 18:18), but this was exceptional. When the law was not quite definite, recourse was made to the divine oracle (Lev 24:12; Num 15:34). . . . Sentence was pronounced after the hearing of the case, and the judgment was carried out (Josh 7:24f.). (Levertoff, 1156)

The book of Susanna attributes to Daniel the innovative procedure of questioning witnesses separately. Judges accepted the testimony of men of standing and good repute. When two elders, appointed as judges (Sus 5), tried to force themselves on Susanna, she cried out, drawing a crowd. When the elders charged that they saw her in the garden with a young man, "Because they were elders of the people and judges, the assembly believed them and condemned her to death" (41). Daniel intervened, however, protesting that the people had condemned Susanna "without examination and without learning the facts" (48). Demanding that they return to court, the rest of the elders invited Daniel to sit with them, "for God has given you the standing of an elder" (50). Daniel then ordered that the two accusers be brought in and examined separately. When they did not agree under which tree they saw Susanna and the alleged young man together, their false testimony was exposed, and Susanna was vindicated.

16.3 The Sanhedrin

Interpreters have struggled to construct the history of the Sanhedrin from scattered references in the Gospels and Acts, Josephus, and the Mishnah (much of this section appears in Culpepper, 531–32). The challenge is compounded by the fact that there are so few references in Josephus, and the Mishnah (ca. 200 CE) portrays the Sanhedrin as a body of scholars adjudicating religious matters, following procedures that do not accord with Josephus and the New Testament. The word *synedrion* occurs in both the singular (Matt 5:22) and the plural (Matt 10:17; Mark 13:9) in the Gospels. In the singular it occurs both with (Matt 26:59; Mark 14:55; 15:1; Luke 22:66) and without the definite article (John 11:47) and can be translated as "the Sanhedrin" or "a sanhedrin," council, or assembly. Luke 22:66 reads, "When day came, the elders of the people, both chief priests and scribes, came together, and they brought him [Jesus] to their council [*synedrion*]" (author's trans.). John says the chief priests and scribes called together a council (*synedrion*; 11:47) before arresting Jesus. Acts refers to "the council" or "the Sanhedrin" fourteen times.

Nineteenth- and early twentieth-century scholars, trying to synthesize these historical sources, proposed that there were one, two, or three *synedria* in Jerusalem with differing functions. The revised edition of Schürer's *History of the Jewish People in the Age of Jesus Christ* (vol. 2, 1979) provides a definitive statement of the majority view. The first reference to this aristocratic council comes from the Greek era, although rabbinic tradition traces it to Moses' seventy elders (Num 11:16). Josephus first mentions a council of elders (*gerousia*) in the time of Antiochus the Great (223–187 BCE; *Ant.* 12.138). The term *synedrion*, denoting the Jerusalem council, first appears (in *Ant.* 14.165–179) when the young Herod the Great had to give an account of his actions in Galilee before this body. When Herod returned as king, he executed most of the Sanhedrin (*Ant.* 14.175; cf. 15.5) and formed a new Sanhedrin. Under Archelaus (4 BCE–6 CE), the authority of the council was restricted to Judea. Although it was controlled by the high-priestly aristocracy, who were predominantly if not exclusively

Sadducees, we do not know how appointments to this body were made (Schürer, 2:213).

In the New Testament, the Sanhedrin appears to be the supreme Jewish court (*boulē*, "council," in Luke 23:51). There is no evidence of a plurality of institutions with differing functions. The Sanhedrin handled judicial decisions that could not be rendered by lesser courts and were not reserved for the Roman governor (Schürer, 2:218). After the destruction of Jerusalem in 70 CE, "the Sanhedrin ceased to exist in its previous form" (Schürer, 2:209).

The Mishnah defines which cases can be heard by lesser courts of three or twenty-three judges (m. Sanh. 1:1, 6; 3:1) and specifies that to have a Sanhedrin of twenty-three judges, a "city" must have a minimum of 120 men (m. Sanh. 1:6), but it is unclear whether this system functioned in Judea or Galilee prior to the destruction of the temple. The Babylonian Talmud declares that an authorized scholar may decide money cases sitting alone (b. Sanh. 4b–5a). This legal system, however, is a later entity, idealized, and retrojected into the pre-70 era: "In all this there is nothing historical" (Schürer, 2:215; so also Saldarini, 978).

Martin Goodman, James S. McLaren, and E. P. Sanders have mounted a compelling challenge to the majority view by assessing the references in Josephus case by case. In short, they argue that there is insufficient evidence for the existence of the Sanhedrin as it has traditionally been understood:

> There was no body that combined judicial and legislative powers, there were no appointments for life, Palestinian Jews did not all line up behind one of the two parties (no one ever includes the Essenes), the two small parties did not seat representatives in a parliament, changes of government did not just shift the numerical balance of power in an otherwise unchanged body, and legislation was not passed by the majority vote of either one or more standing legislative and judicial bodies. This whole picture is a scholarly invention. (Sanders, 747; see further, 742–71)

While admittedly we know little of the composition of the council under various rulers or how one became a member of the Sanhedrin, or council, it nevertheless appears as a Jewish judicial body in Jerusalem from the second century BCE until the destruction of the city in 70 CE. Moreover, it appears to have served an essential function in administering national and religious law and adjudicating major crises. The chief priests and the aristocracy collaborated with the Romans, maintained order, and assured that taxes were paid: we see them working in the Gospels in that capacity (Hengel and Deines, 58; Luz, 438–46).

16.4 Reflections

Our concern is with the role of local judges in Galilee. The evidence sketches a fuzzy picture of overlapping legal systems, Jewish and Roman. We may assume that there was some system for hearing minor civil and criminal cases in the cities and towns of Galilee, following the historic precedents in Israel's Scriptures, but the evidence is sparse.

According to Josephus, Gabinius, governor of Syria, established five councils (*synedria*, *Ant.* 14.41; *synodous*, *J.W.* 1.170; see Kennard). Josephus himself heard cases, established councils (*synedria*, *J.W.* 1.537), sought to keep peace in Galilee by making seventy of the Galilean authorities "assessors to the cases . . . [he] tried, and obtained their approbation of the sentences . . . pronounced" (*Life* 79). It may be argued that Josephus attributes to Moses the system he is familiar with:

> As rulers let each city have seven men long exercised in virtues and in the pursuit of justice. . . . Let the judges have power to pronounce what sentence they think fit; always provided that no one denounce them for having received a bribe to pervert justice or bring forward some other charge to convict them of not having pronounced aright; for they must be influenced neither by lucre nor by rank in declaring judgement, but must set justice above all. . . . But if the judges see not how to pronounce upon the matters set before them—and with men such things oft befall—let them send up the case entire to the holy city and let the high priest and the prophet and the council of elders meet and pronounce as they think fit. (*Ant.* 4.214–218)

Uncertain as the situation may be for Judea, it was probably simpler in Galilee. Sherwin-White finds no evidence in Josephus of any developed legal system outside the Herodian cities (128). Herod Antipas settled cases that came before him or delegated them to one of his associates or clients. Sepphoris and Tiberias would have had magistrates who heard cases or appointed judges. Most cases, however, would have been settled in the towns and villages by the assemblies and leaders of the synagogue.

Current research on the origin and functions of synagogues in Galilee suggests that they originally served as meeting places of the community for social, political, and religious purposes generally, which were in any case closely related in Galilean village life (Sherwin-White, 128, 133–34; Runesson, 164). Community leaders (Luke 11:43; 20:46) and assemblies met in the synagogues, which probably served as local courts also. Mark 5:22 refers to "one of the leaders of the synagogue" (*archisynagōgōn*) and Luke 8:41 to "a leader of the synagogue" (*archōn tēs synagōgēs*). Matthew 9:18 omits the reference to the synagogue, thereby transforming the man into a magistrate (*archōn*; Boring, 237). Josephus charges that Albinus, prefect of Judea following the death of Festus, "accepted ransoms from their relatives on behalf of those who have been imprisoned for robbery by the local councils" (*hypo tēs par' hekastois boulēs*; *J.W.* 2.273).

We may return to Jesus' warning that his followers would be hauled before synagogues, rulers, and authorities (Luke 12:11). Immediately following the warning, someone asks Jesus to compel his brother to divide the family inheritance with him. Jesus responds, "Friend, who set me to be a judge or arbitrator over you?" (12:14). This brief exchange suggests that any teacher or leader could have served as a judge or arbiter where no official judges or courts were available. Jesus' response further suggests that judges were normally appointed: "Who set me to be a judge?" Roman governors or city magistrates could serve as judges or appoint judges, while Jewish towns and villages turned to their elders to resolve civil disputes, property issues, and debts and to impose judgment for crimes. In both Jewish and Roman litigations, the plaintiff was responsible for bringing the defendant to court. Jesus could therefore counsel his followers, "Come to terms quickly with your accuser while you are on the way to court with him" (Matt 5:25). Sherwin-White finds this reference to have "a very un-Roman and un-Greek ring to it" (133). Indeed, "the absence of Graeco-Roman colouring is a convincing feature of the Galilean narrative and the parables" (138–39).

Care for the widows and orphans was the chief characteristic of justice and the mark of a true judge. Judges were expected to refuse bribes and judge rightly: "He who refuses to a suppliant the aid which he has power to give is accountable to justice. . . . These and many similar regulations are the ties which bind us together" (Josephus, *Ag. Ap.* 2.207). Conversely, those who do not "look out for the widow or the orphan . . . are lawless judges" (Barn. 20.2; cf. Did. 5.2; T. Mos. 5.6). Ultimately, the Jews looked to God for justice. As Sirach reminded his students, "The Lord is the judge, and with him there is no partiality. He will not show partiality to the poor; but he will listen to the prayer of one who is wronged. He will not ignore the supplication of the orphan, or the widow when she pours out her complaint. Do not the tears of the widow run down her cheek as she cries out against the one who causes them to fall?" (35:15–19).

Works Cited in Chapter 16

Ando, Clifford. 2016. "Legal Pluralism in Practice." Pages 283–94 in du Plessis, Ando, and Tuori.

Boring, M. Eugene. 1995. "The Gospel of Matthew." *NIB* 8:87–505. Nashville: Abingdon.

Culpepper, R. Alan. 2021. *Matthew*. NTL. Louisville: Westminster John Knox.

Derrett, J. D. M. 1971–72. "Law in the New Testament: The Parable of the Unjust Judge." *NTS* 18:178–91.

du Plessis, Paul J., Clifford Ando, and Kaius Tuori, eds. 2016. *The Oxford Handbook of Roman Law and Society.* Oxford: Oxford University Press.

Goodman, Martin. 1987. *The Ruling Class of Judaea: The Origins of the Jewish Revolt against Rome (A.D. 66–70).* Cambridge: Cambridge University Press.

Harris, Jill. 2010. "Courts and the Judicial System." Pages 85–101 in *The Oxford Handbook of Jewish Daily Life in Roman Palestine.* Edited by Catherine Hezser. Oxford: Oxford University Press.

Hengel, Martin, and Roland Deines. 1995. "E. P. Sanders' 'Common Judaism,' Jesus, and the Pharisees." *JTS* 46:1–70.

Kennard, J. Spencer, Jr. 1962. "The Jewish Provincial Assembly." *ZNW* 53:25–51.

Levertoff, Paul. 1982. "Judge." *ISBE* 2:1156. Rev. ed. Grand Rapids: Eerdmans.

Lewis, Naphtali, Yigael Yadin, and Jonas Greenfield, eds. 1989. *The Documents from the Bar-Kokhba Period in the Cave of Letters: Greek Papyri and Aramaic and Nabatean Signatures and Subscriptions.* JDS 2. Jerusalem: Israel Exploration Society.

Luz, Ulrich. 2005. *Matthew 21–28.* Translated by James E. Crouch. Hermeneia. Minneapolis: Fortress.

Martin, Dale B. 1990. *Slavery as Salvation: The Metaphor of Slavery in Pauline Christianity.* New Haven: Yale University Press.

May, James M. 1988. *Trials of Character: The Eloquence of Ciceronian Ethos.* Chapel Hill: University of North Carolina Press.

McLaren, James S. 2015. *Power and Politics in Palestine: The Jews and the Governing of Their Land: 100 BC–AD 70.* London: Bloomsbury.

Metzger, Ernest. 2005. *Litigation in Roman Law.* Oxford: Oxford University Press.

———. 2013. "An Outline of Roman Civil Procedure." *Roman Legal Tradition* 9:1–30.

Rüfner, Thomas. 2016. "Imperial *Cognitio* Process." Pages 257–69 in du Plessis, Ando, and Tuori.

Runesson, Anders. 2017. "Synagogues without Rabbis or Christians? Ancient Institutions beyond Normative Discourses." *JBV* 38:159–72.

Saldarini, Anthony J. 1992. "Sanhedrin." *ABD* 5:975–80.

Saller, Richard P. 1982. *Personal Patronage under the Early Empire.* Cambridge: Cambridge University Press.

Sanders, E. P. 2016. *Judaism: Practice and Belief, 63 BCE–66 CE.* Minneapolis: Fortress.

Schürer, Emil. 1973–79. *The History of the Jewish People in the Age of Jesus Christ (175 B.C.–A.D. 135).* Revised and edited by Géza Vermès, Fergus Millar, M. Black, and P. Vermès. Vols. 1–2. Edinburgh: T&T Clark.

Scott, Bernard Brandon. 1989. *Hear Then the Parable: A Commentary on the Parables of Jesus.* Minneapolis: Fortress.

Sherwin-White, A. N. 1963. *Roman Society and Roman Law in the New Testament.* Oxford: Clarendon.

Ste. Croix, G. E. M. de. 1954. "Suffragium: From Vote to Patronage." *The British Journal of Sociology* 5:33–48.

Walton, Steve. 2022. "Trying Paul or Trying Rome? Judges and Accused in the Roman Trials of Paul in Acts." Pages 107–21 in *Reading Acts Theologically.* LNTS 661. London: T&T Clark.

Part V

Religious Leaders

Chapter 17

Pharisees

Pharisee and Tax Collector (Luke 18:10–13)

*A*lthough Pharisees appear frequently in all four Gospels, only one parable features a Pharisee. In a classic example of a reversal that turns the hearer's worldview upside down, Jesus condemns the Pharisee for his self-righteous arrogance and praises the tax collector for his humility. The parable presumes that hearers held Pharisees in high regard or at least knew their reputation for meticulous piety. Two related questions require our attention: Who were the Pharisees? Were they common in Galilee early in the first century?

17.1 A Survey of the Sources

Our knowledge of pre-70 Pharisaism comes from Josephus, the New Testament, rabbinic sources, and references in the Qumran scrolls. But each of these presents challenges for the historian: the apocryphal writings that have often provided information for other chapters in our quest for "the people of the parables" do not mention the Pharisees. Recent scholarship has examined each of these sources intensively, casting doubt on much that was once widely accepted. A generation ago Joseph Sievers aptly commented, "We know considerably less about the Pharisees than an earlier generation 'knew'" (138). Research during the past twenty-five years has only confirmed Sievers's prescient observation, with the result that students of the New Testament must now keep an open mind and question all that was once taught about the Pharisees.

Earlier interpreters often turned to the etymology of the Greek, Hebrew, and Aramaic terms for Pharisees for clues to their identity, but this approach offers little help. Matthew Black offers three possible etymologies for the name. First, it may mean "one who is separate," but Black notes that although the Greek term *pharisaios* (Hebrew, *parash*; Aramaic, *perash*) means "separate" or "distinguished" (by their practices and beliefs), it is not clear from what or whom the Pharisees separated. The Pharisees did not separate themselves from the rest of society as did the Essenes: "The Pharisees . . . cultivate harmonious relations with the community" (Josephus, *J.W.* 2.166). Were the Pharisees so named because (a) they separated from the priestly interpreters of the law, (b) they descended from the Hasidim who separated from the followers of Judas Maccabeus in 163 BCE, or (c) they separated themselves from the unclean "people of the land" (*'am ha'areṣ*)? Second, the name may designate the Pharisees as "interpreters" (those who divide or interpret the Scriptures). Or, third, it may be a pejorative name drawn from the Aramaic word for "Persian," used by the Sadducees to denigrate the Pharisees for accepting foreign doctrines (such as angels and resurrection). Matthew Black concludes, "No single theory can be said to hold the field to the exclusion of any other" (776).

17.1.1 Josephus

Writing for a Roman audience, Josephus characterizes the Pharisees as one of three or four "schools" (*haireseis*) among the Jews, the one most widely accepted (*J.W.* 2.119, 162–163; *Ant.* 13.171–173; 18.11, 15). Josephus draws parallels between the Pharisees and the Stoics for his Greco-Roman audience; thus, Pharisees "simplify their standard of living, making no concession to luxury" (*Ant.* 18.12). In a rather self-serving account of his early life, Josephus claims that, at the age of sixteen, he determined to gain personal experience of these three "schools." Setting forth on "a thorough investigation," he completed "hard training and laborious exercises," then spent three years as a devoted disciple of an ascetic, Bannus, who, much like John the Baptist, "dwelt in the wilderness, wearing only such clothing as trees provided, feeding on such things as grew of themselves, and using frequent ablutions of cold water, by day and night, for purity's sake." At the age of nineteen, Josephus began to follow "the rules of the Pharisees" (*Life* 10–12; for a skeptical assessment of this account, see Mason, 105–8). Yet, Josephus summarizes the teachings of the Pharisees much more briefly than his longer description of the Essenes (*J.W.* 2.120–161).

Using Josephus as a primary source requires the interpreter to recognize the differences between his works *The Jewish War* and *The Antiquities of the Jews* (Richardson, 253–55; see above, 2.3), determine when Josephus is drawing material from sources (esp. Nicolaus of Damascus), and prioritize Josephus's descriptions of specific incidents involving the Pharisees over his summary statements (Sanders, 632). In his summary statements Josephus says, "The Pharisees are considered the most accurate interpreters of the laws, and hold the position of the leading sect" (*J.W.* 2.162; cf. 1.110; *Ant.* 17.41; 18.12; *Life* 191). They taught "certain regulations handed down by former generations and not recorded in the Laws of Moses, for which reason they are rejected by the Sadducaean group" (*Ant.* 13.297). The latter have "the confidence of the wealthy alone, while the Pharisees have support of the masses" (*Ant.* 13.298). We may well suspect that Josephus is exaggerating the popularity of the Pharisees, however, when he claims that they are "extremely influential among the townsfolk; and all prayers and sacred rites of divine worship are performed according to their exposition" (*Ant.* 18.15; cf. 13.288, 298). Even if exaggerated, however, this statement suggests wide acceptance of the Pharisees' piety. Similarly tendentious are Josephus's claims that the Sadducees submit "unwillingly and perforce" to "the formulas of the Pharisees, since otherwise the masses would not tolerate them" (*Ant.* 18.17) and that, while the Pharisees are "affectionate to each other and cultivate harmonious relations with the community," the Sadducees are, "even among themselves, rather boorish" and rude (*J.W.* 2.166). The Pharisees were also more lenient in punishments than the Sadducees, but they were not monolithic; the school of Hillel was more lenient than the school of Shammai (*Ant.* 13.294; cf. Acts 5:17). The Pharisees were also distinguished by their beliefs regarding fate or God's providence, angels, and the resurrection of the dead (*Ant.* 13.171–172; 18.12–15).

Josephus first mentions the Pharisees during the time of Jonathan (161– 143 BCE; *Ant.* 13.171). They played an active role in the Hasmonean upheavals, opposing John Hyrcanus (137–104 BCE), Alexander Jannaeus (103–76 BCE), and the Sadducees. As allies of Salome Alexandra (76–67 BCE), they enjoyed a brief period of ascendancy, during which they took vengeance on their enemies, the aristocrats (*J.W.* 1.110–114). The situation changed with the coming of the Romans in 63 BCE. When six thousand Pharisees refused to take an oath to Caesar and to Herod the Great, Herod fined them, but the wife of Pheroras (Herod's younger brother) paid the fine for them (*Ant.* 17.41–42). Then, when the Pharisees prophesied that the crown would be taken from Herod and passed to Pheroras, Herod put their leaders to death (*Ant.* 17.43). Near the end of Herod's life, two teachers, probably Pharisees (Judas and Matthias), incited their followers to pull down the Roman golden eagle Herod had placed over the main entrance to the temple. For this, Herod had them put to death (*J.W.* 1.648–655; *Ant.* 17.149–167). Judas the Galilean led an uprising against the Romans in 6 CE with the support of Saddok, a Pharisee (*Ant.* 18.4, 23), but Josephus does not mention the Pharisees again for sixty years of his history, when they reappear during the war against Rome in 66–70. For that period, we must turn to the New Testament, where several Pharisees are identified by name: Simon (Luke 7:40, 43, 44), Nicodemus (John 3:1–10; 7:50–52; 19:39–40), Gamaliel (Acts 5:34–39; 22:3), and Paul (Acts 23:6–9; 26:5; Phil 3:5).

17.1.2 The Gospels and Acts

The New Testament suggests that the Pharisees continued to be politically influential during the period Josephus passes over in silence (John 11:47; Acts 23:6), and some Pharisees became followers of Jesus (Acts 15:5). Paul was a Pharisee, indeed, the only Pharisee from this period whose writings have survived (Fredriksen, 113, 125–35). For our present purposes, the Gospel accounts are central. All four Gospels depict the Pharisees as Jesus' frequent critics; in the Synoptic Gospels Jesus repeatedly condemns them as hypocrites. Yet each Gospel must be studied individually because each treats the Pharisees with different nuances. Later, we will return to the Gospels when we take up the question of the role of the Pharisees in Galilee.

We do not know where any of the Gospels were written; the theories are only more or less convincing. The traditional view is that Mark was written in Rome (e.g., Bacon and Incigneri), but some interpreters locate it in Galilee (e.g., R. H. Lightfoot, Marxsen, Kelber, and Roskam) or Syria (Marcus). Clifton Black (237) concludes, judiciously, "Our relevant evidence is strong enough to lend support to a location of Mark's Gospel in Rome; at the same time, it remains too equivocal to nail that theory down" (see further Culpepper 2007, 25–29).

The Pharisees appear as Jesus' primary antagonists in Mark, challenging Jesus for eating with "sinners and tax collectors" (2:16), allowing his disciples to pluck grain on the Sabbath (2:24), healing on the Sabbath (3:1–6), and allowing his disciples to eat with unwashed hands, contrary to "the tradition of the elders" (7:1–5). The Pharisees demand a "sign from heaven" (8:11) and test Jesus regarding the debated issue of divorce (10:2, 4); the temple authorities send "some Pharisees and some Herodians to trap him in what he said" (12:13; cf. 3:6). Mark also reports that some Pharisees and scribes were sent from Jerusalem to investigate Jesus' activities and teachings (3:22; 7:1). The debate that follows concerns the authority of "the tradition of the elders," food laws, purity, and what defiles a person. Jesus warns his disciples to beware of "the yeast" (i.e., the teachings) of the Pharisees (8:15). Notably, although the Pharisees act in concert with the scribes and Herodians, they play no role in the arrest, trial, and crucifixion of Jesus.

Proposals regarding the provenance of Matthew center on Antioch and Syria, with other interpreters favoring Palestine, Galilee, and Caesarea

Maritima (Culpepper 2021, 26–27). Only Matthew says the report about Jesus spread "throughout all Syria" (4:24). Notably, those who advocate a site other than Antioch generally postulate a more uniformly Jewish setting, whereas Antioch more easily accounts for the diversity of traditions Matthew draws upon, for its relationships with other early Christian writings, and for the Gospel's rapid reception in other areas.

Matthew intensifies the hostility between Jesus and the Pharisees (Culpepper 2017, 207–11), with both vehemently condemning the other. John the Baptist calls the Pharisees and Sadducees "you brood of vipers" (3:7). The Pharisees say Jesus casts out demons by Beelzebul, the ruler of the demons (9:34; 12:24). Jesus responds with the tirade in Matthew 23, repeatedly calling the scribes and Pharisees "hypocrites" (23:2, 13, 15, 23, 25, 27, 29). Matthew also associates the Pharisees with the Sadducees (3:7; 16:1, 6, 11, 12) and clarifies that by yeast Jesus meant "the teaching of the Pharisees and Sadducees" (16:12).

Jesus declares that "not one jot or one tittle" will pass from the law (5:17 KJV) and proceeds to interpret the law while contrasting his teaching with what his followers have heard (5:21–48). Jesus also contrasts the practice of piety he teaches with that of the Pharisees, saying, "Unless your righteousness exceeds that of the scribes and Pharisees, you will never enter the kingdom of heaven" (5:20). Jesus' followers should give alms, pray, and fast, but they should do so in secret, not to be seen by others (6:1–6, 16–18). The issues at stake between Jesus and the Pharisees are the same in Matthew as in Mark: eating with tax collectors and sinners (Matt 9:11), fasting (9:14), purity and the tradition of the elders (15:1–20), and divorce (19:3). Although the Matthean Jesus acknowledges the authority of the scribes and Pharisees, who "sit on Moses' seat," he instructs the crowds and his disciples, "Do whatever they teach you and follow it; but do not do as they do, for they do not practice what they teach" (23:3). Matthew therefore portrays Jesus as standing both closer to the Pharisees and in sharper debate with them. Both emphasize keeping the law (5:17–20; 22:34–40), even tithing mint, dill, and cumin (23:23); but Jesus charges that the Pharisees are "blind guides," who "have neglected the weightier matters of the law: justice and mercy and faith" (23:23–24; cf. Mic 6:8). Matthew 23 ends with Jesus uttering the chilling words, "Truly I tell you, all this will come upon this generation. 'Jerusalem, Jerusalem, the city that kills the prophets and stones those who are sent to it! How often have I desired to gather your children together as a hen gathers her brood under her wings, and you were not willing! See, your house is left to you, desolate'" (23:36–38). As in Mark, the Pharisees are not mentioned in the Matthean passion narrative, but in Matthew they go with the chief priests to ask Pilate to station guards at Jesus' tomb (27:62).

Luke is the most difficult Gospel to locate geographically. It was probably written by a gentile in an urban setting. Still, its portrayal of the Pharisees is more nuanced than those of Mark and Matthew. Luke introduces the Pharisees with the report that "while Jesus was teaching, Pharisees and teachers of the law were sitting near by (they had come from every village of Galilee and Judea and from Jerusalem)" (5:17). Luke picks up the same scenes and themes one finds in Mark and Matthew. The scribes and the Pharisees accuse Jesus of blasphemy (5:21), eating with tax collectors (5:30), not teaching his disciples to fast (5:33), allowing them to pluck grain on the Sabbath (6:2), and healing on the Sabbath (6:7). Luke comments that by refusing John's baptism "the Pharisees and the lawyers rejected God's purpose for themselves" (7:30). Luke's Pharisees also invite Jesus to dinner, where Jesus finds fault with them over matters of purity, washing, and tithing mint and herbs, but neglecting justice and the love of God, and seeking "the seat of honor in the synagogues" (7:36–50; 11:37–43). After the lawyers complain, "When you say these things, you insult us too" (11:45), he pronounces woes on them also. After this, the scribes and the Pharisees were hostile toward him, cross-examined him, and sought to catch him in something he said (11:53–54). Jesus responded, "Beware of the yeast of the Pharisees, that is, their hypocrisy" (12:1).

On one occasion, however, the Pharisees warn Jesus that Herod (Antipas) wants to kill him (13:31). Although some have taken this text as evidence of Luke's more positive view of the Pharisees, nothing to this point has prepared readers to understand the Pharisees' warning as a benevolent act (Darr, 105–6; Gowler, 236–41). Jesus knows full well that he will die in Jerusalem (9:22; cf. 13:33), and his response highlights "the Pharisees' ironic misunderstanding; . . . this is a journey to the place of death, not the escape from death that the Pharisees urge" (Tannehill, 153).

Nevertheless, at a Sabbath meal in the home of "a leader of the Pharisees," Jesus heals a man with dropsy, then tells a parable about seeking the places of honor and admonishes them to invite the poor, crippled, lame, and blind when they give a banquet (14:1–13). When the Pharisees and scribes grumble that he eats with sinners (15:2), Jesus responds with the parables of the lost sheep, the lost coin, and the prodigal son. In a side comment, Luke labels the Pharisees as "lovers of money" (16:14). When the Pharisees ask when the kingdom of God will come, Jesus responds, not with signs "that can be observed; . . . the kingdom of God is among you" (17:20–21). The parable of the Pharisee and the tax collector praying in the temple follows in 18:10–14; the last we see of them in this Gospel is when the Pharisees order Jesus to make his disciples stop celebrating his entry into Jerusalem (19:39). Again, the Pharisees have no part in the crucifixion of Jesus.

In sum, Luke presents "a well-formed and heavily reinforced pejorative image of this leadership group" (Darr, 115) as "a paradigm of imperceptiveness" (Darr, 86). The stereotypes Luke applies to the Pharisees—hypocrisy (12:1), greed and wickedness (11:39), grumbling or murmuring (5:30), and love of money (16:14)—are "general tropes of vilification" (Löhr, 175). David Gowler observes, however, that although the Pharisees oppose Jesus, "to a great extent [they] remain separate from the other Jewish leaders" (299).

In the Gospel of John, the Pharisees emerge as Jewish leaders (3:1; 7:48; 12:42) closely associated with other leaders and the chief priests (7:32, 45; 11:47, 57; 18:3). The Jerusalem Jews who send priests and Levites to interrogate John the Baptist are Pharisees (1:19, 24). At first, at least, the Pharisees are at some distance from Jesus. Hence the sending and the hearing of reports (4:1; 7:32). Acting in concert with the chief priests, they send subordinates to seize Jesus (7:32, 45), and the officers report back to them (7:32, 45–47; 18:3). The Pharisees are distinguished from the crowd, for whom they show some disdain (7:45–49). Following John 9:17 they blend with "the Jews" (cf. 9:16, 18; 9:40; 10:19). By this point the Jews have been provoked to take official action against Jesus. By means of this pattern of characterization, the evangelist lays the blame for much of the Jews' opposition to Jesus at the Pharisees' feet. If the unbelief of the world is represented by the Jews, then in similar fashion the hostility of the Jews toward Jesus is concentrated in the Pharisees (Culpepper 1983, 130–31). Nevertheless, Nicodemus, introduced as a Pharisee, challenges other Pharisees (7:50–52; cf. 19:38–42), showing that they were not homogeneous in their response to Jesus (Poplutz, 125). In this regard, Saldarini ventures, John provides a glimpse of the role of the Pharisees in the mid-first century, when "some Pharisees had great influence in Jerusalem" (1988, 197). Alternatively, the power ascribed to the Pharisees in John may reflect instead the situation late in the first century or early in the second century (Martyn, 84–89).

The references to Pharisees in Acts, though few, are informative. Gamaliel, "a Pharisee in the council" (5:34; 22:3), is probably the elder Gamaliel, the father of Simon (m. Avot 1:17–18) and the grandfather of Rabban Gamaliel (m. Avot 1:16; Stemberger, 242–43). Luke praises Gamaliel, "a teacher of the law, respected by all the people"; Josephus says that Simon "was a native of Jerusalem, of a very illustrious family, and of the sect of the Pharisees, who have the reputation of being unrivalled experts in their country's laws" (*Life* 119; cf. *J.W.* 4.159). Gamaliel offers judicious counsel regarding Jesus' followers: "Fellow Israelites, consider carefully what you propose to do to these men. . . . Keep away from these men and let them alone; because if this plan or this undertaking is of human origin, it will fail; but if it is of God, you will not be able to overthrow them—in that case you may even be found fighting against God!" (Acts 5:35, 38–39).

Paul claims that this Gamaliel was his teacher (Acts 22:3). At the Jerusalem conference, some believers who were Pharisees demanded that Paul's gentile converts be circumcised and keep the law (15:5). Although the emphasis on the unanimity of the early church in Acts (1:14; 2:46; 5:12) may influence its report of the result of the conference, "the whole church," presumably including the Pharisaic believers, agreed "unanimously" (15:22, 29) to a compromise resolution.

Later, when Paul appears before the council, some of whom are Pharisees, he shrewdly identifies himself as a Pharisee, the son of a Pharisee (cf. Phil 3:5–6), and claims that he is on trial "concerning the hope of the resurrection of the dead," which Acts explains was accepted by the Pharisees but not by the Sadducees (23:6–9). In his trial before Agrippa, Paul reiterates his claim: "I have belonged to the strictest sect of our religion and lived as a Pharisee" (26:5). These references reaffirm the high esteem in which Pharisees were held, their role as Jewish leaders in Jerusalem, and their belief in the resurrection.

The portrayal of the Pharisees in Acts, as in the Gospels, is therefore rhetorically shaped but in its own way. First, non-Christian Pharisees defend the early believers, then Pharisees who are Christians maintain the imperative of circumcision before acceding to the church's decision. Finally, Paul serves as a paradigm for how Jews, and Pharisees in particular, should respond to the gospel of the resurrection of Jesus (Gowler, 300–301).

The Gospels, especially Matthew and John, paint the Pharisees as Jesus' antagonists, so it is difficult to extract an unbiased picture of them from the New Testament. In Luke, the Pharisees invite Jesus to eat with them on several occasions. The Pharisees condemn Jesus for eating with tax collectors, healing on the Sabbath, letting his disciples pluck grain on the Sabbath, and eating with unwashed hands. Jesus responds condemning them for hypocrisy, practicing their piety before others, desiring the prominent seats in the synagogue, emphasizing minor things while neglecting the weightier, and failing to practice what they teach. In John and Acts, the Pharisees appear among the Jewish leaders in Jerusalem, at times acting in concert with the chief priests. We will consider the question of their presence in Galilee below.

17.1.3 Qumran Scrolls

References in the Qumran scrolls to "the Seekers-After-Smooth-Things" (Noam, 55) or "those looking for easy interpretations" (García Martínez, 195) are often regarded as criticisms of the Pharisees.

> [On Nahum 2:12:] [Its interpretation concerns Deme]trius, king of Yavan, who wanted to enter Jerusalem on the advice of those looking for easy interpretations, [but he did not go in because God did not deliver Jerusalem] into the hands of the kings of Yavan from Antiochus up to the appearance of the chiefs of the Kittim. (4QpNah frags. 3–4 I, 2–3; García Martínez, 195)
> [On Nahum 2:13:] Its interpretation concerns the Angry Lion [who filled his den with a mass of corpses, carrying out rev]enge against those looking for easy interpretations, who hanged living men [from the tree, committing an atrocity which had not been committed] in Israel since ancient times, for it is horrible for the one hanged alive from the tree. (4QpNah frags. 3–4 I, 6–8; García Martínez, 195)
> [In the next two columns, the pesher on Nahum adds that the Seekers-After-Smooth-Things] walk in treachery and lies. (frags. 3–4 II, 2)
> Those who misdirect Ephraim, who with their fraudulent teaching and lying tongue and perfidious lip misdirect many; kings, princes, priests and people together with the proselyte attached to them, (frags. 3–4 II, 8–9)
> whose evil deeds will be exposed to all Israel in the final time and many will fathom their sin, they will hate them and loathe them for their reprehensible arrogance. . . . The simple people of Ephraim will flee from their assembly and desert the ones who misdirected them, (frags. 3–4 III, 3–5)
> whose council will die and whose society will be disbanded; they shall not continue misdirecting the assembly and simple [folk] shall no longer support their advice." (frags. 3–4 III, 6–7; García Martínez, 196–97)

The commentary on Hosea similarly castigates the people for listening to "those who misdirect them and acclaim them [. . .] and will revere them like gods in their blindness" (4QpHos[a] frag. 1 II, 5–6; García Martínez, 192). These references vividly polemicize against a group that gives "easy interpretations" of the law in their directions and counsel to the "kings, princes, priests and people" "from Antiochus up to the appearance of the chiefs of the Kittim," descriptions that accord well with Josephus's accounts of the Pharisees in the Hasmonean period. The Essenes therefore withdrew to Qumran to study the law and live in purity.

Particularly illuminating are the fragments of 4QMMT (García Martínez, 77–85), which appears to be a letter addressed to someone in authority, exhorting him to follow the interpretations of the Essenes rather than interpretations that appear later in rabbinic sources and hence probably represent the views of the Pharisees on a wide range of issues: "the sacrificial offerings, the red heifer, the sanctity of Jerusalem and the temple and its halakic consequences, purity laws, priestly gifts, and the prohibition against incest" (Noam, 60). The letter ends, "Reflect on all these matters and seek from him so that he may support your counsel and keep far from you the evil scheming and the counsel of Belial, so that at the end of time, you may rejoice in finding that some of our words are true. And it shall be reckoned to you as in justice when you do what is right and good before him, for your good, and that of Israel" (4QMMT 114–118; García Martínez, 79). Vered Noam concludes, "The stringent Qumran legislation is quite similar to an early tradition, practiced at the start of the second century BCE, whereas the Pharisaic position must have been a novelty" (71; cf. 78–79).

17.1.4 Rabbinic Sources

After the destruction of Jerusalem and the temple in 70 CE, the chief priests and Sadducees ceased to hold power, the Essenes at Qumran were wiped out with its destruction (in 68). We have no evidence concerning Essenes who may have lived elsewhere, but the remaining Zealots perished at Masada (in 73–74). According to conventional understanding, during the following decades prominent Pharisees gathered at Jamnia and began the process of defining how faithful Jews could continue to be obedient to the law without temple, sacrifices, or priests. What emerged was the classic articulation of Judaism in the rabbinic writings: the Mishnah, which collects the oral tradition of the Pharisees; the Tosefta (supplement); and later the Talmuds and midrashim (commentaries).

Recent scholarship has questioned both the significance of Jamnia and the continuity between the Pharisees and later rabbis. Shaye Cohen argues that while there probably was a close connection between the post-70 rabbis and the pre-70 Pharisees, the early rabbis (the Tannaim) "display little interest in establishing themselves as Pharisees" (1984, 39). Gamaliel and Simon, Gamaliel's son or grandson, are named in Mishnah Avot; but no rabbi is ever called a Pharisee, not even Johanan ben Zakkai, the leader at Jamnia, who spent a period of his life between 20 and 40 CE in Arav, five miles NNE of Sepphoris (m. Shabb. 16:7; 22:3; Neusner, 1962, 23–26; Freyne, 315). Beliefs and practices ascribed to the Pharisees by Josephus and the New Testament are also common among the rabbis, "notably the belief in a combination of fate and free will, the belief in the immortality of the soul and resurrection, the acceptance of ancestral traditions in addition to the written law, and the meticulous observance of the laws of purity, tithing,

Shabbat, and other rituals" (Cohen, 1984, 37). On the other hand, there is no evidence for the Pharisees believing that the oral law was revealed to Moses, as the rabbis maintained. For Cohen, Jamnia marked the end of sectarianism, embracing a plurality of views. Debate was encouraged, and legal opinions were ascribed to individuals by name: "This is not the work of a sect triumphant but of a grand coalition" (1984, 42).

Cohen's reassessment of the evidence for continuity between the Pharisees and the early rabbis has been advanced by Günter Stemberger, who cites "the very poor personal connection" between the Pharisees and the rabbis. The Tannaim never call the pre-70 teachers by the name "Pharisees," as does later tradition (b. Qidd. 66a; Stemberger, 241, 246). Josephus never mentions Hillel. The Mishnah juxtaposes the Pharisees and Sadducees only once (m. Yad. 4:6–7). Pharisaic legislation regarding agricultural tithes and table fellowship is not maintained post-70 but "recovered" only later. Stemberger's conclusion is sweeping: "We may not reconstruct Pharisaic thought and halakah based on rabbinic texts. The year 70 certainly was no radical break; but much that was carried on was also transformed. This makes it most difficult to evaluate continuity and change" (254).

Daniel Boyarin reads the traditions regarding the "Council of Jamnia" not as a history of events but a history of interpretations, comparing the imaging of Jamnia in the Talmuds to Athanasius's construction of the significance of the First Council of Nicea (325 CE), which was then accepted at the First Council of Constantinople in 381. Cohen regards Jamnia as a council that "created a society based on the doctrine that conflicting disputants may each be advancing the words of the living God" (1984, 51). As the Talmuds say, "It is taught, a heavenly voice went out and said, 'These and these are the words of the Living God, but the Law is like the School of Hillel.' Where did the voice go out? Rabbi Bibbi said in the name of Rabbi Yoḥanan, 'In Yavneh the voice went out'" (y. Yebam. 1.6; cf. b. 'Erub. 13b and b. Gitt. 6b). Boyarin argues in response: "Cohen is right, I think, but the Yavneh [Jamnia] that he describes is a product of the late myth-making discourse of the Talmuds" (29, 60–62). In current scholarship, therefore, Jamnia, the early rabbis, and the pre-70 Pharisees fade further into the mists of history and interpretation.

17.2 Pharisees in the First Century

As this survey of our sources demonstrates, each one confronts interpreters with complex issues, and each presents the Pharisees in a different light. The Pharisees evolved over time, from their appearance in the second century BCE through the period of Herod and his sons, in the decades lead-ing up to the First Jewish Revolt (66–70), and later. The work of clarifying the identity and social status of the Pharisees is ongoing, so at best we can offer only a reading of current perspectives on Pharisees in the first century.

Historians have attempted to trace the development of specific traditions and distinguish their earliest layers. Regarding the pre-70 Pharisaic teach-ers, "We do not have tales of how they taught, nor do we even have inter-nal evidence that they organized circles of disciples. Perhaps they did; we cannot claim that they 'must have' done so" (Neusner 1971, 3:152). Jose-phus may give us a glimpse into the activities of certain Pharisees when he refers to "their lectures on the laws" (*J.W.* 1.649) and to "men especially dear to the people because they educated the youth, for all those who made an effort to acquire virtue used to spend time with them day after day" (*Ant.* 17.149). Josephus's references to the Pharisees' interpretation of the law and their teaching activities fit descriptions of the early synagogues as places for prayer and the reading of Scripture (see above, 3.2; 6.5; Deines, 89; and Saldarini 1988, 291–97). Pharisees may not have established or controlled the synagogues before the second century CE, but, like Jesus, they prob-ably found it a natural venue for their teachings (Hengel and Deines, 32). Josephus relates a speech by Nicolas of Damascus, Herod's adviser, appeal-ing to Marcus Agrippa, a friend of Augustus, on behalf of the Ionian Jews. Nicolas asserts: "Nor do we make a secret of the precepts that we use as guides in religion and in human relations; we give every seventh day over to the study of our customs and law, . . . through which we can avoid com-mitting sins" (*Ant.* 16.43–46). This reference to the Jews' Sabbath activi-ties describes study, presumably in the synagogues, of their "customs and law" and "precepts" (Hengel and Deines, 33).

The Pharisees practiced a strict piety, especially in matters of purity, agri-cultural tithing, Sabbath observance, divorce, and table fellowship, appeal-ing to both the law and oral tradition (Neusner 1973, 81–96, summarizing his three-volume work [1971]; and Sanders, 649–57). According to Jose-phus, they were known for their belief in fate or providence, human free-dom, affirming the oral tradition handed down to them, the immortality of the soul, and rewards or punishments after death (*Ant.* 13.171–172, 297; 18.12–15; *J.W.* 2.162–163). They were more lenient in punishments than the Sadducees, and the school of Hillel was more lenient than the school of Shammai (*Ant.* 13.294; Acts 5:17, 34–39).

Sanders concludes that while the Pharisees were not aristocrats, many were probably landowners who had time for study. While the Pharisees did not govern or control, they were popular, their interpretation of the law was respected, and they exercised influence by persuasion. They were "neither leisured nor destitute" (637; cf. Hengel and Deines, 34). Since the Pharisees were typically not among the elite, most would have been subordinate officials, bureaucrats, craftsmen, merchants, or "retainers." Drawing on the work of social historians of the Greek and Roman Empires, Saldarini contends,

> The governing class maintained its position with the assistance of what Lenski calls retainers, whose roles in society were military, governing, administrative, judicial and priestly. These retainers were mostly townspeople who served the needs of the governing class as soldiers, educators, religious functionaries, entertainers and skilled artisans; it is here we find the Pharisees and scribes [Kautsky, 323–28; Lenski, 243–66]. (Saldarini 1988, 37–38)

Virtually all the references to Pharisees in our sources—except for the Gospels—concern their activities in Jerusalem and Judea. In the Gospel of John especially, they are associated with the chief priests and Jewish leadership. The Synoptics (Matt 15:1; Mark 3:22; 7:1; Luke 5:17), John (1:19, 24; 7:32; cf. 4:1), and Josephus (*Life* 190–191, 196–197, 216) all refer to Pharisees in Jerusalem sending or being sent to Galilee to investigate, variously, John the Baptist, Jesus, and Josephus. We turn therefore to the question at the center of our study: What can we say about Pharisees in Galilee?

17.3 Pharisees in Galilee

The judgment of scholarship regarding Pharisees in Galilee is predominantly negative: Morton Smith declares, "The synoptics' picture of a Galilee swarming with Pharisees is a further anachronism" (157); Shaye Cohen agrees: "The Pharisaic movement was centered in Jerusalem and did not become influential in Galilee until after the Bar Kokhba war (132–135 CE)" (2002, 226). Horsley observes, "The statements that they look for deference in public and seats of honor at feasts and assemblies (Mark 12:38–39; Luke 11:43) suggest periodic visits to villages and towns, as might be expected from those whose social role has recently been constructed as 'retainers' of the temple-state in Jerusalem" (152). Since Pharisaism "was largely restricted to Jerusalem and the larger towns of Judea," John Meier suggests Jesus' confrontations with the Pharisees probably occurred "in and around Jerusalem, when Jesus came on pilgrimage to the great feasts—just as John's Gospel intimates" (336).

Others allow that some Pharisees resided in Galilee, perhaps from the time of the Hasmonean settlement there. Saldarini's assessment of the geographical range of the Pharisees is relevant: "The evidence is tenuous, but if Pharisaism was known and influential outside of Judea, the most likely sphere of influence would be Jewish communities in the Semitic areas to the north, including Galilee, the Damascus area to the northeast [cf. Acts 9:2], the rest of southern Syria and greater Syria beyond [cf. Matt 4:24]" (1988, 293). Seán Freyne located specific cities where Pharisees could be found: "Pharisaism had made certain inroads into the province [Galilee] prior to 70 C.E. and both Josephus and the gospels suggest that its greatest successes were in the settlements along the lake front—Tiberias, Taricheae [Magdala], Caesarea Philippi, and probably Capernaum, Chorazin and Bethsaida also" (322).

Archaeological evidence confirms widespread use of stone vessels (which did not retain impurity), some produced in lower Galilee (esp. at Kefar Hananya and Kefar Shikhin; Fiensy and Strange, 2:98–101, 181–85), as well as *miqva'ot* and first-century synagogues in Galilee (Strange, 250–51), but these material remains are not exclusively or definitively Pharisaic. In addition to Pharisees, the Essenes, priests, Levites, and apparently other Jews practiced ritual purity during this period.

17.4 Reflections

The first point that must always be emphasized is that Christian sources have misrepresented and stereotyped Pharisees across the centuries, branding the Pharisees as hypocrites, condemning them for Jesus' crucifixion (a role that none of the Gospels supports), and making them representative of all Jews. This misrepresentation is so pervasive that it is virtually impossible now to separate the Pharisees from the invective that has been heaped upon them. Our review of the sources and their interpretations in current scholarship finds, in contrast, that the Pharisees were widely respected by other Jews for their interpretation of the law, their teachings, and their stringent efforts to obey the law and the oral tradition that had come down to them. When the Matthean Jesus says, "Unless your righteousness exceeds that of the scribes and Pharisees, you will never enter the kingdom of heaven" (5:20), he points to those who were the most faithful among them in living righteously.

Current scholarship has also shown how elusive the Pharisees are, obscured by the sources in which they appear, evolving over time, sharing much in common with other Jews, and vigorously debating among themselves. The irony is that some scholars (W. D. Davies, J. Louis Martyn, followed by Morton Smith, and Seán Freyne) argued that the proliferation of

Pharisees in the Gospels reflects the Jamnian period rather than Jesus' ministry, while others have argued that Jamnia was either too late or not significant enough to have influenced the Gospels (Daniel Boyarin). Yet, the debates between Jesus and the Pharisees that are attested across the various sources and strata of the Gospels must arise from some historical context, either during Jesus' ministry or later, or both. But it cannot be neither. Still, regardless of its generative context, the role of the Pharisees in the Gospels clearly appears to be exaggerated, and the Pharisees have been stereotyped as Jesus' opponents—with tragic consequences throughout the church's history.

In the Gospels, Jesus is often shown in dialogue with Pharisees over issues the Pharisees debated among themselves (Neusner 1973, 81–96; Neusner 2007; Sanders, 649–57; Freyne, 320; Meier, 320–21):

Figure 4

Purity	Handwashing, unclean food	Mark 7:1–23
	Washing bowls	Matt 23:25–26
Agricultural tithing	Mint, dill, cumin	Matt 23:23
Sabbath observance	Plucking grain	Mark 2:23–28
	Healing	Mark 3:1–6; Luke 13:10–17; 14:1–6; John 5:1–18; 9:1–34
Table fellowship	Eating with tax collectors	Matt 9:10–13//Mark 2:15–17; Luke 5:29–32; 19:1–10
Divorce	A certificate of divorce	Matt 19:3–8//Mark 10:2–9

Jesus and the Pharisees both appealed to their fellow Jews, but they followed different approaches to the interpretation of the law (Matt 22:34–40). Jesus was less concerned about issues of purity, table fellowship, and Sabbath observance (see below, 21.9) but adopted a more radical prohibition of divorce. Matthew has Jesus affirming tithing even of herbs but condemning the Pharisees for neglecting "the weightier matters of the law: justice and mercy and faith" (23:23). Amid the threats to Jewish customs and traditions in that period, such debates were common among various groups and movements.

The rise and fall of Pharisaic activism in support of or opposition to various rulers, continuing into the period of the Herods, and the localization of the Pharisees primarily in Jerusalem and Judea—all these facts call for caution in assessing their role as Jesus' opponents in Galilee. Reports that the Pharisees in Jerusalem sent men to investigate Jesus follow from the Gospel accounts that crowds were coming to Jesus and responding to his healing and teaching. Yet an inference that, because Pharisees were concentrated in Jerusalem, no Pharisees were in Galilee is unwarranted.

A modest clarification may be to note the settings of Jesus' debates with Pharisees in Galilee concerning issues identified with pre-70 Pharisees. To put it another way, where are debates over the law reported in Galilean settings? The controversy stories in Mark 2:1–3:6 are particularly significant. Even if the arrangement of these stories is Mark's handicraft, as Joanna Dewey has demonstrated, the combination of Galilean settings and issues of concern to the Pharisees suggests that Jesus encountered Pharisees among the crowds in Galilee.

Figure 5

Mark 2:16	Capernaum, toll booth	Eating with tax collectors
Mark 2:23–26	Grainfields	Plucking grain on the Sabbath
Mark 3:1–6	A Galilean synagogue	Healing on the Sabbath (Pharisees and Herodians)

In earlier chapters, we found the settings of these controversy dialogues to be entirely credible: meeting tax collectors at a tax office or toll booth in Capernaum, walking through grainfields in Galilee, and entering synagogues in Galilee. In these traditional stories we also meet Galilean Pharisees devoted to the observance of the law, seeking to maintain purity in their communities, and debating with Jesus over what it means to live righteously under the law. This brief tabulation of debates with Pharisees over typical Pharisaic concerns in common settings in Galilee supports Saldarini's conclusion: "The contention that the early church put the Pharisees in all the Galilean disputes or moved the disputes with the Pharisees from a Judean to a Galilean location lacks cogency" (1988, 291; cf. Saldarini 1992, 295–96).

Works Cited in Chapter 17

Black, C. Clifton. 1994. *Mark: Images of an Apostolic Interpreter.* Columbia: University of South Carolina Press.
Black, Matthew. 1962. "Pharisees." *IDB* 3:774–81.

Boyarin, Daniel. 2000. "A Tale of Two Synods: Nicaea, Yavneh, and Rabbinic Ecclesiology." *Exemplaria* 12:21–62.

Cohen, Shaye J. D. 1984. "The Significance of Yavneh: Pharisees, Rabbis, and the End of Jewish Sectarianism." *HUCA* 55:27–53.

———. 2002. *Josephus in Galilee and Rome: His Vita and Development as a Historian.* CSCT 8. Leiden: Brill.

Culpepper, R. Alan. 1983. *Anatomy of the Fourth Gospel.* Philadelphia: Fortress.

———. 2007. *Mark.* SHBC. Macon, GA: Smyth & Helwys.

———. 2017. "Matthew and John: Reflections on Early Christianity in Relationship to Judaism." Pages 189–219 in *John and Judaism: A Contested Relationship in Context.* Edited by R. Alan Culpepper and Paul N. Anderson. RBS 87. Atlanta: SBL Press.

———. 2021. *Matthew.* NTL. Louisville: Westminster John Knox.

Darr, John A. 1992. *On Character Building: The Readers and the Rhetoric of Characterization in Luke-Acts.* Louisville: Westminster John Knox; repr., Wipf & Stock, 2020.

Deines, Roland. 2014. "Religious Practices and Religious Movements in Galilee: 100 BCE–200 CE." Pages 78–111 in vol. 1 of *Galilee in the Late Second Temple and Mishnaic Periods: Life, Culture, and Society.* Edited by David A. Fiensy and James Riley Strange. Minneapolis: Fortress.

Dewey, Joanna. 1980. *Markan Public Debate: Literary Technique, Concentric Structure and Theology in Mark 2:1–3:6.* SBLDS 48. Chico, CA: Scholars Press.

Fiensy, David A., and James R. Strange, eds. 2015. *The Archaeological Record from Cities, Towns, and Villages.* Vol. 2 of *Galilee in the Late Second Temple and Mishnaic Periods.* Minneapolis: Fortress.

Fredriksen, Paula. 2021. "Paul, the Perfectly Righteous Pharisee." Pages 112–35 in Sievers and Levine.

Freyne, Seán. 1980. *Galilee from Alexander the Great to Hadrian, 323 B.C.E. to 135 C.E.* University of Notre Dame Center for the Study of Judaism and Christianity in Antiquity 5. Wilmington, DE: Glazier.

García Martínez. *See* Bibliography of Ancient Sources and Translations

Gowler, David B. 1991. *Host, Guest, Enemy, and Friend: Portraits of the Pharisees in Luke and Acts.* New York: Lang.

Hengel, Martin, and Roland Deines. 1995. "E. P. Sanders' 'Common Judaism,' Jesus, and the Pharisees." *JTS* 46:1–70.

Horsley, Richard A. 1996. *Archaeology, History, and Society in Galilee.* Valley Forge, PA: Trinity Press International.

Kautsky, John H. 1982. *The Politics of Aristocratic Empires.* Chapel Hill: University of North Carolina Press.

Lenski, Gerhard E. 1966. *Power and Privilege: A Theory of Social Stratification.* New York: McGraw.

Löhr, Hermut. 2021. "Luke-Acts as a Source for the History of the Pharisees." Pages 170–84 in Sievers and Levine.

Martyn, J. Louis. 2003. *History and Theology in the Fourth Gospel.* 3rd ed. NTL. Louisville: Westminster John Knox.

Mason, Steve. 2021. "Josephus's Pharisees." Pages 80–111 in Sievers and Levine.

Meier, John P. 2001. *Companions and Competitors.* Vol. 3 of *A Marginal Jew: Rethinking the Historical Jesus.* ABRL. New York: Doubleday.

Neusner, Jacob. 1962. *A Life of Rabban Yohanan ben Zakkai, ca. 1–80 C.E.* StPB 6. Leiden: Brill.

————. 1971. *The Rabbinic Traditions about the Pharisees before 70*. 3 vols. Leiden: Brill.

————. 1973. *From Politics to Piety: The Emergence of Pharisaic Judaism*. Englewood Cliffs, NJ: Prentice-Hall.

————. 2007. "The Pharisaic Agenda: Laws Attributed in the Mishnah and the Tosefta to Pre-70 Pharisees." Pages 313–27 in Neusner and Chilton.

Neusner, Jacob, and Bruce D. Chilton, eds. 2007. *In Quest of the Historical Pharisees*. Waco, TX: Baylor University Press.

Noam, Vered. 2021. "Pharisaic Halakah as Emerging from 4QMMT." Pages 55–79 in Sievers and Levine.

Poplutz, Uta. 2013. "The Pharisees: A House Divided?" Pages 116–26 in *Character Studies in the Fourth Gospel*. Edited by Steven A. Hunt, D. François Tolmie, and Ruben Zimmermann. WUNT 314. Tübingen: Mohr Siebeck.

Richardson, Peter. 2004. *Building Jewish in the Roman East*. Waco, TX: Baylor University Press.

Saldarini, Anthony J. 1988. *Pharisees, Scribes, and Sadducees in Palestinian Society: A Sociological Approach*. Grand Rapids: Eerdmans.

————. 1992. "Pharisees." *ABD* 5:289–303.

Sanders, E. P. 2016. *Judaism: Practice and Belief, 63 BCE–66 CE*. Minneapolis: Fortress.

Sievers, Joseph. 1997. "Who Were the Pharisees?" Pages 137–55 in *Hillel and Jesus: Comparative Studies of Two Major Religious Leaders*. Edited by James H. Charlesworth and Loren L. Johns. Minneapolis: Fortress.

Sievers, Joseph, and Amy-Jill Levine, eds. 2021. *The Pharisees*. Grand Rapids: Eerdmans.

Smith, Morton. 1978. *Jesus the Magician*. San Francisco: Harper & Row.

Stemberger, Günter. 2021. "The Pharisees and the Rabbis." Pages 240–54 in Sievers and Levine.

Strange, James F. 2007. "Archaeology and the Pharisees." Pages 237–51 in Neusner and Chilton.

Tannehill, Robert C. 1986. *The Narrative Unity of Luke-Acts: A Literary Interpretation*. Philadelphia: Fortress.

Chapter 18

Priests and Levites

Good Samaritan (Luke 10:30–35)

*I*n the parable of the good Samaritan, the only parable in which priests or Levites appear, they "pass by on the other side," leaving the injured man in the ditch. In contrast to the chief priests and the high priest, who are prominent in the Gospels' passion narratives, neither ordinary priests nor Levites receive much notice in the New Testament. Levites appear only two other times: in John 1:19, where the Jews send priests and Levites from Jerusalem to question John the Baptist (at "Bethany across the Jordan," 1:28); and in Acts 4:36, where Barnabas is identified as a Levite from Cyprus.

By the first century, both priests and Levites officiated in the temple, with the priests administering the sacrifices and the Levites carrying out secondary tasks. The focus in this chapter is on the roles of these two groups, with only passing attention to the evolution of the high priests and the families of the chief priests. The relationship between priests and Levites prior to the early Roman period sets the context for understanding their roles in the first century.

18.1 Origins and Early History

The origins of these two cultic groups are both inscribed and enshrouded in the Hebrew Scriptures. The priests represented the tribes of Israel before God and made sacrifices on their behalf: "So Aaron shall bear the names of the sons of Israel in the breastpiece of judgment on his heart when he goes into the holy place, for a continual remembrance before the LORD" (Exod 28:29). Genealogies were traced and rewritten to establish the claims of one group or the other because priestly legitimacy was based on lineage,

267

descent from Levi, Aaron, or Zadok. The priests were descendants of Levi through Aaron (Exod 28:1; 1 Chr 6:1–15, 49–53). Complicating the matter, the term "Levite" refers variously to descendants of Levi, son of Jacob and Leah (Gen 35:23), and to the professional class of second-rank priests. Second Temple sources claim the true priestly line of descent ran through Zadok, a descendant of Aaron (1 Chr 24:1–3). In protest against the corruption of the Jerusalem priesthood by anointing high priests who were not Zadokites (see below, 18.3), the priestly community at Qumran traced their lineage to Zadok (CD IV, 2–4; 1QS V, 1–3, 8–10). Regarding these histories and genealogies, Robert Kugler cautions that the literature "only occasionally reflects what actually happened and more often presents what its authors wished had happened, or hoped would be the case" (2010, 1096).

According to the pentateuchal accounts, Aaron and his sons were appointed to serve as priests (Exod 28:1–4, 41; 29:9; 40:15), administer the burnt offerings (Lev 1:5–17), the grain offerings (Lev 2), and the sin offerings (Lev 4). Priests examined skin diseases, pronounced them clean or unclean (Lev 13), made the appropriate offerings (Lev 14), and inspected the houses of the diseased (14:34–48). A priest entered "the sanctuary inside the curtain before the mercy seat that is upon the ark" (16:2) to "make atonement for the people of Israel" (16:34) on the Day of Atonement. Priests were anointed with oil (21:10). They could not attend to a dead body (21:11) and could only marry a virgin: "A widow, or a divorced woman, or a woman who has been defiled, a prostitute, these he shall not marry. He shall marry a virgin of his own kin, that he may not profane his offspring among his kin" (21:14–15). Blemishes, various diseases, broken bones, deformities, and impairments disqualified one from serving as a priest (21:17–23). Offerings could be eaten only by the priest, his wife and children, and his slaves (22:10–13). Priests also assessed the values of human beings, animals, and fields promised by a vow to God (27:1–23). During the preexilic period, priests officiated in sanctuaries throughout Israel. Deuteronomy does not distinguish two classes of priests: all of them are Levitical priests.

The descendants of Levi were not given an allotment of land (Deut 18:1–2), as were the other tribes, but were assigned certain towns and pasturelands (Josh 14:4; 21:1–3; 1 Esd 5:46). Nevertheless, provisions were made for Levites to own houses in the cities assigned to them (Lev 25:32–33) and in Ezekiel's vision they have allotments near Jerusalem (48:8–14). Why were Levites deprived of land? Accounts of the early Levites (Gen 34; 49; Exod 32; Num 25, esp. 25:11–13; Deut 33) all "hold in common the tradition that the Levites were chosen for special treatment as a result of an act of violence" (Baden, 103). Tensions and rivalries among the royal priests can be seen as early as the period of the monarchy, with Solomon's dismissal of Abiathar (1 Kgs 2:27, 35; Nurmela, 49). Ezekiel 44:10–16 explains the second-class priesthood as punishment for cultic infidelities, while restricting altar priesthood to the Zadokites, who remained faithful when the people of Israel and the Levites went astray (Ezek 44:15; 48:11; Kugler 2010, 1096–97). The origin of the Levites as second-class cultic officials can be traced to Josiah's attempt (ca. 640–609 BCE) to centralize the cult in Jerusalem by closing the other sanctuaries. The discovery in 2012 of an Iron Age temple and sacred vessels at Tel Motza, near Jerusalem, dating from the ninth century BCE, provides rare evidence of one such sanctuary (cf. Tel Moza Excavation website). The priests at rival sanctuaries either lost their livelihood or found a place in the temple in Jerusalem, where they were assigned lesser duties, which may have given rise to the distinction between priests and Levites (Nurmela, 70–74; Cook).

According to tradition, Aaron was the first high priest (Lev 8; Josephus, *Ant.* 20.225). The references to Jehoiada (2 Kgs 12:9 [12:10 Masoretic Text]) and Hilkiah (2 Kgs 22:4, 8; 23:4; 2 Chr 34:9), the senior priest at the time of Josiah's reform, as high priests (*hakohen hagadol*) do not settle the question of whether the high priesthood can be traced to the preexilic period (Rehm, 309). A genealogy begins with "the chief priest Seraiah" (2 Kgs 25:18; Neh 11:11), who was executed in exile by Nebuchadnezzar (Jer 52:21, 27), and continues with Jehozadak (1 Chr 6:14–15). His son, Joshua, is the first high priest of the Second Temple (Hag 1:1 et passim; Zech 6:11). Josephus continues the genealogy through the time of Herod and his sons (*Ant.* 20.224–251).

Until the centralization of the cult in Jerusalem, there was no structure to support the high priesthood, and even thereafter the high priest was simply the chief cultic official. Even following Hezekiah and Josiah, the king was the supreme political and religious authority (Rooke, 120–21).

18.2 The Persian and Hellenistic Periods

A letter from the Jews at Elephantine in Egypt (CAP, no. 30; 408 BCE), addressed to "Jehohanan the high priest," confirms that there was a hierarchical order of priests in Jerusalem at this time (Adler, 198–99). The return to Jerusalem (Ezra 2:36–54; Neh 7:39–56) and the rebuilding of the temple prompted further definition of roles among the priests and Levites. While the Aaronide priests administered the sacrifices at the altar, the Levitical priests carried out supportive tasks, including teaching (2 Chr 35:3; 1 Esd 9:49; Neh 8:9) and settling "cases of dispute and assault" (Deut 21:5). The priestly writer declares that God commanded Moses:

Bring the tribe of Levi near, and set them before Aaron the priest, so that they may assist him. They shall perform duties for him and for the whole congregation in front of the tent of meeting, doing service at the tabernacle; they shall be in charge of all the furnishings of the tent of meeting, and attend to the duties for the Israelites as they do service at the tabernacle. You shall give the Levites to Aaron and his descendants; they are unreservedly given to him from among the Israelites. But you shall make a register of Aaron and his descendants; it is they who shall attend to the priesthood. (Num 3:6–10)

Because the Levites had no allotment of land, tithes were paid to the Levites, who paid a tenth of the tithe to the priests. Nehemiah explains the procedure for collecting the tithes.

The priest, the descendant of Aaron, shall be with the Levites when the Levites receive the tithes; and the Levites shall bring up a tithe of the tithes to the house of our God, to the chambers of the storehouse. For the people of Israel and the sons of Levi shall bring the contribution of grain, wine, and oil to the storerooms where the vessels of the sanctuary are, and where the priests that minister, and the gatekeepers and the singers are. (Neh 10:38–39; cf. 12:44)

This two-tiered organization of the cult was secured by 1 and 2 Chronicles (ca. 300 BCE): "One of the Chronicler's great innovations is to further define the roles of the Levites: they are given various and sundry assignments as singers, musicians, gatekeepers, treasurers, judges, and scribes and 'the descendants of Solomon's servants'" (Kugler 2009, 610; cf. Ezra 2:41–43, 55–58). The priests maintained a superior status above the Levites, who were divided into two groups: musicians and below them the gatekeepers.

Jehoiada assigned the care of the house of the LORD to the levitical priests whom David had organized to be in charge of the house of the LORD, to offer burnt offerings to the LORD, as it is written in the law of Moses, with rejoicing and with singing, according to the order of David. He stationed the gatekeepers at the gates of the house of the LORD so that no one should enter who was in any way unclean. (2 Chr 23:18–19; cf. 5:11–12; 31:2; 35:15; Ezra 7:24; Neh 10:28)

The Levites took no part in the sacrifices. According to 1 Chronicles 23:4–5, David specified their duties as directing the work in the temple, serving as officers and judges, gatekeepers, and offering praises to the Lord. Furthermore, their duty shall be to assist the descendants of Aaron for the service of the house of the LORD, having the care of the courts and the chambers, the cleansing of all that is holy, and any work for the service of the house of God; to assist also with the rows of bread, the choice flour for the grain offering, the wafers of unleavened bread, the baked offering, the offering mixed with oil, and all measures of quantity or size. And they shall stand every morning, thanking and praising the LORD, and likewise at evening, and whenever burnt offerings are offered to the LORD on sabbaths, new moons, and appointed festivals, according to the number required of them, regularly before the LORD. (1 Chr 23:28–31; cf. *Ant.* 7.363–367)

The Levites did not have access to the court of the priests, the sanctuary, or the altar (Num 18:2–3; m. Kelim 1:8). They were musicians, gatekeepers, and temple police (Philo, *Spec. Laws* 1.156; m. Mid. 1:1; see the history in Nurmela).

Some of the priests and Levites continued to live in towns and villages around Jerusalem (Ezra 2:70; 7:7; Neh 7:73; 11:20). Both the priests and the Levites were enrolled "according to their ancestral houses" (2 Chr 31:17). Since these offices were hereditary, it was imperative to ensure the purity of the lineage. Priestly genealogies were maintained in public registers (Neh 7:64; 1 Esd 5:38–40; Josephus, *Life* 6; *Ag. Ap.* 1.34–35). Documents dating to the third century BCE emphasize the importance of the Levitical lineage of Israel's priests (esp. the Aramaic Levi Document; Jub. 30; 32; 1 En. 12–16; Kugler 2009, 611). Rigid rules governed the marriage of priests (Lev 21:7; Ezek 44:21–22; Josephus, *Ag. Ap.* 1.33; m. Qidd. 3:12), and priests often married the daughter of a priest. In the high-priestly families, a daughter was sometimes married to her father's brother.

Throughout the Second Temple period, the priests' duties continued to be making sacrifices (Sir 50:1–21), teaching (Hag 2:10–19; Mal 2:7), interpreting the Torah (Josephus, *Ag. Ap.* 2.184–187), and giving oracles (Zech 7:3; Kugler 2010, 1096). The priests and Levites were organized in families or courses, first 21 courses (Neh 10:3–9), then 22 (12:1–7, 12–21), and finally 24 courses (1 Chr 24:1–19; Josephus, *Life* 2). The final list appears to be Maccabean because it puts first the family to which the Maccabees belonged, Jehoiarib (Jeremias, 199). Each course served in the temple for a week at a time, beginning on the Sabbath, and all of them served during the three pilgrimage festivals (Josephus, *Ant.* 7.365–366; *Ag. Ap.* 2.108). Luke's account of the annunciation of the birth of John the Baptist to Zechariah reflects this arrangement: "In the days of King Herod of Judea, there was a priest named Zechariah, who belonged to the priestly order of Abijah. His wife was a descendant of Aaron, and her name was Elizabeth" (Luke

1:5). First Chronicles lists Abijah among the descendants of Aaron (24:3–4, 10; Neh 10:7; 12:4, 17) and affirms, "These had as their appointed duty in their service to enter the house of the LORD according to the procedure established for them by their ancestor Aaron, as the LORD God of Israel had commanded him" (1 Chr 24:19).

18.3 The Hasmonean Period

The upheavals of the Maccabean Revolt and Hasmonean period corrupted and destabilized the temple cult. When Antiochus IV ascended to the throne (175 BCE), Onias III, the rightful Zadokite high priest, was in Antioch, apparently to answer charges of disloyalty brought against him by the Tobiads, the rival pro-Hellenist family. His brother, Jason, traveled to Antioch and met with Antiochus. Rather than supporting Onias III, however, Jason offered to pay more taxes and a onetime tribute if Antiochus appointed him (Jason) as high priest. Although no Seleucid ruler had assumed authority to appoint a high priest, Antiochus readily agreed. Fourth Maccabees charges, "Jason changed the nation's way of life and altered its form of government in complete violation of the law" (4:19). His appointment as high priest gave him the power to make changes in Jerusalem, but it was the Seleucid backing rather than the office itself that gave him intrinsic power (Rooke, 325). Under Jason,

> there was such an extreme of Hellenization and increase in the adoption of foreign ways because of the surpassing wickedness of Jason, who was ungodly and no true high priest, that the priests were no longer intent upon their service at the altar. Despising the sanctuary and neglecting the sacrifices, they hurried to take part in the unlawful proceedings in the wrestling arena after the signal for the discus-throwing, disdaining the honors prized by their ancestors and putting the highest value upon Greek forms of prestige. (2 Macc 4:13–15)

Three years later, Menelaus, a Tobiad whom Jason had sent to Antioch with the annual tribute, offered Antiochus twice the annual taxes that Jason was collecting. Again, Antiochus agreed and appointed Menelaus as high priest even though he was not from the Zadokite lineage and therefore had no claim to the office (4:23–29). Menelaus had Onias III murdered (4:34). When Menelaus himself was later killed by the Seleucid monarch, the office of high priest passed to Alcimus (162–159 BCE; 1 Macc 7:9).

In response to the unrest in Jerusalem, Antiochus tore down its walls and built a fortress, probably for defense against the Ptolemies. He erected altars and ordered the Jews to sacrifice swine to Zeus Olympus. Mattathias, who was a priest but not a Zadokite, had moved from Jerusalem to Modein (1 Macc 2). When the Seleucid officers sought to enforce the king's orders in Modein, Mattathias killed a Jew who came forward to offer the sacrifice, then killed one of the officers and tore down the altar. Calling out to his fellow townsmen, "Let everyone who is zealous for the law and supports the covenant come out with me," he led his followers into the hills (2:27–28). When Mattathias died shortly thereafter, one of his sons, Judas the Maccabee (the Hammer) became the leader of the rebellion. For the rest of the story, see chapter 1 above.

Whether there was a high priest following the death of Alcimus in 159 is uncertain. In 152 BCE, Alexander Balas appointed Jonathan (the brother of Judas Maccabeus) as high priest (152–143/142 BCE). Ironically, Jonathan was now the political, religious, and military leader of the Jews and an appointee of the Seleucids. When Jonathan was killed in 142 (1 Macc 12:46–50), leadership of Judea passed to his brother, Simon, and the Hasmoneans continued to occupy both the royal and high-priestly offices until the Roman conquest (see Seeman). Under the Hasmonean high priests, the aristocratic priests prospered.

The corruption of the high priesthood during these years elicited a strong reaction in some quarters. The Essenes withdrew to Qumran, where they cultivated a priestly community (1QS V, 1–7; VIII, 5–6, 8–9; IX, 6; CD III, 18–IV, 4; 4qFlor I, 3–4) and lived in purity (1QS V, 13; VI, 16–17; 1qSa I, 8–17; II, 3–10; CD X, 6–8; XV, 15–17). References to "the wicked priest" in 1QpHab (VIII, 8, 16; IX, 8; XI, 4; XII, 2, 8) reflect their animosity toward the Jerusalem priesthood (CD V, 6–7).

18.4 The Early Roman Period

The high priest Joseph called Caiaphas, the son-in-law of Annas (high priest, 6–15 CE), is best known for his role in the Gospels. Although he was the longest-serving high priest of the first century, remarkably little is recorded elsewhere about his tenure. Josephus (*Ant.* 18.33–35) says only that "he was appointed by the governor Gratus in 18 CE, remained throughout Pilate's governorship (26–36), and was removed by Vitellius, the legate of Syria, in 36 or 37 CE" (Reinhartz, 12). His long tenure probably indicates that he worked well with the Romans and maintained order.

In 1990 an ossuary (a limestone box for bones) inscribed with the name "Caiaphas" was found about two miles south of Jerusalem's Old City. The inscription on the box, which contained the bones of a sixty-year-old man and other members of his family, reads *Yehoseph bar Qayapha'* on one end and *Yehoseph bar Qapha'* on the side. The spelling of the name has been contested, but it is possible that the ossuary, now housed in the Israel Museum, contained the remains of this most famous of the high priests (Evans, 327–29).

The essential priestly duties continued unchanged until the destruction of the temple in 70 CE. Josephus says there were 20,000 priests (*Ag. Ap.* 2.108), and E. P. Sanders agrees: "We cannot do better than take Josephus's word for it" (132). Jeremias's calculations arrive at a similar number: 18,000 priests and Levites in the time of Jesus (204). Also, Jeremias calculated that "each course consisted of an average of 300 priests and 400 Levites, and was accompanied by a group of lay representatives from its district [m. Bik. 3:2]. The keys of the temple and the 93 vessels were ceremoniously handed over by the course going off duty (*Ag. Ap.* 2.108)" (206).

Priests heard confessions, accepted sacrifices, butchered animals, sprinkled blood, ate the meat of sacrifices, recited Scripture, prayed, burned incense, and blew trumpets (*shofarot*) during the temple services (Sanders, 133–34). Wine was forbidden to the priests when they were on duty (Josephus, *Ant.* 3.278–279; *J.W.* 5.228–229). The Letter of Aristeas (150–100 BCE) provides a vivid description of the priests at work in the temple, emphasizing their silence, devotion, and exertion.

> The ministering of the priests was absolutely unsurpassable in its vigor and the arrangement of its well-ordered silence. All work hard of their own accord, with much exertion, and each looks after his appointed task. Their service is unremitting, sharing the sacrifices, some undertaking the carrying of wood, others oil, others wheaten flour, others the sweet spices, others offering burnt offerings of the parts of the flesh—all of them exerting their strength in different ways. (Let. Aris. 92)

Aristeas also praises the priests' skill in butchery: "They divide the legs of the bullocks with both hands, though they are more than two talents in weight in almost every case, and then with an upward movement rip off with each hand in an amazing way a sufficiently large portion with unerring accuracy" (93). When one gets tired, "They have a rest room set aside, where those who are resting sit down. When this happens, some of those who are rested stand up with alacrity, but no one orders the arrangements of their ministry" (94).

Not all the priests were aristocratic. Priests were not to grow their own food (Sanders, 293), but the ordinary priests and Levites probably had other work, like serving as masons or scribes (Hengel and Deines, 50). Babatha's legal documents (see above, 5.4; 7.8) provide evidence of the work of scribes in Ein Gedi, Petra, and perhaps even Maḥoza. The temple administration would have required a sizeable cadre of scribes, some of whom were probably Levites (Sanders, 296). Josephus adds that priests served as judges, "for the appointed duties of the priests included general supervision, the trial of cases of litigation, and the punishment of condemned persons" (*Ag. Ap.* 2.187; cf. m. Sanh. 1:3). In a change that Josephus resented (ca. 64 CE), Agrippa II allowed the Levites to sing from memory rather than hold heavy scrolls and to wear linen like the priests (*Ant.* 20.216–218).

18.5 Priests in Galilee

It is striking that Jesus never interacts with a priest or Levite in Galilee. When Jesus healed a leper, he ordered him, "Go, show yourself to the priest, and offer the gift that Moses commanded, as a testimony to them" (Matt 8:4//Mark 1:44//Luke 5:14; cf. Luke 17:14), complying with the Mosaic law. Although it is not clear, Jesus presumably directs the man to a local priest. In the passion narratives, the chief priests and the high priest are principal actors; ordinary priests are not mentioned. The possible exception is Matthew's improbable allegation that the (chief?) priests devised a plan to give money to the soldiers guarding Jesus' tomb if they would say his disciples stole his body while they were asleep (28:12–13). References to priests are also scarce in Acts: some priests came to the disciples while they were teaching in the temple (4:1), and "a great many of the priests became obedient to the faith" (6:7).

Although some texts refer to priests living outside of Jerusalem, we have no explicit reference to priests in Galilee before the destruction of the temple in 70 CE. This does not mean there were no priests or Levites in the Galilean towns and cities, although most priests probably lived in Judea, closer to the temple, since they had regular duties there. Josephus reports that during the revolt the Zealots, after casting lots, appointed Phanni, a priest who lived in Aphthia, an otherwise unknown village, who "scarcely knew what the high priesthood meant" (*J.W.* 4.155–156).

Where evidence is lacking, we can only make reasonable assumptions, as does Sanders: "It is not unreasonable to suppose that a few thousand priests and Levites lived in Jerusalem in Josephus' day. The rest lived in the cities of Judaea and Galilee, but we have no idea of their distribution. . . . If aristocratic priests lived anywhere other than Jerusalem, Sepphoris is the most probable city. We may assume, in any case, that the ordinary priests were scattered through the main parts of the country" (279–80). Josephus adds suggestive information in the course of narrating his activities in Galilee early in the First Jewish Revolt. Whereas his fellow priests, Joazar and Judas, accepted the tithes the Galileans brought to them, amassing "a large sum of money," Josephus chose not to accept them (*Life* 63, 80). Whether "Josephus thought that priests also were entitled to tithes, not just the 10 percent from Levitical tithes," is debated (Udoh, 256–57). On the other hand, it appears that the people were used to paying tithes locally (Udoh, 274–75).

When the authorities in Jerusalem sent a delegation to remove Josephus, they included two priests, instructing them to ascertain the reason for the Galileans' support of Josephus. If it was because he was a priest, they were to answer that they too were priests (*Life* 198). The discovery of the stone in the synagogue at Migdal bearing images apparently associated with the temple suggests a close association between Galilean Jews and the temple (see above 3.2; 5.4). Josephus refers to Joseph ben Illem, a priest in the time of Herod the Great, who served in place of the high priest when the high priest was defiled because he had a wet dream (*Ant.* 17.166–167). Rabbinic sources say this Joseph was from Sepphoris (b. Yoma 12b; Jeremias, 194, n. 146; Freyne 1980, 285). Josephus, however, does not say that Joseph ben Illem came from Sepphoris, and he never says that the city was a center of priestly families (Miller, 252–54).

Although the Galileans' support for Josephus and their readiness to pay their tithes argue in favor of their attachment to Jerusalem and their practice regarding tithing, the situation may have been more complicated. About the same time, Rabbi Simeon ben Gamaliel and Rabban Johanan ben Zakkai wrote a letter to men in upper and lower Galilee, reminding them that the tithe due in the fourth year had not been collected (b. Sanh. 11b; Freyne 1980, 282). Were some Galileans reticent to send tithes to Jerusalem rather than give them to local priests? Did some Galileans chafe at paying a portion of their produce to priests who may have been rich landowners? Clearly, our knowledge of the activities of priests and Levites in Galilee is limited in the extreme.

18.6 Reflections

Related to these questions is the overarching issue of the place of the temple in the lives and practices of Galilean Jews. The material remains—including *miqva'ot*, cooking and dining pottery, oil lamps, and tombs and ossuaries—point to a close relationship between Galilean Jews and Jerusalem on one hand and provide signs of a cultural divide between the wealthy Judean priests and the rural population of Galilee on the other. Seán Freyne's observation that Josephus presented Jews in Galilee and Judea as having "a shared symbolic world-view, of which the Jerusalem temple was the central focal point" (1987, 607), seems now to be confirmed by archaeology (Berlin, 467–69). At the same time, excavations in Jerusalem and Galilee fill out scenes of two different cultures.

> In the first century C.E., Jerusalem's wealthiest residents entertained in formal dining rooms of Hellenistic style, prepared Roman dishes in Italian-style pans, and used beautifully decorated serving dishes and individual place settings. They built elaborate, public display tombs whose large courtyards and impressive facades provided a classicizing backdrop for opulent funeral ceremonies. Formal dining and elaborate funerals were practices previously confined to Judean royalty—both the Hasmonean kings and Herod, in the first century B.C.E. Their adoption by Jerusalem's elites likely accompanied and fostered a sense of social superiority. At this same time Jews in Galilee and Gaulanitis chose to live by a very different cultural ethic, in which even a few decorated serving vessels had no place. (Berlin, 467)

The artifacts from these cultures "reflect a marked fissure between Jerusalem elites, including some priests, and the majority of Jews living in the Judean countryside, Galilee, and Gaulanitis. Over the course of the first century C.E. that fissure probably weakened the link between position and moral authority, which in turn created a space and platform for new voices and different agendas" (Berlin, 470). Seen in this context, Jesus may well have been one of those "new voices" filling the space and calling Galileans to prepare for the coming of God's kingdom, which would vanquish Roman domination and establish justice: "Your kingdom come. Your will be done on earth as it is in heaven" (Matt 6:10). Preparation for the coming kingdom required confrontation of the Jerusalem aristocracy in the temple. Jesus' threat to the stability of Jerusalem could not be tolerated, however, and led quickly to his death. Nevertheless, this sequence of events does not support a dichotomy according to which Jesus was received in Galilee but rejected in Jerusalem. The Synoptic Gospels attest to opposition in the Galilean towns and villages also (Matt 11:21; Mark 6:3–6; Luke 4:28–29; Freyne 2001, 310); in Jerusalem he encountered the full force of the joint interests of the Jewish aristocracy and the Romans.

Works Cited in Chapter 18

Adler, Yonatan. 2022. *The Origins of Judaism: An Archaeological-Historical Reappraisal.* AYBRL. New Haven: Yale University Press.

Baden, Joel S. 2011. "The Violent Origins of the Levites: Text and Tradition." Pages 103–16 in Leuchter and Hutton.

Berlin, Andrea M. 2005. "Jewish Life before the Revolt: The Archaeological Evidence." *JSJ* 36.4:417–70.

Cook, Stephen L. 2011. "Those Stubborn Levites: Overcoming Levitical Disenfranchisement." Pages 155–70 in Leuchter and Hutton.

Evans, Craig A. 2006. "Excavating Caiaphas, Pilate, and Simon of Cyrene: Assessing the Literary and Archaeological Evidence." Pages 323–40 in *Jesus and Archaeology*. Edited by James H. Charlesworth. Grand Rapids: Eerdmans.

Freyne, Séan. 1980. *Galilee from Alexander the Great to Hadrian, 323 B.C.E. to 135 C.E.: A Study of Second Temple Judaism.* Wilmington, DE: Glazier.

———. 1987. "Galilee-Jerusalem Relations according to Josephus' Life." *NTS* 33:600–609.

———. 2001. "The Geography of Restoration: Galilee-Jerusalem Relations in Early Jewish and Christian Experience." *NTS* 47:289–311.

Hengel, Martin, and Roland Deines. 1995. "E. P. Sanders' 'Common Judaism,' Jesus, and the Pharisees." *JTS* 46:1–70.

Jeremias, Joachim. 1969. *Jerusalem in the Time of Jesus.* Translated by F. H. and C. H. Cave. Philadelphia: Fortress.

Kugler, Robert A. 2009. "Priests and Levites." *NIDB* 4:596–613.

———. 2010. "Priests." *EDEJ*, 1096–99.

Leuchter, Mark A., and Jeremy M. Hutton, eds. 2011. *Levites and Priests in Biblical History and Tradition.* AIL 9. Atlanta: Society of Biblical Literature.

Miller, Stuart S. 2015. *At the Intersection of Texts and Material Finds: Stepped Pools, Stone Vessels, and Ritual Purity.* JAJSup 16. Göttingen: Vandenhoeck & Ruprecht.

Nurmela, Risto. 1998. *The Levites: Their Emergence as a Second-Class Priesthood.* SFSHJ 193. Atlanta: Scholars Press.

Rehm, Merlin D. 1992. "Levites and Priests." *ABD* 4:297–310.

Reinhartz, Adele. 2011. *Caiaphas the High Priest.* Columbia: University of South Carolina Press.

Rooke, Deborah. 2000. *Zadok's Heirs: The Role and Development of the High Priesthood in Ancient Israel.* Oxford: Oxford University Press.

Sanders, E. P. 2016. *Judaism: Practice and Belief, 63 BCE–66 CE.* Minneapolis: Fortress.

Seeman, Chris. 2013. *Rome and Judea in Transition: Hasmonean Relations with the Roman Republic and the Evolution of the High Priesthood.* New York: Lang.

Udoh, Fabian E. 2020. *To Caesar What Is Caesar's: Tribute, Taxes, and Imperial Administration in Early Roman Palestine (63 B.C.E.–70 C.E.).* 2nd ed.. BJS 343. Providence, RI: Brown University.

Part VI

Outcasts

Chapter 19

Samaritans

Good Samaritan (Luke 10:25–37)

"*T*he Good Samaritan" is the most widely known of the characters in Jesus' parables. Anyone who stops to help another person is apt to be called "a good samaritan" (often not capitalized). Webster's dictionary offers a definition of "Samaritan" as "one ready and generous in helping those in distress"—hardly a definition one would have gotten in Galilee or Judea!

Only in the last several decades has the study of the Samaritans, the Samaritan Pentateuch, Second Temple Judaism, and excavations on Mount Gerizim brought the history, beliefs, and practices of the Samaritans into clearer focus. The Samaritans wrote no histories before the Byzantine period, so we depend on fragmentary, polemical, and at points erroneous accounts, especially by Josephus. Jewish and Christian histories have regularly denied that the Samaritans were Israelites, labeling them "Cutheans," from Babylonia, based on 2 Kings 17:24. Archaeological discoveries now require extensive corrections to earlier histories, especially for the Persian, Hellenistic, and Hasmonean periods.

19.1. The History of Samaria and the Samaritans

Although there are multiple references to Samaria in the Old Testament, especially in 1 and 2 Kings and 2 Chronicles, the only reference to Samaritans is in 2 Kings 17:29: "But every nation still made gods of its own and put them in the shrines of the high places that the people of Samaria [*hasomeronim*] had made, every nation in the cities in which they lived." The name may derive from its etymology, "Keepers of the Law" or "Guardians of the Torah," rather than from geography (Mor, 1). The term "Samaritans" is therefore ambiguous, sometimes meaning inhabitants of Samaria

(Samarians), and at other times designating religious or ethnic monotheists (Samaritans) who worshiped the God of the patriarchs (Hall, 40; Zangenberg, 394, n. 3). By the first century CE, Samaria had a very diverse population, which also included Jewish settlers (from the Hasmonean period) and gentiles (e.g., Sidonians and descendants of Macedonian, Seleucid, and Roman soldiers settled in Samaria).

Samaria sat between the coastal plain on the west and the Jordan River valley on the east, Galilee to the north, and Judea to the south (Avi-Jonah, 151–54). The coastal plain produced grain, and the hill country exported wine and olive oil. The main north-south road ran from Ginaea (Jenin) in the north through Shechem and Gofna (Jifna) in the south and was intersected by east-west roads at each of these three points (Zangenberg, 398–402). Herod's harbor at Caesarea Maritima provided a point of entry for construction materials for Sebaste and export for Samaria's produce.

19.1.1 Origins

Origins are almost by definition obscure, yet the obscurity of Samaritan origins has allowed scholars to point to a wide range of events as marking the beginning of Samaritanism: the building of an altar at Shiloh, the introduction of foreign peoples following the Assyrian conquest, the construction of the temple on Mount Gerizim (Kartveit 2009, 351), divergent responses to the Seleucids during the reign of Antiochus IV (175–164 BCE), the destruction of the Samaritan temple by John Hyrcanus (Knoppers, 218–19; Wardle, 29–30), and the work of the Samaritan leader Baba Rabba in the third century CE (Crown 1991b). A related issue is identifying when Israelites became Jews. Did Samaritans diverge from Judaism, or are both "paternal traditions of the People of Israel" (Tsedaka, 419) that developed their own special traditions? Another question concerns the origin of the Samaritan Pentateuch. The following paragraphs review key moments in the history of Samaria (see further Pummer 2010).

The Samaritans claim to be Israelites, descendants of the tribes of Ephraim and Manasseh, and Yahwists. Abraham and Jacob built altars at Shechem (Gen 12:6–7; 33:18–20). According to the Samaritans, the Lord commanded Moses and Joshua to build an altar on Mount Gerizim. Whereas the Hebrew text of Deuteronomy 11:29–30 reads, "Set the blessing on Mount Gerizim, . . . beyond the Jordan, some distance to the west, in the land of the Canaanites who live in the Arabah, opposite Gilgal, beside the oak of Moreh" (cf. Deut 27:12; Josh 8:33; 9:7), the Samaritan Pentateuch adds, "near Shechem" (Magen 2008a, 4). God cursed the house of Eli at

Shiloh because of the corruption and immorality of Eli and his sons (1 Sam 2:27–36; 1 Kgs 2:27; Ps 78:60; Jer 7:12; Anderson 1992, 941).

On the other hand, 2 Kings 17:17–34, probably penned at the time of Ezra, Nehemiah, and Chronicles and later cited by Josephus (*Ant.* 9:277–291), says the Samaritans are descendants of the nations the Assyrians settled in Israel:

> The people of Israel continued in all the sins that Jeroboam committed; they did not depart from them until the LORD removed Israel out of his sight, as he had foretold through all his servants the prophets. So Israel was exiled from their own land to Assyria until this day. The king of Assyria brought people from Babylon, Cuthah, Avva, Hamath, and Sepharvaim, and placed them in the cities of Samaria in place of the people of Israel; they took possession of Samaria, and settled in its cities. (2 Kgs 17:22–24)

These verses appear to state that *all* the Israelites were exiled, and thereafter Samaria was populated by gentiles, "Cutheans," as they came to be called. Ferdinand Dexinger corrects this reading: "The report in II Kings 17 is not a description of historical facts but a postexilic polemic with the purpose of justifying the rejection of the Gentile worshippers of the God of Israel, who were living in the former northern kingdom" (1981, 91). Kartveit adds, "The idea of a separation or schism or split presupposes that there was a unity, which is doubtful. If anything, the returnees created the split or the separation by not cooperating with the people of the land" (2009, 370; cf. Kartveit 2018, 3–18).

The issue is whether some Israelites remained in Samaria following the Assyrian deportation, maintaining continuity with their traditions. Josephus says the Assyrian king "transported all its [Samaria's] people to Media and Persia" and took "other nations from a region called Chūthos" and settled them in Samaria (*Ant.* 9.278–279). According to 2 Kings 17:18, only "the tribe of Judah . . . was left." Sargon II's inscriptions [*ANET*, 284–85] say, however, that he deported 27,290 Israelites from Samaria (cf. 2 Kgs 18:11). Because the imported foreign people did not worship the God of Israel, the author of 2 Kings says the Assyrian king sent one of the deported priests back to teach them "the law of the god of the land" (17:27). In this way, a syncretistic cult arose, worshiping the God of Israel but also foreign gods and practicing child sacrifice (17:29–34): "But every nation still made gods of its own and put them in the shrines of the high places that the people of Samaria had made" (2 Kgs 17:29).

Contrary to 2 Kings 17, the Chronicler attests that at least a remnant, perhaps a majority, of the northern Israelites continued to live in Samaria following the Assyrian conquest (Schur, 21; Tsedaka, 420). Others fled to Jerusalem, the Jordan valley, and surrounding areas. According to the Chronicler, Hezekiah and Josiah attempted to curtail the syncretistic practices in Samaria and centralize worship in Jerusalem (2 Chr 30:1, 10–11, 25). The foreign peoples arrived in waves over time (Ezra 4:2, 10) and settled in various areas. At least some Samaritans participated in the worship in Jerusalem (Jer 41:5) until its destruction by the Babylonians (587 BCE). The disparity between Kings and Chronicles may have originated among the deportees in Babylon. Yitzhak Magen concludes, "We believe that the reports in Chronicles of a surviving remnant in Samaria are based on the historical reality, while the Book of Kings conceals the existence of a remnant in Israel. The Assyrian conquest left a large Israelite population in Samaria" (2008a, 6; cf. Magen 2007, 187; Dexinger 1981, 107).

19.1.2 The Persian Period

During their exile in Babylon, the Israelites from the tribes of Judah and Benjamin (Ezra 1:5) resisted assimilation and maintained their identity by emphasizing monotheism, the Torah, and purity of descent. The Jewish community in Babylon would continue for centuries, as evident by the Babylonian Talmud a millennium later. In their view, they were the chosen people. Consequently, those who returned to rebuild Jerusalem following the Edict of Cyrus the Great in 538 BCE (Ezra 1:1–4; cf. the Cyrus Cylinder: https://www.britishmuseum.org/collection/object/W_1880-0617-1941) held different views from those who had stayed in Judah during the exile; they resisted mingling with non-Israelites.

Jerusalem lay in ruins; Samaria was the stronger of the two. Some of the people in the area offered to help rebuild the temple: "We will build with you. For we obey your Lord just as you do and we have been sacrificing to him ever since the days of King Esar-haddon of the Assyrians" (1 Esd 5:65–66). Zerubbabel refused, however: "You have nothing to do with us in building the house for the Lord our God, for we alone will build it for the Lord of Israel, as Cyrus, the king of the Persians, has commanded us" (5:67–68). In response, these "adversaries of Judah and Benjamin" (Ezra 4:1) cut off their supplies, wrote a letter to King Artaxerxes (4:7–24), and impeded construction of the temple for two years (1 Esd 5:69–70; Josephus, *Ant.* 11.84–88). When Darius succeeded Artaxerxes, the Samaritans asked Darius to rescind his order that they pay tribute to the Jews to help build the temple, but Darius rejected their petition (*Ant.* 11.114–119).

When Nehemiah arrived in 445 BCE to rebuild the walls of Jerusalem, he was opposed by the governors of the neighboring territories: Sanballat in Samaria, Tobiah in the trans-Jordan (Ammon), and Geshem, leader of the Arab tribes in what would become Idumea. Political intermarriages were common. Continuing the insistence on maintaining the purity of Israel, Ezra and Nehemiah forbade intermarriage with non-Jews (Ezra 10; Neh 13:23–27).

During this period, Nehemiah's adversary—Sanballat, a Samaritan of Israelite descent—built the first stage of the temple on the top of Mount Gerizim (Magen 2008a, 10; Magen 2008b, 103; Pummer 2018, 58), likely in an effort to maintain Samaria's superiority over Judah. Josephus claims that the Samaritan temple was built on the same plan as the Jerusalem temple (*Ant.* 13.256). A letter (CAP, no. 30, 408 BCE) from the Jewish community in Elephantine (Egypt) refers to "the sons of Sanballat governor of Samaria" and requests assistance from both the Samaritans and the Jews to help them rebuild their temple.

In the context of addressing intermarriage, Nehemiah writes, "One of the sons of Jehoiada, son of the high priest Eliashib, was the son-in-law of Sanballat the Horonite; I chased him away from me. Remember them, O my God, because they have defiled the priesthood, the covenant of the priests and the Levites" (Neh 13:28–29). According to Josephus, Sanballat established a line of Samaritan priests who were descendants of the Jerusalem high priest's family by marrying his daughter to the high priest's son.

> But Sanballat promised not only to preserve the priesthood for him but also to procure for him the power and office of high priest and to appoint him governor of all the places over which he ruled, if he were willing to live with his daughter; and he said that he would build a temple similar to that in Jerusalem on Mount Gerizim—this is the highest of the mountains near Samaria—and undertook to do these things with the consent of King Darius. (*Ant.* 11.310–311)

Sanballat may also have recruited priests and Levites from Jerusalem to serve in Samaria (Magen 2008a, 13). Once again, however, there is no evidence to corroborate Josephus's claim that the Samaritan priesthood derived from Jerusalem (Purvis 1986, 88). Nevertheless, the emergence of priests at the Samaritan temple was another step in the rift between Jews worshiping in Jerusalem and Samaritans worshiping on Mount Gerizim. As Dexinger observes, "Once such rival groups exist they tend to establish criteria for legitimacy and for mutual excommunication" (1981, 102).

Josephus gives a confusing and erroneous account that places the building of the temple on Mount Gerizim not in the Persian period but at the time of Alexander the Great's conquest of Palestine. Sanballat's daughter

Nikaso was married to Manasses, the brother of the Jewish high priest; thus Sanballat promised his son-in-law he would build a temple on Mount Gerizim similar to the one in Jerusalem with the consent of Darius III (336–331 BCE; *Ant.* 11.309–311). Whether this Sanballat was Nehemiah's adversary or a later descendant with the same name is debated (Pummer 2009, 114–18, 139–40, 147–50). Writing in 1923, Arthur E. Cowley saw the source of the confusion: "Josephus has gone astray by confusing the two kings Darius and the two officials Bigvia, and then filled his history largely by imagination" (110). Josephus adds that division among the Jews served the interests of the king (*Ant.* 11.323), showing that Darius did not distinguish between Jews and Samaritans. According to Josephus, when Alexander invaded Palestine, Sanballat shifted his allegiance to Alexander and sent 8,000 men to join the siege of Tyre (*Ant.* 11.321). In response, Alexander consented to Sanballat's building the Samaritan temple and appointing Manasses as its high priest (*Ant.* 11.324; 13.256).

Excavations on Mount Gerizim now prove that the Samaritan temple was built in the fifth century BCE, not in the time of Alexander (Magen 2007; 2008a, 16; Pummer 2009, 150). A second phase of building occurred during the reign of Antiochus III, early in the second century BCE. A small golden bell, which probably once hung from the fringes of the high priest's ephod, was recovered in the excavation of the temple area (Magen 2007, 170).

Aside from its chronological inaccuracy, Josephus's account clearly disparages the Samaritans, calling them "Cutheans; their temple was built with the approval of Alexander, not by divine command; and the first high priest was a renegade Jew, who had married a foreigner and whose ambition was the reason why the temple was built in the first place" (Pummer 2009, 118).

19.1.3 The Hellenistic Period

Samaritans initially supported Alexander the Great, but after he moved on to Egypt, they revolted and burned alive Andromachus, the governor appointed by Alexander. When Alexander returned from Egypt, the leaders of the revolt and their families, some two hundred men, women, and children, fled to a cave in Wadi ed-Daliyeh, north of Jericho, where they were discovered and massacred. Papyri, coins, seals, and other items recovered from the cave shed light on the material culture and language of Samaria in that period (Pummer 1989a, 175–77). Alexander destroyed the city of Samaria and built Shechem as a gentile military and administrative center, so the Samaritans moved to Mount Gerizim and settled around the temple.

Josephus is confused about the distinct populations: gentiles at Shechem and Samaritans on Mount Gerizim. His bias remains constant, however. He charges that the Samaritans "alter their attitude according to circumstance and, when they see the Jews prospering, call them their kinsmen" (*Ant.* 9.290–291). When the Samaritans saw how Alexander treated the Jews in Jerusalem honorably, they professed to be Jews, but Shechem was "inhabited by apostates from the Jewish nation" (*Ant.* 11.340). When the Jews were in trouble, however, the Samaritans "deny that they have any kinship with them [the Jews], thereby indeed admitting the truth[;] but whenever they see some splendid bit of good fortune come to them, they suddenly grasp at the connexion with them, saying that they are related to them and tracing their line back to Ephraim and Manasseh, the descendants of Joseph" (*Ant.* 11.340–341). Moreover, "whenever anyone was accused by the people of Jerusalem of eating unclean food or violating the Sabbath or committing any other such sin, he would flee to the Shechemites, saying that he had been unjustly expelled" (*Ant.* 11.346–347). Herold Weiss points out Josephus's bias: he "chooses to exhibit his dislike of the Samaritans by presenting them as Sabbath breakers who welcome other Sabbath breakers" (384).

The situation was more complex with periods of collaboration between the elites in Samaria and Jerusalem (Knoppers, 174). The city on Mount Gerizim flourished during the Ptolemaic period (301–198 BCE). Two inscriptions from Delos, dated 250–175 BCE and 150–50 BCE respectively, attest a synagogue at Delos at that time and that they sent offerings to Mount Gerizim (Pummer 1989a, 141, 150–51; Magen 2008a, 20; cf. Runesson, 185–87). A second phase of construction of the Samaritan temple began under Antiochus III (Magen 2008b, 103, 176), as did work on the temple in Jerusalem. Evidently Antiochus III (ca. 242–187 BCE) did not discriminate between Jews and Samaritans.

Rivalry between Jews and Samaritans and their respective temples intensified, with each claiming to be the older sanctuary and hence the legitimate one. Josephus boasts that when the matter was presented to Ptolemy Philometor (186–145 BCE), he ruled that the Jerusalem temple had been built in accordance with the laws of Moses and put the Samaritan delegation to death (*Ant.* 13.74–79). Josephus's bias again makes it difficult to judge the veracity of his claims. Ben Sirach (ca. 195–180 BCE) professed the same bias: "Two nations my soul detests, and the third is not even a people: those who live in Seir and the Philistines and the foolish people that live in Shechem" (50:25–26).

Josephus further asserts that during the Ptolemaic period the Samaritans did "mischief to the Jews by laying waste their land and carrying off slaves" (*Ant.* 12.156). Josephus relates this activity somewhat ambiguously to Onias II's refusal to pay tribute to Ptolemy III (246–221 BCE). Josephus's bias is again evident, raising questions about the origin of this report and its historicity (Pummer 2009, 156–61). Samaria emerges once again in the Maccabean period. When Antiochus IV Epiphanes ordered reprisals against the Jews, he did not distinguish between the Jews and the Samaritans. "He [Antiochus IV] left governors to oppress the people: at Jerusalem, Philip, by birth a Phrygian and in character more barbarous than the man who appointed him; and at Gerizim, Andronicus; and besides these Menelaus, who lorded it over his compatriots worse than the others did" (2 Macc 5:22–23).

Either willingly (according to Josephus) or unwillingly (according to 2 Macc 6:2), the Samaritans renamed their sanctuary for Zeus. According to Josephus, a group of Sidonians in Samaria, without consent of the priests, sent a delegation to Antiochus IV, declaring that they were not Jews and requesting that the temple be named the temple of Zeus Hellenios, a request that Antiochus granted (*Ant.* 12.257–261). Menahem Mor suggests that the petition came from Samaritan Hellenists who presented themselves as "Sidonians of Shechem" to distance themselves from the Jews (15). Pummer responds, "Had the Samaritans been as thoroughly Hellenized as *Ant.* 12.257–264 makes it appear, the Samaritans would hardly have demanded that their sacrifices go to Mt. Gerizim" (2009, 178). Josephus simply reports the incident because it portrays the Samaritans as cowards and liars.

According to 2 Maccabees, which Josephus never follows, the change of name was forced on the Samaritans: "Not long after this, the king [Antiochus IV] sent an Athenian senator to compel the Jews to forsake the laws of their ancestors and no longer to live by the laws of God; also to pollute the temple in Jerusalem and to call it the temple of Olympian Zeus, and to call the one in Gerizim the temple of Zeus-the-Friend-of-Strangers, as did the people who lived in that place" (6:1–2). The fact that this move did not lead to a counteraction in Samaria, as it did in Jerusalem, "suggests a totally different religious and cultural atmosphere" in Jerusalem and Samaria, with Samaria accepting Hellenism more tolerantly (Freyne, 266). Yet, "if both sides, the Samaritans and the Jews, suffered the same fate during Antiochus' persecution, why didn't they cooperate and fight together against the Seleucids? Why didn't the Samaritans join the Maccabean Revolt? The answer to this question is that we are dealing with two different groups that could never cooperate, not even when they faced a common enemy" (Mor, 15). At least in this situation, the ancient proverb "My enemy's enemy is my friend" did not apply. First Maccabees, which records that Judas Maccabeus sent his brother Simon to rescue Israelites in Galilee from the gentiles and bring them to Jerusalem (5:14–23), suggests that "even from an early period Galilean attachment to the Jerusalem temple was unwavering" (Freyne, 275).

19.1.4 The Hasmonean Period

The traditional date for the destruction of the Samaritan temple has been 128 BCE, but that date has now been shown to be incorrect. Coins found at the site continue until 112–110 BCE (Magen 2008a, 27; Bourgel, 506, 511; cf. Josephus, *Ant.* 13.249, 254–257; *J.W.* 1.61–63). More important than the date of the destruction is its severity. The city on Mount Gerizim was not walled, and many of the houses had wood in the walls or roof. Archaeologists found that the outer walls of the houses around the perimeter had been fortified. After the destruction, the bodies were removed, and the city was burned, fulfilling Deuteronomy's prescription of the total destruction and burning of a city that went out from them (13:13–17), thereby also precluding any resettlement (Magen 2008a, 25–26). Anti-Samaritan stories that tied the punishment of the Samaritans to the rape of Dinah appear in the literature of this period (Gen 34; Jdt 9:2–4; Jub 30.5–7; T. Levi 5.3; 7.2–3).

John Hyrcanus was bitterly anti-Samaritan (Josephus, *Ant.* 13.275). Shortly later (108–107 BCE), Hyrcanus's sons mounted a yearlong siege of the city of Samaria (*J.W.* 1.64–65), sacked it, and left it to be "swept away by the mountain-torrents" (*Ant.* 13.281). Hyrcanus ensured that there would be no rival center of power in Samaria and that it would remain under Jerusalem's control, as it did until Rome repopulated Samaria (Horsley, 37). On the other hand, the archaeological evidence reveals that while gentile settlements were destroyed or abandoned, "the Samaritans . . . were apparently allowed to remain on their lands" (Bourgel, 516). Accordingly, Hyrcanus destroyed the temple on Mount Gerizim and the city of priests that had grown up around it (Magen 2008b, 89) to complete his conquest of Samaria and compel Samaritans to bring their offerings to Jerusalem. Bourgel argues, "John Hyrcanus's destruction of the Samaritan temple was intended not as an act of exclusion but as an act of integration of the Samaritans into the Hasmonean state. It was a radical but entirely logical attempt to rally them to his authority as high priest of the Jerusalem temple" (517; cf. Raviv, 70–71). Although some Samaritans participated in sacrifices at the Jerusalem temple (Josephus, *Ant.* 18.29–30) and adopted Jewish purity rituals (Magen 2008a, 42), others were further alienated by the Jews' destruction of their temple. Over a century later, the woman at the well said, "Our ancestors worshiped on this mountain" (John 4:20)!

19.1.5 The Roman Period

Pompey (63 BCE) and Gabinius (57–55 BCE) restored the city of Samaria (Josephus, *J.W.* 1.155–157, 166; *Ant.* 14.74–76) but did not allow the

Samaritans to rebuild their temple. While Gabinius, governor of Syria, was away in Egypt, Alexander (d. 49 BCE), son of Aristobulus II, invaded Samaria, killing Romans and "besieging those who had taken refuge on Mount Gerizim" (*Ant.* 14.100). Herod the Great restored order in Samaria. After Octavian added Samaria to Herod's territory, he rebuilt the city, naming it Sebaste; brought in predominantly gentile settlers; and built a temple dedicated to Caesar on the summit of the hill (*Ant.* 15.292–293, 296–298; *J.W.* 1.403; see Isser, 572–73). One of Herod's ten wives, Malthace, was a native of Samaria; when Herod died, their son Archelaus became tetrarch of Judea, Idumea, and Samaria (4 BCE–6 CE).

During the time of the procurator Coponius (6–9 CE), some Samaritans defiled the temple on the eve of Passover by scattering human bones in it (Josephus, *Ant.* 18.29–30). Did the Samaritans celebrate Passover at the same time as the Jews, and would they not have defiled themselves by handling bones? Again, questions have been raised about the historicity of Josephus's reporting (Pummer 2009, 229–30). That Samaritans could enter the temple may also indicate that, following the destruction on Mount Gerizim, some Samaritans celebrated Passover in Jerusalem (Magen 2008a, 43; Bourgel, 521). Mishnah Rosh Hashanah 1:3 and 2:2 say the Jews used to light beacons to announce the beginning of a new month for Jewish communities outside of Jerusalem, but Samaritan "malpractices" (lighting misleading flares) led the Jews to send out messengers instead of using the beacons.

During the time of Pontius Pilate, in 36 CE, "a con man" or "messianic pretender" (Pummer 2009, 235; Hall, 38–40) persuaded some Samaritans to go with him to Mount Gerizim, where he would show them sacred vessels that Moses had buried there (cf. 2 Macc 2:4–8). His followers may have hoped that the recovery of the sacred vessels would lead to the restoration of the temple or to the coming of their Messiah (the *Taheb*, or Restorer), based on Deuteronomy 18:15, 18. Pilate blocked their ascent of the mountain with cavalry and heavy infantry. Some of the Samaritans were killed, others taken prisoner, and their leaders executed. When the Samaritans brought charges against Pilate before Vitellius, governor of Syria, he ordered Pilate to return to Rome (Josephus, *Ant.* 18.85–89).

Pilgrimages to Jerusalem contributed to the antagonism between Galileans and Samaritans (Freyne, 291). In 52 CE, when Cumanus was procurator, Samaritans massacred Jewish pilgrims at En-Gannim, a border town with Galilee. Josephus charges that Cumanus refused to become involved because he had been bribed by the Samaritans, so the Galileans took up arms and sacked Samaritan villages, leading Cumanus to side with the Samaritans and march against the Jews. The Samaritans then went to Ummidus Quadratus, governor of Syria, seeking redress. Quadratus traveled to

Samaria, where, according to Josephus, he determined that the Samaritans were at fault and crucified both the Samaritan and the Jewish leaders in the conflict. Agrippa the Younger intervened on behalf of the Jews; Emperor Claudius found in their favor and exiled Cumanus (*J.W.* 2.232–246; *Ant.* 20.118–136; Tacitus, *Ann.* 12.54; cf. Freyne, 74–76).

When the Samaritans mustered at Mount Gerizim while the Romans were preoccupied with the siege of Yodefat, Vespasian sent the fifth Roman legion to forestall a Samaritan revolt. Cerealius, the Roman commander, deployed his troops around the base of the mountain, cutting off the Samaritans' water supply. When the Samaritans refused Cerealius's call for them to surrender, his troops wiped them out (Josephus, *J.W.* 3.307–315). In 72 CE, the Romans built the city of Neapolis at the base of Mount Gerizim to keep the Samaritans from returning to their holy site (Magen 2009).

19.2. Samaritan Beliefs and Practices

Samaritanism was and still is a living tradition. In the absence of Samaritan texts from the first century and earlier, it is difficult to say much about Samaritan beliefs and practices during this period. They evolved over time, as is evident from later sources: Samaritan liturgical, halakic, and exegetical texts; and Jewish and Christian accounts.

Samaritans shared many beliefs and practices with Jews. In addition, like the Qumran community, they opposed the Jerusalem temple and priesthood and expected a Mosaic messiah. Both Samaritans and Essenes followed an alternative calendar, and neither group celebrated Purim or Hanukkah (Anderson 1992, 942).

Samaritans continued to use the old Hebrew script for the Torah even when the Jewish scribes adopted the Aramaic script (Purvis 1968, 18–52; Pummer 1989a, 136–38; Anderson 1989, 390–96; Magen 2008a, 68–69, 231–34). The oldest manuscript of the Samaritan Pentateuch is the Abisha Scroll, so-called because it is attributed to Aaron's great-grandson (1 Chr 6:50, "Abishua") in a cryptogram written by a twelfth-century scribe in Nablus (Crown 1975; Crown 1991a). The ancient scroll is a patchwork of texts, the oldest being the text of the end of Numbers and the book of Deuteronomy, which cannot be securely traced prior to Abu'l Fath in the latter half of the fourteenth century. Crown dates this oldest portion of the Abisha Scroll to around 1150, making it "one of the oldest Torah scrolls in the world" (Crown 1991a, 39).

The origin of the Samaritan Pentateuch is still debated. From the time the temple on Mount Gerizim was built, Samaritan priests would have needed a Torah to regulate cultic practice. Was there a common Torah, which the Samaritans revised? Or is the Pentateuch itself "the result of a prolonged collaboration between the two communities" (Knoppers, 178), cooperation in which the Samaritans had an "active role in the production of the Torah" (Römer, 92)? The biblical scrolls from Qumran suggest such a period of collaboration. The priests in Jerusalem and Samaria, for example, both acknowledged the Aaronide pedigree of the other (Knoppers, 190).

A prominent example of Samaritan tradition appears in an expansion of Exodus 20:17, where the Samaritan Pentateuch adds:

> And when it so happens that LORD God brings you to the land of Caanan, which you are coming to possess, you shall set-up there for you great stones and plaster them with plaster and you write on the stones all words of this law. And it becomes for you that across the Jordan you shall raise these stones, which I command you today, in mountain Grizim. And you build there the altar to the LORD God of you. Altar of stones. Not you shall wave on them iron. With whole stones you shall build the altar to LORD God of you. And you bring on it ascend offerings to LORD God of you, and you sacrifice peace offerings, and you eat there and you rejoice before the face of the LORD God of you. The mountain this is across the Jordan behind the way of the rising of the sun, in the land of Caanan who is dwelling in the desert before the Galgal, beside Alvin-Mara, before Sechem. (Samaritan Pentateuch in English: stepbible.org/?q=version=SPE|reference=Exo.20; cf. Dexinger 1981, 108–9)

A fragment of Deuteronomy 27:4–6 found at Qumran contains a similar text, reading "Gerizim" instead of "Ebal" (https://foundationjudaismchristianorigins.org/ftp/dead-sea-scrolls/unpub/DSS-deuteronomy.pdf). At issue is the formation of the Pentateuch in the exilic and postexilic periods. What are the earliest readings? Where have Jews and Samaritans introduced new readings? Over time, both traditions probably introduced new, variant readings (Hjelm, 13–75, 282–85).

In addition to the dispute about the proper holy place (Mount Gerizim or Jerusalem), the other major dispute between Jews and Samaritans concerned belief in the resurrection of the dead. Kutim, one of the minor tractates of the Talmud, says, "When shall we receive the Samaritans? When they renounce Mount Gerizim and acknowledge Jerusalem and the resurrection of the dead" (2:8; Magen 2008a, 66). Belief in the resurrection of the dead is not found in the Pentateuch and therefore was not accepted by Samaritans until later in their history (Dexinger 1989, 281–84; Lehnardt). Neither was the resurrection accepted by the Sadducees (Acts 23:8). The development and relationship between the various strands of Samaritan eschatology—including the *Taheb* (messiah), the new eon or time of Divine favor, and the resurrection of the dead, among others—are still unclear (Dexinger 1989, 292). When Jews as well as Samaritans began to build tombs to the patriarchs before the destruction of the Jerusalem temple in 70 CE, Samaritans built tombs in Samaria and the Transjordan. They venerated Moses especially, since he was given the Torah, and Deuteronomy 34:10 says, "Never since has there arisen a prophet in Israel like Moses, whom the LORD knew face to face." Although Deuteronomy 34:6 says no one knew Moses' burial place, the Samaritans built a worship site at Jebel Siyagha on Mount Nebo, perhaps as early as the Hellenistic period. If so, it might explain why John Hyrcanus attacked Madaba and Samagah in the Transjordan after destroying the Samaritan temple and town on Mount Gerizim (Magen 2008a, 66–67).

Earlier we have noted that *miqva'ot* were common in Judea and Galilee from the first century BCE until the second century CE (see above, 3.2), evidencing the heightened importance of ritual purity. It is significant, therefore, that Samaritans seem to have adopted this practice during the Hasmonean period, perhaps forced to do so by John Hyrcanus (Magen 2008a, 68, 183–86, 194). Samaritan priests would have maintained strict purity, just as the Jewish priests did, including avoidance of gentile impurity. Again, archaeological finds fill gaps in our literary sources. The Samaritans did not use imported (gentile) vessels. Magen reports, "Seven large cisterns unearthed at the sacred precinct of Mt. Gerizim bear witness to the large quantity of water needed for the rite and for purification, and almost every residential house on the Mount contained a rock-cut or built and plastered stone bath" (2008a, 184). In addition, a small vat was found at an olive press, no doubt so that workers would not communicate uncleanness to the oil (see above, 10.3). The laws concerning priestly purity became obsolete for the Samaritans following the destruction of their temple, explaining the paucity of Samaritan *miqva'ot* during the Roman period (Magen 2008a, 184–85).

Samaritan communities survived but could not return to Mount Gerizim until the fourth century, when they built a synagogue there. Other Samaritan synagogues from the same period are identifiable because they face Mount Gerizim or contain Samaritan inscriptions, but the orientations of the synagogues are not always consistent (Magen 2008a, 117–80; Pummer 2018, 51–54).

Some rituals and practices originated in antiquity, although others have arisen or changed across the centuries (Pummer 1989b). Today, Samaritans wash before they pray, but the origin of this practice is unclear. Amulets of bronze, silver, and stone have been preserved since the Roman-Byzantine period, and Samaritans wrote the Decalogue on their doorposts, in accord with Deuteronomy 6:9. Circumcision was strictly practiced, and the Samaritan Pentateuch of Genesis 17:14 adds, "on the eighth day." Observance of the Sabbath is fundamental for Samaritans, as it is for Jews. Passover is their most important festival, and they celebrate it on Mount Gerizim, worshiping outdoors whenever possible, as in generations past, but it is not always celebrated on the same dates as the Jewish Passover. The Samaritans also celebrate Shavuot (the giving of the law, Pentecost), the Day of Atonement, and Sukkot (Booths).

19.3. Reflections

The Gospels present varying accounts of Jesus' teachings regarding the Samaritans, no doubt reflecting to some degree differing perspectives among the evangelists and their communities. Matthew (alone) has Jesus instructing the disciples, "Go nowhere among the gentiles, and enter no town of the Samaritans, but go rather to the lost sheep of the house of Israel" (10:5–6); also, in Matthew (20:29) and Mark (10:46) Jesus does not travel through Samaria but through Jericho. Josephus, who (as we have seen) regularly disparages the Samaritans, reports that Jews traveled through Samaria "for rapid travel" because "Jerusalem may be reached in three days from Galilee" (*Life* 269). The alternate route, preferred by Galileans who wanted to avoid Samaria, led down the Jordan River valley to Jericho and up to Jerusalem. In Luke 9:52 and John 4:1–42, Jesus travels through Samaria with his disciples. In Luke, Jesus also travels "through the region between Samaria and Galilee" (17:11), then through Jericho (18:35; 19:1), while John never mentions Jericho. John reports Jesus' conversation with a Samaritan woman at the well near Sychar (John 4), explaining, presumably for gentile readers, that "Jews do not share things in common with Samaritans" (4:9).

Luke records two events in Samaria. First, when messengers whom Jesus sent ahead entered "a village of the Samaritans," the Samaritans would not receive him, prompting the offer of James and John to "command fire to come down from heaven and consume them" (9:52–54). The way Luke refers to the village may be very specific: not merely a village in Samaria but a Samaritan village as opposed to a gentile village. The question is whether in the first century some towns and villages in Samaria were predominantly gentile while others were Samaritan (Raviv, 71–72; Magen 2008a, 81–83).

The ambiguity of the term "Samaritan," which can have a geographical or an ethnic/religious sense, clouds the interpretation of key passages.

Josephus generally uses "Samarian" geographically, that is, to designate inhabitants of Samaria (Böhm, 147–51; Isser, 575), but at times to refer to inhabitants with an Israelite heritage (*Ant.* 12.257). Josephus is not always consistent. Discussing *Jewish Antiquities* 12.154–156, Crown observes, "In this account the Samaritans are described by Josephus as *Samareis*, a term which he appears to reserve for the Greek colons of Samaria in the part of his work relating to this period, and it is likely that these were not Samaritan Jews but Greek settlers in Samaria who were pro-Ptolemaic" (1991b, 28–29). But as Crown also notes, Josephus uses the same term for "the Samaritans who worshipped at the temple on Mount Gerizim" in *Antiquities* 13.74; in 12.257, where he is also writing of those who worshiped on Mount Gerizim, he uses *hoi Samareitai*.

John is similarly ambiguous, referring to the woman at the well both as "a woman of Samaria" (*gynē ek tēs Samareias*, 4:7) and as "a Samaritan woman" (*hē gynē hē Samaritis* and *gynaikos Samaritidos*, 4:9). Similarly, John says that Jesus came to "a city of Samaria" (*polin tēs Samareias*, 4:5; cf. Acts 8:5); but then, after the woman says, "Our ancestors worshiped on this mountain," John reports that "many Samaritans [*Samaritōn*] from that city believed in him" (4:39), and the Samaritans (*hoi Samaritai*) "asked him to stay with them" (4:40). John's explanation that "Jews do not share things in common with Samaritans" (4:9) presumably means ethnic/religious Samaritans.

Returning to the issue raised above, Luke 9:52, Matthew 10:5, and Acts 8:25 all refer to a "city/village(s) of the Samaritans" (*Samaritōn*) in a context in which the meaning may be religious: Samaritan as opposed to gentile cities or villages in Samaria. A Samaritan village would have been more likely to deny hospitality to Jews on their way to Jerusalem; giving the term a religious sense, the Matthean Jesus forbids the disciples to enter a village of Samaritans (10:5). To date, excavations reveal a common material culture, making it difficult to distinguish Samaritan from Jewish communities (Pummer 1989a; Zangenberg, 405, 408–13). We can hope that future excavations will clarify whether gentiles and Samaritans in Samaria were generally segregated or lived in the same towns and villages.

At least when Luke reports that the one leper (out of ten) who returned praising God was a Samaritan (17:16), and that a Samaritan stopped to help the beaten and robbed man on the road to Jericho, he means not a gentile from Samaria but a Samaritan as distinct from a Jew. The same may be said for the woman at the well in John 4. In a culture of bitter polemic and denigration of Samaritans by Jews, therefore, Jesus—or at least the Jesus traditions known to Luke and John—provide a corrective challenge.

Works Cited in Chapter 19

Anderson, Robert T. 1989. "Samaritan Pentateuch: General Account." Pages 390–96 in Crown.

———. 1992. "Samaritans." *ABD* 5:940–47.

Avi-Yonah, Michael. 2002. *The Holy Land from the Persian to the Arab Conquest (536 B.C.–A.D. 640): A Historical Geography.* Rev. ed. Jerusalem: Carta.

Böhm, Martina. 1999. *Samarien und die Samaritai bei Lukas: Eine Studie zum religionshistorischen und traditionsgeschichtlicen Hintergrund der lukanischen Samarientexte und zu deren topographischer Verhaftung.* WUNT 111. Tübingen: Mohr Siebeck.

Bourgel, Jonathan. 2016. "The Destruction of the Samaritan Temple by John Hyrcanus: A Reconsideration." *JBL* 135:505–23.

Cowley, Arthur E. 1923. *Aramaic Papyri of the Fifth Century B.C.* Oxford: Clarendon.

Crown, Alan D. 1975. "The Abisha Scroll of the Samaritans." *BJRL* 58:36–65.

———, ed. 1989. *The Samaritans.* Tübingen: Mohr (Siebeck).

———. 1991a. "The Abisha Scroll—3,000 Years Old?" *bRev* 7.5:13–21 passim, 39. cojs. org/alan-d-crown-abisha-scroll/.

———. 1991b. "Redating the Schism between the Judeans and the Samaritans." *JQR* 82:17–50.

Dexinger, Ferdinand. 1981. "Limits of Tolerance in Judaism: The Samaritan Example." Pages 88–114 and 327–38 [notes] in *Aspects of Judaism in the Graeco-Roman Period.* Vol. 2 of *Jewish and Christian Self-Definition.* Edited by E. P. Sanders. Philadelphia: Fortress.

———. 1989. "Samaritan Eschatology." Pages 266–92 in Crown 1989.

Dušek, Jan, ed. 2018. *The Samaritans in Historical, Cultural and Linguistic Perspectives.* SJ 110. SS 11. Berlin: de Gruyter.

Freyne, Séan. 1980. *Galilee from Alexander the Great to Hadrian, 323 B.C.E. to 135 C.E.: A Study of Second Temple Judaism.* Wilmington, DE: Glazier.

Hall, Bruce. 1989. "From John Hyrcanus to Baba Rabbah." Pages 32–54 in Crown 1989.

Hjelm, Ingrid. 2000. *The Samaritans and Early Judaism: A Literary Analysis.* JSNTSup 303. Sheffield: Sheffield Academic.

Horsley, Richard A. 1995. *Galilee: History, Politics, People.* Valley Forge, PA: Trinity Press International.

Isser, Stanley. 2008. "The Samaritans and Their Sects." Pages 569–95 in *Cambridge History of Judaism.* Vol. 3, *The Early Roman Period.* Edited by William Horbury and W. D. Davies. Cambridge: Cambridge University Press.

Kartveit, Magnar. 2009. *The Origin of the Samaritans.* Cambridge: Cambridge University Press.

———. 2018. "Anti-Samaritan Polemics in the Hebrew Bible? The Case of 2 Kings 17:24–41." Pages 3–18 in Dušek.

Knoppers, Gary N. 2013. *Jews and Samaritans: The Origins and History of Their Early Relations.* Oxford: Oxford University Press.

Lehnardt, Andreas. 2010. "Massekhet Kutim and the Resurrection of the Dead." Pages 175–92 in Mor and Reiterer.

Magen, Yitzhak. 2007. "The Dating of the First Phase of the Samaritan Temple on Mount Gerizim in Light of the Archaeological Evidence." Pages 157–211 in *Judah and the Judeans in the Fourth Century BCE.* Winona Lake, IN: Eisenbrauns.

———. 2008a. *The Samaritans and the Good Samaritan.* JSP 7. Jerusalem: Israel Antiquities Authority.

———. 2008b. *A Temple City.* Vol. 2 of *Mount Gerizim Excavations.* JSP 8. Jerusalem: Israel Antiquities Authority.

———. 2009. *Flavia Neapolis: Shechem in the Roman Period.* Jerusalem: Israel Antiquities Authority.

Mor, Menahem. 1989. "The Persian, Hellenistic and Hasmonean Period." Pages 1–18 in Crown 1989.

Mor, Menachem, and Friedrich V. Reiterer, eds. 2010. *Samaritans: Past and Present, Current Studies.* SJ 53. SS 5. Berlin: de Gruyter.

Pummer, Reinhard. 1989a. "Samaritan Material Remains and Archaeology." Pages 135–77 in Crown 1989.

———. 1989b. "Samaritan Rituals and Customs." Pages 650–90 in Crown 1989.

———. 2009. *The Samaritans in Flavius Josephus.* TSAJ 129. Tübingen: Mohr Siebeck.

———. 2010. "Samaritanism—A Jewish Sect or an Independent Form of Yahwism?" Pages 1–24 in Mor and Reiterer.

———. 2018. "Synagogues—Samaritan and Jewish: A New Look at Their Differentiating Characteristics." Pages 51–74 in Dušek.

Purvis, James D. 1968. *The Samaritan Pentateuch and the Origin of the Samaritan Sect.* HSM 2. Leiden: Brill.

———. 1986. "The Samaritans and Judaism." Pages 81–98 in *Early Judaism and Its Modern Interpreters.* Edited by Robert A. Kraft and George W. E. Nickelsburg. Atlanta: Scholars Press.

Raviv, Dvir. 2021. "Settlement and History of the Northern Judean Hills and Southern Samaria during the Early Hasmonean Period." Pages 53–72 in *The Middle Maccabees: Archaeology, History, and the Rise of the Hasmonean Kingdom.* Edited by Andrea M. Berlin and Paul J. Kosmin. ABS 28. Atlanta: SBL Press.

Römer, Thomas. 2018. "Cult Centralization and the Publication of the Torah between Jerusalem and Samaria." Pages 79–92 in *The Bible, Qumran, and the Samaritans.* Edited by Magnar Kartveit and Gary N. Knoppers. SJ 104. SS 10. Berlin: de Gruyter.

Runesson, Anders. 2001. *The Origins of the Synagogue: A Socio-Historical Study.* ConBNT 37. Stockholm: Almqvist & Wiksell.

Schur, Nathan. 1989. *History of the Samaritans.* Frankfurt am Main: Lang.

Tsedaka, Benyamim. 2012. "Reevaluation of Samaritan Studies Due to the New Discoveries in Excavations and Research." Pages 419–25 in *Die Samaritaner und die Bibel: Historische und literarische Wechselwirkungen zwischen biblischen und samaritanischen Traditionen = The Samaritans and the Bible: Historical and Literary Interactions between Biblical and Samaritan Traditions.* Edited by Jörg Frey, Ursula Schattner-Rieser, and Konrad Schmid. SJ 70. Berlin: de Gruyter.

Wardle, Timothy. 2018. "Samaritans, Jews, and Christians: Multiple Partings and Multiple Ways." Pages 15–39 in *The Ways That Often Parted. Essays in Honor of Joel Marcus.* Edited by L. Baron, J. Hicks-Keeton, and M. Thiessen. ECL 24. Atlanta: SBL Press.

Webster's Ninth New Collegiate Dictionary. 1989. Springfield, MA: Merriam-Webster.

Weiss, Herold. 1998. "The Sabbath in the Writings of Josephus." *JSJ* 29:363–90.

Zangenberg, Jürgen. 2006. "Between Jerusalem and the Galilee: Samaria in the Time of Jesus." Pages 393–433 in *Jesus and Archaeology.* Edited by James H. Charlesworth. Grand Rapids: Eerdmans.

Chapter 20

Bandits

Good Samaritan (Luke 10:25–37)

*T*ypically, little is said about the robbers or bandits in expositions of the parable of the good Samaritan. Some expositors say the Jericho road was notoriously dangerous, a point to which we will return below; but what do we know about bandits in Galilee and Judea? How prevalent was banditry? Were bandits folk heroes, like Robin Hood? Were they supported by the local populace, and on whom did they prey?

20.1 Definition

The parable says that the traveler "fell among" or "fell into the hands" (*periepesen*) of robbers (*lēstais*, Luke 10:30), but this term can have various meanings, from revolutionaries to highway robbers, and Josephus uses it for various groups. Shaye Cohen concludes that in the Galilean narratives of both *Life* and *The Jewish War*, "*lēstai* usually refers to men who were primarily brigands, only secondarily, and not always, revolutionaries"; but he cautions that each occurrence must be investigated (211). Martin Hengel offered a more nuanced definition: "*lēstēs* is a classical Greek word derived from *lēïs,* booty, *or lēïzomai,* to seize as booty. It is synonymous with *harpax* [Luke 18:11; 1 Cor 5:10–11; 6:10] although this has the meaning more of a robber of another's property, while *lēstēs* is rather a criminal, often armed and violent" (24). The term is often translated as brigand: "one who lives by plunder, usually as member of a band" (*Webster's*). One-word glosses do not take us very far, however. The debate over the interpretation of this term and what it tells us about ancient Galilee has evolved over the past fifty years, progressively clarifying the Galilean ethos. Martin Hengel's *Die Zeloten* (1961; ET 1989) contended that the term is the

298

most common designation for the Jewish freedom movement, the Zealots, which he thought could be traced continuously from Judas the Galilean (6 CE) to the Jewish Revolt of 66–74 CE, although not every occurrence of this term carries this sense: for example, its use in the parable does not (24, 29). David Rhoads (1976) and Richard Horsley and John Hanson (1985) found no evidence of the Zealots as a movement during the period between Judas the Galilean and the outbreak of the First Jewish Revolt. This conclusion calls into question the widespread understanding that Galilee was a hotbed of revolutionary sentiment during this period—a view Seán Freyne (1980) challenged.

Richard Horsley distinguished the use of *lēstai* to identify "social bandits" from "violent insurrectionary activity," although he finds little evidence related to bandits in Galilee in the first half of the first century CE (1995, 259). Horsley drew upon Eric Hobsbawm's work (1963, 1969, 1973) on social banditry as a form of "pre-political rebellion" in peasant societies. Among its characteristics, drawn from Eric Hobsbawm, Horsley lists: (1) "Social banditry arises in traditional agrarian societies where peasants are exploited by governments and landowners." (2) "Such banditry may increase in times of economic crisis, caused by famine or high taxation." (3) Social bandits "often function as champions of justice for the common people, and usually enjoy the support of local peasants." (4) "Banditry occurs regularly in areas and periods of administrative inefficiency" (Horsley and Hanson, 48–51; McGing, 161–63, lists nine characteristics). Some of these conditions are characteristic of banditry in general. The distinguishing feature of social banditry is its close connection with and support by the peasantry.

John Kloppenborg examined Horsley's appeal to the model of social banditry and found it wanting. Studies of banditry in other times and cultures (Blok, Driessen, Sant Cassia, Slatta) find that Hobsbawm's model does not fit the data (Kloppenborg 2009, 462). B. C. McGing, for example, surveyed Egyptian papyri, finding, "There is no trace in the papyri of what Hobsbawm presented as the classic route into banditry—the commission of a crime, especially murder, which ordinary people, but not the state, regard as in some sense justified or honourable" (174). Nor did he find any trace of bandits as romantic heroes (179–82). Nevertheless, there are instances of collusion between bandits and establishment interests (182–83). After reviewing Josephus's references to banditry in Galilee, Kloppenborg concludes, "There is little evidence of two key features of social banditry: that Galilean bandits enjoyed the support of the peasantry and that they refrained from preying on their own villagers" (2009, 467). Thomas Grünewald reached the same conclusion, but he reduces banditry to a single mold when he observes that when Josephus speaks of *lēstai*, it is always in reference to "politically motivated usurpers in Judaea" (100): "The Jewish *leistai* were never in any sense social bandits" (109). Complicating the matter further, Josephus uses *lēstai* pejoratively, as a slur, labeling a rival or opponent—a local baron or strongman—as a violent criminal not subject to ordinary legal processes (Kloppenborg 2009, 475–76; Shaw 1984, 23; Freyne 1988, esp. 58, 62–65; Hooff, 111, 113).

Conditions that foster banditry include deteriorating social and economic conditions, debt, poverty, and roving groups of young men, especially shepherds (Josephus, *Ant.* 15.346; 16.272; Kloppenborg 2010, 61–62), army veterans and deserters, and fugitive slaves (Shaw 1984, 28–32; Kloppenborg 2009, 467–81; Fiensy 2022, 132). Bandits no doubt were in Galilee as elsewhere, but the work of Uriel Rappaport (1992) and Morten Jensen (2006; Jensen 2007) shows that, during the long reign of Herod Antipas (4 BCE–39 CE), Galilee was generally peaceful and prosperous (see above 9.1; Deines, 30–31). Even a brief survey of banditry in the ancient world shows that the phenomenon was not limited to Palestine but was common across the Mediterranean world, where it was propelled by poverty, Roman taxation, and inefficient control of marginal areas.

20.2 The Scourge of Robbers

Banditry was so common that it "impinged on the most mundane aspects of Roman social life" and Roman law (Shaw 1984, 8; Hengel, 25). For example, "Among the common causes of death recognized by the laws are old age, sickness, and attacks by bandits" (Shaw 1984, 8–9; Paulus, in *Dig.* 13.6.5.4). Travel was dangerous, especially in the frontier provinces. The apostle Paul boasts that he was constantly in danger "on frequent journeys, in danger from rivers, danger from bandits, danger from my own people, danger from Gentiles, danger in the city" (2 Cor 11:26). The disappearance of travelers was so common (Pliny the Younger, *Ep.* 6.25) that tyrants could say their victims had been attacked or killed by bandits (Hooff, 117). Danger was ubiquitous, "though in varying degrees of intensity, in the empire in all periods of its existence" (Shaw 1984, 10).

Early in his reign, Octavian took steps to address the problem, commissioning one Sabinus to secure peace in the region (Appian, *Bell. civ.* 5.132). Suppression of bandits was expected of Roman governors. The good emperor, king, or governor, like the Good Shepherd (John 10:1, 7–11), would protect his flock from bandits. Yet the extension of Roman power itself fostered banditry by alienating populations and introducing Roman authority, taxation, and the Roman army. In Asia Minor, for example, the Pamphylians and the Isaurians were notorious for their lawlessness (Strabo, *Geogr.* 12.7.2; Dio Cassius, *Hist.* 55.28.3–4).

Egyptian papyri provide graphic accounts of banditry. A husband cautions his wife not to wear her gold jewelry when she travels by boat from the Fayum to Coptos (P.Mich. 3.214, in 297 BCE; Huebner, 104). A certain Petesouchos, traveling to see his sister, had his clothes and money stolen (P.Lille 1.6, in 3rd c. BCE; Huebner, 104–5). Another traveler, Seos, lost his clothing as well as his donkeys: "A band of robbers set upon us as we were coming back and took off in possession of a male donkey of mine and a female one. With both of these they carried off the merchandise of which they stripped me" (*SB* 8.9792, from 162 BCE; Huebner, 105).

We may assume that such assaults were as common in Palestine as they were in Egypt. We simply do not have a similar trove of papyri from Galilee or Judea. The Gospels report that two *lēstai* were crucified with Jesus (see below, 20.6). Josephus says that officials traveled with a military escort (*Ant.* 18.112). The Essenes were armed when they traveled (*J.W.* 2.125). As we have seen (above, 9.2), the majority of the populace in the first century lived at or near subsistence level. Droughts, plagues, wars, and debts disrupted the already tenuous cycle of sowing and harvesting, leaving desperate peasants with no alternative but to "rob the rich" and "plunder the poor" to survive (Fiensy 1991, 99; Horsley 2014, 168).

Josephus's lengthy story of two Jewish brothers, Asinaeus and Anilaeus, in Babylonia illustrates this pattern (*Ant.* 18.314–370; Shaw 1993, 179–83). When their father died, their mother apprenticed them in weaving; but after their master beat them, they stole a cache of weapons and retreated to a remote area. There, "young men of the poorest class gathered about them, and these they armed" (*Ant.* 18.315). Later, after Asinaeus was killed, "an indigent horde of scoundrels who held their lives cheap" joined Anilaeus "to gain some ease for the moment" (*Ant.* 18.367). The story is paradigmatic. By becoming bandits, they were able to survive at the margin of society and even gain a measure of power for a brief period (20–35 CE; Shaw 1993, 183). Such roving bands preyed on the populace (Josephus, *J.W.* 2.253, 581–582; 4.406; *Ant.* 16.271–272; 17.285; 20.124, 185). The result was a spiral of impoverishment and emigration (*Ant.* 20.256).

In some instances, the authorities allowed the brigands to rove undisturbed in exchange for tribute (Josephus, *Ant.* 15.344). Strabo gives an account of Pompey's suppression of banditry in Iturea, with pertinent comments about the bandits' relationship with the local farmers: "Now all the mountainous parts are held by Ituraeans and Arabians, all of whom are robbers, but the people in the plains are farmers; and when the latter are harassed by the robbers at different times[,] they require different kinds of help. These robbers use strongholds as bases of operation" (Strabo, *Geogr.* 16.2.18; cf. Josephus, *Ant.* 14.38–40). Among the "strongholds" Pompey destroyed were mountain fortresses, caves, and a castle.

20.3 Brigands in Judea and Galilee

For data regarding banditry in Galilee, we are almost entirely dependent on Josephus, who describes outbreaks of banditry in three periods: in the latter part of the first century BCE, early in the first century CE, and leading up to the First Jewish Revolt. In light of the issues raised earlier regarding social bandits, close attention must be paid to Josephus's labeling of different groups as *lēstai*, whom they robbed, and who supported them.

20.3.1 Hezekiah, the Brigand Chief

After Caesar appointed Hyrcanus to the high-priesthood, Antipater, an Idumean, became the effective leader and appointed one of his sons, Phasael, as governor of Jerusalem, and the other, Herod (who became "the Great") to authority in Galilee. Although only fifteen (Josephus, *Ant.* 14.158; 15.203), Herod immediately set about purging Galilee of bandits. His first adversary was Hezekiah, the brigand chief (*archilēstēs*), whose band had been ravaging the Syrian frontier. Hezekiah "was no ordinary highwayman, but rather a Hasmonean supporter, who may indeed have been forced to adopt robber tactics due to the defeat of Peitholaus" (Freyne 1980, 211–12; so also Grünewald, 95). Peitholaus had been second in command in Jerusalem before deserting with a thousand men to support Aristobulus (Josephus, *J.W.* 1.172), but he was caught and executed by the Roman general Cassius. When Herod killed Hezekiah and many of his band (in 46 BCE; *Ant.* 14.159; *J.W.* 1.204), the Syrians celebrated him as a hero: "Up and down the villages and in the towns the praises of Herod were sung, as the restorer of their peace and possessions" (*J.W.* 1.205; *Ant.* 14.160), but the mothers of the men who had been murdered by Herod begged the king to bring Herod to judgment (*Ant.* 14.168). Hezekiah was clearly not a small-time robber. His activities were part of the larger political turmoil of this frontier region (Freyne 1988, 55–57; Horsley 1995, 260–63).

20.3.2 Herod the Great and the Galilean Brigands

When Varro, governor of Syria, wrote to Augustus Caesar about this problem (in ca. 23 BCE), Caesar instructed him to drive out the brigands and assign Galilee to Herod the Great (*Ant.* 15.345). Josephus's description of the brigands' strongholds gives new meaning to Jesus' reference to "a den of robbers" when he quotes Jeremiah 7:11 in the temple (Mark 11:17 par.).

> For it was really not easy to restrain people who had made brigandage a habit and had no other means of making a living, since they had neither city nor field of their own but only underground shelters and caves, where they lived together with their cattle. They had also managed to collect supplies of water and of food beforehand, and so they were able to hold out for a very long time in their hidden retreat. Moreover, the entrances (to their caves) were narrow, and only one person at a time could enter, while the interiors were incredibly large and constructed to provide plenty of room, and the ground above their dwellings was not high but almost level with the (surrounding) surface. The whole place consisted of rocks that were rugged and difficult of access unless one used a path with a guide leading the way, for not even these paths were straight, but had many turns and windings. (*Ant.* 15.346–348)

The brigands in Galilee were so numerous that Herod had to mount "a campaign against the cave-dwelling brigands," who were "inflicting on the inhabitants evils no less than those of war" (*J.W.* 1.304). The nature of the brigands' activities is open to debate. Were they pillaging indiscriminately, raiding villages? Or attacking the elite and their property? Or were they "indigenous Galilean villagers waging guerrilla warfare" (Horsley 2014, 1:169) against the new king appointed by the Roman emperor? Although Herod took three battalions of infantry and a squadron of cavalry, Josephus says the brigands were undaunted because they "combined the experience of seasoned warriors with the daring of brigands" (*J.W.* 1.305).

Even after Herod defeated the brigands in a fierce battle and chased them across the Jordan, a remnant remained in the caves in the sheer cliffs on Mount Arbel (near Tiberias). "The king was, consequently, for long baffled by the impracticable nature of the ground, but at length had recourse to a most hazardous scheme. By means of ropes he lowered the most stalwart of his men in cradles and so gave them access to the cavern-mouths; these men then massacred the brigands and their families, hurling in firebrands upon those who resisted" (*J.W.* 1.311; cf. *Ant.* 14.423–430). Having wiped out the resistance, Herod appointed Ptolemy as commander of that region and moved on to Samaria. When he left, however, violence broke out again, and Ptolemy was killed. Herod was forced to return, put down the rebels, and demolish their fortified places. This time, he imposed a fine of 100 talents on the cities that protected them (*Ant.* 14.433), which suggests support for the rebels among the local populace.

20.3.3 Judas Son of Hezekiah

When Herod the Great died (4 BCE), rebels reappeared in Jerusalem, Idumea, and Perea. At Sepphoris, Judas, the son of Hezekiah the brigand-chief, raised an army of followers, equipping them with arms from the royal arsenal (Josephus, *J.W.* 2.56): "He [Judas] became an object of terror to all men by plundering those he came across in his desire for great possessions and his ambition for royal rank, a prize he expected to obtain not through the practice of virtue but through excessive ill-treatment of others" (*Ant.* 17.272).

Another aspirant to royalty, Simon, one of Herod's slaves, was particularly strong and handsome. "Elated by the unsettled conditions" following Herod's death, he gathered a force of men, proclaimed himself king, and plundered and burned the royal palace at Jericho (*Ant.* 17.273–274; *J.W.* 2.57–59). Another outlaw named Athronges, "a mere shepherd," wore a royal diadem and appointed his four brothers as generals of armed bands to carry out raids, killing Romans and their supporters. Like his father Hezekiah, Judas as well as Simon and Athronges all seem to have been driven by political ambitions; they do not fit the model of social bandits (Grünewald, 95–96).

These men "were making the whole of Judaea one scene of guerilla warfare" (*J.W.* 2.65), Josephus declares, clearly for the benefit of his Roman patrons: "And so Judaea was filled with brigandage. Anyone might make himself king as the head of a band of rebels whom he fell in with, and then would press on to the destruction of the community, causing trouble to few Romans and then only to a small degree but bringing the greatest slaughter upon his own people" (*Ant.* 17.285).

20.3.4 Judas the Galilean

Brigandage flared again in Judea in 6 CE, when Archelaus, tetrarch of Judea, was deposed and Augustus appointed Coponius as procurator "with full powers, including the infliction of capital punishment" (Josephus, *J.W.* 2.118). Judas, a Galilean identified by Josephus as a sophist who founded his own sect, incited revolt. Because Judas was an itinerant teacher who called followers, Jesus may have had to distinguish himself and his movement from this rebel (so Theissen, 109–16). In *Jewish Antiquities*, Josephus says Judas was from Gamla and relates his fury to the census that Quirinius carried out, assessing the value of property held by Jews (18.1–4). Judas "threw himself into the cause of rebellion" (18.4), saying that the assessment amounted to slavery, calling his countrymen "cowards for consenting to pay tribute to the Romans" rather than "having God for their lord" (*J.W.* 2.118), and advocating bloodshed if it proved necessary. Consequently, Josephus charges that Judas and his fellow rebel, Saddok, started a "fourth school of philosophy," which eventually culminated in the First Jewish Revolt sixty years later (*Ant.* 18.23–25; see also Acts 5:37). Hengel identified Judas the Galilean as Judas the son of Hezekiah and followed Josephus in making him the founder of the Zealots (293, 331), but both assumptions are dubious (Rhoads, 48–60; Horsley 2014, 1:169–70). On the contrary, Rhoads concludes, "The revolt of Judas the Galilean in Judea in 6 C.E. was relatively small and ineffective," and only in a limited sense was he "one of the formulators of the later national call for freedom from the Romans" (59, 60). Moreover, Rhoads finds that "the absence of evidence for conspiratorial revolutionary activity in Josephus' account of the period from 6 to 44 C.E. is striking" (64).

20.3.5 The Peasant Strike

Cooler heads prevailed when a revolt threatened to erupt in 39 CE. Jews in Alexandria had defiantly refused to make the obligatory sacrifices to Emperor Gaius. In response, Gaius (Caligula) ordered Petronius, governor of Syria, to erect his statue in the temple at Jerusalem (Josephus, *J.W.* 2.184–187). No doubt exaggerating a very real threat, Josephus claims that "many tens of thousands faced Petronius on his arrival at Tiberias" (*Ant.* 18.271), urging him not to defile the temple in this way. The Jews said they would die first. For forty days, they neglected their fields even though it was time to sow the seed (18.272). Rallying to head off the crisis, Jewish leaders appealed to Petronius to write to Gaius and point out that "since the land was unsown, there would be a harvest of banditry, because the requirement of tribute [taxes] could not be met" (18.274). Fortunately, Gaius died before his order was carried out (*J.W.* 2.203).

20.3.6 Brigands under the Procurators

The following decades were marked by ineffective Roman procurators, famine, and growing anarchy. Not surprisingly, Josephus records the steady rise of brigandage in these years. Cuspius Fadus (44–46 CE) purged Judea of robber bands, executing both Tholomaus, an archbrigand who terrorized

Idumea (*Ant.* 20.5); and Theudas, who claimed he was a prophet and could part the Jordan River (*Ant.* 20.97–99; Acts 5:36; Smith, 514–15). When Samaritans murdered a Galilean pilgrim on his way up to Jerusalem with a large company of pilgrims, many of the Jews in Jerusalem abandoned the festival and began to ravage Samaritan villages. Yet the Roman procurator Cumanus (48–52 CE) would not avenge the Galileans, who sought the help of Eleazar son of Dinaeus, "a brigand who for many years had had his home in the mountains" (*Ant.* 20.121). Then, when Cumanus marched against them, "The people dispersed and the brigands returned to their strongholds," but "from that time the whole of Judaea was infested with bands of brigands" (*Ant.* 20.124).

Another outbreak of brigandage followed an incident in the temple, sparked by a Roman soldier. At this time, one of Caesar's slaves named Stephen was attacked "on the public road leading up to Bethhoron" and robbed of his baggage (Josephus, *J.W.* 2.228). Cumanus sent troops to round up the villagers from the area and reprimanded them for not arresting the robbers (2.229). These brigands were also led by Eleazar, son of Deinaeus. Cumanus led troops from Caesarea, capturing and killing many of the brigands. Leaders from Jerusalem convinced the others to cease their pillaging lest it "bring down the wrath of the Romans on Jerusalem." Although the brigands dispersed, many of them, "emboldened by impunity, had recourse to robbery; . . . raids and insurrections, fostered by the more reckless, broke out all over the country" (2.238).

Felix (procurator, 52–60 CE) captured the brigand chief Eleazar the son of D[e]inaeus, who had ravaged the country for twenty years, and sent him to Rome for trial (*Ant.* 20.161), which means that he was particularly notorious, "a member of the bandit elite" (Grünewald, 97). It is probably telling that Eleazar was later remembered among the rabbis as "one who prematurely tried to free the Jews" (Song Rab. 2.18; Isaac, 180). Josephus adds, "Of the brigands whom he [Felix] crucified, and of the common people who were convicted of complicity with them and punished by him, the number was incalculable" (*J.W.* 2.253–254).

When Festus (procurator, 60–62 CE) succeeded Felix, "Judaea was being devastated by the brigands, for the villages one and all were being set on fire and plundered" (*Ant.* 20.185), so he too "proceeded to attack the principal plague of the country: he captured large numbers of the brigands and put not a few to death" (*J.W.* 2.271). The situation only got worse under Gessius Florus (procurator, 64–66 CE; *Ant.* 20.255–256). A new species of banditti, the *sicarii* (dagger men), sprang up in Jerusalem, so-called because they "committed murders in broad daylight in the heart of the city," especially during the festivals, "when they would mingle with the crowd, carrying short daggers concealed under their clothing, with which they stabbed their enemies" (*J.W.* 2.254–255; cf. *Ant.* 20.185–187, 208–210).

20.3.7 John of Gischala

John of Gischala, who emerges in the early days of the Jewish Revolt (66–67 CE), provides an interesting case study in the factors leading to brigandage, the close relationships between lawlessness and violence, and political alliances (Grünewald, 100–105). Josephus's tendentious account reflects the intense rivalry and animosity between this John and Josephus, making it difficult to get a true picture of John's actions.

After outbreaks of violence in Syria and Scythopolis, the authorities in Jerusalem sent Josephus to Galilee to encourage the brigands and rebels to lay down their arms. Although the Galileans attacked Sepphoris because it was loyal to Rome, Cohen judges that "the peasants reserved most of their fear for the brigands and most of their hatred for the cities" (230). Tiberias was divided, with some residents eager for revolt against Rome. The latter, following one Justus, set fire to villages belonging to Gadara and Hippos, east of the Jordan.

At Gischala, John was at first a moderate, like Josephus, seeking to restrain revolutionary sentiment (*Life* 43; Rappaport 1982, 481–82). Nevertheless, a strong animosity grew between them. After men from Gadara, Tyre, and other cities sacked and burned Gischala, John defeated them, then returned to rebuild Gischala with money his men raised (extorted?) from the wealthy. John acted in defense of his city against neighboring gentile cities, not against the Romans (Rappaport 1982, 485).

When John visited Tiberias, he persuaded Justus to join him in opposing Josephus. Josephus met with John at Gischala, reporting that he found him eager for revolution and ambitious to take command (*Life* 70). First, according to Josephus, John bribed Josephus's colleagues to allow him (John) to control all the grain stored in the province. Then he arranged to supply the Jews at Caesarea Philippi "pure" olive oil at ten times the price of oil in Gischala (*Life* 75). Josephus belittles John, his archrival in Galilee, by labeling him a brigand, "who at the outset practiced his trade alone, but afterwards found for his daring deeds accomplices, whose numbers, small at first, grew with his success. . . . With their help he plundered the whole of Galilee" (*J.W.* 2.587–589). Both wealthy landowners and small villages needed protection from the brigands. Seeing that he could not disarm the brigands, Josephus "persuaded the people to pay them as mercenaries; remarking that it was better to give them a small sum voluntarily than to submit to raids upon their property" (*Life* 77–78). As Morton Smith observed, the bandits were ready to work for anyone who could pay them (530). Josephus charged the brigands not to attack their countrymen or the Romans (*J.W.* 2.581–584; *Life* 244), but John continued to induce the Galileans to follow him and turn against Josephus (*Life* 87; *J.W.* 2.593). John even sought to kill Josephus on various occasions. Each time, Josephus eluded him. Shaye Cohen estimates, "Josephus and John could never count on more than about 5000 each and most of these will have been *lēstai*, bandits, not all of whom were revolutionaries" (202). As always, however, we must consider that Josephus's numbers are probably inflated. Even Josephus's writings are not consistent in their descriptions. In *The Jewish War*, John is portrayed "not simply as a revolutionary but as a brigand and tyrant, but the stock quality of much of this language makes the whole picture highly suspect" (Freyne 1980, 238); in *Life*, John is more moderate and never called a brigand (Rhoads, 123–24).

When Josephus approached Sepphoris, the people were alarmed and called Jesus, "the brigand chief, on the borderland of Ptolemais," to protect them (*Life* 105–106), which he agreed to do and marched against Josephus. However, Josephus tricked the brigand, forced him to surrender, and then let him go.

John of Gischala persisted in his attempts to get cities in Galilee to abandon Josephus, but without success. At one point, however, "brigands and the promoters of the disturbance," fearing that they would be called into account for their activities, went to burn Josephus's residence (*Life* 145–148). Once again, and in several subsequent events, the hero of this story eluded his adversaries. Ultimately John sent a contingent to Jerusalem, seeking to have himself appointed in Josephus's place (*Life* 189–193). Rhoads reads John's actions as showing that he was a moderate who accused Josephus of being a revolutionary extremist (128–29). Only later did John become a revolutionary.

When Josephus considered returning to Jerusalem, the Galileans feared that his departure "would leave them an easy prey to the brigands" (*Life* 206). Some of the leaders in Jerusalem, acting on their own, sent orders to remove Josephus, but he thwarted the plot by sending his own delegation to Jerusalem (*Life* 266–267, 309). With his position secure, Josephus stripped John of his support by threatening to burn the homes of any of John's followers who did not lay down their arms (*Life* 368–372). Outmaneuvered, John remained in Gischala (*J.W.* 2.632). Later, when Titus demanded the surrender of Gischala, John decided to join the revolt, abandoned Gischala, and fled to Jerusalem. There, he first supported the provisional government, then allied with the Zealots, rising in power until he and Simon bar Giora, another brigand who became the commander of the Jewish forces in the defense of Jerusalem, controlled the doomed city, tyrannizing the people and plundering the wealthy (*J.W.* 5.439–441; Rhoads, 130–35, 140–48; Rappaport 1982, 487–93; Smith, 539–42).

Josephus focuses on the most notorious of the brigands and those who became involved in uprisings and the First Jewish Revolt. Still, he repeatedly emphasizes the pervasiveness of the problem. Many brigands were driven by desperation, landlessness, and hunger. Some fell in with larger bands. Others followed would-be prophets, messiahs, and kings (Simon, Herod's former slave; Athronges). Strongmen, bandit chiefs, arose in remote towns and frontier areas (Hezekiah, John of Gischala); raiding and pillaging sometimes evolved into guerrilla warfare, requiring the intervention of Herod or one of the procurators. There is no indication, however, that the robbers in Jesus' parable were other than bandits preying on passing travelers.

20.4 The Jericho Road and the Good Samaritan Inn

The Roman road from Jerusalem to Jericho may have followed the earlier "Arabah Road" (2 Kgs 25:4–5; Jer 39:4; 52:7), known from the First Temple period. The middle section followed the same route as the modern highway (Dorsey, 204–6). Travel increased under the Hasmoneans and Herodians, when the road was used by caravans of traders and Jewish pilgrims on their way to Jerusalem for the festivals. Strabo says that when Pompey seized Jerusalem, he "destroyed the haunts of robbers and the treasure-holds of tyrants. Two of these were situated on the passes leading to [Jericho]" (*Geogr.* 16.2.40). The area was ideal for brigands: remote, rugged, with wadis and caves, "desert and rocky, . . . wild and barren" (Josephus, *J.W.* 4.474). Danger increased in the Roman and later periods when travel along this route increased. In the time of Herod, bands of robbers who raided caravans going to Damascus were protected by the Nabateans (*Ant.* 16.276, 282–283).

The Hasmonean kings and Herod built winter palaces near Jericho. Herod also built a palace on a hill just north of the road to Jericho, east of the Mount of Olives, near Ma'ale (ascent) Adummim, which appears in Joshua 15:7 but not as an inhabited site. Remains of structures and caves date from the Second Temple period. The site was identified in the Byzantine period (Eusebius, *Onom.* 24.9, number 70; Notley and Safrai, 26), and a fort was built there to protect travelers against the bandits (Isaac, 201). Jerome (ca. 342–420) interpreted *Adummim* as coming from *adom* (red) in reference to *dam* (blood), but the soil in the area is red enough that the name may refer to its color (Wilkinson, 149; see further Magen 2008, 281–313).

20.5 Reflections

Life was hard. One wonders how people survived the dangers and threats—hard labor, disease, and famine, all compounded by social and political upheaval and the banditry it produced. Jesus' preaching of God's mercy and love, his wondrous healings, and his announcement of the imminent coming of God's eschatological rule offered hope in a desperate time.

But violence ultimately consumed Jesus too. The crowds and the stories they told about him attracted the attention of the authorities. When Jesus entered Jerusalem, cheered by a crowd of excited followers, then overturned tables and disrupted activities in the temple, nervous and wary leaders identified him as yet another *lēstēs* (cf. John 11:47–48; Acts 5:36–38), conspired against him, and came after him "with swords and clubs," as for a *lēstēs* ("rebel," Matt 26:55). The Johannine Jesus interprets his death in relation to the *lēstai*: he broke the cycle of violence by laying down his life to protect his sheep from *lēstai* (John 10:1, 8, 10, 15). Ultimately, the crowd chose Barabbas, the *lēstēs* (John 18:40), and the Romans crucified Jesus between two *lēstai* (Matt 27:38, 44).

Works Cited in Chapter 20

Blok, Anton. 1972. "The Peasant and the Brigand: Social Banditry Reconsidered." *Comparative Studies in Society and History* 14:494–503.

Cohen, Shaye J. D. 2002. *Josephus in Galilee and Rome: His Vita and Development as a Historian.* Columbia Studies in the Classical Tradition 8. Leiden: Brill.

Deines, Roland. 2014. "Galilee and the Historical Jesus in Recent Research." Pages 11–48 in Fiensy and Strange, vol. 1.

Dorsey, David A. 1991. *The Roads and Highways of Ancient Israel.* Baltimore: Johns Hopkins University Press.

Driessen, Henk. 1983. "The 'Noble Bandit' and the Bandits of the Nobles: Brigandage and Local Community in Nineteenth-Century Andalusia." *Archives européennes de sociologie* 24:96–114.

Eusebius. *Onomasticon.* See Bibliography of Ancient Sources and Translations

Fiensy, David A. 1991. *The Social History of Palestine in the Herodian Period: The Land Is Mine.* Lewiston, NY: Mellen.

———. 2022. "Bandits and the Galilean Economy: Was the Galilee Prosperous or Desperately Poor?" Pages 126–39 in *Taxation, Economy, and Revolt in Ancient Rome, Galilee, and Egypt.* Edited by Thomas R. Blanton IV, Agnes Choi, and Jinyu Liu. RMCS. London: Routledge.

Fiensy, David A., and James R. Strange. 2014. *Life, Culture, and Society.* Vol. 1 of *Galilee in the Late Second Temple and Mishnaic Periods.* Edited by David A. Fiensy and James R. Strange. Minneapolis: Fortress.

Freyne, Séan. 1980. *Galilee from Alexander the Great to Hadrian, 323 B.C.E. to 135 C.E.: A Study of Second Temple Judaism.* Wilmington, DE: Glazier.

———. 1988. "Bandits in Galilee: A Contribution to the Study of Social Conditions in First Century Palestine." Pages 50–67 in *The Social World of Formative Christianity and Judaism: Essays in Tribute to Howard Clark Kee.* Edited by Jacob Neusner et al. Philadelphia: Fortress.

Grünewald, Thomas. 2004. *Bandits in the Roman Empire: Myth and Reality.* Translated by John Drinkwater. London: Routledge.

Hengel, Martin. 1989. *The Zealots.* Translated by D. Smith. Edinburgh: T&T Clark.

Hobsbawm, Eric J. 1963. *Primitive Rebels: Studies in Archaic Forms of Social Movement in the 19th and 20th Centuries.* 2nd ed. New York: Praeger.

———. 1969. *Bandits.* New York: Delacorte.

———. 1973. "Social Banditry." Pages 142–57 in *Rural Protest: Peasant Movements and Social Change.* Edited by Henry A. Landsberger. New York: Barnes & Noble.

Hooff, Anton J. L. van. 1988. "Ancient Robbers: Reflections behind the Facts." *Ancient Society* 19:105–24.

Horsley, Richard A. 1995. *Galilee: History, Politics, People.* Valley Forge, PA: Trinity Press International.

———. 2014. "Social Movements in Galilee." Pages 167–74 in vol. 1 of Fiensy and Strange.

Horsley, Richard A., and John S. Hanson. 1988. *Bandits, Prophets, and Messiahs: Popular Movements in the Time of Jesus.* San Francisco: Harper & Row.

Huebner, Sabine R. 2019. *Papyri and the Social World of the New Testament.* Cambridge: Cambridge University Press.

Isaac, Benjamin. 1984. "Bandits in Judea and Arabia." *HSCP* 88:171–203.

Jensen, Morten Hørning. 2006. *Herod Antipas in Galilee.* WUNT 215. Tübingen: Mohr Siebeck.

———. 2007. "Herod Antipas in Galilee: Friend or Foe of the Historical Jesus?" *JSHJ* 5: 7–32.

Kloppenborg, John S. 2009. "Unsocial Bandits." Pages 451–84 in *A Wandering Galilean: Essays in Honour of Seán Freyne.* JSJSup 132. Leiden: Brill.

———. 2010. "Pastoralism, Papyri, and the Parable of the Shepherd." Pages 47–70 in *Light from the East: Papyrologische Kommentare zum Neuen Testament.* Edited by Peter Arzt-Grabner and Christina M. Kreineker. Wiesbaden: Harrassowitz.

Magen, Yitzhak. 2008. *The Samaritans and the Good Samaritan.* JSP 7. Jerusalem: Israel Antiquities Authority.

McGing, B. C. 1998. "Bandits, Real and Imagined, in Greco-Roman Egypt." *BASP* 35.4:159–83.

Rappaport, Uriel. 1982. "John of Gischala: From Galilee to Jerusalem." *JJS* 33:479–93.

———. 1992. "How Anti-Roman Was the Galilee?" Pages 95–102 in *The Galilee in Late Antiquity.* Edited by Lee I. Levine. Cambridge, MA: Harvard University Press.

Rhoads, David M. 1976. *Israel in Revolution 6–74 C.E.* Philadelphia: Fortress.

Sant Cassia, Paul. 1993. "Banditry, Myth, and Terror in Cyprus and Other Mediterranean Societies." *Comparative Studies in Society and History.* 35:773–95.

Shaw, Brent D. 1984. "Bandits in the Roman Empire." *P&P* 105:3–52.

———. 1993. "Tyrants, Bandits and Kings: Personal Power in Josephus." *JJS* 44:176–204.

Slatta, Richard. 2004. "Eric J. Hobsbawm's Social Bandits: A Critique and Revision." *A Contracorriente: A Journal on Social History and Literature in Latin America.* Spring, 22–30. https://acontracorriente.chass.ncsu.edu/index.php/acontracorriente/article/view/45.

Smith, Morton. 1999. "The Troublemakers." Pages 501–68 in *The Early Roman Period*. Vol. 3 of *The Cambridge History of Judaism*. Edited by William Horbury et al. Cambridge: Cambridge University Press.

Theissen, Gerd. 2009. "Jesus as an Itinerant Teacher: Reflections from Social History on Jesus' Role." Pages 98–122 in *Jesus Research: An International Perspective*. Edited by James H. Charlesworth and Petr Pokorny. Grand Rapids: Eerdmans.

Webster's Ninth New Collegiate Dictionary. 1989. Springfield, MA: Merriam-Webster.

Wilkinson, John. 2002. *Jerusalem Pilgrims before the Crusades*. 2nd ed. Warminster, UK: Aris & Phillips.

Part VII

Jesus

Chapter 21

Jesus the Galilean

*T*he incarnation entails a specificity of time and place that is seldom recognized. The Gospel of John affirms that "the Word [*logos*] became flesh and dwelt among us" (1:14 RSV). The Word was eternal, but the flesh-and-blood human being was born to a human mother and raised in a village in Galilee, where he was taught a craft by his earthly father. He was influenced by his mentor, John the Baptist, and his ministry was shaped by the environs, history, culture, economy, religion, and politics of Galilee. Jesus' parables open a window on Galilee; likewise, Galilee places Jesus' ministry in context. Eduard Schweizer observes, "The characteristics which distinguish Jesus from the masses are not biographical data—his family, his particular training, his early abilities and successes" (39). These formative factors were much the same for any first-century Galilean, so what was typical of "the masses" also applied to Jesus. For what distinguished him, we have to look elsewhere, especially to his own words and works. Nevertheless, the dramatic increase in knowledge regarding first-century Galilee in recent decades means that constructions and proposals regarding the historical Jesus that do not fit what we have learned about Galilee are not convincing. The following paragraphs sketch a general profile of Jesus by accommodating the Gospels' accounts to our current understanding of Galilee.

21.1 Jesus of Nazareth

As strong as the christological identification with Bethlehem was, Jesus' historical identification with Nazareth persisted. The designation "Jesus of Nazareth" appears in all four Gospels and in Acts. Luke explains how Jesus came to be born in Bethlehem (because of the census; 2:1–4); Matthew explains how he came to be raised in Nazareth (because of the Herods and through Joseph's dreams; 2:22–23).

Nazareth was so insignificant during earlier periods that it is not mentioned in the Hebrew Scriptures, nor does Josephus mention it. To identify him, the crowds in Jerusalem said, "This is the prophet Jesus from Nazareth in Galilee" (Matt 21:11), locating Nazareth "in Galilee" (cf. Mark 1:9; Luke 1:26; 2:4). Others said, "Surely the Messiah does not come from Galilee, does he?" (John 7:41). Nathaniel scoffed, "Can anything good come out of Nazareth?" (1:46).

Located on the south side of the Nazareth Ridge, about three miles southeast of Sepphoris, Nazareth was an obscure agricultural village with fewer than 400 inhabitants. A major road ran from Ptolemais, past Sepphoris, to Tiberias (Reed, 117; Strange 2015, 171–72). Topographically, Nazareth was oriented toward Sepphoris rather than the Jezreel Valley, which lay to the south, 350 feet lower in elevation (Reed, 115). The southern exposure was ideal for growing grain, olives, and legumes (see above, ch. 10). Remains of cisterns, tunnels, olive presses, winepresses, granaries, and grinding stones confirm these agricultural pursuits. A spring, now called Mary's Well, provided water part of the year; cisterns collected water for the dry periods.

Excavations have revealed Jewish tombs from the Herodian period, a few of which contained modest artifacts and cheap jewelry but no public buildings, marble, or frescoes (Reed, 131). Caves in the soft limestone hillsides were used for storage, and modest houses were attached to them. Little remains of the ancient houses, suggesting that they were built with stacked, unhewn stones and had dirt floors, although remains of two courtyard houses (see 3.4) have been found. The artifacts point to occupation from the late Hellenistic period (3rd c. BCE) by Jews of modest means: bronze Hasmonean coins, Herodian lamps, local pottery, two *miqva'ot*, and limestone vessels. Jonathan Reed concludes, "All the archaeological evidence from the Roman Period points to a simple peasant existence at Nazareth. It also points to a *Jewish* Nazareth" (Crossan and Reed, 69; cf. Strange 1992; Strange 2015, 175–77; Lloyd, 132–35). Such a small village probably did not have a synagogue, however. Instead, the "synagogue" was probably in a private home or a place where they gathered outdoors (Claussen and Frey, 240, 244).

21.2 Jesus' Family and Childhood

When Jesus spoke at the synagogue in Nazareth, Mark says folks in his hometown were amazed: "Is not this the carpenter, the son of Mary and brother of James and Joses and Judas and Simon, and are not his sisters here with us?" (6:3). Based on this reference, Jesus had four brothers and at least two sisters. Matthew reads "all his sisters" (13:56), implying more than two. For Jesus' mother to have had this many pregnancies would not have been unusual, but to have this many *living* children was remarkable. We do not know whether Mary and Joseph lost any children in infancy, but it is statistically probable that they did. David Fiensy notes, "Were you a female, we can speculate that, after marrying as a teenager, you might have eight to ten pregnancies, five live births, and lose two of the five children in childhood"; "43 out of 100 children died by the age of twenty" (2020, 299). Men were typically older than their brides and had a life expectancy of only 38 years. Seventy percent of children lost one parent by the time they were sixteen (see 4.1). Since Joseph is not mentioned in the verses cited above, he had presumably died; but if Jesus had at least six living younger siblings, Joseph lived through Jesus' childhood, perhaps into his teenage years. Luke 2:42–52 places Joseph with the family when they went to Jerusalem for Passover when Jesus was twelve.

According to the Gospels, Joseph was a *tektōn*, a craftsman. Justin Martyr (2nd c.) says Joseph was a carpenter who made plows and yokes (*Dial.* 88). Epictetus (*Diatr.* 1.15.2) says a *tektōn* worked with wood, whereas bronze was the material of statuary. Less frequently the term designates a mason, sculptor, or stoneworker (BDAG, 995). In the Protoevangelium of James 9.2, Joseph constructs buildings. It is possible that Joseph maintained a carpenter's shop, making farming implements and tools. Given the population of Nazareth, it is also likely that he traveled at least from time to time to work in construction at Sepphoris and perhaps other sites (Oakman, 176–82; Fiensy 2007, 74–80). Josephus indicates that the massive building projects of the Herods, especially the temple in Jerusalem, required thousands of workers. "For [Herod] prepared a thousand wagons to carry the stones, selected ten thousand of the most skilled workmen, purchased priestly robes for a thousand priests, and trained some as masons, others as carpenters, and began construction only after all these preparations had diligently been made by him" (*Ant.* 15.390). When the construction of the temple was finally completed, Josephus claims that 18,000 laborers were put out of work (*Ant.* 20.219). Even if Josephus's numbers are inflated, the point is clear: the massive building projects created the need for slaves and work for traveling workers. As artisans, therefore, Joseph's family "lived simply, but they lived without anxiety and without want" (Fiensy 2007, 70).

Jesus probably learned Joseph's craft (Matt 13:55) and was therefore a carpenter himself (Mark 6:3). According to the Gospel of Thomas 77, Jesus said, "Split a piece of wood, and I am there" (Robinson, 126). Making a christological point from what may have been a common proverb (Dodd, 386), Jesus declared, "The Son can do nothing on his own, but only what he sees the Father doing; for whatever the Father does, the Son does likewise" (John 5:19).

If Joseph died while Jesus was a teenager, Jesus, as the eldest son, would have stepped into his father's shoes and supported the family by working as a carpenter or builder. He may also have traveled around towns and cities in Galilee, preparing the way for his itinerant ministry. Some of Jesus' sayings and parables may also be based on his early experiences: a neighbor knocking on the door after the family had bedded down for the night (Luke 11:5–8), and a widow seeking justice from an unjust judge (18:2–5).

21.3 Jesus' Education

We know more about Jesus than any other first-century Galilean, but modern scholarship has taken divergent views on the issue of Jesus' literacy. Ernst Knauf (348), for example, contends, "There is no doubt that Jesus could read the Hebrew Bible" (so also Meier 1991, 1:268–78; Evans, 80–88). The gospel traditions remember Jesus both as literate and illiterate. The evangelists not only drew upon different traditions regarding Jesus' literacy, they represented him differently for their intended readers. Moreover, the evangelists appear to have been members of well-educated communities. According to Mark 6:3, the people of Nazareth were amazed because they knew he was a carpenter (*tektōn*) and knew his family; he was not educated. Where did he get such wisdom? According to Luke 4:16, however, Jesus stood in his home synagogue to read, took the scroll, and read the passage in Isaiah. In John 7:15, when Jesus stood in the temple teaching, the people were astonished: "How does this man have such learning [lit., 'know letters'], when he has never been taught?" Craig Evans argues that this refers to "formal, scribal training" (80), but the same idiom appears frequently in nonliterary papyri (Kraus 1999, 434; Kraus 2007, 181), including Babatha's documents, where someone else signs for her because she "did not know letters" (see above, 5.4). In John, Jesus responds, "My teaching is not mine but his who sent me" (John 7:16; cf. 6:45). Yet Jesus taught in the synagogues and in the temple, confronted the scribes and Pharisees and priests, quoted and interpreted Scripture, and bested his opponents in such confrontations. Jesus taught and interpreted Scripture, but unlike the scribes, "he taught them as one having authority" (Mark 1:22), a higher authority than the scribes.

Chris Keith traces both the traditions that Jesus was illiterate and that he was scribal literate to the earliest memories of Jesus: "This tension was part of the received tradition from the outset" (181). Different groups, with varying levels of literacy, interpreted Jesus' actions differently. As a Galilean carpenter, the son of a carpenter in a village as small as Nazareth, Jesus was probably only "craftsman-literate" (Keith, 169; see above, 5.4 and 5.6). Jesus' disciples were also "uneducated [*agrammatoi*] and ordinary men" (Acts 4:13). Eventually, however, "the stream of Jesus-memory in which Jesus appears as a legitimate scribal-literate teacher predominated over the stream in which he is denied scribal literacy" (Keith, 156).

Jordan Ryan responded that one cannot draw inferences about an individual from data about the group to which the individual belongs, and one need not be scribal literate to read the Scriptures. Ryan argues that by participating in "synagogue culture," Jesus "attained a level of literacy higher than craftsman's literacy" (188). This argument pushes us beyond the evidence, however. Even if there was a synagogue in Nazareth, as the Gospels indicate, did the "synagogue culture" entail not only the public reading and interpretation of Scripture but also instruction in reading? We do not know. This level of education was generally found only in the homes of the elite, who had slaves or could afford to employ a tutor (see 5.4).

Even if the educational resources were available in Galilee, would the son of a *tektōn* have the time or support needed to learn to read unpointed Hebrew? The answer must remain "probably not." To date, excavations at Nazareth have found "no public inscriptions whatsoever," which Reed saw as "instructive of the level of illiteracy and lack of elite sponsors," and the same was true of Capernaum (131, 156–65).

21.4 Physical Description

Early sources contain no description of Jesus, but it is reasonable to assume that he shared the physical characteristics of other Galileans of his time. Studies in osteoarchaeology, the analysis of bones, provide data on diseases, the kind of work one did, causes of death, life expectancy, and average height. One sample includes remains of 227 individuals found in eight caves in and around Samaria (Nagar and Torgeë). Other samples contain remains found elsewhere in Palestine, providing a current database of about 1,600 individuals (Fiensy 2020, 189). Calculating a person's stature from the length of the femur, the average height of Palestinian males in the Hellenistic and early Roman periods was about 165.5 centimeters, or 5 feet, 5 inches; and 147 centimeters, or 4 feet, 10 inches for females (Nagar and Torgeë, 169; Fiensy 2020, 193). Therefore, it is a fair conclusion that these figures, give or take an inch or two, apply to Jesus and Mary, and to Jesus' followers, the twelve disciples, Mary Magdalene, and others. Based on these samples, men probably weighed about 140 pounds. Jesus' skin tone would have been olive-brown, with brown eyes, brown or black hair, and a short beard (Taylor, 168).

21.5 Jesus and John the Baptist

Because the church would not have created the story of Jesus' baptism by John, given the rivalry between the two movements, "Jesus' being baptized by John is one of the most historically certain events ascertainable by any reconstruction of the historical Jesus" (Meier 1994, 129). According to Luke, John was the son of a priest (Zechariah) and Mary's kinswoman (Elizabeth; Luke 1:5, 36). Mark describes John as "clothed with camel's hair, with a leather belt around his waist" (1:6), and crying in the wilderness, "Prepare the way of the Lord" (1:3; Isa 40:3). John's dress was that of a prophet (2 Kgs 1:8; Zech 13:4). John's diet of locusts (Lev 11:21–22) and wild honey (1 Kgs 14:3; 2 Kgs 18:32; Rev 10:9–10) identified him as a "wilderness man." He ate what was available: locusts (*akris*, grasshoppers; less probably carob pods or fritters [*egkris*] made from desert plants; BDAG, 39) and "uncultivated honey," whether from plants or bees (Kelhoffer, 97–99). For a while, Judas Maccabeus and his men also kept themselves alive in the wilderness "on what grew wild" (2 Macc 5:27), and the Martyrdom of Isaiah (2.11) describes a group of prophets who ate only "wild herbs (which) they gathered from the mountains."

John preached "a baptism of repentance for the forgiveness of sins" (Mark 1:4), and crowds of people went out to be baptized by him (1:5). The specific site of John's baptisms is unknown, but archaeologists working at Wadi el-Kharrar, along a spring-fed stream east of the Jordan, have found baptismal pools and churches dating to the fourth century (Khouri). The site is consistent with John 1:28, which refers to "Bethany beyond the Jordan" (RSV); and with the Pilgrim of Bordeaux (333 CE), who said that Jesus was baptized five miles north of the Dead Sea (http://andrewjacobs .org/translations/bordeaux.html).

The Essenes at Qumran, not far from where John was baptizing, practiced repeated self-administered washings, and it is possible that John was influenced by their practices. Like the Essenes, he called fellow Jews to repent and prepare for the coming eschatological events. The following lines from the Manual of Discipline illustrate the similarities: "God will refine, with his truth, all man's deeds, and will purify for himself the configuration of man, ripping out all spirit of injustice from the innermost part of his flesh, and cleansing him with the spirit of holiness from every irreverent deed. He will sprinkle over him the spirit of truth like lustral water (in order to cleanse him) from all the abhorrences of deceit and from the defilement of the unclean spirit" (1QS IV, 20–22; García Martínez, 7). Josephus's description of John the Baptist similarly connects repentance, baptism, and justice:

> But to some of the Jews the destruction of Herod's army seemed to be divine vengeance, and certainly a just vengeance, for his treatment of John, surnamed the Baptist. For Herod had put him to death, though he was a good man and had exhorted the Jews to lead righteous lives, to practise justice towards their fellows and piety towards God, and so doing to join in baptism. In his view this was a necessary preliminary if baptism was to be acceptable to God. (*Ant.* 18.117–118)

In spite of these similarities, there is no evidence that John had lived with or was influenced by the community at Qumran. His prophetic call for Israel to repent may have been a rebellion against his priestly family (Luke 1) or an echo of the Essenes' condemnation of the Jerusalem priesthood (Meier 1994, 27). Regardless, since his parents were somewhat older than usual and given the mortality rates of the time, it may be that John had lost one or both of his parents before he took up the prophets' mantle.

Although Jesus accepted John's baptism and his call for Israel to repent, their ministries were both similar and different. Matthew especially emphasizes the similarities (21:23–27, 28–32; Davies and Allison, 1:289–90; Culpepper 2021, 406–7). Jesus echoes John's words, proclaiming, "Repent, for the kingdom of heaven has come near" (Matt 3:2; 4:17). The Matthean Jesus' repeated warnings about the coming judgment also echo both John's preaching (3:7–12) and the Dead Sea Scrolls (Culpepper 2021, 22–23). An eternal fire is "prepared for the devil and his angels" (Matt 25:41). The wicked will be banished to "Hades" (11:23; 16:18), Gehenna (5:22, 29–30; 10:28; 18:9; 23:15, 33), a "furnace of fire" (13:42, 50), "eternal punishment" (25:46), and "the outer darkness" (8:12; 22:13; 25:30), amid "weeping and gnashing of teeth" (8:12; 13:42, 50; 22:13; 24:51; 25:30).

According to the Gospel of John, Jesus drew some of his first disciples from John's followers (1:35–37) and conducted a parallel ministry (3:22–24; 4:1): he and/or his disciples baptized those who came to him (3:22; 4:2). Nevertheless, Jesus' ministry was very different. He was an itinerant, traveling through Galilee: he was not an ascetic (Matt 11:7–19), and he healed the sick and worked wonders (11:2–16), while "John performed no sign" (John 10:41).

21.6 Jesus and the Galilean Prophets and Charismatics

Géza Vermès found in the Gospels' portrayals of Jesus "the true heir of an age-old prophetic religious line" (1973a, 69) also represented by other Galilean holy men, especially Honi the Circle Drawer and Hanina ben Dosa. Like John the Baptist, they continued the prophetic tradition represented especially by Elijah (cf. Matt 11:14; 16:14; 17:3–4, 10–12). Their contemporaries believed that these holy men were like Elijah (1 Kgs 17:1): by praying, they were able to control natural phenomena (Vermès 1973a, 90).

21.6.1 Honi the Circle Drawer

The Mishnah connects Honi with Simeon ben Shetah (ca. 80 BCE). Josephus locates Honi in the struggle for power between Hyrcanus and Aristobulus before 63 BCE. Honi became known as "the Circle Drawer" after the people asked him to pray for rain during a drought. First, he told them to bring in the Passover ovens, which were made of dried clay, so that they would not be softened by the rain. When he prayed but the rain did not fall, he drew a circle and stood within it, vowing he would not leave the circle until it rained. He appealed to God: "I am like a son of the house before thee." When it began to sprinkle, he said, "Not for such rain have I prayed but for rain that will fill the cisterns, pits, and caverns." When it rained violently, he said, "Not for such rain have I prayed, but for rain of goodwill, blessing and graciousness." When it rained steadily until Jerusalem began to flood, the people asked him to pray that it would stop. Simeon ben Shetah complained in frustration that he could do nothing about Honi's impertinence before God because God granted his requests, like a father granting the requests of his son (m. Ta'an. 3:8).

Josephus refers to this story by way of introducing Honi as "a righteous man and dear to God." Honi hid during the civil war between two Hasmonean contenders, but he was taken to the camp of Hyrcanus's supporters and asked to place a curse on Aristobulus. When he refused because God's people were attacking God's priests and asked instead that God not grant their request, they stoned him to death (*Ant.* 14.22–24).

21.6.2 Hanina ben Dosa

While it cannot be established that Honi was a Galilean, the Talmud reports that, before 70 in the first century, Hanina lived in 'Arava, a small town north of Sepphoris (y. Ber. 7c; Vermès, 1973b, 58; Goodman, 608–10). The Mishnah introduces Hanina in the tractate on prayer, which says, "The pious men of old used to wait an hour before they said the *Tefillah*, that they might direct their heart toward God" (m. Ber. 5:1). A few lines later the rabbis report that Hanina "used to pray over the sick and say, 'This one will live,' or 'This one will die.' They said to him, 'How knowest thou?' He replied, 'If my prayer is fluent in my mouth[,] I know that he is accepted; and if it is not[,] I know that he is rejected'" (m. Ber. 5:5). So great was Hanina's reputation for piety that when he died the rabbis said, "The men of good deeds ceased" (m. Soṭah 9:15; see also m. Avot 3:10–11; b. Ber. 17b, 33a, 34b, 61b; b. Pesaḥ. 112b; b. Taʿan. 24b–25a; b. Yoma 53b; b. Ḥul. 86a).

Vermès's interpretation of Honi and Hanina as Galilean charismatics has been widely influential (Moller) yet critiqued by others. Meier in particular found that the rabbinic sources emphasized their efficacious prayer rather than their miracle working and that the earliest traditions do not connect either of them with Galilee (Meier 1994, 588; see below, 21.8). The connection of piety, prayer, sonship, and control over nature in these traditions still resonates with Jesus. In one of his early works, James D. G. Dunn found the twin pillars of Jesus' religious experience to be his sense of sonship and his experience of empowerment by the Spirit, especially in the context of prayer. At the same time, Jesus' sense of sonship was not unique, even though it was the foundation for his self-consciousness and his sense of mission (1975, 37, 39). Other expressions of the connection between sonship and knowledge of God, such as we find in Matthew 11:27, appear in the wisdom literature, where the righteous one "professes to have knowledge of God, . . . calls himself a child [son] of the Lord," and "boasts that God is his father" (Wis 2:13, 16). Dunn concludes, "Jesus thought of himself as God's son and as anointed by the eschatological Spirit, because in prayer he experienced God as Father and in ministry he experienced a power to heal which he could only understand as the power of the end-time and an inspiration to proclaim a message which he could only understand as the gospel of the end-time" (1975, 67). Thus Jesus explained, "If it is by the finger of God" (Luke 11:20; cf. Exod 8:19), "by the Spirit of God" (Matt 12:28), "that I cast out demons, then the kingdom of God has come upon you."

Whatever one makes of the relevance of Honi and Hanina ben Dosa for understanding Jesus and the religious atmosphere of Galilee in the first century, they do not represent adequate models for Jesus' itinerant ministry, his proclamation of the coming kingdom, his exorcisms and healing, or his teaching in parables. As W. D. Davies has cautioned, the thesis "that Galilee was especially connected with the Messiah as the scene of the Messianic Age, must be treated with great reserve" (231); "Galilee found much to object to in Jesus, as he found much to condemn in it" (241).

21.7 Jesus' Itinerant Ministry

Whatever drove Jesus to be an itinerant, others interpreted his nomadic ministry in light of the model of Elijah (Theissen, 108–9), who was divinely directed: "The word of the LORD came to him, saying, 'Go from here and turn eastward,'" then, "Go now to Zarephath, which belongs to Sidon, and live there; for I have commanded a widow there to feed you'" (1 Kgs 17:2–3, 9). Matthew 4:13 says Jesus left Nazareth and made his home in Capernaum, where he may have stayed with Peter and Andrew (Mark 1:29) as he began to proclaim the coming kingdom of God (or "of heaven," Matt 4:17). When his disciples reported that the people were looking for him, Jesus responded, "Let us go on to the neighboring towns, so that I may proclaim the message there also; for that is what I came out to do." Mark adds, "He went throughout Galilee, proclaiming the message in their synagogues and casting out demons" (1:38–39//Matt 4:23). Some days later, he returned to Capernaum, "and it was reported that he was at home" (Mark 2:1). Traveling from village to village and then returning to Capernaum seems to have become Jesus' pattern, at least in Mark (Baergen; Zeichmann; Dube, 80–87). In a summary verse, Matthew characterizes Jesus' ministry as itinerant, without reference to Capernaum: "Then Jesus went about all the cities and villages, teaching in their synagogues, and proclaiming the good news of the kingdom, and curing every disease and every sickness" (9:35).

Sociologically, there were probably multiple reasons why Jesus and his disciples chose to become marginal itinerants: "It is not much of a stretch, then, to imagine a scenario in which their hardship provoked them to abandon work and live as drifters, especially if they were heavily indebted" (Myles, 106; cf. Josephus, *Ant.* 18.314–370). Nevertheless, the impulse that drove Jesus was deeper than the socioeconomic conditions. Martin Hengel highlighted Jesus' call for a select group—not everyone—to forsake family ties and obligations, renounce possessions, follow him, and join him in the prophetic work of announcing the coming of God's kingdom and the judgment (71–73). "These ideas," Hengel contends, "occur in contexts where the traditional order and its standards are repeatedly broken down, or indeed rejected outright"; they can be seen "most clearly in the apocalyptic prophets and popular Zealot leaders" (34). Some of Jesus' sayings reflect his itinerant lifestyle: "Foxes have holes, and birds of the air have nests; but the Son of Man has nowhere to lay his head" (Matt 8:20//Luke 9:58); and "Let the dead bury their own dead" (Matt 8:22//Luke 9:60). These sayings cast Jesus as displaced, destitute, and marginalized from home and society, but apparently by choice rather than circumstances (Brawley, 2–3; Myles, 112–34).

The Gospels record the names of only a few cities and villages, but it appears that Jesus frequented two main areas in Galilee: (1) the central region near his hometown (Nazareth, Cana, and Nain) and (2) around the Sea of Galilee (Capernaum, Bethsaida, and Gennesaret on the northwestern shore; Chorazin, two miles north of the lake and west of the Jordan). It is likely that he taught at the synagogue in Magdala. At times, he also withdrew or made excursions into the region of Tyre and Sidon, to Caesarea Philippi, and across the lake to the east. The Gospels never record that Jesus visited Sepphoris or Tiberias, which has been explained in various ways. Eric Meyers claims that this silence is deliberate and artificial: "It strains credulity to imagine any sort of ministry of Jesus in Galilee without coming into contact with the populations of either Tiberias or Sepphoris" (61). Seán Freyne suggests it was "principled, based on Jesus' views of the values represented by these cities and his own call to minister to those who had become victims of their elitist lifestyle" (2004, 144–45; cf. Freyne 1997, 55; Schröter, 59–60).

Several justifications have been advanced for Jesus' strategy of itinerancy. First, it was the most effective way for him to reach all Israel. He may have visited as many towns and villages as he could, then sent his disciples out to reach others (Mark 3:14; 6:7–13 par.; Luke 10:1–17). According to Matthew, Jesus explicitly limited their mission to "the lost sheep of the house of Israel" (10:5–6) and assured them that they "will not have gone through all the towns of Israel before the Son of Man comes" (10:23).

Jesus chose neither the wilderness (in contrast to John the Baptist) nor Jerusalem but Galilee as the locus of his ministry. Summary statements in all four Gospels specify that he taught in the synagogues (Matt 4:23; Mark 1:38–39; Luke 4:15–16; John 18:20), where the Law and the Prophets were read and discussed (Ryan, 125–69). The Gospels also contain samples of Jesus' teachings, set both in the synagogues and elsewhere. He affirmed the authority of the law but taught a new interpretation of it (Matt 5:21–48; 9:13; 12:7; 22:38–40). He taught "not as the scribes" but "as one having authority" (Mark 1:22): "They were all amazed, and they kept on asking one another, 'What is this? A new teaching—with authority!'" (Mark 1:27).

Nevertheless, Jesus was rejected in many places: Nazareth (Mark 6:4–6; Luke 4:28–29), Chorazin and Bethsaida (Matt 11:21//Luke 10:13), and even Capernaum (Matt 11:23/Luke 10:15). So he warned his disciples that they would be persecuted also (Matt 5:10–12; John 15:20). When they were rejected, they were to shake the dust off their feet and go on to the next village (Matt 10:14, 23; Mark 6:11//Luke 9:5; 10:11).

A further reason for his itinerancy was to avoid capture (Theissen, 121; Lloyd, 58–62). Jesus had reason to fear Herod Antipas after he beheaded

John the Baptist. When Antipas heard about Jesus and his disciples, he was reported to have said, "John, whom I beheaded, has been raised" (Mark 6:16). On various occasions Jesus took the disciples and withdrew to desolate places, across the Sea of Galilee, to the region of Tyre and Sidon, to Caesarea Philippi, or east of the Jordan. He may have been preaching to Jews in these areas also, but his periodic withdrawals may have been timed to allow the crowds to dissipate and the reports of his activities to cool down. As reports of his teaching and healing spread, "Jesus could no longer go into a town openly, but stayed out in the country; and people came to him from every quarter" (Mark 1:45).

Stirring up the people was dangerous (Luke 23:5; John 7:1). Josephus wrote the following about John the Baptist's arrest: "When others too joined the crowds about him, because they were aroused to the highest degree by his sermons, Herod [Antipas] became alarmed. Eloquence that had so great an effect on mankind might lead to some form of sedition, for it looked as if they would be guided by John in everything that they did" (*Ant.* 18.118). Jesus' activities too could have given rise to hopes, suspicions, or fears that he sought a change in the political order (Schröter, 64).

One result of Jesus' itinerancy is that because he would have repeated his teachings for different audiences, his disciples learned them by their sheer repetition and repeated them when they were sent out to preach (Hengel, 81–82; Theissen, 120–21). A further consequence of Jesus' charismatic and itinerant lifestyle may be that he did not marry, as would have been normal for a Jewish man. Various explanations have been advanced for Jesus' apparently remaining single: he was too poor to marry, he was an ascetic, he formed a monastic community, he expected the end to come imminently (Fiensy 2020, 308–11, responds to each of these proposals). Appealing to Max Weber's attributes of a charismatic (Weber, 1:215, 241–45), David Fiensy plausibly suggests that "Jesus as a charismatic leader renounced his possessions and family and lived the life of an itinerant teacher, demanding also that his closest disciples—at least temporarily—do the same" (2020, 313).

21.8 Jesus as Healer

The description of Jesus that appears in Josephus (*Ant.* 18.63–64) contains three passages that appear to be later insertions by a Christian copyist. The remainder, which probably comes from Josephus (Meier 1991, 59–69), identifies Jesus as a "wise man" (*sophos anēr*) and a doer of *paradoxōn ergōn*, "surprising feats" (Feldman, LCL) or "startling deeds" (Meier 1991,

61), which presumably included his work as a healer. In addition, Josephus reports, he was "a teacher of such people as accept the truth gladly."

Marcus Borg addresses the issue of the authenticity of the Gospel accounts of Jesus' healings: "Behind this picture of Jesus as healer and exorcist, I affirm a historical core. In common with the majority of contemporary Jesus scholars, I see the claim that Jesus performed paranormal healings and exorcisms as history remembered. Indeed, more healing stories are told about Jesus than about any other figure in the Jewish tradition. He must have been a remarkable healer" (Borg and Wright, 66). Understanding Jesus' work as a healer, however, requires a brief overview of medicine and healers in antiquity.

Early in the second century BCE, Jesus ben Sirach, a Jewish wisdom teacher who embraced the authority of the Torah while facing the transformation of Jewish culture by the new wave of Hellenism, grudgingly advised his pupils to avail themselves of the healing arts of physicians, while at the same time warning them to seek God's healing help first. Listen for his ambivalence:

> Honor physicians for their services,
>   for the Lord created them;
> for their gift of healing comes from the Most High,
>   and they are rewarded by the king.
> The skill of physicians makes them distinguished,
>   and in the presence of the great they are admired.
> The Lord created medicines out of the earth,
>   And the sensible will not despise them.
> . . . .
> My child, when you are ill, do not delay,
>   But pray to the Lord, and he will heal you.
> Give up your faults and direct your hands rightly,
>   And cleanse your heart from all sin.
> Offer a sweet-smelling sacrifice,
>   and a memorial portion of choice flour,
>   and pour oil on your offering, as much as you can afford.
> Then give the physician his place, for the Lord created him;
>   do not let him leave you, for you need him.
> There may come a time when recovery lies in the hands of physicians,
>   for they too pray to the Lord
> that he may grant them success in diagnosis and in healing,
>   for the sake of preserving life.
>
> (Sir 38:1–4, 9–14)

So, pray first, but go to a physician; recovery may lie in the physicians' hands, for they too pray. Sirach recognizes both the ancient lore and contemporary medicine; the sacred and the professional; the importance of prayer, offerings, and cleansing your heart from sin on the one hand, and pharmaceutical science and medicines from the earth on the other. His bridge between the two is that God created both (cf. Temkin 1991, 89–90; Kee 1986, 19–21; Kee 1992, 660–61).

Views regarding physicians and healers were in flux in Second Temple Judaism (Hogan; Vermès 1973a, 59–69). The traditional view was that God sent illnesses as punishment for sin. Therefore, one should repent and pray for healing (Kee 1986, 12–16; Wilkinson, 54–56). Sirach takes a mediating position, retaining the traditional view but making a place for physicians and herbalists. Jubilees (10.10–13) and 1 Enoch (7.1) treat medical knowledge as wisdom revealed to humans. Other writers (1QapGen XX, 16–19) maintain the traditional view, leaving little place for physicians and healers. On the other hand, a "medical report" found at Qumran that describes ailments and treatments shows that Hellenistic medicine was known among the Essenes (Kee 1986, 46–47). In Tobit, the archangel Raphael becomes the healing angel. Consulting a physician only made Tobit's eye condition worse, but Raphael heals Tobit and instructs Tobias about how to use fish parts to chase away a demon. Rebecca Raphael concludes from these sources that "1 Enoch, Tobit, and Jubilees all prescribe a medical function to angelic intermediaries" (711).

Walter Wilson refined John Pilch's model of three sectors—the professional, the popular, and the folk—noting that healers can be official or unofficial and they can operate with supernatural or natural assumptions, resulting in four sectors (Wilson, 29; Pilch, 25–27, 77–86; cf. Stanley, esp. 135–65).

Figure 6

	Supernatural	Natural
Official	Cultic	Professional
Unofficial	Charismatic	Folk

Cultic healers were priests in temples or cultic centers of gods associated with healing (Asclepius and Isis) who could lead pilgrims seeking healing through the sacred rites. A fourth-century CE inscription contains a list of healings attributed to the priests of Epidaurus (Boring, Berger, and Colpe, 64). The cult of Asclepius was known in Phoenicia, and there was a healing center near Sidon (McCasland, 223; cf. Nutzman). Josephus refers to the thermal springs at Hammat Tiberias (*J.W.* 2.614; *Ant.* 18.36; cf. Pliny the Elder, *Nat.* 5.70–72); Hygieia, the daughter of Asclepius, appears on a bronze coin struck by Tiberias in 99 and again in 108 CE (McCasland, 224). *Professional* healers, the smallest of the four sectors, were generally trained in one of the Hippocratic schools, sought natural causes and therapies, and expected remuneration for their services (Temkin 1991, 10–13). The Hippocratic tradition split into three schools of thought: (1) dogmatics, who investigated the causes of diseases; (2) empiricists, who relied on accumulated experience; and (3) methodists, who emphasized therapy and rejected both etiological research and mere experience (Temkin 1956, xxv–xxx). Most sick people relied on *folk* healers, often family members administering traditional folk remedies with a dose of superstition. *Charismatic* healers displayed personal powers and claimed access to spiritual or magic means of healing, which John Meier describes as "manipulation of various (often impersonal) supernatural forces or the coercion of a deity in order to obtain a desired concrete benefit" (1994, 549).

Jesus would have been identified as a charismatic healer. Apollonius of Tyana and Hanina ben Dosa (m. Ber. 5:5, quoted above) are often cited as examples of charismatic healers. Meier's assessment of these traditions is that (1) the sources describing Apollonius and Hanina are not contemporary with them; and (2) in the case of Hanina (and Honi the Circle Drawer), the wonder is the power of his prayer rather than his miracle working (1994, 576–601). Jesus' healings and exorcisms were distinctive because they demonstrated the power of the kingdom he announced: "But if it is by the finger of God that I cast out the demons, then the kingdom of God has come to you" (Luke 11:20).

As the quotation from Sirach above illustrates, the traditional, sacred, and folk approaches to healing were in conflict with the newer, secular, and professional approaches, which were slowly gaining ground. Most people probably sought help from folk healers and spiritual direction from priests and community religious leaders. Illness was culturally and religiously defined as the result of sin, so it was assumed that healing required forgiveness or purification. Physical symptoms were the result of a direct cause, whether divine punishment or demon possession. In many cases, illness brought shame, pollution, or uncleanness, and therefore ostracism from family and society (cf. Prayer of Nabonidus, 4Q242). In Matthew and Mark, the demoniacs lived in tombs (burial caves). The hemorrhaging woman would have been forbidden to marry, have sexual relations, or participate in religious activities. To reenter society, a leper was required to show oneself to the priest and offer the proper sacrifices. Healing was understood as regaining wholeness or *shalom*: physical, social, and spiritual well-being.

Healings and exorcisms were commonly accepted in that era. Josephus's praise of Solomon reveals much about how exorcisms were viewed (cf., however, Mark 3:22): "And God granted him [Solomon] knowledge of the art used against demons for the benefit and healing of men. He also composed incantations by which illnesses are relieved, and left behind forms of exorcisms with which those possessed by demons drive them out, never to return" (*Ant.* 8.45). Josephus adds, "This same form of healing remains quite strong among us until today" (8.46, trans. Begg and Spilsbury). He personally witnessed an exorcism performed by a certain Eleazar in the presence of Vespasian. The exorcist put a ring under the nose of the possessed man that had a root prescribed by Solomon. The scent drew the demon out. When the man fell down, the exorcist forbade it to return, invoking the name of Solomon and reciting one of Solomon's incantations. Then the exorcist commanded the demon to overturn a basin of water as it left to confirm Solomon's wisdom and how God had favored him (8.47–49).

Finally, we must give at least a passing nod to the question of historicity. On what basis can the claim be made that the healing miracles ascribed to Jesus are any more credible than those attributed to other ancient healers? Meier recalls Morton Smith's probative observation in one of his seminars: "Without his miracles, Jesus would never have attracted both the enthusiasm and the opposition that marked and finally ended his public life" (Meier 1994, 3). Jesus was not just a prophet and teacher but also one known as a healer and wonder-worker. The church fathers also spoke of Jesus as a physician (Wilkinson, 63, citing Ign., *Eph.* 7.2; Clement of Alexandria, *Paed.* 1.1.1; 1.2.6; 1.8.64; 1.12.10; Origen, *Cels.* 2.67; Origen, *Hom. Lev.* 8.1; Eusebius, *Hist. eccl.* 10.4.11). Even if these reports have been embellished over time, healings and exorcisms were integral to Jesus' preaching of the kingdom of God.

21.9 Jesus and Purity

Jesus departed from the dominant religious practice among Galilean Jews with respect to purity defined as separation from unclean things. Ritual impurity was highly transmissible, "contagious," but purity was not transmissible by contact (Hag 2:11–13; Holmén, 2721). As we have seen, the material culture of first-century Galilee attests to the widespread practice of purity, with its *miqva'ot* and stone vessels, purity at meals, and separation from gentiles (see above, 3.2, 3.4, 10.3), yet Jesus (Luke 11:37–38) and his disciples (Matt 15:2, 20; Mark 7:1–5) did not wash before eating, and Jesus ate with the unclean. It may be that common people were not concerned about being touched by unclean people unless they were entering the temple, but the unclean touched the tassels (*tzitzit*; Num 15:38–39) of Jesus' garments, perhaps so as not to transmit their uncleanness (Matt 9:20; 14:36; Magness, 120). Nevertheless, Jesus seems to have observed Jewish dietary laws because in the early chapters in Acts, Peter and the disciples observe the Levitical food laws (10:14), which implies that Jesus did not teach otherwise. The comment in Mark 7:19, "thus he declared all food clean," therefore probably owes more to Pauline practice than to Jesus (Culpepper 2021, 10–11).

Jesus' challenge to the observance of ritual purity was sweeping (Mark 7:14–23//Matt 15:10–20). One is not made unclean, he taught, by what one eats or what one touches: "There is nothing outside a person that by going in can defile, but the things that come out are what defile" (Mark 7:15//Matt 15:11). True purity is a matter of the heart, thought, will, desires, and speech. Jesus therefore ate with tax collectors, touched lepers, asked for a drink from a Samaritan woman, and traveled in gentile areas. In this disregard for conventional practice, Jesus returned to the piety of Israel's prophets. Isaiah called for purity in actions: "Wash yourselves; make yourselves clean; remove the evil of your doings from before my eyes; cease to do evil, learn to do good; seek justice, rescue the oppressed, defend the orphan, plead for the widow" (1:16–17). Amos called for justice: "Let justice roll down like waters, and righteousness like an ever-flowing stream" (5:24). True piety, therefore, requires purity of heart, justice, and mercy, rather than distinction between common and holy, or clean and unclean (cf. Culpepper 2021, 286–90; Dunn 2003, 573–77; Fiensy 2007, 147–80; Schröter, 113–19).

The Gospels also suggest that when Jesus healed, he delivered the sick and possessed from their uncleanness. When Naaman the Syrian came to Elisha, the prophet sent him to wash in the Jordan River: "Go, wash in the Jordan seven times, and your flesh shall be restored and you shall be clean" (2 Kgs 5:10). Healing both involved cleansing and was a sign of cleansing. As Matthew tells the story, a leper came to Jesus and knelt before him, saying, "Lord, if you choose, you can make me clean." Jesus stretched out his hand and touched him, saying, "I do choose. Be made clean!" and "Immediately his leprosy was cleansed" (Matt 8:2–3//Mark 1:40–42//Luke 5:12–13; 17:14). Similarly, when the hemorrhaging woman touched Jesus, power flowed from Jesus to her with the result that she was healed and cleansed (Mark 5:27–30). When he took the dead girl's hand, she was revived. In none of Jesus' contacts with unclean persons do the Gospels ever intimate that Jesus became unclean. On the contrary, they became clean (Viljoen 2014a; 2014b), or as Tom Holmén put it, "The impurities of the unclean do not transfer to Jesus; instead, Jesus' purity transfers to the unclean" (2743).

The Gospel of John develops Jesus' power to heal and cleanse as a recurring motif (Blomberg, 223–332). Jesus follows John the Baptist, who declares that while he baptized with water, Jesus will baptize "with the Holy Spirit" (1:33). The stone vessels used for purification are filled with good wine: the first of Jesus' signs (2:1–11). Later, Jesus' disciples debate with a Jew about purification (3:25). John is ambiguous, but Jesus (3:22) and/or his disciples baptized others (4:2). Jesus was the source of "living water" (4:10–14; 7:37–39). He healed the man at the Pool of Bethesda, not the stirring of the waters (5:1–9, NRSV, n.). When the blind man washed himself in the Pool of Siloam, which John pointedly says "means Sent," he "came back able to see" (9:7). When Jesus washed his disciples' feet, he declared that they were clean, all of them except Judas (13:10–11), then commented, "You have already been cleansed by the word that I have spoken to you" (15:3). Although John and the Synoptics differ on many points, on this topic they speak with one voice: Jesus was the source of true purity (Blomberg, 370–71).

21.10 Jesus' Announcement of the Coming Kingdom

Jesus called for repentance, announcing the imminent coming of the kingdom of God: "There are some standing here who will not taste death until they see that the kingdom of God has come with power" (Mark 9:1; Culpepper 2013, 82). Jesus pointed ahead to God's future deliverance of the faithful and judgment on the wicked. Yet his eschatology was restrained: he rejected the search for signs and the calculation of times (Matt 12:38–39; 16:1–4; 24:3, 30; Acts 1:6–8). The renewal of Israel in the coming kingdom was already present in his ministry, where it was manifest in his preaching to the poor, the hungry, and the outcast; his exorcisms; his repentant followers, their open table fellowship, and the new community he was creating. The ethic of this new community was based on justice for the poor and oppressed; dignity and care for women, children, the sick and disabled; and piety oriented around love and inclusion, rather than purity, privilege, or ritual.

Galileans found familiar figures and situations in Jesus' parables and aphorisms: a woman sweeping her dirt floor, another kneading bread, neighbors arriving late, farmers sowing precious seed on rocky ground, children playing in the marketplace, fishermen sorting their catch, shepherds searching for lost sheep and separating sheep and goats, men waiting for work, vineyard owners seeking laborers for the harvest, a younger son leaving home to seek a better life, persistent widows and unjust judges, unjust stewards, and travelers falling among thieves. Jesus challenged his hearers to live into a different world, one populated by masters who forgive debts, a contrite tax collector, a compassionate Samaritan, and a generous vineyard owner who takes care of his day laborers.

God's rule would restore the land promised to Abraham and his descendants. Robert Brawley summarizes Jesus' message persuasively: "In the midst of development of cities and estates in imperial systems that stripped land and its resources from peasants, Jesus declared his homelessness in solidarity with the poor and dispossessed" (5). Jesus gave hope to the Galileans, calling them to repent, forgive, and live justly and compassionately with a pure heart. Although the modern world is so different from Jesus' Galilean context, the basic human issues remain the same. For "those who have ears to hear," Jesus' parables still announce God's infinite love, deliverance for the poor, comfort for those who mourn, and judgment on those who turn a deaf ear to the plight of the poor.

Works Cited in Chapter 21

Baergen, Rene Alexander. 2013. *Re-Placing the Galilean Jesus: Local Geography, Mark, Miracle, and the Quest for Jesus of Capernaum*. Toronto: University of Toronto.

Begg and Spilsbury. *See* Bibliography of Ancient Sources and Translations: Josephus, *Judean Antiquities*

Blomberg, Craig L. 2023. *Jesus the Purifier*. Grand Rapids: Baker Academic.

Borg, Marcus J., and N. T. Wright. 1999. *The Meaning of Jesus: Two Visions*. San Francisco: HarperSanFrancisco.

Boring, M. Eugene, Klaus Berger, and Carsten Colpe, eds. 1995. *Hellenistic Commentary to the New Testament*. Nashville: Abingdon.

Brawley, Robert L. 2011. "Homeless in Galilee." *HvTSt* 67.1. http://www.hts.org.za/index.php/HTS/article/view/863.

Claussen, Carsten, and Jörg Frey, eds. 2008. *Jesus und die Archäologie Galiläas*. Biblisch-Theologische Studien 87. Neukirchen-Vluyn: Neukirchener.

Crossan, John Dominic, and Jonathan L. Reed. 2001. *Excavating Jesus: Beneath the Stones, Behind the Texts*. Rev. ed. San Francisco: HarperSanFrancisco.

Culpepper, R. Alan. 2013. "Contours of the Historical Jesus." Pages 67–85 in *The Quest for the Real Jesus*. Edited by Jan van der Watt. BibInt 120. Leiden: Brill.

———. 2021. *Matthew*. NTL. Louisville: Westminster John Knox.

Davies, W. D. 1974. *The Gospel and the Land: Early Christianity and Jewish Territorial Doctrine*. Berkeley: University of California Press.

Davies, W. D., and Dale C. Allison, Jr. 1988. *The Gospel according to Saint Matthew 1–7*. Vol. 1. ICC. Edinburgh: T&T Clark.

Dodd, C. H. 1963. *Historical Tradition in the Fourth Gospel*. Cambridge: Cambridge University Press.

Dube, Zorodzai. 2020. *Jesus, the Best Capernaum Folk-Healer: Mark's Aretalogy of Jesus in the Healing Stories*. Eugene, OR: Pickwick.

Dunn, James D. G. 1975. *Jesus and the Spirit*. Philadelphia: Westminster.

———. 2003. *Jesus Remembered*. Grand Rapids: Eerdmans.

Evans, Craig A. 2012. *Jesus and His World: The Archaeological Evidence*. Louisville: Westminster John Knox.

Fiensy, David A. 2007. *Jesus the Galilean: Soundings in a First Century Life*. Piscataway, NJ: Gorgias.

———. 2020. *The Archaeology of Daily Life: Ordinary Persons in Late Second Temple Israel*. Eugene, OR: Cascade.

Freyne, Seán. 1997. "Town and Country Once More: The Case of Roman Galilee." Pages 49–56 in *Archaeology and the Galilee: Texts and Contexts in the Graeco-Roman and Byzantine Periods*. Edited by Douglas R. Edwards and C. Thomas McCollough. Atlanta: Scholars Press.

———. 2004. *Jesus, a Jewish Galilean*. London: T&T Clark.

García Martínez. *See* Bibliography of Ancient Sources and Translations

Goodman, Martin. 1999. "Galilean and Judaean Judaism." Pages 596–61 in *The Early Roman Period*. Vol. 3 of *The Cambridge History of Judaism*. Edited by William Horbury et al. Cambridge: Cambridge University Press.

Hengel, Martin. 1968. *The Charismatic Leader and His Followers*. Translated by James Greig. New York: Crossroad.

Hogan, Larry P. 1992. *Healing in the Second Temple Period*. Göttingen: Vandenhoeck & Ruprecht.

Holmén, Tom. 2011. "Jesus and the Purity Paradigm." Pages 2709–44 in *Handbook for the Study of the Historical Jesus*, vol. 3. Edited by Tom Holmén and Stanley E. Porter. Leiden: Brill.

Kee, Howard Clark. 1986. *Medicine, Miracle and Magic in New Testament Times*. SNTSMS 55. Cambridge: Cambridge University Press.

———. 1992. "Medicine and Healing." *ABD* 4:659–64.

Keith, Chris. 2011. *Jesus' Literacy: Scribal Culture and the Teacher from Galilee*. LNTS 413. London: T&T Clark.

Kelhoffer, James A. 2005. *The Diet of John the Baptist: Locusts and Wild Honey in Synoptic and Patristic Interpretation*. WUNT 176. Tübingen: Mohr Siebeck.

Khouri, Rami G. 2005. "Where John Baptized: Bethany beyond the Jordan." *BAR* 31:34–43.

Knauf, Ernst Axel. 2003. "Writing and Speaking in Galilee." Pages 336–50 in *Zeichen aus Text und Stein: Studien auf dem Weg zu einer Archäologie des Neuen Testaments*. Edited by S. Alkier and J. K. Zangenberg. TANZ 42. Tübingen: Francke.

Kraus, Thomas J. 1999. "'Uneducated,' 'Ignorant,' or even 'Illiterate'? Aspects and Background for an Understanding of ΑΓΡΑΜΜΑΤΟΙ (and ΙΔΙΩΤΑΙ) in Acts 4.13." *NTS* 45: 434–49.

———. 2007. "John 7:15B: 'Knowing Letters' and (Il)literacy." Pages 171–83 in *Ad Fontes: Original Manuscripts and Their Significance for Studying Early Christianity: Selected Essays*. TENTS 3. Leiden: Brill.

Lloyd, J. A. 2022. *Archaeology and the Itinerant Jesus: A Historical Enquiry into Jesus' Itinerant Ministry in the North*. WUNT 564. Tübingen: Mohr Siebeck.

Magness, Jodi. 2011. *Stone and Dung, Oil and Spit: Jewish Daily Life in the Time of Jesus*. Grand Rapids: Eerdmans.

McCasland, S. Vernon. 1939. "The Asklepios Cult in Palestine." *JBL* 58:221–27.

Meier, John P. 1991. *The Roots of the Problem and the Person*. Vol. 1 of *A Marginal Jew*. ABRL. New York: Doubleday.

————. 1994. *Mentor, Message, and Miracles*. Vol. 2 of *A Marginal Jew*. ABRL. New York: Doubleday.

Meyers, Eric M. 1997. "Jesus and His Galilean Context." Pages 57–66 in *Archaeology and the Galilee: Texts and Contexts in the Graeco-Roman and Byzantine Periods*. Edited by Douglas R. Edwards and C. Thomas McCollough. Atlanta: Scholars Press.

Moller, Hilde Brekke. 2017. *The Vermes Quest: The Significance of Geza Vermes for Jesus Research*. LNTS 576. London: Bloomsbury.

Myles, Robert J. 2014. *The Homeless Jesus in the Gospel of Matthew*. Sheffield: Sheffield Phoenix.

Nagar, Yossi, and Hagit Torgeë. 2003. "Biological Characteristics of Jewish Burial in the Hellenistic and Early Roman Periods." *IEJ* 53.2:164–71.

Nutzman, Megan. 2017. "'In This Holy Place': Incubation at Hot Springs in Roman and Late Antique Palestine." Pages 281–304 in *Gods, Objects, and Ritual Practice*. Edited by Sandra Blakely. Atlanta: Lockwood.

Oakman, Douglas E. 1986. *Jesus and the Economic Questions of His Day*. SBEC 8. Lewiston: Mellen.

Pilch, John J. 2000. *Healing in the New Testament: Insights from Medical and Mediterranean Anthropology*. Minneapolis: Fortress.

Raphael, Rebecca. 2010. "Healing." *EDEJ*, 709–11.

Reed, Jonathan L. 2000. *Archaeology and the Galilean Jesus: A Re-Examination of the Evidence*. Harrisburg, PA: Trinity Press International.

Robinson, James M., ed. 1977. *The Nag Hammadi Library in English*. New York: Harper & Row.

Ryan, Jordan J. 2017. *The Role of the Synagogue in the Aims of Jesus*. Minneapolis: Fortress.

Schröter, Jens. 2014. *Jesus of Nazareth: Jew from Galilee, Savior of the World*. Translated by Wayne Coppins. Waco, TX: Baylor University Press.

Schweizer, Eduard. 1970. *The Good News according to Mark*. Translated by Donald H. Madvig. Richmond: John Knox.

Stanley, Christopher D. 2023. *Paul and Asklepios: The Greco-Roman Quest for Healing and the Apostolic Mission*. LNTS 639. London: T&T Clark.

Strange, James F. 1992. "Nazareth." *ABD* 4:1050–51.

————. 2015. "Nazareth." Pages 167–80 in *The Archaeological Record from Cities, Towns, and Villages*. Vol. 2 of *Galilee in the Late Second Temple and Mishnaic Periods*. Edited by David A. Fiensy and James R. Strange. Minneapolis: Fortress.

Taylor, Joan E. 2018. *What Did Jesus Look Like?* London: T&T Clark.

Temkin, Owsei, trans. 1956. *Soranus' Gynecology*. Baltimore: Johns Hopkins University Press.

————. 1991. *Hippocrates in a World of Pagans and Christians*. Baltimore: Johns Hopkins University Press.

Theissen, Gerd. 2009. "Jesus as an Itinerant Teacher: Reflections from Social History on Jesus' Role." Pages 98–122 in *Jesus Research: An International Perspective*. Edited by James H. Charlesworth and Petr Pokorny. Grand Rapids: Eerdmans.

Vermès, Géza. 1973a. *Jesus the Jew*. New York: Macmillan.

————. 1973b. "Ḥanina ben Dosa." *JJS* 24:51–64.

Viljoen, François P. 2014a. "Jesus Healing the Leper and the Purity Law in Matthew." *IDS* 48.2 (art. #1751), 7 pages. http://www.scielo.org.za/pdf/ids/v48n2/04.pdf.

————. 2014b. "The Law and Purity in Matthew: Jesus Touching a Bleeding Woman and Dead Girl (Matt. 9:18–26)." *NGTT* 55.1–2. https://ngtt.journals.ac.za/pub/article/view/535.

Weber, Max. 1968. *Economy and Society: An Outline of Interpretive Sociology*. 3 vols. Edited by Guenther Roth and Claus Wittich. Translated by Ephraim Fischoff et al. New York: Bedminster.

Wilkinson, John. 1998. *The Bible and Healing: A Medical and Theological Commentary*. Edinburgh: Handsel.

Wilson, Walter T. 2014. *Healing in the Gospel of Matthew: Reflections on Method and Ministry*. Minneapolis: Fortress.

Zeichmann, Christopher B. 2017. "Capernaum: A 'Hub' for the Historical Jesus or the Markan Evangelist?" *JSHJ* 15:147–65.

Index of Scripture and Other Ancient Sources

Index of Modern Authors

Index of Subjects

Printed in the USA
CPSIA information can be obtained
at www.ICGtesting.com
CBHW031016060324
5006CB00001B/1